MISSION EUROPE

MISSION EUROPE
THE SECRET HISTORY OF THE WOMEN OF SOE

KATE VIGURS

YALE UNIVERSITY PRESS
NEW HAVEN AND LONDON

For information about this and other Yale University Press publications, please contact:
U.S. Office: sales.press@yale.edu   yalebooks.com
Europe Office: sales@yaleup.co.uk   yalebooks.co.uk

Set in Minion Pro by IDSUK (DataConnection) Ltd
Printed and bound in the UK by Bell & Bain Ltd, Glasgow

Library of Congress Control Number: 2025931213
A catalogue record for this book is available from the British Library.
Authorized Representative in the EU: Easy Access System Europe, Mustamäe tee 50,
10621 Tallinn, Estonia, gpsr.requests@easproject.com

ISBN 978-0-300-27269-7

10 9 8 7 6 5 4 3 2 1

This book is dedicated to two great men in my life.
To John Waller, whose passion for authenticity, humanity
and compassion inspired me to tell stories of motivation,
bravery and self-sacrifice.
And to my father, who has always been the voice of reason, the
calm in the storm, and who has made me question and push
myself beyond what I believed to be possible.
My gratitude to them both is unwavering.

To Die . . .
To die . . . so young to die . . . no, no, not I.
I love the warm sunny skies,
Lights, songs, shining eyes.
I want no war, no battle cry –
No, no . . . Not I.

But if it must be that I live today
With blood and death on every hand,
Praised be He for the grace, I'll say
To live, if I should die this day . . .
Upon your soil, my home, my land.

Hannah Szenes, 1941
(Translated from Hebrew by Dorothy H. Rochmis)

Remembering the dead is a sign of life. It is keeping alive what can never be a history or death, for our survival as humans.

Mies Bouhuys

'Resistance'
From *Someone Asks the Question*

Resistance doesn't begin with big words
but with small deeds

like a storm with a soft rustling in the garden
or the cat that suddenly goes off its head

like broad rivers
from a small spring
hidden in the forest

like a conflagration
with the same match
as you light your cigarette

as love with a look
or a touch or something in a voice that strikes you

asking yourself a question
that's where resistance starts
and then asking someone else the same question.

Remco Campert
(Translated from the Dutch by Donald Gardner)

CONTENTS

	List of Illustrations	*x*
	Abbreviations	*xii*
	Prologue	1
1	Mission Polska	18
2	The Uprisings	49
3	Mission Française	67
4	*Nacht und Nebel*	95
5	Mission Belgique	121
6	Mission Nederlands	151
7	Beyond 'Englandspiel'	180
8	Mission Danska	205
9	Escape and Evasion	232
10	Mission Palmach	261
11	Death Be Not Proud	281
	Epilogue	306
	Endnotes	*309*
	Bibliography	*334*
	Acknowledgements	*341*
	Index of Training Schools	*342*
	General Index	*343*

ILLUSTRATIONS

1. Matilde Carré of the INTERALLIÉ network. © The National Archives, KV2 926.
2. Jeanne Bohec, SOE RF Section. © Musée de la Résistance en ligne.
3. A recruitment poster for the Corps féminin.
4. A memorial to the 'Merlinettes' at Ravensbrück. Author's own image.
5. Elaine Madden, SOE. Image courtesy of Sue Elliott.
6. The Wright aircrew team. © RAF Harrington Museum.
7. Rennée Lippens, SOE T Section. © The National Archives, HS9 928 1.
8. Women of the Special Allied Airborne Reconnaissance Force. Image courtesy of Insigne.
9. Trix Terwindt in hospital after the liberation of KZ Mauthausen. © Stadtarchiv der Ortsbürgergemeinde St. Gallen, PA von Fels, Tr. 201, Fotoalbum 3, 1944–53, S,13,1.
10. The 'Englandspiel' memorial in The Hague. Author's own image.
11. Secret agent Jos Gemmeke. Nationaal Militair Museum, Soesterberg.
12. Blackbridge House, STS 32c, Beaulieu. Author's own image. With permission from Angy and Antony Lewis.
13. The *Hongerwinter*, 1944–5. © Maria Austria Instituut.
14. A Lancaster aircraft over Ypenburg.
15. King Christian X of Denmark. © Danish Freedom Museum.

16. Varinka Muus. © Danish Freedom Museum.
17. Varinka and Flemming Muus. © Danish Freedom Museum.
18. Surica Braverman and Haviva Reik with other Palmach fighters. © United States Holocaust Museum.
19. Hannah Szenes in uniform. © United States Holocaust Museum.
20. Conti Street prison, Budapest. Author's own image.
21. The Hannah Szenes parachute memorial, Budapest. Author's own image.

ABBREVIATIONS

ARP   Air Raid Protection
ATS   Auxiliary Territorial Service
BEF   British Expeditionary Force
D/F   direction-finding (van)
DZ   drop zone
FANY   First Aid Nursing Yeomanry
LZ   landing zone
MI(R)   Military Intelligence (Research)
NN   *Nacht und Nebel* (night and fog)
RAF   Royal Air Force
RCAF   Royal Canadian Air Force
RF   République française
SAB   Students Assessment Board
SIS   Secret Intelligence Service
SOE   Special Operations Executive
STS   Special Training School
USAAF   United States Army Air Force
W/T   wireless telegraphist
WVS   Women's Volunteer Service

PROLOGUE

As the sun rose over a little border town between Yugoslavia and Hungary, a young couple could be seen walking together in the weak sunlight. The girl, in her early twenties, was cheerful, excited even, as she prepared herself to undertake a short but extremely dangerous journey for which she had spent several months preparing.

The couple made their way to a safe house, where, at 7 a.m., they were met by the head of the Yugoslavian partisan group with whom they had spent the last three months. He had been assigned to help them over the border into Hungary. As they greeted each other, he announced they would be leaving in fifteen minutes.

As the minutes ticked by, the anticipation built, and the young girl recalled what had brought her to this point: her immigration to Palestine from Budapest; training at agricultural school; working on a kibbutz; recruitment into the Palmach;[1] jumping into Yugoslavia with a parachute strapped to her back; the weeks spent hiding in the forest with Tito's partisans. It all seemed to have passed by in the blink of an eye. In only a few minutes' time, she would cross between Yugoslavia and Hungary to begin her perilous mission. She tried to make light of the situation; she told jokes and recalled all the funny situations of the last few weeks.

That girl was Hannah Szenes, her partner Reuven Dafne.

The day before, following a four-hour trek to the safe house to rejoin members of their unit, Hannah and Reuven had spent much of the night in deep conversation. After an early supper, they went into the nearby orchard, where they discussed the finer details of their mission, covering their various means of communication, contacts, codes and everything else relevant to the work. They agreed their secret code would be 'United Kibbutz Movement Sdot Yam Caesarea'.[2]

Although Hannah was confident and self-assured, she begged Reuven to give her a cyanide pill to take with her just in case she should fall into enemy hands and wish to end her life. He refused. He felt it was his duty to instil yet more self-confidence in her and to remove any doubts she may have had about her forthcoming work. By giving her a pill, he felt he would reinforce any fears or misgivings she might have.

Reuven, however, had his own misgivings about the situation. He felt that they were under-prepared, and he was not satisfied with the arrangements that had been made for Hannah's crossing, but she insisted that she would not be delayed for anything or anyone. 'She absolutely refused to wait another day, another hour'; all of Reuven's efforts to persuade her to wait 'just a trifle longer' came to nothing.[3] She told him she was going to cross without further delay. 'That was that,' he recalled, 'the matter was settled.'[4]

In fact, Hannah had previously told him that she wished to go to the border alone; she did not want them both to go into the 'danger zone' at the same time unless it became necessary. She wanted one of them to be able to continue with their mission should the other fall. Reuven said that she 'seemed to be like someone about to embark on an experience she had been looking forward to for years', such was her excitement and determination.[5]

When the time came, they left the safe house together but walked in opposite directions to the border in case nosy villagers were watching and might report them and give them away to the enemy. Holding back a storm of emotion, Hannah shook hands with Reuven; the pair thanked one another for everything that had gone before, and then Hannah said, 'til we meet again – soon, I hope, in enemy territory.' She walked away. At the turn in the road, she spun on her heel and waved goodbye.[6]

The two would never meet again.

■ ■ ■

Hannah was one of three women selected to be part of the Palmach, an acronym for Pelugot HaMahatz, a Jewish fighting force totalling thirty-two. Palmach's missions were on behalf of two organisations – Special Operations Executive (SOE) and MI9, an organisation that specialised in escape and evasion. Members of the Palmach worked for a branch within MI9 known as IS9 or Room 900. Palmach agents were trained in various methods of communication and infiltration by SOE before being dropped into enemy-occupied territory with the main aim of offering aid to beleaguered European Jewry.

SOE selected and trained many agents for a variety of missions across occupied Europe, although they did not necessarily oversee or supervise their missions once agents were in the field.

SOE was created in 1940, following months of the aptly named 'phony war' with an effective stalemate on both sides of the Channel. This was broken by the invasion of Denmark and Norway on 9 April, the battle for France (10 May–25 June), and the invasion of the Low Countries. In just over six weeks, German armed forces overran Belgium and the Netherlands, captured Paris, forced the humiliating surrender of the French government and drove the British Expeditionary Force (BEF) back over the sea to England in the evacuation of Dunkirk.

In the wake of these events, and fearing for the future, the British government recognised that a new body, independent of the War Office, was required to arm, aid, train and equip those in these occupied countries who wished to resist the Nazi regime by any means, but in particular by sabotage and subversion.

SOE was created from existing Foreign Office departments, one of which was EH (formed in 1938 at Electra House, after which it was named). The principal task was to develop methods of influencing

German opinion. Section D (for destruction) would also be absorbed into SOE; this proved a little more complicated because, although technically it was part of the Foreign Office, it was also part of the Secret Intelligence Service (SIS), with whom SOE was to have a fractious relationship. The aim of Section D (also set up in 1938) was to target Germany's infrastructure and defend Britain against sabotage. The third department to be absorbed into SOE was MI(R) (a research section of the General Staff at the War Office, established in 1939 to handle irregular warfare, including weapons development).

The idea for the formation of a new organisation that would incorporate all the above had been proposed in several government memos throughout the spring and summer months of 1940. On 1 July a meeting was convened at the Foreign Office chaired by the foreign secretary Lord Halifax and the plan was discussed. The Minister of Economic Warfare Hugh Dalton held that 'there was a clear distinction between "war from without" and "war from within", and that the latter was more likely to be better conducted by civilians, than soldiers', thus laying the land for myriad people from different walks of life to become part of this unique organisation.[7] It was also decided that a coordinator should be appointed, who would look at the problem 'as a whole' and report solely to the prime minister, thus allowing him to 'override any departmental objections'.[8]

The following day Dalton wrote to Halifax suggesting the new organisation's remit would be to 'co-ordinate all action by way of subversion and sabotage against the enemy overseas'.[9] On 16 July the prime minster wrote to Dalton asking him to accept the task of forming Special Operations Executive. Three days later, the formal charter of SOE, written by Neville Chamberlain, was circulated, and on 22 July it was formally approved by the War Cabinet. Churchill gave the new head of SOE the much-quoted directive to 'set Europe ablaze', and the organisation lasted as long as his tenure as prime minister.[10]

SOE was made up of different sections, which worked in occupied European countries, including (but not restricted to) France, the

Netherlands, Belgium, Poland, Hungary, Norway, Denmark, Yugoslavia, Greece, Italy and Albania. Force 136 operated in the Far East.[11]

Arguably the most lauded SOE section was 'F', the independent French Section. F attempted to work across the whole of France and ignore the tensions that were developing between the occupied and unoccupied zones, as well as between Marshal Philippe Pétain and General Charles de Gaulle (the self-professed leader of the Free French in exile), from whom F Section was kept secret. There was a desire for a political dynamic in which the British government achieved a resistance that was not inspired by or directed by the Free French.

F Section is perhaps the best known for several reasons: the first is the strategic importance and geographical proximity of France to Great Britain in relation to the planned Allied invasion of the Continent (D-Day). Britain and France not only needed to maintain a good political relationship, but Britain also wanted to influence the way that the war in France was fought by the resistance, so they could have confidence and control when planning the invasion.

Another reason is the resistance 'myth' that was perpetuated by de Gaulle after the war and embodied in his speech of 25 August 1944 at Paris city hall:

> Why should we hide the emotion which seizes us all, men and women, who are here, at home, in *Paris that stood up to liberate itself and that succeeded in doing this with its own hands? . . .* Paris! Paris outraged! Paris broken! Paris martyred! But Paris liberated! Liberated by itself, *liberated by its people with the help of the French armies, with the support and the help of all France,* of the France that fights, of the only France, of the real France, of the eternal France![12]

His implication was that France fought alone with no outside help, its people only ever resisting and never collaborating with the enemy.

Therefore they were all resistance heroes, with no shame or culpability. This 'myth' went unchallenged for decades.

Another reason that F Section is so well known is its employment of a relatively high number of female agents (thirty-nine out of approximately four hundred and thirty F Section agents were women). The utilisation of French-speaking women to become F Section agents was inspired by the relative abundance of potential candidates and the comparative ease of insertion into their operational areas (as opposed to the challenges faced when infiltrating agents over longer distances such as into Poland).

The post-war popularity of these women agents was vast. The newspapers gazetted their decorations and reported on the war crimes trials, which catapulted them to heroine status, making many of them into household names. There is a wealth of biographical and autobiographical works, films and television programmes featuring the women agents, including *This Is Your Life*. Some of them became so well known that it was – and often still is – mistakenly believed that F Section comprised only women, and that it was the only section to make use of them.

Outside of F Section, however, only a few women were employed as agents by SOE. Their experiences and missions have been largely overlooked by historians and authors, an imbalance that this work aims to rectify. Within these pages you will find the stories of other women agents who had links to SOE or were employed directly by them during the war across Europe and parts of Scandinavia.

After its formation in 1940, SOE grew rapidly, and 'reached its maximum expansion in the late summer and early Autumn of 1944, when its total British strength was probably just under 13,000 . . . the total includes about 450 ATS, 60 WAAF and 1,500 FANY as well as nearly 1,200 civilian women: [totalling] about 3,200 women.'[13]

The relatively small number of women recruited for active service behind the lines appertains to the perception that the Second World War 'was a war fought by men – both in conventional and unconventional war'.[14] There was no coordinated effort or official route by which women could be recruited, trained and infiltrated as secret agents from Great Britain. Recruiting was somewhat haphazard, and women ended up in SOE sometimes more by luck than anything else. A dropped book at a party, sending photographs of the French coast to the wrong address or working at the bar of a hotel used by spies are just a handful of the bizarre ways in which women were recruited.

While SOE sections other than F did train and use women as agents, the numbers were small. SOE historian M.R.D. Foot wrote, 'So few of the agents SOE sent to the low countries were women – three went to the Netherlands [N Section] and two to Belgium [T Section] – that the author hopes today's feminists will forgive him for writing, as a rule, in the male gender only.'[15]

The role of women was not always official, and many women involved with SOE in occupied countries were not officially employed by them, nor did they receive formal SOE training either in the UK or in other territories operated by SOE. They should, however, still be counted among SOE's ranks as they participated in the war in other ways, such as working with the local resistance – undertaking work in the illegal press, escape lines, intelligence, safe houses, as couriers and so on.

Some were locally recruited resisters. 'In Italy an estimated third of partisans were women; but although even the communists, according to the Italian resistance veteran "Elena" (Carla Capponi), were happy for women to carry bombs, because they were less liable to be challenged by the Germans, they were reluctant to accept them as equal combatants.' Tito's followers in Yugoslavia and the resistance forces of ELAS in Greece included a higher proportion of women soldiers than the French Maquis.

The perception described above, that women were not equal to men and should not carry arms, was not unusual. Historian Charles Cruickshank states, 'In the nature of things they were restricted to unobtrusive backroom jobs, acting as couriers or providing backup for male counterparts. They did not take part directly in the actions

in the field for which the men are remembered, although their secondary role was often of vital importance to the success of the men'.[16]
Women undertook certain roles within the resistance, but there was
a line that the majority did not cross – they did not become involved
in active warfare.

Despite this, women in the resistance proved to be of vital importance. In Norway, for instance, women did not join SOE in the traditional sense (i.e. being trained in the UK and being infiltrated behind
the lines) but they did assist SOE in other ways. For example, while
the main Norwegian resistance group Milorg mainly recruited men,
'many women of all ages actively supported the secret army in a variety of roles, especially in communications and the supply services . . .
Mrs Elsa Endresen . . . made her flat in Oslo available as a safe house
. . . and as a repository for important documents . . . she also acted as
a courier, carrying secret papers in her handbag'.[17]

In Oslogjengen (the Oslo gang), 'Fru Solveig Wideroe found offices for its members when accommodation was scarce' and 'nursed
a wounded member of the gang for three weeks while the Gestapo
searched the immediate neighbourhood for him'.[18] Another member,
Fru Gudrun Collet, provided them 'with essential food for more than
two years'.[19] In Nordland, women assisted SOE missions in a variety
of ways, including when Ingegjerd Hole (a dentist) picked up and
moved a number of mortars in her car to prevent the Germans from
finding them. Four women from the Grannes family also helped SOE.
One of these was Liv, who provided members with special passes 'to
allow them to move freely round the area'. She was also tasked to go
through the packs of resting Germans to make sure they did not have
any direction-finding equipment on them.[20] She came under Gestapo
suspicion and was sent to England, where 'for the rest of the war she
worked for the SOE Norwegian Section at HQ in London'.[21]

The majority of women employed by SOE were based in the UK.
The First Aid Nursing Yeomanry (FANY) was a volunteer corps that
had been set up in 1907 and had become the most highly decorated

auxiliary unit of the Great War. During the Second World War, FANY supplied administrative, secretarial, domestic and teaching staff. A significant number of them also worked as cipher staff and wireless operators, offering a lifeline for those who worked in the field.[22]

The wireless operators were based at Grendon Underwood and Poundon in Buckinghamshire and, 'like the other women's services, they became absolutely indispensable, and their discretion was impeccable'.[23] They received messages from agents working in the field and sent messages from HQ back to them. It was vital that they were swift and accurate. Agents depended on them, not only for vital supplies of weapons, equipment and 'bods', but also for their ability to transmit quickly. This could save an agent from the dreaded wireless direction-finding equipment and potential capture.[24]

FANY members also worked as ambulance drivers for the British Red Cross, the American Ambulance Corps GB and the British Committee for the French Red Cross. A convoy of ten ambulances with forty FANY drivers was sent to Finland. In September 1944, twenty-three FANYs of No. 1 Motor Ambulance Convoy were among the first women to cross the Channel.

The FANYs worked alongside the approximately 24,000 Poles who had escaped from Poland at the outbreak of war to form fighting units in Scotland. FANY provided them with drivers, clerks, cooks and administrative services. There was a FANY mobile canteen unit in France with the Poles, returning via Saint-Malo during the BEF withdrawal.

Other FANY wartime work was as radio officers, encryption specialists, wireless operators, radar operators and personal assistants (drivers, coders and decoders) in the UK, North Africa, Italy, India, Ceylon and the Far East.

Many of the women who went on to become active agents in the field had their FANY rank as their cover, but not all countries used women for undercover work. For example, the idea was mooted to send women behind the lines in Italy, but because only the 'toughest' and most 'illness free FANYs' could be considered, the idea never came to fruition.[25] Instead women undertook roles such as personal assistants to section heads, coders and conducting officers.

Cruickshank states that, 'In the early days of the India mission a few women, both locally recruited and posted from Britain, served as secretaries, typists, and cipher clerks'.[26] These included FANYs. The need for more personnel grew and in South East Asia the 'increased need for W/T operators and cipher clerks made it necessary to recruit women in larger numbers'.[27] By 1944, 'the FANY complement eventually increased to over 600, of whom 400 were engaged in signals work, including 130 on ciphers, 126 on W/T operation and six fingerprint experts ... most were at the main radio stations in Colombo (234) and Calcutta (135)'.[28]

During the Second World War the number of FANYs totalled 6,000, of which 2,000 were in SOE. They were to become extremely highly decorated for their gallantry once more.[29]

■ ■ ■

The women who were to become SOE agents, or who were to work alongside the organisation, usually received training from the Special Training Schools (STS) and SOE instructors. These courses could be held in the UK, at Massingham (near Algiers), in Palestine or Cairo. It is insightful to have an understanding of agents' training, as this played a vital part in their role as agents across the European theatre of war. In 1940, SOE instructor Major Tommy Davies devised a training programme that every student-agent had to complete before being infiltrated into Europe. At this stage the training was just for male agents, as women had not yet been recruited, but women would come to take these courses in the years to come.

The programme consisted of four stages. The first was preliminary school, the aim of which was to identify unsuitable recruits and reject them as soon as possible. Successful recruits then went on to paramilitary training on the west coast of Scotland, followed by parachute school at Ringway Aerodrome near Manchester. Finally, there was a finishing school at a variety of country houses on the Beaulieu estate in the New Forest, Hampshire. Here agents would receive training in fieldcraft to prepare them for the reality of life in occupied territory. An additional course was aimed at agents who had been selected to be wireless operators so that they could hone their wireless skills and Morse code technique.

The courses were not always undertaken in this order and were fairly flexible, sometimes being adjusted to meet the needs of the organisation, or to reflect the talents (or limitations) of the trainee in question. Therefore, not all recruits had the same amount of training, or undertook the courses in the same order.

Once women were recruited and started attending the training courses (from 1942), they undertook preliminary training with the men but only received basic paramilitary training and did not attend the Scotland courses. It was only after the introduction of the Students' Assessment Board in mid-1943 that women went to Arisaig.

On the preliminary course, trainees were known strictly by codenames and the two-week course was conducted undercover. Inquisitive locals were told that commando training was going on, and potential agents sometimes believed the same themselves. The training included 'physical training, weapons handling, unarmed combat, elementary demolitions, map reading, fieldcraft and basic signalling'.[30] Agents who failed this training would be sent to the 'cooler' at Inverlair in Inverness-shire to live out the war and forget the things they had been taught.

The paramilitary course taught recruits how to deal with the tougher side of life as an agent and was held on the rugged west coast of Scotland at ten shooting lodges in the Arisaig and Morar areas of Inverness-shire. The course lasted between three and five weeks and tested a recruit to their limits. It included physical training, silent killing, unarmed combat, weapons handling, demolition, map reading, compass work, fieldcraft, elementary Morse and raid tactics.[31]

In addition to silent killing and knife training, an SOE recruit was taught 'instinctive shooting' and how to use various firearms, including the Sten gun, Bren gun, Thompson submachine gun, PIAT (Projector, Infantry, Anti-tank) and hand-held pistols such as the Colt .32 and Colt .45. They were also introduced to foreign weapons such as the Mauser, Browning and Flaubert, which they might come across when in the field.

Demolition and explosives training was essential, as sabotage was part of SOE's remit. Trainee agents were also instructed in the use of plastic explosive, which varied from Nobel 808 (a volatile, rubbery substance that smelled strongly of almonds) to plastic explosive (PE2), which was much safer to handle, had no smell or taste, and could be moulded into a variety of shapes such as cow dung, fruit or even logs.[32] The demolitions course usually lasted twenty-four hours, in the form of several one-hour lectures. Students were taught about the types of fuses and the various types of explosives to use on different targets.

Rail sabotage was carried out (using dummy explosives) with the cooperation of the West Highland Line, who also supplied the school with a train. Students were taught how to lay charges and fog signals and then hide. While practising, some trainee agents inadvertently blew up a bridge at Loch Morar, as well as the pier at Swordland (STS 23b).

Most importantly, they were taught that demolition must never fail, and spent hours familiarising themselves with various incendiary devices, Molotov cocktails, hand grenades and booby traps.

Major Aonghais Fyffe (security liaison officer for the training schools in Scotland) said:

> there was no distinction between the sexes and all suffered the same rigours of physical training in the early hours of wintry mornings, the same mud, muck soakings in peat bogs on fieldcraft and the same sore muscles and aching joints from the Arisaig form of unarmed combat. After all, when they were crawling flat to the ground over the peaty marshes of Loch nan Uamh, they were all just bods in battledress.[33]

The more unorthodox aspects of the course were taught by Eric Fairbairn and William Sykes, two former Shanghai policemen, who had been given complete freedom by the director of SOE operations and training, Lieutenant Colonel Gubbins, to teach whatever skills and methods they liked. 'Take no bloody notice of anyone but me,' he told them.[34] While the two instructors initially split their time between Arisaig and Inverailort, their techniques were taught at other sites, where agents learned that it was simply a case of kill or be killed: 'When dealing with an utterly ruthless enemy who has clearly expressed his intention of wiping this nation out of existence, there is no room for any scruple or compunction about the methods to be employed in preventing him.'[35]

Parachute training was usually held at Ringway (now Manchester International Airport) and in the case of the Palmach agents the parachute school was at Ramat David in Israel. For Polish agents and Cichociemni (Polish Special Forces), there was preliminary training from the parachute tower at Largo House, Fife. Students did at least two, but ideally five, jumps, but usually more from aircraft and static balloons. When being infiltrated into the 'field' they may have had to jump from altitudes as low as 300 to 400 feet, meaning only ten to fifteen seconds in the air. The training was nerve racking – some refused to jump and some were injured.

Those chosen for wireless training were sent on a course that would help perfect their skills. These were at various locations across the UK, including Thame Park in Oxfordshire. Most students had to start their wireless operator training from the very beginning by learning Morse code, gradually working up their speeds to in excess of twenty-two words per minute. Trainees were sent on clandestine exercises with their wireless sets and learned how to transmit in locations where trees, mountains or tall buildings would impair their ability to do so clearly. They learned how to fix their wireless sets, deal with signal jamming and to include pre-determined security checks in their messages so that the listening posts in England could ascertain whether the messages were genuine, being sent under duress or even being sent by the Nazis.

At Beaulieu in the New Forest all recruits, whether wireless operator or courier, received their final training: 'They were taught the elements of clandestine techniques and security; above all the importance of looking natural and ordinary while doing unnatural and extraordinary things.'[36] Beaulieu was the place where agents learned the reality of what it would be like to live in France and what being a secret agent really meant.

Agents were taught about the importance of false documents, papers and cover stories, and learned to recognise various military uniforms. They were taught various methods of contacting one another through the use of letter boxes, cut outs (an intermediary) or dead drops. Beaulieu was also the place where agents would become at one with their cover; they would learn every tiny detail of their character and would be questioned from time to time on their cover story.

An agent's progress at Beaulieu would be tested in 'schemes' lasting forty-eight, seventy-two or even ninety-six hours. These tested the agents' ability in making contact with a 'cut out'; tailing someone in a city; losing someone who was following them. Longer schemes involved contacting a supposed resistance member.

At Beaulieu there was also a mock interrogation, whereby agents were dragged from their beds at any time of the night and forced to withstand a Gestapo-style interrogation (without physical violence). This was the nearest agents would come to a Gestapo interrogation without undergoing the real thing. It was draining mentally and physically and was a part of the course that many recruits dreaded.

Although this was a fairly standardised plan of events, every agent and every mission was different, and each country section had different specifications and locations. Examples of this will be highlighted throughout the book where these differ from what is listed above.

■ ■ ■

As with any book about SOE, I am somewhat limited by the material that is available. The main sources drawn upon for *Mission Europe* are the SOE files at the UK National Archives. Released some thirty years ago, many of these files contain a wealth of information about agents' personal lives, training, missions and fates. Some also have a post-mission 'interrogation' or interview in which agents themselves relay information about their work, their experiences and their relationships with other SOE colleagues. For those who survived incarceration it also gives a clear understanding of their thoughts immediately after their return from the prisons or concentration camps.

However, while the collection of files for F Section appears to be almost complete, the records of other sections are not. A system of 'weeding' was put in place immediately post-war, whereby FANYs and other personnel were set to work destroying files.

SOE's head of codes Leo Marks was disturbed to discover that a 300-page cipher report, as well as lengthy reports on Holland and Belgium, had been mislaid, and that 90 per cent of his wireless records had disappeared.[37]

In addition, a fire at Baker Street on 17 January 1946, which resulted in a FANY named Barbara Hare being hospitalised, caused the damage or destruction of approximately 87 per cent of the SOE files, some of which related to the activities of SOE FANY agents. These numbers are constantly under review by historians, and it is now believed that significantly fewer files were destroyed, but no exact number has been forthcoming. As with any organisation of this nature, a conspiracy theory is never far away, and even Marks believed it was not 'accidental'.[38]

Regardless of whether the Baker Street fire was deliberately started or not, the result of the fire and 'weeding' means that the SOE historian is left with a small proportion of the original records, access to some of which is still restricted by the Official Secrets Act. Those that do exist are subject to censorship: this occurs in files that have potentially incriminating or damaging material. Large sections of writing are blocked out or even removed from files altogether.

Censorship may have occurred during the war years, when there were strict rules, or even after the war to prevent potentially detrimental accusations of reprisals or unnecessary loss of life. Censorship was also employed to stop information falling into the wrong hands, such as those of journalists or sensation-mongers. The significance of this is that an SOE scholar will never be able to construct a complete picture of an agent or of a particular SOE section simply by using primary source printed material. Other sources need to be utilised.

Material that can offer more information on certain agents includes the rich holdings of audio archives at the Imperial War Museum. These have been thoroughly consulted and are a crucial element of the research carried out for this book (although errors have still been found and some interviewees' claims are untenable). The work of Martyn Cox and colleagues in producing filmed interviews with many FANY and former agents for the 'Legasee' project has proved to be invaluable. Another source of interviews has been the Danish Resistance Museum Archive in Copenhagen and archives belonging to Sue Elliott and the BBC, who interviewed Elaine Madden in great depth, and who have very kindly allowed me to use these sources for this book.

Foreign sources include: Archiwa Państwowe (Warsaw), Elżbieta Zawacka Foundation (Toruń), Warsaw Uprising Museum Archive (Warsaw), Danish Resistance Museum archives (Copenhagen), National Archives (Copenhagen), the Institute for National Remembrance (Budapest), the Aviodrome (Lelystad), Crash Luchtoorlog- en Verzetsmuseum (Aalsmeer), Museum 1940–1945 (Dordrecht), Dutch Resistance Museum (Amsterdam), Oranjehotel (The Hague).

Site visits have included: Conti Utcai prison (organised by the Committee of National Remembrance, Hungary) and Margit Boulevard prison in Budapest; Ravensbrück former concentration camp memorial site, Germany; the Danish Resistance Museum and sites related to Operation 'Carthage' in Copenhagen; Szucha Street Gestapo HQ; Pawiak prison and streets linked to the uprising in Warsaw; and the Elżbieta Zawacka museum and grave in Toruń.

Several women of note were not afforded the opportunity to work with SOE but still deserve recognition for their wartime roles, either as secret agents or for their work within intelligence. These include the communist Ursula Kuczynski, also known as 'Agent Sonya', whose spy work during and after the Second World War included being a bomb maker and saboteur. Also Marie-Madeleine Fourcade, who was the leader of the highly successful French resistance network ALLIANCE and later an employee of MI6. Some women, such as Andrée de Jongh, worked on escape lines. She was a member of the Belgian resistance and was the driving force behind the creation and success of the Comet escape line, which helped over 770 people cross the Pyrenees to safety.

This book includes agents who were either recruited or trained by SOE but who undertook missions from other organisations such as MI9, IS9, who worked on SOE's behalf or alongside them in the field but without official recruitment, and those who undertook specific SOE missions.

This book is organised by country – a chronological approach was deemed to be confusing. Each country's experience of occupation and resistance varies greatly. The chapters are ordered by the date of Nazi invasion. Each chapter is chronological within itself so as to gain an overall view of the occupation and resistance movements in each country.

These women are explored in a way that will not only bring them the recognition they deserve, but will also offer a critique on their work in order to gain a better understanding of the unique and invaluable roles they played behind enemy lines.

1

MISSION POLSKA

I am not the silent one, I am the one who was allowed to jump.

Elżbieta Zawacka[1]

As the darkness of the cold autumn night gave way to daybreak on 1 September 1939, the citizens of the sleepy Polish town of Wieluń awoke in sheer terror to the sound of bombs screaming through the skies. Discombobulated and confused, the people of the town had no idea what was happening as, all around them, the air strikes continued. They did not understand why. There were no military targets there and no cause that they knew of for any conflict, but still the bombs fell, hour after hour, all day and well into the evening. The aggressors showed no mercy, attacking the hospital, destroying most of the houses and strafing civilians as they fled these scenes of carnage and destruction. The nearby towns of Działoszyn, Radomsko and Sulejów were also bombed.

At the same time, the early morning skies over the Baltic Sea were lit up, not by the rising sun but by the blaze of burning buildings and flashes of gunfire. The resultant smoke hung over the waters like a dark mist. The attacker was a German battleship named the *Schleswig-Holstein*, a hulking beast of a ship that had seen action during the Great War. At 4.45 a.m., the ship's guns had opened fire on the fortress on the Westerplatte Peninsula in Gdansk, Poland. The cacophony grew louder as the gunfire intensified. The German troops, who had until this point lain low on board the vessel, spilt onto the shoreline, ready to ambush anyone they found. The shots fired in this heavy naval bombardment and the attack on Wieluń ushered in a new dawn of global suffering, highlighting the worst and the best traits of humanity – the Second World War had begun.

There was no declaration of war and, therefore, no real chance for Poland to defend herself against the 1.5 million troops who stormed the 1,750-mile-long border between Nazi Germany and Poland. The Germans came from all directions and utilised air, land and sea to take back what they believed to be theirs: the lands, the forces and the German pride that had been taken from them in the Treaty of Versailles of 1919. They came to conquer and colonise.

The undermanned Polish defences were overwhelmed by Hitler's *blitzkrieg* (lightning war). The country fell to its knees as its airfields were destroyed. German ships and U-boats attacked the Polish navy. The major cities of Katowice, Krakow and Warsaw were torched, and their fleeing civilians were strafed indiscriminately by machine guns from German aircraft. Poland never stood a chance.

Hitler had it all planned. He had carefully orchestrated and stage-managed a performance, complete with costumes, choreography, entrances and exits to make the world believe that it was Poland, not Germany, who was the agitator. Hitler was only acting in what he called 'justifiable self-defence' against Polish attacks on German soil the previous night.

And so it was that the night before, 31 August 1939, in the border town of Gleiwitz, SS men dressed in Polish army uniforms had stormed one of Germany's radio stations from which they broadcast an anti-Nazi message in Polish. A Silesian farmer named Franciszek Honiok had been arrested the previous day and brought to the station. Dressed in a Polish uniform, he was killed and his body left at the entrance of the transmitter station.

Germany staged twenty such bogus Polish incursions into their territory. 'Criminal' prisoners from camps such as Sachsenhausen and Dachau were dressed in Polish uniforms and killed by German soldiers on sight. Their bodies were then posed to create a ghastly spectacle. All this was done to create the illusion of the two sides being involved in a series of gun battles, giving the impression that it was the Poles who had invaded Germany, not the other way around.

'The Polish State has refused the peaceful settlement of relations which I desired, and has appealed to arms,' Hitler wrote of the fake attacks in his proclamation to the army. 'In order to put an end to this lunacy, I have no other choice than to meet force with force from now on.'[2]

Despite the elaborate charade, to the world outside it was clear that this was a ruse and that Hitler's invasion had been planned for weeks. The invasion plan, codenamed 'Fall Weiss', ended nearly two decades of relative freedom.[3] However, Great Britain and France had pledged to fight in Poland's defence should the Germans invade, and much to Hitler's surprise, they kept their word.

They issued ultimatums for Germany to withdraw troops from Poland immediately or risk war. When Hitler learned of the British demand, he sat in stony silence before demanding to know, 'What now?' World War Two had begun.

■ ■ ■

On 17 September 1939, the Soviet Union declared any previous treaties with Poland void because, under German occupation, the state no longer existed. The Soviets then invaded, with the aim of partitioning Poland on the pretext of protecting the Polish territories of Ukraine and Byelorussia, as well as supposedly liberating the minorities who were being persecuted by Polish 'overlords'. Stalin also hoped to regain territory lost after the Great War. On 8 October, German-occupied Poland was divided almost in half.

Following the invasion by Soviet forces, nearly a million Polish citizens were deported to gulags. In 1940, the Narodný Komissariat Vnutrennikh Del (NKVD), the Soviet secret police, carried out a series of mass executions of Polish victims, including half the officer corps of the army. The Katyn massacre, as it became known, left nearly 22,000 dead. The west of Poland had been absorbed into Germany; the east was under Soviet rule, leaving the central section as occupied Poland, known as the General Government. The occupation was to be brutal, and Poland would be utterly destroyed.

The compulsion to resist was strong within Poland, from the General Government to the absorbed territories, and the contributions of Polish intelligence services had an immense impact on Allied intelligence capabilities. Poland's intelligence operations were widely accepted as the best in the world at the outbreak of the war. At the time of the invasion in 1939, British intelligence had few assets in Poland and relied on Polish intelligence sharing their own findings. Polish intelligence also had great success in decoding signals traffic from Germany. Their expertise in this regard was crucial to breaking the Enigma code. The underground SZP (Służba Zwycięstwu Polski, or Service for the Victory of Poland) was later integrated into the ZWZ (Związek Walki Zbrojnej, or the Union of Armed Struggle) and finally became the AK (Armia Krajowa, or Home Army) on 14 February 1942. The AK was Poland's primary source of resistance, and they forged strong connections with SOE.

The Polish SOE (Section P) is an under-studied field, in part due to archival happenstance. The Polish Section's relationship with Britain suggested an uncomfortable asymmetry of power. Cold War politics further strained the examination of this era. Added to this, the loss of some records – caused by a fire, 'weeding' and a general lack of care – led to some of the remaining records being placed into the less accessible holdings of the SIS archive.[4]

The Polish Section was officially based in Whitehall but actually ran out of 64 Baker Street.[5] Its origins date to July 1939, when intelligence officers met in the War Office to discuss guerrilla operations in Poland in the event of a German invasion.[6] Major Edmund Charaszkiewicz, who oversaw paramilitary operations in Poland, proposed a plan for both paramilitary activity and partisan warfare.[7] The following month,

Britain set a mission to keep tabs on military developments in Poland and ensure the AK was acting in accordance with Allied strategic goals.[8]

The premise of the Polish Section was established in June 1940 in a War Office meeting between senior Polish intelligence officers and the British Military Intelligence Research Section MI(R).[9] The Poles then created a new department, the Sixth Bureau, led by Józef Smoleński. On 22 July, along with the official SOE sign-off, the Polish Section was officially established. Initially staffed with only fourteen officers, it soon became a larger organisation whose duties included liaising with the Poles and serving as a transportation service, bringing agents and supplies to destinations specified by the Polish Sixth Bureau.[10] Typically, SOE selected members of the Polish forces in the UK and trained them as agents.[11]

In return for their work, the AK received supplies from SOE, although in context, the total was not that impressive, just 600 tonnes.[12] The material aid was provided against a loan, as agreed in August 1940.[13] Poland remained dependent on Britain for equipment and materials. This was a challenge for their operations: agreement to their requests was not guaranteed and they never knew what items would actually be provided.[14]

SOE could not give direct orders to the AK, which remained an independent organisation.[15] The SOE Polish Section trained and dispatched platoons to serve in the AK.[16] The Polish Section had seven training schools and students completed courses in marksmanship, underground warfare, sabotage, liaison, intelligence, armaments and anti-tank operations, propaganda and parachuting.[17]

■ ■ ■

Only one woman passed through this training course. She had come to London on a courier mission for the Polish Home Army and was desperate to get back to Poland to continue her work. She was the only woman to be trained as one of the elite Cichociemni, or Silent Unseen (Polish Special Forces), and to jump back into occupied

Poland to undertake a role in the Warsaw Uprising and subsequent liberation of Poland. She was richly decorated after the war and given the rank of general, alongside her friend and compatriot Maria Wittek. Her name was Elżbieta Zawacka.

■ ■ ■

Elżbieta Magdalena Zawacka was born in the medieval town of Toruń, a place filled with history and beauty. Toruń was the birthplace of the renowned medieval mathematician and astronomer Nicolaus Copernicus, as well as the place where the recipe for gingerbread was invented. The former fortress town (once a member of the Hanseatic League), with its vivid orange rooftops and majestic cathedral, lies on the banks of the River Vistula.

Elżbieta was born on 19 March 1909, the seventh of eight children. Her parents were Ladysław Zawackie (a court clerk) and his wife Maria. At this time, Toruń was under Prussian occupation, so, while her parents spoke a little Polish at home, the children learned and spoke German. In spite of this, she and her family (like many others) were fiercely patriotic. Being able to speak German meant that Elżbieta was able to attend a German school, and she began her education at the age of six, while the Great War raged across Europe. In 1918, her brother Jan died of pneumonia, aged just seventeen. The following year, the Treaty of Versailles was signed, and Toruń became part of Poland once more.[18] After five years, Elżbieta moved to the Foru Municipal School for girls, passing her 'matura' exams in June 1927.

More than anything, Elżbieta wanted to study at Gdansk University of Technology, where her brother Ali was undertaking his degree. But financial restraints meant that she was unable to go. Instead, she started to work as a mathematics tutor, eventually saving enough money to enrol in the Faculty of Mathematics and Natural Sciences at the University of Poznań. She worked as a postal clerk during the holidays to finance the following year's study. It was there that she crossed paths with Marian Rejewski, whose contribution to the

Allied war effort would be the staggering accomplishment of cracking the Enigma code.

A clever and devoted student, Elżbieta passed her degree in 1931, obtained her Masters in 1935 and obtained her state teaching certificate in 1936. This allowed her to teach mathematics in public and private schools in both German and Polish.

In 1930, while she was in the midst of her studies, Elżbieta was invited to attend a meeting on 'the newly founded academic regiment' of PWK (Przysposobienie Wojskowe Kobiet, or Female Military Training).[19] Their aim was to train Polish women to be prepared in the event of another war breaking out. Out of curiosity, she went along with her college friend. By the end of the meeting, she was convinced that this was not only a great cause but that she should be a leading figure within it. She joined immediately and received training as a student of the PWK academic troop, passing her instructor's course at a camp in Garczyn in July 1931. 'From then on,' she wrote, 'until 1939, I spent all of my summers in PWK camps, or performing various instructor and command functions, improving my own qualifications.'[20]

Elżbieta continued to teach mathematics, science and physical education, but all of her spare time was taken up with PWK, which she clearly enjoyed, and which gave her a sense of purpose and belonging. With her coiffured blonde hair, piercing blue eyes and toned physique, she was the picture of health; her new outdoors lifestyle seemed to agree with her. She founded school troops and extra-curricular school units and worked as a district commander in Koło, Somplono and Tarnowskie Góry, where she was also the commander of the local PWK circle until 1936. In 1937, at the request of PWK's commander-in-chief (C-in-C), Maria Wittek, she took a two-year teaching break, and following a two-month 'high-level instructor course' in Warsaw, she was appointed head of the Silesian District PWK, a position she held until the outbreak of war in September 1939. Elżbieta also organised two instructor courses in Katowice on behalf of Supreme HQ and developed the network of nineteen District Headquarters in her area, as well as running numerous summer camps.

Excelling at her job, Elżbieta undertook her work with passion and dedication – qualities that she instilled in her thousands of young female students. She also trained these students on behalf of the newly formed PWK Social Emergency Service (SES) in 'self-defence, rescue and sanitation, anti-aircraft and gas, economics and social self-help', all in preparation for the day they should go to war. This was a threat that was now becoming a very real possibility.[21]

To help prepare the rest of the Polish population for the prospect that war was inevitable, PWK organised training trips to local villages so Polish women could undertake auxiliary work (approximately a million were trained in a matter of weeks). They launched a propaganda campaign that garnered support from Polish radio and newspapers.[22] In addition, there were 'registration offices for volunteers, activities . . . to raise awareness of the need to prepare for the defence of the country, and a network of aid centres for the army and evacuated population was created. Until the last days, border social camps operated, which had to be closed down as an emergency' when Germany attacked.[23]

To say that Poland was not prepared for war is a vast understatement. The work of Elżbieta Zawacka, Maria Wittek and the many other women of PWK who trained and prepared for war in a number of ways illustrates that Poland did everything it could to be ready to fight back. The dedication of these women is exemplary and, while much lauded in Poland, is under-recognised in wider Second World War studies.

In August 1939, PWK instructors received instructions that, at the outbreak of war, they would be mobilised to the Women's Auxiliary Service. On 26 August, while leading a PT and military training course at Spała, Elżbieta received her mobilisation order and was told to report to Katowice. There, with a team of SES instructors, she organised aid to the beleaguered army and civilians trying to flee from the German border, including 'drops of milk' stations to provide sustenance. Sometimes they were too late, and in her memoirs, she recalled, somewhat chillingly, that the towns of Imielin and Mikołów were 'liquidated' on 2/3 September. Her other work included manning phone lines and helping to destroy important files to ensure they did not fall into enemy hands.

On 1 September, war broke out: 'There was no declaration, only an "official" war,' spat Elżbieta in a post-war interview. She continued:

> The Germans fell in a terrible mass of tanks on the entire western border! They were immediately on the entire front . . . Because the Polish military authorities knew that we would not be able to maintain this extremely long border line, so everyone was to retreat beyond the Vistula . . . the army was to retreat. The Silesian units were ordered to withdraw and, among others, we, the PWK women, were ordered to withdraw from Katowice.[24]

The day after the German invasion, on 2 September, Elżbieta was told to leave Katowice. The mood was still 'combative', she recalled.[25] The district command centre was stormed by angry women demanding weaponry such as grenades and guns, but the SES continued their work, helping the waves of refugees through Katowice. That evening, Elżbieta, along with twenty to thirty other people, including uniformed PWK instructors, SES workers and scout instructors, boarded a bus. The town was 'deserted', she recalled. The next day the Germans entered it and began a 'bloody liquidation of the resistance'.[26] They had escaped just in time. But the journey was far from easy.

Following the line of army retreat, they went east to Olkusz. They needed to get to the closest crossing over the Vistula, which was at Korczyn, and they 'headed for the nearest bridge' to get across (the bridge is always the most critical link in all military movements).[27] The party reached Olkusz, but the Germans were close by, and the Poles themselves had blown up the bridge at Korczyn. The following day, the party split. The scout leaders took the bus and continued the journey to Krakow, while the rest went on foot, following the course of the river through several towns. A few kilometres away from their destination of Sandomierz, they were picked up in wagons and carts and driven a short distance. No doubt this came as a welcome relief for their sore feet and troubled minds. They then completed the journey on foot.

However, when they arrived at the bridge, a scene of chaos greeted them. Everyone from the town was at the banks of the river trying to cross the bridge, which was already overcrowded and practically impassable. Horses were neighing and rearing, and crowds of people pushed and jostled. Somehow, the PWK group made it to the front, where the bridge commander saw them and, recognising their uniforms, allowed them to cross. As they reached the other side of the river the bridge was blown up behind them, the clouds of smoke and debris adding to the chaotic situation they had left behind.

Arriving late at night in Kraśnik, Elżbieta had to shake the exhausted station master awake to find out what time the next train was. 'The last train is about to leave,' he said solemnly. They boarded, along with a plane crew who had destroyed their own aircraft so the Germans could not use it. Eventually, the group reached Lublin. Here, at the 'Soldier's house', Elżbieta reported to the commander, a woman named Stefania Hajkowicz, who was Maria Wittek's deputy. Stefania had found herself in Lublin on her way to Lwów, where, according to Elżbieta, 'the best-functioning auxiliary service battalion operated'. Because of this, Elżbieta was to 'report to Lwów' immediately.[28] She hitched a lift in a passing car and arrived the same night, assuming the role of commander of the city's women's civil defence unit.

She took part in the defence of Lwów by organising women's units for 'anti-aircraft, gas and fire defence'. She recalled:

My group was assigned to anti-tank defence. We got a large gymnasium. There was no electricity, no light, very little water, so we got a dynamo from somewhere and lit up this big gymnasium. There were huge piles of empty bottles, and we filled them with gasoline as anti-tank defence. This was our task. We were just waiting for the bomb to hit our room! It was full of gasoline vapor so it would be great to catch fire! . . . When the tanks came, there was a bang – with those gasoline tankers. We blew up more than one tank there![29]

Elżbieta firmly believed that the city would succeed in defending itself, so when the news came on 22 September that Lwów had capitulated, she was saddened, describing it as a 'terrible day, that knife in the back . . . it was cruel, shocking . . .'[30] However, the town had been under siege and the decision to capitulate was made to save the starving citizens and prevent the city from suffering further damage.

Elżbieta had applied to work in an anti-tank position but had not yet taken up her post when the Germans started to withdraw and the Red Army entered the city. She was informed that she now had three options available to her: go as a prisoner to the Germans, go back to civilian life or, third, 'go to the Rusk'.[31]

After everything she had been through and experienced, Elżbieta now had to make some serious decisions that would affect her life and career. Disturbed by radio reports that the Germans had occupied Pomerania and that Pomeranians were being arrested and deported, she feared for her parents, who were still in Toruń. Not knowing whether they were alive or dead, Elżbieta decided to return home and reported to her superiors that she was leaving.

She managed to cross the bridge at the San River with a friend, after which she boarded a freight train and reached Krakow. From there, with a combination of walking and hitchhiking, she made it back to Toruń. She found her parents safe in their apartment – presumably a humble dwelling, as any significant building would have been requisitioned by the Germans. She discovered that her father, having served in the Pomeranian army, which was regarded as German, had been and would continue to be left alone.

Knowing this came as a huge relief, and she was able to continue in her work, safe in the knowledge that her parents were relatively free from danger. Elżbieta set off for Warsaw the next day: 'After all,' she said, 'I am a soldier, and the war is not over.'[32]

She decided to return to the army. The journey from Torún to Warsaw took her through Poznań. She described the city as 'dead, empty and alien'.[33] She was shocked at how much Poland had changed: 'This Polish city was all in . . . Hitler's colours: black-white-red. The whole city was colourful, in German colours! I went to my dormitory. I look [and] there is a large German banner hanging.'[34]

Once back in Warsaw, Elżbieta caught up with friends and reported to Maria Wittek. She was sworn in as a soldier of the Service for Poland's Victory and given an order to return to Silesia. She was glad of this and keen to go as she knew the area well, having been a PWK instructor there for several years. Taking the pseudonym 'Zelma', she managed to recruit 200 former PWK women in Upper Silesia and organised them to work in subversive activities, including sabotage, intelligence and counter-intelligence. Elżbieta's skill continued to be rewarded, and she was made head of communication in a sub-division of the Zagłębie Dabrowskie (the Union of Armed Struggle, which later became the Home Army).[35] Her looks played a part: as a young woman fluent in German with blonde hair and blue eyes, she could move with relative ease across the borders between Germany and the General Government.

As a result, she was given a mission: to build routes to the West. The ZWZ needed to be in contact with the government in exile in London, 'so a Warsaw–London connection was absolutely necessary and ran through Budapest . . . they needed people with the language'. She was to go to Warsaw.[36] At her first meeting, she was ordered to wait for a message 'regarding the assignment' she was to be given. The password was 'The white dress is ready.' Thus began her career as a courier.[37] She changed her name from 'Zelma' to 'Zo', as it was shorter to type and send by Morse code. She chose it because it was short for her sister-in-law's name, Zofia.

Over the coming months, she undertook the enormous task of establishing a courier route through Europe on behalf of Zagroda, the Home Army's Foreign Communication Department. The route she established was through Berlin to Alsace, from Alsace to France and then on to England.

Her first trip was in December 1940, and she was accompanied by a friend codenamed 'Ela'. They travelled together to Katowice. The train was hot and overcrowded, but they managed to find a spot for two. They kept each other busy lest they fall asleep and accidentally speak Polish, which would give them away. They had to make sure they spoke German, in which they were both fluent. This would protect them and maybe even save them. The next night was spent with Elżbieta's aunt in Chorzów, then (changing to German ID cards) they travelled to Berlin, where they went to their safe house. With their nerves frayed, the two women entered the house, where Elżbieta recalled their host 'Eli' burning something that Ela had brought. The two then left for the Tiergarten where they planned to visit a café; Elżbieta decided to stay behind, as she was worried for her safety. She decided to break off all contact and as a result she never saw Ela again.[38]

Being both remarkably pragmatic and self-effacing, 'Zo's' own testimony of missions after this time is surprisingly slim. She simply says, 'It's enough that in April 1942 (because I served these two years in "Zagroda"), I had already crossed borders almost a hundred times, and there were plenty of them ...'[39] After the hundredth time, she stopped counting.

Her work included transporting mail and carrying money (transferred from the Polish government in exile). She also organised courier routes through to the West on behalf of the Foreign Communication Department of KG ZWZ AK (the main HQ of the Union of Armed Struggle for the Home Army). This was codenamed 'Circus' and had couriers running routes from Poland to Berlin to Stockholm, Poland to Lorraine to Paris, and Poland to Bern. Elżbieta was helped in her job by the contacts that she had made along the way. Teachers and former students in schools where she had taught and colleagues from the WSK (Wojskowa Służba Kobiet, or Military Women's Service) assisted in her intricate and dangerous endeavours.

In addition to her underground work, Elżbieta continued teaching in Warsaw under a pseudonym, as well as continuing her own studies at the Secret Polish University. This had been set up in the wake of the German invasion, which saw all universities closed and many of the lecturers incarcerated or brutally executed as part of AB-Aktion, in September 1939. However, some professors continued to teach, despite the threat of death, giving secret lessons in private apartments, churches or other suitable buildings. These clandestine classes, which were taught in the utmost secrecy, meant that many students, including Elżbieta, were able to continue their studies.

■ ■ ■

Meanwhile, another agent of Polish origin was successfully working undercover on and around the Polish border. Polish-born aristocrat Krystyna Skarbek (also known as Christine Granville) was in Ethiopia with her second husband Jerzy Gizycki at the outbreak of war. Krystyna was described as 'quite lovely, fragile, small-boned and delicately made. She was very attractive . . .'[40] Married at eighteen, she quickly divorced and moved to Kenya, where she met Gizycki, whom she soon married. In September 1939, the couple decided to go to London to see what they could contribute to the war effort. Selfless and loyal with a passion for the outdoors, Krystyna was the ideal candidate for clandestine work.

In late 1939 she was able to arrange a meeting with George Taylor of SIS, and convinced him of her usefulness before revealing a plan she had devised to travel to Hungary. As a result, she was recruited into Section D (part of SIS), a rare achievement for a woman, let alone one who was not a British national. However, her 'flaming' patriotism and 'smart' looks made an 'excellent' first impression on the recruiters, and she was described as 'a person of quite outstanding courage with exceptional charm and powers of persuasion'.[41] Her fluency in Polish, French and English, in addition to her contacts in Warsaw and across Poland, were exactly what Section D needed, and she was offered a job. She accepted the role, which would be to open lines of communication between Hungary and Poland (as the latter was effectively cut off from the outside world with all news and propaganda controlled by the Germans).

On 21 December 1939, she departed for Hungary and soon established a route into Poland. She crossed the border from neutral Hungary into Poland six times and Slovakia eight times. This latter route was especially perilous as Slovakia was collaborating with the Germans and actively hunting escaping Poles. Krystyna was 'instrumental in effecting the return to the UK of the first escaped British prisoners of war' and organising 'one of the most efficient routes in Central Europe for the escape of Allied nationals'.[42] She often skied across the border, taking and receiving intelligence reports to the resistance circuits that were developing in Poland. She delivered much-needed money to help them finance their activities. She also carried wireless codes and coding books, and even microfilms, which she hid inside her ski gloves. On one occasion, the film she carried contained the first evidence of the German preparation for the invasion of the Soviet Union, codenamed Operation 'Barbarossa'.

Fellow Pole Andrzej Kowerski worked alongside Krystyna, and although he had lost a leg in a shooting accident, he excelled at his work in smuggling Polish soldiers and Allied prisoners of war (POWs) over the border. The pair had 'somewhat complex personalities' but a desire to work together, each believing the other unable to look after themselves without the other's 'supervision'.[43] The situation became even more 'complex' when, on more than one occasion, Kowerski asked Krystyna to marry him. Each time he was rebuffed, and she remained married to Gizycki. But the two did become lovers and made an impressive duo.

Together, they 'gathered intelligence on river and rail transport between Germany and Romania, as well as tracking the movements of border guards between Yugoslavia and Slovakia'.[44] In addition, they continued smuggling Polish airmen out of the country, enabling them to join the Allied war effort. This work involved travelling thousands of miles in extremely strenuous conditions and under constant risk of betrayal or arrest. The pair became mentally and physically exhausted, and Krystyna fell seriously ill.

It is impossible to know whether their arrest in Budapest on 24 January 1941 was a result of their becoming slower or less astute due to the increasing pressures on their health and physical well-being, or whether it was simply fate. The Gestapo succeeded in closing the net around them, arrested them and took them away for interrogation. They gave nothing away, and so the Gestapo employed more brutal means of questioning to extract what they wanted from them, interrogating and beating Kowerski for nineteen hours without a break. He spent that night in Hadik prison and, when brought back for interrogation the following day, was surprised to see that Krystyna had been brought in and was as 'pale as paper'.[45]

Despite already being unwell, Krystyna had a plan to get them out of prison. Biting down on her tongue hard enough to make it bleed, she proceeded to cough up blood, telling the interrogators that she thought she had tuberculosis. An X-ray confirmed that she had scars on her lungs (previous damage from exhaust fumes) and the doctor concluded that she was both very ill and highly contagious. She should, therefore, be released immediately.

She was smuggled out of Hungary in the boot of a car belonging to the British ambassador, with Kowerski (who had also been released) following in another car behind them. Crossing the border into Yugoslavia, the pair continued overland to SOE Headquarters in Cairo but did not receive the hero's welcome that they undoubtedly deserved. Instead, they were greeted with suspicion. They had passed through Vichy-controlled Syria without any issue – a journey that (in SOE's minds) could only be accomplished if they were double agents. They were held at Cairo SOE HQ while the London office investigated them both. After a considerable period, Krystyna was vindicated, partly due to her earlier work carrying the microfilms that had alerted the Allies to Operation 'Barbarossa'.

SOE, which had by now absorbed Section D, deliberated over whether to send Krystyna back to Hungary or Poland but concluded that it was too hazardous. She remained in Egypt and then moved on to Palestine and North Africa where she undertook intelligence work. She also began SOE training in coding, Morse code, wireless transmission, weapons and explosives, parachuting and silent killing in preparation for a time when she might return to occupied Europe.

■ ■ ■

Disaster struck for Elżbieta Zawacka in May 1942, when several of her resistance colleagues were arrested, including her sister Klara. Elżbieta was in town to deliver a suitcase full of money and went to visit her sister. As usual, she threw a pebble at the window to announce her arrival, but there was no reply, no light came on and Klara did not open the door. Realising that something was very wrong, Elżbieta dashed to her sister's neighbour who, on seeing her, turned pale and tried to shut the door in her face. Elżbieta put her foot in the doorway and asked what had happened: 'The Gestapo was [here] yesterday!' came the reply. They 'took Klara to the police'.[46]

Klara had been betrayed, and to make matters worse, it was by a PWK colleague called Saba. Under brutal electric shock torture, she had given away Elżbieta's details and her surname Zawacka, by which means the Gestapo had found Klara as well as her parents and sister in Toruń. After interrogation at Mysłowice prison, Klara was deported to Ravensbrück.[47] Over a hundred people lost their lives because of the Silesian round-up, and it was something that Elżbieta could never forgive or forget.

Meanwhile, Elżbieta knew that she had to get out as soon as she could, but it was after 11 p.m. and she needed to stay somewhere. She stayed at a friend's house for a few hours before leaving for the railway station at 5 a.m., where she took the next train out of town. At Katowice, she checked in her suitcase (giving the receipt to a pharmacist there who was sympathetic to the underground movement). Demonstrating great bravery, she then stayed on the platform of the station to warn couriers and resisters arriving there that the Gestapo were active in the area and were on their trail. It was only when she thought that she herself might be in imminent danger that she stopped and took a train bound for Krakow.

On arrival, she went to a friend, telling her that she was being followed. She asked her friend to warn others, fearing she would not be able to withstand the rigours of Gestapo interrogation and inevitable torture if she was arrested. Suddenly the reality of what she was doing had hit home hard, and she became afraid. She managed to inform Maria Wittek that someone was betraying them and that she was being followed before boarding a train to Warsaw.

Her nerves on edge, she sat down and covered herself with her coat, thinking she would then be safe, but she spotted a German soldier and decided to move to another carriage. The hours passed slowly. All the while, she was terrified of being caught. As the train approached Silesia at around 1 a.m., she realised it was not necessarily her they wanted, but rather those she might lead them to. She decided that she had to escape. Leaving her purse, jacket and shoes, she went to the toilet compartment. Drawing her breath deeply and steeling her nerves, she jumped from the moving train, hitting the gravel below her hard. The train pulled away, and although sore and tired, she was saved. Her steely determination was unhindered, and she continued to Warsaw to await her next mission.

Elżbieta was now *brûlé*, or 'blown', and could not return to work for Zagroda. Instead, she was to go on a mission to London. Her job would be to arrange communication between Warsaw and London. 'London underestimated it a bit,' she said. 'It didn't know the difficulties we had: that for us, for example, a five-minute delay of a connecting link could mean the death of several people because we would already think that there was a mistake, something would be eliminated, something would fall through, and so on.'[48] However, she was determined that she would make it through, especially as her task was twofold.

When Maria Wittek found out about Zo's mission to London, she asked her to undertake another one on behalf of PWK. Wittek explained that the women's army was only an army in name, and it had no statutory rights. Women also did not hold rank. Elżbieta was 'a Master of Mathematics, a graduate of so many instructor courses' but did not hold any rank, not even that of a private. She was paid to do as she was told, not to think for herself.[49]

Wittek prepared documents to be taken to London to demand that women were given soldiering rights, and she instructed Elżbieta on what to say and how to behave in the presence of the Polish government in exile to help settle the matter. 'It sounded incredible to us,' Elżbieta said, 'that in occupied Warsaw there was talk that I would be in London! After all, the occupation closed Poland completely, on all sides! There was no way out of occupied Warsaw.'[50] Her job was not only to prepare reports on Poland to deliver to the government in exile in London, but also to return and report back. She had to leave occupied Poland and then find a means to return. She was being asked to achieve the impossible, but if anyone could find a way, she could.

From August 1942, she prepared for her missions, all the while keeping her head down so as not to bring attention to herself. For example, she was not allowed to travel by public transport in case she was arrested (as she knew too many names and addresses). Fake documents were prepared for her, and she studied all the various elements of Zagroda, 'cramming and drilling' a lot of details into her head, a task she found 'tedious'. She also had to work on her language skills to perfect her French, English and Spanish.[51]

After four months of preparation, Elżbieta was finally ready. However, just before she was due to depart, she received the devastating news that her brother Egon had died (probably of typhus) in Auschwitz concentration camp, where he had been held prisoner along with thousands of other Polish citizens. With her family imprisoned and one of her brothers dead as a result of German maltreatment, she was more determined than ever to play her part in the war, and on 20 December 1942, she set off. Her excellent travel documents named her as Elizabetha Kubica, a representative of a German oil company with offices in Warsaw and Paris, and her clothes were elegant and fashionable, befitting a woman in her job. In her pocket she carried a brass cigarette lighter, secreted inside of which were over 500 pages of microfilm printed with the KG mail (Main HQ), marked 18F/12.[52]

She crossed from Poland into Germany, and then from Germany to Paris. In her usual, slightly flippant way (that seems to understate any peril that she was in) she said that this was 'not dangerous considering the good documents'.[53] In Paris she met 'couriers or emissaries who were taking the same or a different route to London'.[54] But first, she needed to cross between occupied and Vichy France. This was no simple task and required planning as well as bravery. If caught, she would be arrested, interrogated and perhaps, worse still, tortured. She looked around for a sure-fire way to make good her escape and eventually found the ideal solution.

She hid in the water tender of a locomotive. Lying on a wooden board that was mounted above the waterline, she stowed herself away for the journey. But while waiting for the train to leave she learned of the arrest of a man called Wilski, who had been caught while traversing the same route. This trail was 'blown', and it was clear that her planned route across the Pyrenees was not secure. Disheartened, she made the difficult decision to get off the train. She had been ordered to cross 'only in complete safety', and despite her best efforts, she could not find a 'reliable' route.[55] After a month biding her time and learning Spanish, she decided not to risk it, and dejectedly returned to Warsaw with 18F/12 still firmly in her pocket.[56]

Nevertheless, Elżbieta was desperate to leave Warsaw and undertake her mission. She did not wait long before setting off again, hellbent on making it to England via France, Spain and Gibraltar. This time, she carried not only the cigarette lighter but also a key, embedded in which were 'several hundred type-written pages' on microfilm.[57] Carrying the same documents as on her previous mission, she followed the same route from Warsaw to Berlin to Paris. At a checkpoint, her papers were withheld by a German official. Convinced that she had finally been caught, Elżbieta went to a hotel near Cadet metro station and awaited her fate. Her thoughts were racing; how could she get out of this, where could she go, to whom could she turn? She realised that being on the run without her papers was futile, so she just waited. The next morning, she returned to the command post and there the soldier returned her papers. 'This is what the stamps should look like,' he said, having apparently withheld Elżbieta's to compare against another document that he had believed to be fake.[58]

Then, to her intense disappointment, the crossing was cancelled again as it was believed to be too dangerous. Instead of returning to Warsaw, Elżbieta sought the help of the train guard who had helped her on her previous aborted journey, to try again to get her across the French demarcation line. Once again, she climbed behind the locomotive, up a narrow ladder, down through a hole in the tender and into the wagon, this time accompanied by eight French volunteers who wanted to join the army and fight.

Turning her coat inside out so it remained clean, she crouched down, waiting for the train to depart. They all lay down on the boards above the water, laid out like sardines in a tin. Dark, cramped and uncomfortable, the fugitives stayed very still lest they make a noise and be caught. The tension mounted as the train set off. Shortly after, the engine suddenly spurted filthy water out, completely drenching the nine stowaways. They all had to lie in the wet and cold until the train finally reached Vichy. She may have been tired and bedraggled, but Elżbieta had made it out of danger at last.

Elżbieta and her travelling companions soon boarded a train for Toulouse, taking the opportunity to make a diversion and marvel at the medieval splendours of Carcassonne, a beautiful walled city filled with winding streets, taverns and gargoyles. The complete medieval citadel, with its many towers, red-brick houses and shallow-pitch terracotta tile roofs, was far removed from the horrors and privations of war. 'I forgave myself this,' she reminisced, '[to visit] a town like this, straight out of the Middle Ages . . . [it was] a wonderful thing.'[59] No doubt it gave her a much-needed break and a chance to be somewhere away from the greyness and deprivation that wartime seemed to lend to most cities' appearances. Here, she could finally move about without the constant fear of arrest. She was away only for a few hours, and then the whole party went to Toulouse.

From there, they took the mountain train that wound its way up the narrow track along the precipitous slopes. As it approached the border, some of the party lost their nerve, fearing they would have their fake IDs checked and that these might not pass inspection. Jumping from the slow-moving train, they ran alongside it until it was safe to jump back on. Elżbieta remained on board 'with excellent papers, a credible legend [cover story], money and good preparation, remaining composed and calm'.[60] Her calm demeanour was no doubt improved by the fact that 'women in this part of Europe were checked less zealously than in Poland'.[61]

Eventually, they all arrived safely in Tarascon. Close to Arles and Avignon, the town sits on the east bank of the Rhône and was connected by several bridges to the similarly sized town of Beaucaire.[62] Replete with a castle, picturesque town squares and churches, the town was associated with fairy tales and legends going back many centuries. For this party, however, it took on the far more pragmatic role of providing them with a way out of France and into neutral Spain.

Elżbieta found a hotel while her travel companions went out to find a guide to take them over the Pyrenees. They were successful and obtained the help of Paku (also spelt Paquo in some documents), a Spaniard who told them to meet in a mountain shelter the following day. But when they arrived for this rendezvous, they were caught by a German patrol. One by one, the Germans checked everybody's ID cards and backpacks. The boys claimed to be selling espadrilles, but on inspection, the contents of their backpacks betrayed the fact that they were on a hiking expedition, and they were arrested. Knowing that her backpack contained chocolate and her secret messages hidden in the key and cigarette lighter, Elżbieta grabbed her coat and purse and slipped past the end of the line and onto the next floor of the hut, where there was a servant's door that led to a restaurant. She later said, 'You don't know how a person feels in such a situation, he is unconscious, and a thousand thoughts are running through his head.'[63]

She got to the restaurant, turned up the music and grabbed a waitress's apron before returning to the hall, pretending to be a servant. As she was climbing the stairs, Paku grabbed her and threw her out of the window. She landed near a snow-laden bush where she hid. Wearing only a light frock, she was bitterly cold. The snow was falling heavily and she pondered if this was a betrayal. Maybe for money? Or was it carelessness or simply coincidence? After some time, a man threw a 'smelly jacket' over her, but she remained hidden in the snow until she heard the French being loaded into the truck and driven away.[64]

The man who gave her his jacket was called Gilbert; he had seen everything that had occurred and, after that, the two of them became firm friends. She had escaped arrest but had 'no way to go further and no money.' She stayed overnight in the hut and waited for the next expedition to leave.[65]

> We set off . . . very early in the morning. There were much fewer of us, only a few smugglers. Spain was very poor, had little industry,

and smuggling of electrical appliances was very frequent and dense, naturally duty-free. We joined such an expedition. We hit the road. It was a bright, cold night. We've been hiking for probably an hour. I was very tired because it was uphill. We walked a little further and I went on strike – I can't do it anymore. I lay down and said, 'I won't go any further.' Then the guide started kicking me and the kicking helped, it turns out. I sat down and then I actually got up and we moved on. We had to cross a stream. No one knows how it happened – one of the smugglers had a revolver and a shot was fired. A shot at the border is always an event, so our entire smuggling team scattered around the foothills, hiding wherever they could. There were still marble remains of an ancient Roman bath. I hid behind a marble column and after several hours of standing there, I was shaking and didn't know what to do . . . anyway, I waited and someone sent by Paku looked for me, found me there and I spent the night in the village again.[66]

The third time, Gilbert and Elżbieta were accompanied by two Jewish refugees. Paku led them through the mountains, which he claimed to know like the back of his hand. After stopping to eat in a hut, Paku warned them that the next leg of the journey would be difficult, through wild mountainous terrain. He led them at a 'sharp march' through the high Pyrenees, jumping from rock to rock while a violent snowstorm was breaking.[67] Though Elżbieta considered herself 'a young, tall, athletic 33-year-old', the others started to struggle. The Jews especially were already weak.[68] At one point, one of them stopped and refused to go any further. Elżbieta gave him a small bag of sugar, which momentarily revived him, but he was left behind and the others forged ahead in the blizzard. Cold, wet and exhausted, they came across a stone hut. Huddling for warmth between Gilbert and Paku, Elżbieta managed to get two or three hours' sleep before they moved on again in the darkness of the early morning.

But now, Paku seemed quite disorientated, and it appeared that they had lost their way. It was only when they saw the frozen hand of the Jew they had left behind the previous night sticking out of the snow that they realised they had doubled back. Elżbieta was saddened by the sight. He had frozen to death 'alone, weakened, no warming second body'.[69] They trudged on, but they had lost faith in their guide. Completely exhausted, their lips swollen and cracked with only snow to quench their thirst and with nothing left to eat, they took it in turns to lead. When they stopped to rest, they found a German cigarette packet on the floor, and then they heard German voices – they were still in France. They began to run down the mountain. Fording an icy stream the men grabbed Elżbieta by her arms and lifted her over it. Then came a dry riverbed full of stones, and they 'ran down that bed' managing not to break their ankles.[70]

On seeing a watchtower, Paku finally recognised where they were. They saw two guards coming towards them and hid behind a rock to let them pass. After they had walked for a 'long, long time', they came to a mountain shelter, where the men tucked her up in an eiderdown and let her sleep before heading back to Tarascon, right back where they had started their dreadful journey a few days before.[71]

Despite all this, Elżbieta was undaunted. She had to get to England with the microfilm messages and to relay Wittek's report. Her fourth and final attempt to cross the Pyrenees was a success, albeit somewhat unorthodox. This time, there were four of them – Elżbieta, Gilbert and two Frenchmen. Their guide took them by a completely different route that led sharply up the mountains. Elżbieta later recalled, 'He didn't take into account that we were tired, I'm so tired, I cannot take it anymore, we reach a valley, I lie down . . .'. From there, she watched the sunrise.[72] She spoke of the 'burning mountains', describing how the 'sun rises from the horizon, which is much lower than the mountains, it illuminates the peaks from below, and they start to burn . . . a strange intense pink-red colour . . . [it is] something wonderful.' Walking quietly, they saw mountain eagles and chamois. Suddenly, their guide pointed to a tall peak and told them it was Spain. Then he announced that he was tired and did not want to go any further. Spinning on his heel, he turned and walked away, leaving them with no map, no compass and no guide.

The group split up; the two Frenchmen went one way, Elżbieta and Gilbert the other. The snow was bright, the sun was beating down and they were getting hot and frustrated. But they carried on, over a high peak and down into 'some kind of pass'.[73] The mountains below them were getting lower. Sliding down some slopes, walking across others, they eventually reached a stream near a mountain village. While Elżbieta rested, Gilbert went on a reconnaissance to gather information. When he came back, he informed her that they were not in Spain after all – they were in Andorra.[74]

She was taken to a local hall, where she ate her fill of a plate of delicious fried potatoes under the supervision of local soldiers, who made her feel uneasy. When Gilbert returned with a British gentleman, perhaps a spy, whom they called 'Mister Robert', she explained to him in broken English that she was a Polish emissary and was expected in Barcelona. Fortunately, he believed her and:

> telephoned the English ambassador . . . he sent a car to pick us up . . . We arrived in Santa Julia. On the way we passed our two French companions, but we just waved at them and moved on . . . A hotel had already been booked in Santa Julia, so I could go to bed. My shoes were (alas) torn after those mountain trips, so they bought me some mountain shoes, some espadrilles with a string. We agreed that we would go further the next morning and that they would give us a guide who would take us to Barcelona. I was happy that everything was fine and that I had fulfilled my task.[75]

They set off again late evening. Now there were three of them, and despite having rested, Elżbieta was 'quite broken . . . like a dog made of lead'.[76] When they reached a stone hut, they ate a meagre meal of scrambled eggs cooked over a fire. Since there was 'no lamp, no candles, only a torch', they ate and went to sleep.[77] Waking up to thick fog, it took them a while to notice that there were border guards with rifles close by. Gilbert panicked and ran off, leaving Elżbieta by herself in the hut. But, once the guards had gone, a well-timed sneeze alerted him to where she had hidden, and they were soon reunited.

After several more arduous days of hiking, hiding and living by their nerves, the pair made it to Lerida, the final station of the mountain railway, where they boarded a train bound for Barcelona. Travelling separately so as not to arouse suspicion, the pair arrived in Barcelona in the early morning. After their many adventures together, they now bade each other goodbye. Gilbert went to the French embassy to try to join the French army in Algeria, while Elżbieta went to the British embassy, where she met the ambassador on the stairs and greeted him with the required passwords that proved who she was.

The ambassador immediately sent a telegram to say that Elżbieta had finally arrived and required an aircraft to take her to London. Her tattered clothes and shoes were replaced, and she waited for the aircraft that would take her on the final leg of her exhausting journey to fulfil her missions. But it was not to be. While waiting for the aircraft, Elżbieta took the opportunity to explore the city and was astounded to meet a fellow Polish emissary named Arus walking on a pier overlooking the Mediterranean. Elżbieta was 'happy' that she and Arus were together and could discuss their future plans. She even hoped that they could fly to Great Britain together. But, when the aircraft arrived, there was only one spare seat. 'Naturally,' she said, 'they [took] the man and not the woman because a woman cannot be more important than a man!'[78]

This had been her only chance to fly to Britain. Deprived of the opportunity she had worked so hard for, she 'furiously' demanded that a ticket to Gibraltar be bought for her, and the embassy felt that they could not refuse. Passing through Madrid, she visited museums, saw flamenco dancers and spent the last of her money on a ticket to a bullfight. She then travelled on to Seville and from there to Gibraltar. Finally, she was on British territory, if not yet in Britain itself. She was, however, horrified to discover that they were terrified of spies, and she was subjected to a rather intimate search before she was allowed to stay.

After what seemed like an eternity, she finally obtained a place on a ship that was part of a convoy of nineteen about to leave Gibraltar. She boarded HMS *Stirling Castle* under her new name, 'Elizabeth Watson' – an English woman evacuated from bombed-out Malta. She spent eight days on board the ship, which was also carrying Polish prisoners of war, and it was from them that she learned of the barbaric events of the Katyn massacre. She took Mass with them to celebrate Easter. The convoy sailed up the Atlantic to Ireland and finally came into the port of Bristol on 1 May 1943.[79]

The last passenger to leave the ship, Elizabeth Watson was detained before being collected by an English policewoman. They travelled to London together by train, and she was immediately put into a cell in a prison at 101 Nightingale Lane, part of the Royal Victoria Patriotic School, where foreign aliens were vetted and questioned to ensure they were not spies.[80]

When questioned by MI5 personnel, she gave her name as Zofia Zajowska. Perhaps she thought the English had work to do to gain her trust after everything she had been through. Her arrival had caused some alarm within official circles, and in her SOE file there is a memo dated 1 June 1943 to the effect that 'the lady in question has arrived in this country entirely unknown to the Polish Deuxieme Bureau, and he [the author] wishes to keep this arrival secret from them at all costs . . . an absolutely explicit undertaking should be obtained . . . that the report does not reach the Poles, nor is the arrival of the lady mentioned to them in any form.'[81]

Elżbieta recalled that she had 'very good conditions in prison' and was kept there for two days. It transpired that she should not have been detained at all. Her file states that 'the case of Zofia Zajowska [alias] Elizabeth Watson who was recently detained for a short time at Nightingale Lane ... it was discovered after she had arrived that she was a person who might well have been exempted from detention. Consequently, she was released very quickly.'[82]

Once out of prison, a Polish officer picked her up, and on 4 May, she reported to Colonel Protasewicz at the Commander-in-Chief's staff. She provided her passwords, which were 'I am a member of the Chisholm clan' and 'two thousand and twenty.'[83]

She had already given the mail to the agent Arus, whom she had met in Barcelona, to ensure that it would arrive as quickly as possible. The information could have covered a multitude of subjects concerning: 'U-boats in the Baltic, German troop movements, V1 and V2, Auschwitz, photographs of forged documents, escape routes, German industry, munitions factories, sabotage, Jewish ghettoes and the rising in the Warsaw Ghetto, co-operation with the resistance in Hungary and Germany, Extermination of Poles and Jews.'[84] As a courier, she would not have known the exact nature of the information she carried in case she was caught and interrogated. Therefore, neither would Arus.

She reported to the commander-in-chief, General Sikorski, 'but it was a very short report,' she recalled. 'I thought the General would be curious about what was happening in the Home Army, but he was already so busy with his trip ... He went to the Middle East for an inspection to General Wladyslaw Anders, and, as we know, he died in Gibraltar after his return. Sikorski told me that I would give him a detailed report when he returned from the East, and he never came back ...'[85]

Her first task was a communications mission, to:

track all current courier routes from and to the country in the files of the Commander-in-Chief's Staff to increase security. The roads from London to Warsaw were almost safe (if you could call it that) from the time the Silent Unseen began their service because they took the mail, and within a few hours, the mail was in the country.[86]

However, in the opposite direction it could take many weeks before someone dispatched from Warsaw arrived in London (as demonstrated by her own long and arduous journey). For several weeks, she tracked everything, including dispatches, radio-telegrams and telegrams. She 'managed to complete this first mission. With hard office work [she] connected all the postal routes in one direction and the other.'[87] She also conveyed information about life in Poland, which included travel, trains, frontiers, control of documents, rations, German billets, papers carried, general impressions of Germany, Polish workers in Germany, Soviet penetration and internal politics, which she relayed in full.[88]

The second mission, which had been assigned to her by Maria Wittek, was to make the Polish government in exile 'finally issue an act, a decree by law allowing women to be soldiers'.[89] She attended:

a lot of conferences, explaining what women's service was and in what departments women served. In so many different departments that the civilian population did not know about at all: both the mining service, and the intelligence service, especially communications, sanitary, maintaining contacts for everyone, so that it would hide conspiratorial work. So, there was a huge section of women's work that was not known, but above all, women had no rights.[90]

She was also successful in this mission. In October 1943 a decree was issued that 'women active in the army were soldiers, hence they had the right to promotion and decorations'.[91]

While in London, Elżbieta lived at the stylish Rubens Hotel in Victoria, where the headquarters of General Sikorski's Free State Polish Army was based. She was astounded by the expense and how removed it was from her normal life. She seemed rather put out by the life that the Poles in London were living, observing that they lived very comfortably, with almost no air raids. 'They lived, had their coffees and teas and lived a normal life, whilst in our country we had nothing.'[92] She also found English life curious – how there was a line on the bath so as not to overfill it, that the milkman still delivered milk after an air raid and that the English women were still supposed to wear stockings. The banality of it all struck her; her brother had died in Auschwitz, Poland was in a desperate situation, and here she was talking about stockings, 'but that was London', she quipped.[93]

She met with many prominent politicians during her stay in London, including Polish President Władysław Raczkiewicz, General Władysław Sikorski, Prime Minister Stanisław Mikołajczyk, General Kazimierz Sosnkowski and General Józef Haller – who received her reports of life in Poland and the rights of Polish women in the army.

She worked for two months at HQ, but she was desperate to return to Poland, so she sent a telegram to Warsaw asking for an order to come back. Two arrived: 'Zo is to return!' 'After all', she said, 'I want them to learn about communications and to pass on what I learned to the country, so I had to come back and I wanted to go back to the country.'[94] But the question remained: how? One idea was that she would fly to Switzerland (which was neutral), from there to southern Germany and then 'by my own means (I was a courier, I knew how to do it), to reach Poland. It would take several weeks, all together.'[95] This route was long and convoluted. But there was a quicker way, a way that many Poles had taken before: she could parachute back into Poland.

2

THE UPRISINGS

She was the bravest woman I ever knew, the only woman who had a positive nostalgia for danger. She could do anything with dynamite, except eat it.

Sir Owen O'Malley, British ambassador to
Hungary, regarding Krystyna Skarbek[1]

Elżbieta was the only woman who trained alongside the Cichociemni (Silent Unseen) in order to learn the skills that could be useful to her on her return to Poland. Cichociemni were Polish nationals who parachuted back into Poland after a period of training supported by SOE Polish Section (P). In England, they reported to the Polish government in exile, but when back in Poland, they reported to the Home Army (PWK). This meant that although technically not an SOE agent, Elżbieta was trained as if she were working for SOE and undertook the same rigorous courses as agents from other country sections.

Her SOE personnel file does not detail any of her training or provide training reports; however, it is possible to piece together the courses she undertook and/or attended through her post-war interviews and writings.

The preliminary course was bypassed, presumably because it was a foregone conclusion that she would be returning to Poland and, therefore, did not require an assessment to establish whether she was a viable recruit, which was the course's main purpose. In the ordinary scheme of things, agents would then go to Scotland for the paramilitary course. Elżbieta did not undertake 'difficult physical exercises'. Only men trained at the so-called Monkey Grove, at Largo House in Fife. There they underwent instruction in rock climbing, skiing and weapons handling. The nearby parachute tower was where many Poles began their parachute training with the dreaded static jump. A training school was also set up by General Sosabowski at Inverlochy Castle to teach Cichociemni the skills of espionage, sabotage and silent killing.

As an agent specialising in communication, Elżbieta did not necessarily need this type of training. However, it appears that she undertook some firearms lessons: 'We were taught to shoot from a crouch without aiming with both hands.'[2] They 'literally imagined that behind every bush or house, there was a Gestapo officer, that you had to stand in front of him with a gun in your pants. They had to be taught that this is normal life.'[3] This technique, known as instinctive shooting, was to become intrinsic to the way that they would operate once back in Poland. According to Elżbieta, there was a square on which stood a typical Warsaw tram; it differed only in colour, being brown and not the usual red. Here the recruits were taught how to jump out of it in case of a raid and the need to escape quickly. Of the Scottish course, Elżbieta recalled, 'It was very well organized there in terms of psychology,' but it was not training that she needed; silent killing was not for her. 'I am not the silent one,' she thought, 'I am the one who was allowed to jump.'[4]

To prepare her to jump back into Poland and fight for her country's freedom, Elżbieta had to learn how to parachute from an aircraft while under the cover of darkness. By February 1941, Cichociemni were attending SOE's parachute school at STS 51, Ringway Aerodrome near Manchester, in addition to the course held for the 1st Independent Parachute Brigade at Largo House. Given Elżbieta's reference to a 'parachute tower', it seems that she perhaps did her training at both sites rather than just Ringway.

Either way, she trained with other Cichociemni (all of whom were male) and alongside women from 'other nationalities'.[5] They prepared them by undertaking test jumps, and only when five jumps had gone 'favourably' did they get their wings and pass. These jumps were not for the faint at heart, and Elżbieta remembered that, 'at first, we [had] to get used to being in the air. There [was] a high tower . . . 2–3 storeys high, a huge swing – you sit down and throw it. You're in the air.'[6] The jump from the parachute tower was sudden and more rapid than a jump from an aircraft where the slipstream would slow the descent. If the jump was mistimed or something was amiss, terrible injuries could occur. Elżbieta was not equipped with the correct shoes and, when she landed, she badly sprained both her ankles.[7]

This was not uncommon. Many agents, male and female, injured themselves during training, spraining ankles, breaking legs or smashing their faces against the hole in the floor of the aircraft – known as 'ringing the bell'. Seeing her despair, Elżbieta's instructor tightly bandaged her ankles with elastic for support. Elżbieta was afraid that news would reach London about her accident and that she would be withdrawn from her training and never get the chance to return to Poland. But she need not have feared, and it was soon time to get into an actual aircraft, in this case, a Halifax. 'They had a hole in the ground', she said:

> about 1.5 m in diameter, you had to sit over the hole and look down to get used to how the ground was approaching, etc. There were a few such practice flights. Then we learned how to jump and deploy parachutes. Everyone knew it was a matter of life and death.[8]

Their main concern was whether the parachutes had been packed correctly. Agents placed a lot of trust in those who provided their equipment, and Elżbieta was just glad she was not one of those who held such a responsibility.

Then came the moment they had been waiting for: the first jumps took place. Elżbieta maintained that she was not afraid and that her mind was focused on her duty – to get back to Poland:

> A lot of us entered [the] Halifax. We knew we had to sit on the edge of that hole, keeping well back. The parachute was attached to the plane in such a way that when there was a jerk, it broke off. They warned us that at first, we would fall like a rock before the parachute opens. There were two people sitting down. There was a voice and light signal. First there was a red light, then a green light and the order 'go'. You had to put your feet down quickly and fall. The parachute opened and bliss ensued. A completely blissful moment, pleasant to feel weightless in the air. It didn't last very long, because the ground was getting closer in some unexpected way . . . you also need to keep your knees relaxed and tucked in and try to stay above the ground for a long time so as not to roll . . . I had a good flight.[9]

They did three or four practice or 'sporty' jumps and then an 'operational jump', in which they practised with all the equipment they would carry for the jump back into Poland, items that would weigh them down and make them vulnerable once on the ground – an overcoat, a shovel, two pistols, ammunition and a knife for cutting parachute cords.[10] After this, and to relieve the tension, they undertook some 'fun things', like jumping over water and landing in boats. A little light relief on courses such as this was always a welcome touch.

Relief also came in the form of her billet, which was a 'palace in a beautiful park', presumably Dunham Massey, a charming Jacobean manor house in Altrincham, which housed up to twenty-five parachutists and FANY staff. Elżbieta had a conducting officer to look after her, a sergeant named Fanny who took her everywhere and kept her company, no doubt becoming something of a confidante to Elżbieta, who was the only Polish female on the course. In sharp contrast to the intensity of training days, the evenings had a very 'pleasant, sociable atmosphere'. The FANYs swapped their uniforms for evening dresses and there was 'singing, drinking wine, walking, music. It was very relaxing.'[11]

Whether or not Elżbieta attended the best-known SOE Polish Section training school at STS 43, Audley End House in Saffron Walden, is debatable. Her SOE file does not show any training records, nor does she mention it in any of the memoirs held in Toruń or Warsaw. The course at Audley End was primarily focused on physical fitness, map reading, combat fighting, silent killing, microdot photography, shooting, driving, lock breaking, sabotage, explosives and guerrilla warfare. Elżbieta was, in her own words, a courier and worked in communications, not sabotage. However, Audley End was at its peak in terms of training Cichociemni in the summer of 1943, and it was possibly there that she offered her skills to help prepare agents going back to Poland.

As someone who had recently left, Elżbieta knew what everyday life was like, and she was asked to help the recruits prepare to return to a country that they may not recognise after being absent for a period of the occupation. Teaching was her calling, and she excelled in educating the recruits about changes in clothing, social behaviour and conditions on the streets. She helped them identify acts that would cause them trouble, such as if they were found in the wrong place at the wrong time or if a wireless set was discovered. She told them that they could rely on the existing 'communication service, which is so well organised', but the men could not 'imagine that women could be . . . soldiers.'[12] They found it difficult to believe that women could be in control of a situation that was typically and traditionally male. 'Naturally, they didn't believe', she said, 'they were heroes who were to go straight into the lion's den . . . I tried to tell them what it was like.'[13]

The final SOE school where Elżbieta was based was Station 20a, Pollards Park House, Chalfont St Giles. Alongside was STS 20b, an attractive house just off Nightingale Lane sitting deep in the woods and where black propaganda (among other subjects) was taught. STS 20a was a holding station for Poles and occasionally Czech agents. The cover for the house being a 'transit centre for the wounded' was blown when a passer-by heard gunshots and declared her astonishment at what was really going on. While at STS 20a, Elżbieta shared a room with a FANY by the name of Sue Ryder (later Baroness of Warsaw), and the two remained firm friends throughout their lifetimes. Sue described Elżbieta as both 'gay and frightened . . . courageous rather than fearless.'[14] She recalled a picture that Elżbieta hung on their wall named *A Moment Out of Time*, showing a couple standing on a riverbank holding hands. She knew little else about her, other than that she was a courier from Poland and that she was waiting to go back.[15]

Flights to Poland were extremely difficult to come by due to the length of flight time and the extreme danger in which pilots were placed. Agents could wait at STS 20a for some considerable time, sometimes up to three months. During this waiting period, they would have to kill time and try not to allow the weight of the situation to get to them. Fortunately, Elżbieta's wait was only ten days, but during that time, she made quite the impression on Sue Ryder, who had seen approximately 300 agents pass through the waiting stations. 'In the heightened awareness of life and death, it was quality and not quantity that counted; in the final analysis, faith, loyalty, courage and truth were all that mattered.' Elżbieta exuded every one of those qualities.[16]

On 9 September 1943, Elżbieta's wait was over. Along with Lieutenant Bolesław Polończyk and 2nd Lieutenant Fryderyk Serafiński, Elżbieta was picked up by a car from STS 20a and driven to RAF Tempsford in Buckinghamshire, ready to depart as part of Operation 'Neon 4'. She was already in her 'operational gear' and had been given her guns, with which she was 'very happy'.[17] After a farewell meal, the parachutists were searched to ensure they did not carry or wear anything incriminating or that would show they had recently arrived from the UK. At first, Elżbieta did not understand why she was being searched; she thought it must be because they suspected her of being a communist. She was distraught as 'every piece of clothing, purse, under my watch, every piece of paper' was inspected. In no uncertain terms she told the Home Army officer conducting the examination that he had no right to be doing it. She later realised that they were doing this to everyone, not because they suspected them, but because they wanted them to succeed.[18]

Once they had been handed their suicide pill, the three headed towards the waiting Halifax aircraft. It was still light when they departed. The aircraft climbed smoothly into the autumn sky, quickly reaching the coast, then flying out over the Channel and into the darkness. Elżbieta was soon settled enough to note the 'wonderful view' on such a 'clear night'. She felt she could see right to the 'very bottom' of the sea. She delighted in how it 'sparkled' and 'glowed' and quite simply 'couldn't get enough' of it.[19]

She was clearly excited and in very high spirits; after all this time, she was on her way home. But then, like others on such flights, the cold began to hit her. Her flying suit was lined to keep out the chill, but it was just not warm enough as the temperature in the hold gradually dropped. But she forgot all about the chill when the aircraft suddenly lurched sideways and threw her off balance – the wing had been hit by flak as they flew over Denmark. Luckily, it was not serious, and they managed to get away to safety, deciding to divert over neutral Sweden, which was a longer but much safer route. From there, they flew north to the mouth of the Vistula (which was lit up at night) and then along the river to their destination just outside Warsaw.

Tension began to rise in the hold as the detour had added considerable time, and the agents should have already jumped by now. The fuel gauge was lower than it should be, and time was running out. The three Cichociemni had arranged themselves; their static lines were hooked up and they were ready. They just needed the go-ahead – the green light, the 'go' – but for now, it did not come.

The pilot struggled to find the pick-up point at Solnica. Then he finally spotted it: 'several girls and boys . . . on the ground, back-to-back. [They had] a large electric lantern on their chests, their bodies were arranged in the shape of an arrow, and the arrow was pointing in the direction of the wind so that there would be a sign for the planes how the wind was blowing and what the landing would be like.'[20] The Halifax circled several times. The red light came on – the parachutists were still poised to jump, sitting in a circle around a 'round hole in the floor of the plane', with their legs dangling and the static line hooked up that would release the parachute as they jumped out of the aircraft.[21] The seconds felt like minutes as still they waited and waited.

Then, suddenly, the light turned green, followed by the dispatcher's voice yelling over the roaring engines and gusting wind: 'Go!' The men had told Elżbieta that it was to be ladies first, so she jumped. She remembered that 'the parachute [opened] happily and the earth [came] closer to me, not me to the ground! I totally [felt] like the earth [was] coming to us! . . . I hit my heels hard, but I'm on the ground!'[22] Finally, she was home.

She was greeted by the reception committee, the leader of which enthusiastically ran up to her and took her in his arms, then, realising that she was a woman, jumped back in surprise. A woman parachutist was unheard of. They had to hand over their weapons, ammunition, tools and parachutes. Following various winding roads through the darkness, they arrived at the safe house. Meanwhile, the eleven containers that had been dropped with them were picked up and stored.

They were taken to a farmhouse where they were warmly greeted, fed and given a 'wonderful bed' to sleep in.[23] Waking refreshed, Elżbieta made her way downstairs. Knowing that she needed to leave for Warsaw, the farmer's wife gave her clothing another check and discovered an English label inside her navy-blue silk dress. This would have been enough to give her away but had perhaps gone unnoticed because of the fuss she had made when she was searched at

RAF Tempsford. The labels were burned; she was now ostensibly a normal Polish citizen and could go about her business as if she had been there all along.

Boarding a train near Warsaw, she went to visit her Home Army supervisor Emilia Malessa Marcysia and passed on the news regarding the approval of the regulation of women soldiers. The decree was issued on 27 October 1943: her mission was now complete and had been a huge success. However, Elżbieta was too well known and had to go into hiding immediately. She took cover as a postulant nun and went to Szymanów, near Warsaw, to the nuns of the Immaculate Conception, where she stayed for a month. But 'the thought of the Uprising hung in the air' and she 'couldn't stand it any longer', so she went to Warsaw and received a new assignment with the headquarters of the Women's Military Service, working for Maria Wittek as an inspector.[24] She moved in with the Ursuline Sisters on Dobra Street and waited.

■ ■ ■

While Elżbieta was in hiding, the D-Day landings were successfully carried out in Normandy, France. A month later, Polish national Krystyna Skarbek was recruited into SOE's AMF Section (Massingham), which infiltrated agents from Algiers into southern France. With her previous work in the field, fluency in French and successful completion of SOE's wireless communication and parachute training, she was to be sent to replace an arrested courier to the JOCKEY circuit, which covered the Rhône valley, the Riviera and Grenoble.

Jumping in the early hours of 7 July 1944, she was blown wildly off course by six kilometres. She landed awkwardly, resulting in a bruised coccyx and a broken revolver. But not one to be deterred, she brushed herself down and began work. She had been dropped near Vassieux, in the Vercors region of southern France, and her brief was to mobilise her Polish compatriots in France, of whom there were thousands who had either volunteered under duress or been pressed into work in German forced labour camps or units of the German army. However, first she was to meet the contacts of her circuit leader Francis Cammaerts. After this, she undertook a tour of the Vercors area, which had long been home to an active Maquis group.[25] This particular area would, when the time came, make a perfect base for the landing of Allied forces. The plan, which had been approved by the French authorities in exile, was named the 'Montagnards' (mountaineers) plan.

In the wake of D-Day, hundreds of volunteers congregated at Vercors in anticipation of joining the Maquis in the forthcoming fight, for which airborne troop support had been requested. On 3 July, the Free Republic of Vercors was founded. But the paratroopers never came, and the Maquis became trapped by the Germans.

Over the course of the next few weeks, supplies and weapons were dropped by parachute, culminating on 14 July with a daylight drop of over eight hundred containers dropped from seventy-two American B-17 Flying Fortresses. The Germans launched air attacks to destroy the containers, and the Maquis initially mistook their aircraft for more Allied aircraft – until the planes started to strafe the ground, destroying the equipment and killing or injuring those nearby. Krystyna recalled the strike: 'Having sprayed us lavishly with bombs, the enemy planes then inundated the plateau with dozens of grenades . . . Vaissieux[-en-Vercors] was on fire.'[26] Working under these dangerous conditions, Krystyna helped to unpack supplies and stack them in piles ready to be distributed to the Maquis.

That night, while the villagers made makeshift hospitals and tended to the wounded, Krystyna and Cammaerts spent the night together in a hotel in Saint-Agnan. The following morning, as they were looking out of the bedroom window, they saw a fighter aircraft with a bomb strapped underneath it: 'We could see the pilot's face. I said if he releases it now, we've had it – and on the word "now", he fired.' The bomb skidded across the roof of the hotel and landed in a mound of earth behind the building. It did not go off. Krystyna gripped Cammaerts's hand: 'They don't want us to die,' she said laughingly.[27]

A week later, twenty gliders brought four hundred SS paratroopers who were armed with flamethrowers. They launched a large ground attack in which men, women and children were brutally killed. The doctors, nurses and even patients of the Red Cross hospital hidden in a cave were murdered, and many bystanders deported or shot. It is estimated that 840 French men and women lost their lives in the fight for the Vercors plateau.

Leaving on 22 July, Krystyna narrowly avoided the massacre. Travelling some 100 kilometres in just twenty-four hours, they reached Cammaerts's safe house in Seyne-les-Alpes. The next day Krystyna set off alone to cross the mountains into Italy, where she contacted a partisan group. She helped them in the wake of a German ambush and put them in contact with Major Hamilton, a Jedburgh team leader in the area, whose job was to establish contact with partisans all along the frontier.[28] Together they blew up roads and bridges around Briançon. Krystyna also managed to convince some seven hundred or so Poles (who had been pressed into working for the Germans as guards on the alpine frontier posts at the Col de Larche) to desert their posts and disable their guns.

Later that summer, following the arrest of Cammaerts at a German roadblock, she organised his escape from prison along with two British officers. She cycled 40 kilometres to the Gestapo HQ, declaring herself to be not only a British agent but also the niece of Field Marshal Montgomery. She demanded that the men be released lest the Gestapo staff 'be handed over to the mob' when the Allies invaded the south.[29] She must have been quite convincing, as the prisoners were released just hours before their scheduled execution and made good their escape. A few weeks later, Krystyna's area was liberated. She filed her final report and returned to London. Later, she was described as a 'person of remarkable courage and intelligence' and 'one of the most distinguished of our female agents'.[30]

■ ■ ■

In Poland the tension was mounting as preparations for the Warsaw Uprising were in full swing. The idea behind General Komorowski's Operation 'Tempest' was a series of planned local uprisings against the Germans that would precede the liberation of Poland by the Red Army. Initially, Warsaw was excluded from the plan; however, by July 1944, it became clear that Warsaw would indeed form an integral part of the operation.

After several days of discussion between the leaders of the Home Army and the Polish government in exile, Komorowski announced the outbreak of the uprising on 31 July 1944, after Soviet forces were seen along the east bank of the Vistula. It was anticipated that the uprising would succeed in just a few days, allowing the Soviets to enter and liberate the city.

The order was issued on 1 August 1944. The AK mobilised, and the streets suddenly filled with soldiers, wearing their battalion armbands in red and white and hiding their weapons beneath their clothes as they dashed to the assigned meeting points.

The city was awash with Polish flags, excited civilians and soldiers ready to do whatever it took to liberate their city. The atmosphere was charged and excited. Their time had finally come. After nearly five years of Nazi occupation, the inhabitants of Warsaw were ready to fight back.

The population flocked to assist in any way they could: preparing cellars, tunnelling underground passageways, building barricades with anything they could find – paving stones, bricks, furniture, sandbags, trams, cable reels, even prams. Vehicles were overturned to block roads, and people armed with improvised petrol bombs hurled them at passing German tanks and personnel. Several survivors of the Warsaw Ghetto Uprising joined the fight, although, officially, the AK did not allow Jewish members (since the oath of allegiance was to the Virgin Mary). Some Jews posed as Poles and fought alongside or joined the Polish People's Army, which readily accepted Jewish members in their ranks. After the AK liberation of the Gęsiówka concentration camp (inside the walls of the former Jewish ghetto), a Jewish battalion was formed to join the fight.

Elżbieta was visiting a pharmacy on Dobra Street when she received news of the uprising: 'Someone whispered to me: "It's 'W' time!" – I knew what that meant. I look – it's two o'clock. I run to my apartment, that is, to the Ursuline sisters, and say: "It's 'W' hour!" Today will be "W" hour! The uprising had begun.'[31]

At 5 p.m., she was sitting in a window with her friend Wack, when she saw a Polish patrol marching down Tamka Street, near the university. Potshots were fired, and the patrol began to fall, its members dead and wounded. Jumping down from the window, the pair searched the convent, trying to find something they could use to help. They spotted some stretchers propped against a wall in the hall and picked them up so that they could go onto the street and tend to the wounded. However, the sisters, who were assigned as part of the sanitary section, refused to let them take the stretchers. They were allocated to them so they could do their job of helping the wounded – it was their only way of contributing to the uprising. Elżbieta gave up trying to protest and watched the sisters take the stretcher and go outside. She was horrified to see that the Germans paid no heed to the sisters' red crosses and shot them down mercilessly. She could do nothing to save them, and it was only under cover of darkness that she was able to go out to help them and the others be transferred to a hospital.

Despite the horrors, the city was 'in a state of euphoria' and 'suddenly there were Polish flags . . . they bloomed in the windows. People come out, shout, dance, enjoy!'[32] Underground printing presses churned out news sheets with the latest news. Film crews and photographers recorded events as they happened, with the films later shown in cinemas across Poland, thus making it one of the best-documented actions of the war. The Boy and Girl Scouts managed an entire postal network across the city. But many people were frightened and went into hiding. Some hid in bombed-out cellars to shelter from inhumane weapons such as the Nebelwerfer (a six-barrel rocket launcher). Elżbieta remained locked in her HQ.

Only one person was allowed to act as a liaison at a time, and they were to go to the main HQ, a large PKO building (which was later bombed). The job was dangerous: 'one returns wounded, the other returns shot while crossing Nowy Świat', she said. 'So, the war continues. There are wounded, there are dead. There is a power plant opposite – it is bombed.'[33]

By 3 August, Komorowski was able to report to the Polish government in exile that morale was high in the city as inhabitants rushed to join the AK. Komorowski noted that the Home Army could not 'be compared with the attack of any regular army', since most volunteers were railway men, artisans, clerks and factory workers. They had 'all the drive and enthusiasm of a revolutionary uprising . . . [which] more than made up for the poor quality of arms.'[34]

However, the Soviet offensive had by now been halted. This gave the Germans time to apply their usual calculated and brutal manner to their efforts to crush the entire city and its roughshod army of civilians. 'Warsaw became the scene of long, relentless battles of attrition as the fighting intensified, and the explosions became more frequent – raining debris down onto the city which was choking in a cloud of smoke and dust.'[35]

It was in this atmosphere that Elżbieta received a new order that she and her comrades were to move their HQ to Słowicza Street and set up a field hospital. The building was next to an anti-aircraft pond, which also acted as a water reservoir. The hospital was set up to try to avoid the bombing on the streets and attacks from above. They managed the hospital and took care of those in it as best they could. Food was scarce, supplies even more so, and they were under constant fear of bombardment and sudden death.

After a short time, they received an order to move again, this time to Śródmieście-Południowe. Elżbieta had to cross the barricades. These she greatly admired; they had been made from bags of sugar as it was all that had been to hand. But the journey was an extremely dangerous one, with the group forced to wait until they could get a pass to get across the barricade. Priority was given to those who worked on the front line. As Elżbieta and her comrades were second line, they had to wait a considerable time before they were given the 'right to move to the other side'. Elżbieta recalled being struck by the stupidity of a group of women who carried a sewing machine with them as they had been ordered to make as many armbands as possible, 'as if there were no sewing machines in [Śródmieście]-South! They are carrying a sewing machine through the tunnel and through this barricade!'[36]

Their new premises were on Krucza Street, a large six-bedroom apartment house adorned with a 'large collection of books' and 'beautiful paintings'.[37] The latter were removed by the Ministry of Culture to preserve them. A representative came to the apartment and pointed at various objects. 'This needs to be taken to the basement, and these paintings should be deposited properly.'[38] When they came back from securing the items, the man was gone, along with a jar of tomatoes they had been saving. Elżbieta was remarkably pragmatic about her food being stolen: 'Hunger had already begun in Warsaw, food was already hard to come by, so they saw these jars and took one of them! That's how it was. Nobody blamed them.'[39]

She remembered:

We were there for a long time. I remember one of them managed to bring the Commander-in-Chief, that is, Maria Wittekówna, a few tomatoes from the field, because there were plots of land in Pole Mokotowskie and there were tomatoes there. It was a treat, because you couldn't dream about vitamins anymore, there was no milk at all. To get water, we went to a well, even close to us, which was dug quite deep, but unfortunately shot at, so we often returned with leaky buckets and the precious water gushed out of the holes.[40]

The city of Warsaw became overrun with the decomposing bodies of the dead, which piled up in the streets and filled the courtyards. Death was everywhere and a constant threat for those who still lived in the city, as food, water and supplies were all but gone. The people were exhausted, and the city was on its knees. Warsaw was dying. SOE sent some aid (but very little in comparison to aid sent to other countries) and the Soviets simply sat and watched from across the river as the city slowly but surely died.[41]

On 2 September, after thirty-three days of fighting, the last Polish soldiers left the ruins of the Old Town through the sewers. In mid-September, the Red Army took the district of Praga on the east bank of the Vistula but did not cross the river to aid the beleaguered city. By the end of the month, German forces took control of most of the city, systematically razing it to the ground and killing anyone they found. After sixty-three days of prolonged and bitter fighting, the uprising ended and Warsaw fell into German hands once more.

Together with her colleagues, Elżbieta 'led about 17 soldiers through the sewers to another part of the capital. For thousands, this was the only way out. The acute shortages of food, water, medicines, and dressings were appalling . . . the only food some of us had was yeast from a brewery which we mixed with drops of water and cooked where and whenever possible.'[42]

Many thousands of women had taken part in the fighting – one in seven combatants was female. The women's unit Dysk attacked the Waffen SS supply depots at Stawki, killing German guards and freeing several Jewish forced labourers. These warehouses contained enormous amounts of food, which would help feed the inhabitants of the Old Town. This unit also took part of northern Wola (a district in the western part of Warsaw) during the first week of the uprising. Other women worked as nurses, messengers, couriers and guides in the sewers, or helped drag the badly wounded from the street battles and through dimly lit underground routes that connected one cellar to another.

■ ■ ■

In September, the insurgents were rounded up and marched out of the city, and many ended up in concentration camps. Elżbieta (now promoted to captain) managed to escape, although she had actually been ordered to leave some weeks prior. With a typed silk handkerchief in her pocket, conveying an order from General Tadeusz that the bearer should be given help if required, she travelled to Krakow (codenamed 'Museum') via the convent in Szymanów and Częstochowa, arriving on 2 October 1944. There she was given an order by Home Army HQ to rebuild foreign communication. Gaining access to a working wireless with all the parts she needed, she miraculously managed to re-establish contact with the Polish authorities in London with the message 'that *Zo* is moving to Krakow and that *Zagroda* is moving from burning Warsaw to Krakow. From then on, communication was [to be] via Kraków.'[43] She was ordered to return to London, but finding the route unsafe, she returned to Krakow, successfully re-establishing many of her earlier routes and helping many couriers to pass safely along them.

In February 1945, the Home Army was demobilised. Poland fell to the Soviets and essentially swapped one brutal occupation for another; it would not be free until the 1980s.

Elżbieta no longer had a role and returned home to Torún and her family, and to her pre-war life of teaching. But she soon renewed her underground contacts and became involved in the Delegation of the Armed Forces, working in the communications and distribution department. In 1946, she took up work with Maria Wittek's section of Women's Military Training at the State Office for Physical Education and Military Preparation, thus ending her underground work.

Elżbieta Zawacka's exemplary achievements are a shining example of bravery, courage and selflessness. She not only sought to train and prepare others for wartime by teaching them the necessary skills to become active and useful members of PWK, but continually sought to improve herself with constant training for both her underground work and her university studies. Quick-witted and with nerves of steel, she undertook missions, escapes and journeys that any lesser person would baulk at the very thought of, all the while carrying incriminating documents and luggage. She ensured women's recognition in the Polish auxiliary units and undertook a hazardous mission to London, determined that she would jump back into Poland to continue her work in the fight for freedom. Although not technically an SOE agent, her training within SOE's Special Training Schools served to improve an already phenomenal courier and latterly gave her the accolade of the only female Cichociemni.

In 1951 she was arrested and tortured by the Urząd Bezpieczeństwa (the Security Office). Along with many other Polish resistance fighters and insurgents from the Warsaw Uprising, Zo was considered a threat by the Soviet communist authorities who took power after the war had ended. She was accused of treason and espionage and sentenced to ten years in prison. Fortunately her sentence was shortened, and she was released in 1955. Afterwards she earned a PhD from Gdansk University and became a professor at the Institute of Pedagogy at Mikołaja Kopernika University in Torún. She remained an active member of the World Union of Home Army Soldiers, was involved with the Solidarity movement and received the rank of general in 2006. She died three years later. She is Silent and Unseen no longer.

3

MISSION FRANÇAISE

I had my handbag in one hand and my pistol in the other. I walked up to a farmer and said, 'Good evening.' I scared the wits out of him! He was waiting for an agent named Râteau, but nobody had told him that Râteau was a woman.

Jeanne Bohec[1]

It took just six weeks for France to fall to the Nazis. The invasion began on 10 May 1940 when the tanks and troops of seven Wehrmacht Panzer divisions rolled across the German–Belgian border and crashed through the heavy forests of the Ardennes. The key to their success was *blitzkrieg*, or lightning war – a strategy of rapidly overwhelming anything and everything that lay in their path. The French had put much faith in the Maginot Line, built in the wake of the Great War to protect against another German invasion. This string of defensive concrete fortifications, some 450 kilometres in length, ran along the Franco-German border. They had also believed that the Ardennes forest would be impenetrable to fast-moving armoured formations. But in both of these assumptions they had been proved disastrously wrong.

Outflanking the Maginot Line, the Panzers turned north towards the English Channel and pushed the Allies there back to the coast at Dunkirk. From here the Allies had no choice but to evacuate by sea in any available transport. Warships, tugboats and even fishing vessels came to their aid, undertaking the perilous mission, all the while being strafed from the air by low-flying Luftwaffe aircraft. The scene on the beaches was one of chaos and carnage, as the men who were queuing to embark vessels on the 'mole' were shot and killed, while their vehicles, weapons and supplies lay abandoned along the roads.[2] But for the 'Halt order' issued by local commander Von Rundstedt (in a decision endorsed by Hitler himself), in which the advance of tank divisions was stopped for three days, the Allies could have been annihilated there and then. However, this unexpected respite allowed for an evacuation of a large proportion of the British Expeditionary Force (BEF), along with many French troops, some of whom would return as résistants and SOE agents.

But the humiliation of France was not yet complete. Hitler ordered that the Compiègne Wagon, in which the 1918 armistice had been signed, be removed from the specially created museum in the 'Glade of Armistice' in which it was housed and be taken back to the Rethondes Clearing. It was there that, in a reversal of fortune, this symbol of peace became one of victory for the Germans and shame for the French. Inside the carriage, a second armistice was signed, this time marking the defeat of France. On 22 June, France was split into two, the Occupied Zone under German control and the Unoccupied, or Vichy, Zone, ruled over by the eighty-four-year-old Marshal Pétain. The humiliation complete, the train carriage was taken to Germany and dismantled.

Four days earlier, smarting from the defeat at Dunkirk and Pétain's pleas to the French to cease hostilities and comply with the German occupation, General Charles de Gaulle, the self-professed leader of the Free French in exile, made his now famous 'À tous les Français' (To all Frenchmen) speech. He called upon the French to 'unite . . . in action, in sacrifice and in hope. Our Country is in danger of death. Let us fight to save it. Long live France.'[3] The flame of resistance had been lit.

It was a naive hope, but a hope nonetheless held by SOE staff that all anti-Nazi Frenchmen would work together under a common goal to rid France of the Nazis and bring an end to an occupation that brought fear, deprivation and an uncertainty as to who one could trust or what the future held. It was soon discovered, however, that this unity was not to be and there emerged two distinct camps – those who supported de Gaulle and those who did not. The anti-Nazi elements in Vichy refused to have anything to do with de Gaulle, who in turn rejected anything and anyone who cooperated with Pétain. De Gaulle and his followers saw Pétain as a puppet leader with his regime of collaboration with the Nazis. De Gaulle was also horrified to discover that SOE were infiltrating agents without any real regard for their political affiliations. Since his aim was not only to rid France of the Nazis but to influence the country's post-war politics and leadership (which did not include political parties such as the communists), he was loath to allow them the freedom to operate in France without his authority.

While F Section had been formed in July 1940, its existence was kept from de Gaulle and the Free French authorities, who were 'exceedingly angry' when they found out about it in late 1940 and immediately called for a separate country section to work with the Free French.[4] Reports from SOE agents who had made contact with Gaullists in France showed there was strong support for him and his policies, and that this new section was warranted and viable. So République Française (RF) Section was given the go-ahead – although this did little to dispel the mutual distrust between the two sections. There were bitter tensions between F and RF throughout the war. 'Each of these two sections was sure that its own men and methods were sound, while its rivals were not; each thought the other was unfairly favoured, either by the rest of the SOE machine or by politicians outside it.'[5]

With offices in Berkeley Court off Glentworth Street, RF's head of section, Major Eric Piquet-Wicks, was tasked with liaising with other Free French organisations and personnel. These included André Dewavrin (also known as Colonel Passy), who was appointed

by de Gaulle as head of Service Action and who dealt with operations, and Deuxième Bureau (also known as Service Renseignements,
SR), which dealt with intelligence and counter-espionage. Both were
in constant contact with RF. SR was housed in various locations
across London before settling at 10 Duke Street in March 1942, by
which time the organisation had been renamed twice: in April 1941
to Bureau central de renseignements et d'action militaire (BCRAM)
and in January 1942 to Bureau central de renseignements et d'action
(BCRA). By this time, RF had expanded and taken new offices at 1
Dorset Square. The relationship between the two organisations was
so close that it was as if one could not exist without the other: 'RF
could effect nothing without BCRA ... and without RF, the BCRA
would have had no weapons, and no means of sending its fighting
men into the field.'[6]

However, the 'fighting men' or women differed greatly in terms
of background, political allegiance and stability according to which
SOE section recruited them. F Section was able to draw upon 'bilin-
gual British subjects ... Frenchmen with some English background
and a special affection for Britain and ... Frenchmen who combined
patriotism with distrust for de Gaulle and had energy and initiative
to act independently of his authority'.[7] RF, on the other hand, had a
'pool of plain patriotic Frenchmen, of no great education, and varying degrees of honesty' but with a knowledge of French life and a
passion for de Gaulle's policies.[8] As a result de Gaulle did not recruit
'born leaders' but instead built an army of saboteurs, instructors and
couriers whom he provided with money, arms, explosives and wireless sets, which had in turn been provided by SOE and the British.

These men (women had not yet been given the go-ahead to work
as agents) were trained at Inchmery House near Southampton, with
its own private beach and views across the Solent to the Isle of Wight.
Previously home to the Mitford and Rothschild families, it was
now the Free French training school. Here, SOE provided the facilities and training – although the actual training was not under their

direct control and was reputed to lack 'discipline and order'.[9] From the spring of 1942, it was decided that RF agents should attend the formal SOE training at the Special Training Schools in order to prepare them for their first missions.

It was also in the spring of 1942 that SOE formally started to recruit women agents. Sir Colin Gubbins, director of operations and training at SOE and the organisation's driving force, observed that the usefulness of women had already been proved by the work of Virginia Hall,[10] Krystyna Skarbek (see Chapter 1, 'Mission Polska') and Gilliana Gerson.[11] All three had been recruited and run in a fairly ad hoc manner. Gubbins knew and understood the advantages of the further use of women, and believed there was an important and niche role which only they could fulfil. Thus, SOE sanctioned the systematic recruitment and training of women in larger numbers to work as agents in the field.

The use of women in France is arguably one of the most discussed elements of SOE history, and yet studies have been largely restricted to F Section, with very little written (especially in English) about RF. There is a host of reasons for this. Firstly, the comparatively large proportion of women agents (39 of around 430 agents were female) struck a chord with the British public post-war. Subsequent enquiries led by Dame Irene Ward into the whys and wherefores of recruiting women led to public debate and an official history being commissioned by historian M.R.D. Foot. In the immediate post-war period, there was unprecedented media interest in F Section agents, especially after their names appeared in the gazettes for decorations and the much-publicised war trials of the camp guards responsible for the women's deaths. Vera Atkins had been employed during the war as assistant to the Head of F Section, Maurice Buckmaster, and was now tasked with finding the missing agents of F Section only. This did not include the missing women from RF/BCRA, of whom there were several.

In the 1950s there was a flurry of biographies about certain F Section women, notably Odette Sansom and Violette Szabo, whose compelling stories were also made into films. Thus 'F' led the way in terms of media coverage and subsequent popularity. It is also the case that these women were English, or at least had links to England and therefore fitted the mould as war heroines for the British public; French women were just that – French – and did not garner the same interest or praise. Yet eleven French women were recruited directly into RF Section, and others were recruited in Algiers and, after passing their SOE training in Britain, were infiltrated into France to undertake various missions in the latter stages of the war. There were also women with very close links to SOE who, while not technically SOE agents, deserve to be mentioned within this chapter, starting with an infamous woman who sought to bring the organisation to its knees through treachery and deceit.

Born in Le Creusot on 29 June 1908, Mathilde Carré née Bélard (known to her family as Lily) was the daughter of an engineer and his wife who, soon after her birth, left their infant daughter with her grandfather in the Haut-Jura and moved to Paris. She had a somewhat isolated childhood but frequently saw her parents. In the Great War, her father served at Verdun, but in 1916 he was sent on a mining course at Versailles, where Mathilde and her mother joined him and spent three glorious months together. In 1920, she entered the local lycée, which she described as 'bright and pleasant', before becoming a boarder at the strict Lycée Jeanne D'Arc in Orléans.[12] Following that she attended the Sorbonne, where she studied in the faculty of law.

In May 1932, while still at the Sorbonne, she undertook some teaching in Montmartre. It was here that she discovered men, in particular a thirty-year-old schoolteacher named Maurice Carré, who was well dressed and handsome. She took an instant liking to him. She knew that marrying him would mean undertaking a more frugal lifestyle than she was previously used to, and that her parents would disapprove. In spite of it all she married him in May 1933 – and immediately regretted it. 'The whole affair seemed to be false, comic and a complete illusion,' she recalled.[13] The couple lived apart until she joined him on a posting to Oran in Algeria, where she worked as his assistant.

At the outbreak of war, Mathilde left him and travelled to France, where she became a nurse in L'Union des femmes de France, part of the French Red Cross, and trained at a surgical hospital on the outskirts of Paris. In May 1940, she was posted to a hospital near the Maginot Line. There, she met a dashing lieutenant in the French Foreign Legion called Jean, and they began a tumultuous affair, making love 'under the eyes of an enormous crucifix' in a bishop's cell at the seminary at Cazères-sur-Garonne.[14] She became pregnant but soon miscarried, blaming Jean for the loss of the child. The couple split up, and she found herself on a bridge contemplating suicide. 'However,' she said, 'instead of the Garonne, I decided to fling myself into something else . . . I would fling myself into the war . . . it would be more intelligent to commit a useful suicide.'[15]

That night she went to a restaurant with a friend to mark this positive turning point in her life and met a Polish man by the name of Roman Czerniawski. The next day, they met for a coffee, and soon a 'great bond of friendship' grew between them.[16] He confided in her that he had been a prisoner of war, having been arrested while studying at the Lunéville pilot school. He had managed to escape from the POW camp and returned to Lunéville, where he was harboured by his mistress, who gave him her dead husband's clothes and papers. Under the name of René Borni, he was able to live and move freely around the city. 'His eyes flashed' when he spoke of all of this, and he refused to accept that 'Poland had been defeated'.[17] Mathilde told him that she also refused to believe that France was defeated and that she would do anything to help, 'even if it entails great danger'.[18]

A few weeks after their initial meeting, Czerniawski 'gravely' informed her that he was a spy and had already created an intelligence-gathering network in the Free Zone, and was now planning on doing the same in the Occupied Zone (with the blessing of the Polish government in exile and the heads of the Marseilles network). What was more, he wanted her to help him create this new, 'multi-celled net-work'.[19] Since the new network was working on behalf of the Allies, its 'general' was a Pole whose 'chief of staff' was an 'intelligent [and] brave' Frenchwoman. It was a truly 'inter-Allied' project and was thus named INTERALLIÉ.[20] Mathilde was codenamed 'La Chatte', because she 'walked like a cat' and could 'scratch like one too'.[21]

Despite the fact that they only had their 'enthusiasm', 'ideals' and 'optimistic ignorance', they quickly got to work with the sole aim of 'overthrowing' the Nazis.[22] Czerniawski dispatched the intelligence that he had gathered to London, while Mathilde set about recruiting new agents. These included 'railway workers, policemen, criminals' and even a toilet attendant, who allowed her premises to be used as a 'letter box', which, along with several other buildings across Paris in-cluding hotels and schools, allowed the network to flourish.[23] Renée Borni, the widow who had provided Czerniawski with his cover story, moved to Paris and joined INTERALLIÉ. Codenamed 'Violette', she coded and decoded the wireless messages that were now being sent on behalf of the network. Undertaking this 'tiring and unrewarding work admirably', she and Czerniawski renewed their relationship, much to Mathilde's disgust. She didn't like Renée at all, describing her as 'a typical little provincial woman, and badly dressed'.[24]

Whether Mathilde was actually jealous of the relationship is dif-ficult to ascertain. She maintained that she and Czerniawski were not lovers and that she harboured no feelings for him other than friend-ship and comradeship, despite sharing a flat with him. Their cover was that they were cousins, and she affectionately called him 'Toto'. During this time, Mathilde's husband was repatriated to France. She went to meet him but found him to be 'cross-grained, ill and very dis-agreeable', and, worse still, 'pro-Nazi' and anti-British.[25] She decided that she wanted a divorce and never saw him again.[26] He was posted back to Africa and made several attempts at reconciliation, writing to her parents and even Marshal Pétain, asking for the whereabouts of his wife.

Meanwhile, INTERALLIÉ got to work. Its main aim was to gather as much intelligence as possible to build up a clear picture of the enemy in occupied France for de Gaulle and the Allies in London. They gathered information on the general situation in France: troop movements, military installations, stocks of fuel and electric power stations, munition dumps, industry, press, politics and propaganda. The material was collated and typed onto tissue paper before being sent back to London via a convoluted system that involved hiding notes behind toilet cisterns in certain railway trains travelling to Vichy France, after which they were then taken across the Pyrenees by courier and eventually found their way to an office at SIS HQ in London. Some reports were so long that they were photographed and sent on undeveloped films via Spain. The sheer effort that went into getting the reports into the right hands and the 100 per cent success rate was a testament to the organisation and bravery of all of those involved. The network even nicknamed itself 'La Famille' because of how close-knit and loyal agents were to one another.

On 1 October 1941, Czerniawski was picked up by a Lysander that had been arranged by DF Section (who predominantly ran escape lines across France into the Iberian and Breton peninsula) and was taken to London, where he was to give a report. He was met by the head of Polish intelligence, Colonel Stanislaw Gano, who told him how busy he had been keeping them with the sheer number of reports that INTERALLIÉ was sending. For the next day or so, Czerniawski was quizzed on every aspect of the network, including Mathilde, whom he described as his 'perfect partner'.[27] Afterwards he was taken to see General Sikorski, who greeted him and took him by surprise by pinning the Virtuti Militari to his chest.[28] A few days later he prepared to be parachuted back into France, but 'felt a disturbing uneasiness'.[29]

Czerniawski was dropped by a Whitley bomber over a field near Tours on 9 October 1941 and took the bus back to Paris, where he was reunited with Mathilde and the rest of INTERALLIÉ. A few weeks later, the network celebrated its first anniversary. A small party was laid on at the Villa Léandre with sandwiches and champagne (undoubtedly procured on the black market for the occasion). At 8.15 p.m. the persons gathered sat around the wireless set and heard a message from London: 'Many happy returns to our family in France on the occasion of their anniversary.'[30] But despite all their successes, INTERALLIÉ was beginning to show signs of cracking under the pressure and Mathilde was struggling to keep up with her workload:

> My physical powers of resistance and my nerves began to fail me. Will-power, conceit and also patriotism prevented me from giving up the struggle. The more weary I became, the more I plunged into my work, consuming large quantities of spirits and strong black coffee to keep me up to scratch. I felt that my whole body was hollow, that my heart no longer existed . . .[31]

The next evening Czerniawski dined out with Renée. Walking home, he spotted a man with an upturned collar holding an umbrella. Thinking little of it, they went to bed. They were woken suddenly by the sound of gunshots, after which a man burst into the bedroom. This man was Hugo Bleicher (who would later become famous for the arrests of Odette Sansom and Peter Churchill). An officer in the Abwehr (German Military Intelligence) in Paris, his job was to catch agents and break up resistance networks. That night, he hit the jackpot: the leader of INTERALLIÉ and his girlfriend were now in custody. But he still had Mathilde Carré in his sights and was determined to catch her as soon as possible. He did not have to wait long.

The next morning, Mathilde was out for a walk and upon returning to her flat she saw that her lodger, Alice, was waiting for her: 'Her haggard face betrayed that a tragedy had occurred.'[32] As Alice embraced her, Mathilde noticed that the door behind them was broken and hanging off its hinges.[33] At that moment, a Gestapo officer appeared. 'You have kept us waiting, madame,' he said, and went on to tell her that he had been following her all morning. She remained 'extremely calm' as she was bundled into a car, telling herself that she had at least achieved her aim of a 'useful suicide'.[34] As the car drove away, she saw Renée standing on the street nodding her head. She had presumably identified Mathilde as being 'La Chatte'. Mathilde mused over what had just happened. Had they been betrayed by a collaborator or had they become victims of the efficiency of the Abwehr?[35]

She was taken to Abwehr HQ at the Hôtel Eduard VII, where, after being questioned about her family and husband and whether or not she was Jewish, she spent the night in a prison cell. The next day she was taken to see Bleicher, who told her that everyone else had already confessed and that he had all of Czerniawski's paperwork, as well as her diary. He gave her an ultimatum. She was to keep a rendezvous she had that morning at 11 a.m.; Bleicher would go with her, passing himself off as a member of the network, and then arrest the agent in question. If she did as he said, she would 'be at liberty' by that same evening. 'If you double cross me,' he warned, 'you will be shot immediately and without trial . . . You have committed enough crimes to be shot seven times over . . . Save your own skin and get it into your head that Britain is doomed.'[36]

It only took her a matter of minutes to change sides. She later said that it 'seemed the surest way of one day being able to escape' and that it was 'the greatest act of cowardice of my life'.[37] But her actions do not qualify these sentiments, which she recorded many years later, in 1960. In fact, she was ruthless in her efficiency and ability to sell out her colleagues and friends. The agent in question arrived at the rendezvous that morning, and after some small talk with Mathilde and the new INTERALLIÉ agent (Bleicher), the latter offered him a lift home. As soon as he was in the car, Bleicher told him that he was now in German custody. The agent turned to Mathilde and spat, 'What a slut you are.'[38]

This was only the first in a long line of arrests she facilitated, using her 'little notebook' as a guide, in which she had the names and addresses of thirty-five INTERALLIÉ agents.[39] She accompanied Bleicher as he arrested every one of them.[40] Some of those arrested remained stoically silent. Others cracked under interrogation and gave others away. Within three days, INTERALLIÉ was destroyed. Mathilde told Bleicher everything, including the locations of letter boxes, safe houses and agents' home addresses. With her help, four wireless transmitters were seized and taken to a house in Saint-Germain-en-Laye, nicknamed 'the cattery'. From here the wireless sets were operated by Abwehr officers, who pretended to be members of INTERALLIÉ, sending bogus messages to London. There was no break in their transmissions, as Mathilde had told them everything they needed to know – the codes, the transmission times, even the prearranged security checks.

London was even informed that she was now in charge of wireless operations and from now on would be known as 'Victoire' (Victory). An example of a false piece of information that was sent from 'the cattery' was that three German warships were in Brest harbour for repairs and would be out of service for some time. This overrode the correct intelligence sent by Colonel 'Remy' of RF Section that the repairs had been completed and so those ships left harbour safely, completely unopposed.[41]

Mathilde was directly responsible for this and, worse still, the Allies still believed her to be at liberty. She was 'now collaborating with the Germans as wholeheartedly as she had with the Allies'.[42] She showed no shame and even moved into Bleicher's apartment, becoming his lover. Together, they dined out on foie gras and champagne and attended concerts and parties; he even played the piano for her. She had completely sold herself to the Nazi cause.

On 26 December 1941, Mathilde met SOE Pierre de Vomécourt for the first time at the Café George V on the Champs-Elysées. Bleicher was sitting at the next table. Vomécourt thought a café was too open and dangerous a place – he feared they could be overheard – and so he asked her to come back to his office. Bleicher had no option but to let her go. Vomécourt had met her with the intention of asking her to help him with wireless transmission as his operator Georges Bégué had been arrested in October, and his replacement André Bloch had been arrested a month later. He had no means with which to communicate with London and needed her help. She agreed to help and, of course, reported everything back to Bleicher. In January Vomécourt asked her to procure some 'forged identity documents' and she arrived the next day with 'an impressive collection of passes and identity cards'.[43] The speed of her response and the exceptional quality of the papers made Vomécourt suspicious of Mathilde and, when he challenged her, she admitted she was working (under duress) for the Germans.

Together they hatched a plan that she should persuade the Germans to let her go to SOE HQ in London with him. As far as Bleicher was concerned, she could continue her work as a double agent right from the hub of the action at Baker Street and then return with valuable information and intelligence about SOE, securing its downfall. As far as she was concerned, it was a way out of the mess she had created. In early February, a message was sent to London (supposedly from Vomécourt but actually sent from 'the cattery') requesting the immediate exfiltration of Vomécourt and Mathilde as their lives were in danger. After several misadventures, the two reached England by boat on 27 February.

Mathilde was greeted as 'a welcome and honoured friend'. SOE had decided that she should be left under the impression that her story was accepted as genuine – that she had fled France as she was at risk of arrest by the Gestapo. But the truth was already out: Vomécourt had informed Maurice Buckmaster who and what she was. London sent a message to the fake INTERALLIÉ and told them that Victoire and Vomécourt had arrived safely, and that 'messages will be passed through to the Germans, leading them to suppose that they will both return at the end of April or beginning of May'.[44]

Mathilde made a decision: she was going to do what suited her best. She turned again, from double agent to triple agent, and gave the Allies what they wanted. She told them about 'the cattery' and the *Funkspiel* (radio play). She gave them the names and whereabouts of all the Abwehr officers that she had met and produced the codes that Bleicher had entrusted to her. With this, she hoped to buy her freedom. She was given a flat, but her phone was tapped, her diary monitored and, to begin with, an officer was placed in charge of her movements. He wrote reports on her and how she behaved. He described her as:

> very lazy and will only do what amuses her . . . she is clever, but not as clever as she thinks she is, and has an enormous vanity, and with flattery, it is possible to guide her to a certain extent and for a limited period. On the other hand, she has an enormous arrogance, completely unfounded, and a sense of her own infallibility, which results in the most offensive remarks . . . as long as she gets what she wants, she is perfectly charming and merely asks for more, but at the slightest sign of opposition she will either burst into a fury, ending up in a pathetic scene or if that is not successful act the injured party and become difficult and obstinate and refuse to eat.[45]

On 1 April 1942, a month after they arrived, Vomécourt returned to France under a veil of secrecy: 'It is essential to the plans of LUCAS that no news of his return in France should be leaked out in this country in such a way that information may get into the hands of the enemy.'[46] But somehow, his arrival was noted by the Germans and, on 25 April, he was lured into a trap and arrested. He found himself face to face with Bleicher, who had 'for reasons of his own' helped Vomécourt escape to England.[47] 'I have been betrayed,' Bleicher said. 'Our little cat has been playing a dirty game.' 'Not at all,' Vomécourt replied. 'If anyone has been betrayed by "the cat" it is me.'[48]

News of Vomécourt's arrest reached London some weeks later via the SOE network ADOLPHE run by Pierre Culioli. SOE HQ assumed that Vomécourt might have given way under torture, revealing the true nature of 'La Chatte's' triple treachery. In any case, her usefulness to SOE in London had come to an end and the French, discovering her treachery, had called for her arrest. On 1 July 1942, just days after her thirty-third birthday, she was arrested and taken to Aylesbury prison, where she went on hunger strike. She was moved again to Holloway prison, an imposing Victorian edifice with castellations and huge griffins holding keys in their claws. Six wings radiated from a central tower. She was kept in a cell near those of the condemned women. Little did she know that in a few years' time, she too would be sentenced to death by a French court as a collaborator and enemy of France.

The case of Mathilde Carré, who worked for INTERALLIÉ, the Germans and SOE, is as complex as her personality. Staunchly patriotic at the outset of the war, she soon showed her true colours as an 'utterly egotistical woman who cares for nothing and nobody but herself and her own well-being and pleasures'.[49] Her behaviour was selfish and self-motivated, and as a result of her actions, dozens of people were imprisoned, tortured and murdered. She showed little remorse, and only in her memoirs did she attempt to garner public sympathy by suggesting that she was forced to betray her friends, colleagues and countrymen. She single-handedly destroyed a network, and if she had succeeded in her aims, it is likely that she could have destroyed SOE too.

Fortunately, the war produced patriots as well as traitors, among them the women of de Gaulle's RF Section.

■ ■ ■

The first woman into France on behalf of RF Section was a fiercely proud twenty-one-year-old Breton named Jeanne Bohec. The daughter of a submariner and Great War veteran and his wife, she spent the first ten years of her life following her parents from port to port, believing that if she had been born a boy, she too would have joined the navy like her father. When she turned ten, her father retired and took work in a reserved occupation, and she settled into life at school in Angers, showing a penchant for mathematics and science. In her spare time, she devoured books and was inspired by the stories of women spies in the Great War, like Louise de Bettignies and Léonie Vanhoutte, as well as stories of naval battles. She imagined herself on the bow of a ship or at the periscope of a submarine and 'dreamed of one day fighting against the enemies of France'.[50]

At the outbreak of war, Jeanne was completing her studies at school and wondering where to go next. In March 1940, she heard that the Moulin-Blanc powder chemical plant in Brest was looking for a chemical assistant, and despite the fact that she didn't have the necessary qualifications, she was given a letter of recommendation from a teacher. She sought permission from her father to go for an interview and, grudgingly, he allowed her to attend. Jeanne passed her initial exam and 'was assigned to a laboratory to check the nitrate content of cotton powder'.[51] She worked ten-hour days, six days a week, with 'chemicals that could be bought at any pharmacy, and invented explosives', which were tested on the lawns outside.[52] Many of the employees suffered from burns at one time or another, including Jeanne herself.[53] But this ever-present danger did not deter her.

Jeanne was very politically minded. She opposed the Munich agreement and felt that France 'lacked leaders of the class of those in the other war'.[54] She made up her mind that if Germany invaded, she would go to England and continue the fight from there – and she did not have long to wait. On 18 June, the factory was evacuated. She ran back to her apartment, packed a suitcase and headed down to the port to see if she could find a ship to take her to England. She found a tugboat called *L'Abeille 4* and was allowed to board. At first, there was only a handful of crew – a family and their dog – but the boat soon turned back to pick up some Polish soldiers and pull a ship out to sea. Its duty fulfilled, the boat set out to make the crossing. Jeanne recalled looking back to see that 'the harbour was lined with fires from the coal and petrol depots. High black and white smoke with red and yellow highlights was rising. We could hear the sound of battle, the crash of cannons, the tac-tac-tac of machine guns. No one could be seen along the quays. The enemy had reached the very edge of France. Only the sea was stopping them.'[55] The following morning Brest was occupied by the Germans.

As a refugee without any papers or forwarding address, Jeanne was put into a requisitioned school near Crystal Palace in the suburbs of London. She soon moved into a billet in Dulwich, where she was provided with a bedroom, clothes and food, and attended church. But life in England was alien and strange to her, and she was itching to help with the war effort. She finally heard about de Gaulle and the Free French forces that were being formed under his leadership. Even though she had never heard of him, she rallied to his cause and was dismayed that so few others joined her to support 'this unknown general who had taken up the torch'.[56]

Deciding that she wanted to see him for herself, she boldly took a bus into central London, where he was due to lay a wreath at the statue of Marshal Foch. Trying out her newly acquired knowledge of English, she got a little lost but eventually found her way to the ceremony. Seeing French soldiers for the first time since she had left France had a profound effect on her. She wanted to join the fight but could not serve in the Forces françaises de l'intérieur (FFI) as women were not permitted to join. Nevertheless, she was determined to find a way.

That autumn the Blitz raged across London. The family with whom she was billeted moved and Jeanne found a room in a boarding house, where she made ends meet by sewing and helping out at mealtimes. She got used to the London fog and air raids and celebrated her first English Christmas by playing board games, singing songs and eating Christmas pudding.

That winter, the Corps féminin (CF) was created, based on the model of the Auxiliary Transport Service (ATS). Its aim was to provide personnel to serve in clerical and secretarial functions, thus freeing up men to be mobilised. But this did not interest Jeanne, who frequently visited the FFI HQ at Carlton Gardens to ask if her chemistry skills could somehow be put to use. After several false starts, she eventually signed up to the CF in January 1941.

After two weeks of training, during which she took on the 'martial bearing that distinguishes a soldier from a civilian', Jeanne proudly sewed her 'France' badges, along with the insignia of the Land Forces of the Free French, onto her khaki uniform.[57] This she topped with a 'horrid cap', gas mask and French helmet (for use in an air raid).[58] She set about her work as secretary to the Technical and Armament Service, which was responsible for buying railway and scientific equipment to be used in France.

Working long days, she had eight days off every six months. She spent these on leave in various places provided by the Friends of the Free French Forces for the use of FFI personnel. Destinations included Middlesex, Cornwall and Edinburgh. In London, she delighted in finding a restaurant that served horse meat, steak 'bleu' and pastis, served by a man with a 'magnificent gallic moustache'.[59] She frequented nightclubs and cinemas, joined a dance troupe and 'sometimes we met General de Gaulle, the "Grand Charles", as we called him with love and respect. At the time, we were not "Gaullists". We were simply his first companions, and his presence at our head seemed so natural that we didn't even feel the need to talk about it.'[60]

In late spring 1943, Jeanne was appointed to work in a laboratory (on the premises of the French lycée in London) that was tasked with 'finding the best ways of manufacturing sabotage devices using everyday products that could be bought in chemists'.[61] The results would be destined for the ever-growing French resistance. She helped to develop 'incendiaries, explosives and time-delay devices . . . detonators and a substitute for Bickford cord',[62] all of which became synonymous with SOE and sabotage. Her job was dangerous; her fingers turned yellow and, on one occasion, she was hospitalised for eight days with badly burned fingers. On another occasion, an explosive 'spontaneously decomposed' under her nose, and an explosion blew her colleague's fingers off so violently that she found a fingernail embedded in the curtains some days later.[63]

Soon, BCRA started to send future saboteurs to her to learn the art of sabotage and the 'recipes' for homemade explosives in case they ran out of the provisions provided by the British. It was while doing this that she had an idea of how best her expertise could be used: 'Instead of teaching our little recipes to a few boys here in London, wouldn't it be more rational for me to go and do the same thing myself in France?'[64] Encouraged by the fact that the British were sending women into France to undertake the same work as men, she arranged a meeting with BCRA but was immediately turned down. The French were not sending women to France. They were 'decidedly misogynistic [and] would have none of it'.[65] So she decided to try to join F Section, and was told that as she was FFI she was not eligible. She was stuck: she was arguably one of the most qualified and appropriate recruits, and yet her sex prevented her from being able to undertake what would be an extremely valuable role within SOE, BCRA and the resistance.

One day, Henri Frenay of BCRA visited the laboratory, and Jeanne wasted no time in asking him to plead her case and recommend her again. He agreed, and a few weeks later, she was summoned to Duke Street for an interview. A discussion followed about the work that she proposed to do and the risk involved, which continued over dinner the following evening. Shortly afterwards, she received the news she had been waiting for – she had been accepted by BCRA and was to begin training in preparation for being returned to France.

She was to be part of an assignment that Colonel de Chevigné had been tasked with on behalf of de Gaulle, namely reorganising and leading 'the military action of the French resistance'.[66] He believed that the military organisations suffered setbacks because of their 'close relations with the civil resistance, known, monitored and certainly infiltrated by the Gestapo'.[67] He decided that the two should be mutually exclusive and proposed infiltrating 200–300 officers into France to lead the resistance. Alongside the officers, he would also send wireless operators, secretaries and couriers. The teams would be recruited and trained in the UK and sent out as pre-prepared units with an established hierarchy and method of working already in place. Women were predominantly recruited to be couriers and wireless operators (i.e. subordinate roles: none were recruited as leaders; in that respect, RF was the same as F Section). Their files usually had a paragraph that read along the following lines: 'This lady had been handpicked by Colonel de Chevigné to work as a courier in a new organisation he proposes to establish.'[68] Within weeks, several women were recruited as couriers: Yvonne Gittus, Germaine Grüner, Germaine Heim, Marguerite Petitjean, Josiane and Marcelle Somers. Jeanne Bohec was given the unique role of explosives instructor.[69]

Her training began in September 1943, and she attended STS 6 in Finchampstead. Here she was described as 'intelligent and practical', as well as 'quick, observant and seldom at a loss for ideas'.[70]

Her short stature clearly caused some amusement to the instructors, who marvelled at this 'little person' of 'diminutive stature' who had all the gumption and courage of the men.[71] She is 'a regular little tomboy', wrote Colonel Hodges, who 'seems to enjoy being thrown about by the boys. As soon as she comes into a room, she starts scrapping with one or another of them.'[72] Among her hobbies, it was noted that she made 'homemade explosives', and since she was already well versed in how to make them, she was excused from the paramilitary course in Scotland.[73]

Her parachute course was held in October of that year. The striptease suit was too big for her (it was so-called as it hid a complete civilian outfit underneath and, with one long zip, could be easily and quickly removed), as were her boots, and she suffered such aches and pains that she was forced to walk downstairs backwards. As for the parachute, 'God, it was heavy,' she said.[74] As no one had ever flown before, they were treated to a flight in the Halifax before making three jumps. Despite her nervousness and the fact that she was the only woman, she was on the winning team in a competition between the French and Poles to see which team would land first.[75]

She was taught how to shoot various weapons, including 'pistols and revolvers of all calibres', which she then used in her instinctive shooting course. 'There was a specially prepared room where we had to enter by surprise and shoot immediately,' she recalled. 'There were silhouettes of Germans and a resistance fighter tied to a chair. Each silhouette hit would fall. Of course, it was preferable to spare the prisoner.'[76] She perfected her explosives skills and even learned how to operate a French locomotive. 'Nothing,' she said, 'was left to chance.'[77] Having learned how to pick locks and be the 'perfect burglar', she went on to learn close combat and silent killing, which, despite being 'below the average size', she excelled in.[78] After attending finishing school at Beaulieu, her instructors concluded that she would make an 'excellent instructor in homemade explosives' and that there was little more they could teach her 'in that or in any other subject'.[79]

After a few weeks of waiting, Jeanne was informed by Duke Street that she had been chosen to work in the M3 region (Brittany) as a sabotage instructor, codenamed 'Râteau'. She was the first and only woman to fulfil such a role within SOE.[80] On 26 January 1944, Jeanne was taken to RAF Tempsford. Enjoying a 'meticulous' meal, complete with a bottle of wine followed by coffee and whisky, Jeanne received her final checks and was handed the last items that she would need for her mission. The pistol she received caused much disappointment; it was 'tiny . . . a "lady's pistol" . . . a toy'.[81] She would have liked a more 'serious weapon' but had to make do.[82] The cyanide pill she was also given caused her much distress; as a Christian, she felt she would put her faith in God 'to keep me quiet'.[83] Quietly she took the items and put on her striptease suit, which was far too big, and boarded the aircraft:

During the journey, it was difficult to talk because of the noise of the engine. I closed my eyes and tried not to think about anything.

The weight of the parachute was cutting into my shoulders. I was sitting uncomfortably. But an hour passed quickly. We had to get closer. The dispatcher spoke to the captain. 'We are above the DZ 1. But we can't see anything,' he tells me. The plane turned onto the wing. Another long wait. Decidedly nothing.[84]

There were no lights at the DZ (drop zone) and the pilot decided to turn back for England. The dispatcher removed Jeanne's parachute, which eased the pain that had been mounting on her shoulders, but Jeanne was terribly disappointed not to have succeeded in her attempt to get back to France. She later learned that there had been a series of arrests in the area and that no one had dared come out to meet her at the DZ. A second attempt at infiltration was called off due to bad weather.

Finally, on 29 February 1944, she received a call to get ready. It was a freezing cold night and the wind was blowing fiercely as she drank a hot coffee and donned her jumpsuit once more. She was handed papers, mail, money and the same 'little pistol' as before, and then she boarded the aircraft. A little way into the flight, she felt the call of nature, but getting out of her parachute harness and the cumbersome jumpsuit would be next to impossible, so she had to hang on as best she could. The sight of the DZ couldn't have come quickly enough. The dispatcher hooked her static line, opened the hatch and switched on the red light. She sat on the edge of the hole, her legs 'dangling in the air', marvelling at the French countryside as it passed underneath her.[85]

The light turned green and she 'went through the hole. Immediately there was silence.'[86]

As she got closer to the ground, she realised that the bonfires were 'a long way off', but there was nothing she could do about it.[87] Landing about three fields away from her DZ, she quickly took off her parachute and the oversize striptease suit to reveal smart civilian clothes and was relieved to empty her bladder. With that settled, she could think straight, and she decided to leave her parachute where it was. Cocking her pistol, she walked across the fields to where she could see the bonfires blazing. She walked up to a farmer who was wrestling with an unruly parachute that was attached to one of the containers that had been dropped with her. Seeing such a smartly dressed, pistol-wielding woman in the middle of the DZ, he immediately jumped to the conclusion that she was Gestapo. It seemed that no one had told them that 'Râteau' was a woman. The situation was quickly defused. Then the chief appeared and, seeing her 'small silhouette', quipped, 'What's this? Are they sending us children now?'[88] Once she established (again) that she had just landed and was the person they were waiting for, she was taken to a safe house, where she spent the night before setting off for Paris.

She made the last part of her journey by train. At the station, she had her first taste of French 'ersatz' coffee. Excited at the prospect of a real coffee after so long, she was disappointed to find that it 'was black and hot . . . but that was the only thing it had in common with real coffee. It was bitter, repulsive smelling and, of course, unsweetened.'[89] She did her best to hide her 'surprise and repugnance and swallowed stoically'.[90] Her heart pounding in her chest, she waited for the train that would take her into the capital. After a sleepless night on a sofa and with the nervousness of being so close to the Germans weighing on her mind, she went to her first rendezvous, where she met, among others, Brigitte Friang.

■ ■ ■

Brigitte was sixteen when France was occupied. She had been brought up as a free thinker and was encouraged to speak up for her rights (and those of others) by her liberal parents. They encouraged her to excel in her studies so that she could aim high and get a good job. But her academic studies were cut short when she was expelled from the lycée that she attended for writing Gaullist messages on the school blackboard and etching a Cross of Lorraine and 'V' for victory on the school windows. She just wanted to do 'something, anything against them'.[91] She managed to get into university but, by her own admission, spent all of her time 'discussing ways of resisting' rather than focusing on her studies.[92] It was clear that she was going to become a very active member of the resistance. She fought back in any way she could; she would often steal revolvers from Germans on busy trains or from cloakrooms in restaurants, or slash propaganda posters. 'It was stupid,' she said, 'because the result was not worth the risk that we took.'[93] Just like Jeanne, she was desperate to do her bit and join BCRA.

Brigitte got her wish. In September 1943, a BCRA agent named Jean-François Clouët des Pesruches (codenamed 'Galilée') arrived in Paris to expand and coordinate 'M' group, which covered Normandy, Brittany, Anjou and Touraine. He had heard about Brigitte through a colleague in London and sought her out as soon as he got to Paris, asking her to become his assistant. Eagerly she agreed. Quitting university, she was recruited into BCRA as a P2 (permanent agent) and given the codename 'Galilée II'.

However, she did not tell her parents what she was doing – they still believed that she was attending university. But, hidden away in her bedroom in the dead of night, she was learning how to operate wireless equipment, as well as coding and decoding messages from England. She helped to organise parachute drops and worked as Clouët's cut out.

In November, she decided to leave home. She felt it was unfair to risk the lives of her parents and brothers. She was frequently out after curfew and risked bringing attention to herself and her family when she came home late, night after night. Bidding her parents an emotional farewell, she moved out and 'lived underground – in hotels, with friends'; she was constantly on the move and had to learn to live by her wits, working out who she could and could not trust.[94] Clouët worked with her to perfect her shooting technique by aiming at her own reflection in a looking glass. He also taught her some silent killing techniques and how to throw hand grenades.

She learned how to select drop zones for parachute drops and was often part of the reception committee. To see the parachutes coming down was quite a morale boost.[95] Brigitte was not present the night

Jeanne Bohec landed, but Clouët was part of the reception committee who had been so shocked to discover that their new sabotage expert was a woman.

■ ■ ■

After arriving in Paris, Jeanne Bohec was too nervous to leave her apartment and explore a strange city. She counted down the days until she could return to Brittany and no sooner was she there than she went straight to her parents' home in Rennes. They had not met since before she had left for her work at the chemical plant, and they were delighted to see her, thinking she had come back to stay. Jeanne stayed for a few days but was soon on her way again. 'There is a war on,' she told her father; she had an important mission to fulfil.[96] Promising to stay in touch, she took her bicycle and bade them farewell, cycling 42 kilometres to Pipriac, where her first sabotage pupil, who ran a garage and car repair shop, was waiting for her.

She was staggered to see how much he had managed to collect: 'Plastic [explosive], detonators, time pencils, a Bickford cord, a few Sten submachine guns and cartridges.'[97] She showed him where to lay the charges, how much to use and how to make the explosives himself should he run out. That night, as she lay in bed, her legs ached from her long bicycle ride but her heart was 'full of joy' after months of preparation and training. She had 'finally started to take action. What a long time it had taken!'[98]

From here on in, she was unstoppable. For several weeks, she travelled across the region on her bicycle, teaching members of the resistance how to use explosives: ten boys in Josselin, five men in Loudéac and even a priest in Saint-Brieuc who planned to pass on the 'good word' to his congregation.[99] 'None of them ever showed the slightest surprise at having to deal with a girl who was a sabotage instructor, and I was always treated like any of them,' she recalled.[100]

■ ■ ■

The spring of 1944 saw the arrival of Mauritian-born, twenty-one-year-old Alix d'Unienville. Her family, wealthy French aristocrats, moved to France when she was six years old and she spent her childhood in a château near Vannes in Brittany and in Morbihan. She held dual nationality, which made her case as an RF agent particularly interesting. The family were already planning to evacuate after the fall of France, but de Gaulle's rallying speech in June 1940 made Alix even more determined to get across the Channel so that she could become involved with the war effort. Eventually, the family boarded a crowded ship leaving for England, with Alix clambering up the pilot's ladder. Alix and her mother slept in the hold while the men slept on deck. The Polish Red Cross served food to the troops on board the ship, and what was left was handed out to the families. The British provided tea and, eventually, Alix's mother procured some bacon. The voyage took four long days, and food soon became scarce. On arrival at Plymouth, they were given welcome refreshments by the Red Cross, after which the family made their way to London. The city fascinated Alix, especially the 'astonishing spectacle' of the vast array of uniforms on display on the streets and in the parks.[101] While the Blitz was an intimidating and frightening experience, the lack of rationing (at this point) was welcome, and she enjoyed the wide range of food and clothes that were still in the shops.

Alix's brother had joined the Free French and was tasked with rallying the islands of Madagascar and Réunion to the cause by broadcasting via Mauritius. Alix wrote a few of the radio broadcasts and was soon employed as a secretary at de Gaulle's headquarters in Carlton Gardens. She then moved on to producing propaganda leaflets to be dropped by Allied aircraft over France, and it was through this work that she was recruited into SOE's RF Section.

Due to the nature of her mission, she was allowed to forgo SAB and paramilitary training, undertaking parachute training and the finishing school 'at an agreeable villa in the country' in Beaulieu.[102] In spite of being a little 'unfit' and 'somewhat apprehensive' of her parachute ground training, she successfully jumped three times from an aircraft in February 1944. This was despite high winds and wintry weather conditions.[103] At Beaulieu she demonstrated her strength of mind and courage and was described as 'hard-working', 'intelligent' and likely to 'be well capable of carrying out her duties in the field'.[104]

All she needed now was the chance to prove it. Returning to London, she anxiously awaited news of her mission, which had originally been scheduled for January 1944. She would wait by the phone until noon each day of the full moon period, after which she would spend time with her mother or go to the cinema. On 31 March, Alix was under the weather with flu symptoms and intended to stay in bed for the day. She called in to see if the mission was going ahead and was told, 'No, not today.' So she got back into bed and tried to sleep it off but was awoken at noon by the phone ringing. There had been a change of plan. The message announcing her arrival, 'two angels will make lace tonight', had already been heard by the local resistance. By the next morning, she would be in France.

At the airfield, she underwent the standard checks, then, armed with a small pistol and weighed down by her equipment (such as torches and medical kits), Alix was helped onto the Halifax aircraft. Adding to her load were 2 million francs, which she carried in a pocket in her oversized jumpsuit. This, at least, provided some useful extra cushioning to her backside. She was joined by her colleague 'Cathau' and alongside them were several containers, her personal effects and a suitcase with a further 40 million francs, which would be dropped with them.

The noise of the engines drowned out the conversation that she tried to strike up with her colleague, and so Alix sat in the cold and dark alone with her thoughts. Her hopes of refreshments being served were dashed and she thought how even a tot of rum might have given her a little Dutch courage at such a critical time. When they got over the DZ, the static lines were hooked up and she was told that it was a case of ladies first. Dangling her legs through the hole that had been opened, she waited until the light turned green and, after a brief hesitation, she jumped. Looking down through the darkness, she soon realised that she was plummeting towards some woods. She had no way to steer herself away from the trees. She did her best to protect her face and legs as she crashed through the branches, coming to an abrupt halt in a tree canopy. She could hear dogs barking and realised to her horror that she must be near houses. She tried to release her harness, but to no avail, so she resorted to hacking at it with a knife. Landing deftly on the ground, she had no choice but to leave the parachute where it was and make her way through the woods towards 'Cathau', who was also stuck in a tree. Soon the reception committee appeared out of the woods, and once he was cut down, they were hastily taken to a farmhouse where they dined on fresh milk and rillettes. After staying overnight in a local hotel, the following day she was on her way to Paris.

Under the cover of 'Aline Bavelan', who had been born on Réunion in 1922, moved to France in 1938 to study and was now the wife of a prisoner of war, Alix began work.[105] But despite the fact that she had been employed to be part of a 'civil delegation', her role was 'in fact military', and to reflect this, she was given the rank of Lieutenant.[106] Codenamed 'Myrtil', her main role was 'organisation of transmissions' and attending rendezvous. On one occasion, she was followed by a very persistent man, who pursued her down into the metro. She jumped on the train and at the last second jumped out of the compartment as the doors closed, but he was ready and did the same. Back on the platform, she was convinced that he was going to search or arrest her. Instead, he simply asked her to go out with him for a drink. She had become so embroiled in a world of fear and intrigue that she had almost forgotten that things like this could happen, even in wartime Paris.

4

NACHT UND NEBEL

I pushed the detonators deep into the explosives and tied them together with detonating cord. Finally, after placing half-hour delay pencils at the end of the Bickford cords, I smashed the pencil bulbs. One last look to see if everything was in order and we slipped away quietly.

Jeanne Bohec, SOE RF Section[1]

In March 1944, plans to break RF Section agent Pierre Brossolette from the notorious Gestapo HQ at 84 Avenue Foch in Paris's leafy 16th arrondissement were being hatched by 'Tommy' Yeo Thomas (codenamed 'Shelley'). A friend of Brigitte Friang's, Yeo Thomas had just returned to France with instructions from Winston Churchill to compose a report on the condition of the French resistance ahead of D-Day. However, when he learned of Brossolette's arrest, he decided to try to save him, unaware that Brossolette had committed suicide by jumping from a window at Gestapo HQ, where he had been brutally tortured. Yeo Thomas worked with Clouët on his plan to break Brossolette out of jail and frequently met Brigitte, who became very fond of him.

The date for the rescue was set as 21 March, and Yeo Thomas arranged a rendezvous between his cut out (named Guy) and Brigitte at 9.30 that morning at Alma metro station. She had another meeting on the same morning at the aquarium but had asked someone to attend in her place. Guy told her that Yeo Thomas wanted to meet with her himself at 11 a.m. at Passy metro station. Brigitte asked after a fellow résistant named Chaillot, and Guy told her that he was meeting him at 10 a.m., at the same rendezvous point and time as the one that she had decided not to attend. At that point, she changed her mind and went with him, planning to meet with Yeo Thomas afterwards.

Arriving a few minutes early, Brigitte was disconcerted to see a man in a light-coloured gaberdine overcoat at the entrance to the aquarium. Shaking off her worries, she and Guy continued up the main path, where she spotted another two men wearing raincoats and trilby hats. Then another pair of men dressed similarly came up the path towards them. She had a gut feeling that these men were Gestapo and, worse still, that they were surrounded. She felt like a caged animal. Her heart thumping in her chest, she turned to Guy and whispered that she was going to 'try and get out'.[2] Turning on her heel, she tried to run down the footpath. 'Everything happened in a flash,' she said. 'I found myself on the pavement surrounded by eight men,' all demanding to see her papers.[3] 'It's all right Brigitte,' one of them said to her, 'the game is up.'[4]

Hearing her name used by a member of the Gestapo made her blood boil. Remembering the techniques that Clouët had taught her, she struck him with the heel of her hand in his solar plexus, her pent-up tension increasing her 'strength tenfold'.[5] She remembered thinking to herself, 'I'll show them that a girl of the resistance knows how to die.'[6] Looking over, she saw, to her dismay, that Guy had been handcuffed and was surrounded by Gestapo men, and then she heard gunshots ringing across the park. 'Something struck my back with unparalleled violence. The shock of it sent me reeling headfirst . . . a thick mist seemed to pad me like cotton wool. Through it, I heard dim cries, "pull her dress down. Pull her dress down." '[7] Having gunned her down in broad daylight, they were concerned for her modesty – 'the Gestapo had principles'.[8]

'I was lying on my back', she remembered, 'my legs drawn up. From my abdomen, from underneath my left hand . . . blood was welling out warm and thick.'[9] A man came over and tucked her skirt around her legs. He bent down over her and murmured, 'I am sorry, Madame, that it was such a big-calibre gun, but this is war.'[10] She found humour in this: 'this man who after shooting me came to apologise for using a heavy calibre weapon to do it with!'[11]

She was put into the back of a black Citroën and took much delight in the fact that she bled and vomited all over the upholstery. She was taken to the requisitioned Hôpital de la Pitié, where she was given 'the utmost care and attention Gestapo style'.[12] After being dumped onto the floor on her stretcher, Brigitte was unceremoniously moved to an operating table, where someone took off her clothes and began to sponge away the blood that was covering her body. Fortunately, the bullet had missed all her vital organs and left her with grazed nerves and torn muscles, but that was where her luck ran out.

The Gestapo soon arrived and began their interrogation. She refused to speak to them, and soon 'the blows rained down, from open hands and closed fists'.[13] Fixing her eyes on the clock on the wall, she watched as the second hand ticked round and round. By now, the doctors had 'fled the room in terror' and left her there, stark naked, at the mercy of the Gestapo men who shouted questions and pummelled her with their fists.[14] Sometimes, they hit her wound, but she reacted so violently that they decided to focus on her breasts, limbs and head. They broke her teeth, making her gums bleed, and struck her jaw. She continued to stare at the clock as the minute-hand crawled towards 11 a.m. She should have been meeting with Yeo Thomas. Unbeknown to her, he was at that exact moment being arrested. He would go on to suffer the most brutal torture and privations at the hands of the Gestapo at Avenue Foch, Fresnes prison and later at Buchenwald concentration camp.

During her interrogation, the Gestapo had gone through her handbag, in which she had been carrying her real ID card, meaning that they now had the names and address of her parents. They told her that they had arrested them and would shoot them if she did not give up the information they required. She made the exceptionally difficult decision not to talk as so many lives now depended on her. She was informed that Yeo Thomas and several others had also been arrested and that they had all talked. She was the only one refusing to speak. Although she knew in her heart of hearts that this was a lie, she still had to fight the urge to give in and tell them. She was 'petrified' whenever she heard their footsteps coming down the hallway and the key turning in the door. She began to shake uncontrollably as they dragged her out for another bout of brutal interrogation. Afterwards, she said, 'I was happy, because physically and morally I had stood my ground.'[15] Denied any medication or painkillers, she spent three weeks in La Pitié, during which time she was visited by an army doctor twice.[16]

Clouët tried to rescue her. Disguised in doctor's clothing, he and some other agents borrowed a black Citroën for their getaway car, but the rescue attempt failed and two agents lost their lives. A second rescue attempt was planned, but while they were still working out the details, Brigitte was transferred to Fresnes prison. Thrown into a dirty, flea-ridden cell, she was informed that she was not allowed to sit or lie on the bed during the day; she was to either sit on a hard-backed chair or stand. Explaining that she had an abdominal wound, she asked to see a doctor whom she felt, upon seeing her injury, would give her permission to lie down. The grey-uniformed wardress told her that seeing a doctor was forbidden – her wound was to be used against her in every way possible.

Alone in her cell, Brigitte suddenly felt very lonely and isolated: 'I felt a desperate longing to sob my heart out like some tiny child left all alone. Everything was black, cold. There was no hope anymore.'[17] But she fought back the tears. At night the prison came alive as prisoners banged on walls, tapped Morse on water pipes or talked through ventilation shafts. Despite risking re-opening her stomach wound, Brigitte climbed onto her chair. Taking a deep breath, she shouted through the air ventilator, 'Brigitte, cell 121, arrived yesterday.'[18] Cries of welcome and good luck greeted her ears, and this strange method of communicating became a lifeline to her over the weeks to follow.

After a month or so, she heard a familiar voice through the pipes: 'Hello Brigitte! Tartarin here! Your little dog's doing fine!' Tartarin was Yeo Thomas. He was alive, and he was there in the same prison. Although she could not see him, she finally felt like she had company. The dog to whom he referred was a wooden toy that she had given him as a gift, so there was no mistaking that it really was him. Trembling with joy, she climbed up to the ventilator; this was her chance to tell him that it wasn't her who had betrayed him, something that had caused her sleepless nights lest he blamed her. 'It wasn't me who gave you away,' she said. 'I know that,' came the reply.[19] Giddy with joy, she sank into a deep sleep. Over time, the daily grind of prison life, the interrogations at one of the Gestapo buildings at Rue de Saussaies and the constant pain and hunger gnawed away at her. She began to hallucinate and 'the misery of [her] lot quite overwhelmed [her]'.[20]

■ ■ ■

In March 1944, preparations for D-Day were well under way. De Gaulle made a call for resistance fighters to unite under the banner of the Forces françaises de l'intérieur (FFI) and the diverse groups all over France heeded his request. In spite of the fact that the location of D-Day had not been disclosed, the FFI in Brittany were tasked with blocking the route of some 150,000 German troops and keeping them diverted from finding other routes to Normandy once the invasion had begun. In preparation for this monumental event, many more agents were sent into the field by RF, including forty-seven-year-old Marcelle Somers.

Marcelle was a mother of two children, Josiane and Claude, with whom she escaped from France in June 1940. She then worked for de Gaulle's government in exile and in October 1943 was handpicked by Colonel de Cheveigné to work as a courier.' Meanwhile, her daughter Josiane, who had joined the Corps auxiliaire féminin in 1942 and also worked in de Gaulle's department in London, had been invited for SOE training alongside her mother (her brother Claude was recruited too). During her training, Josiane met and married Claude Gros. Marcelle was infiltrated on 3 May; her mission was to liaise with the chief and recce new drop zones for future infiltrations. Josiane was parachuted into the Charente area of France after D-Day.[21]

A plan to put a nationwide strategy known as 'Plan vert' (Green Plan) in place for D-Day was mooted. The outcome would be that all train lines into Normandy were destroyed to prevent troop and armament movement. As such, hundreds of railways were targeted but first the Allies wanted proof that the resistance could be entrusted with this task and were indeed capable of such acts of sabotage.

To demonstrate their effectiveness, 'it was decided to sabotage all the railway lines in a pre-selected département, with the cuts to be maintained for eight days'.[22] This was to happen simultaneously on the night of 6/7 May. Jeanne Bohec's pupils would blow up the Paris–Quimper line, the Ploërmel–Guer line and all the secondary lines while she took the Dinan–Questembert–Roc-Saint-André line. The time had come to prove themselves, and she was more than ready. However, their supplies were limited. While they had enough plastic explosives, Bickford cord and time pencils, they were lacking the requisite number of detonators, which would mean that the explosions could not succeed. Jeanne gave what supplies they had to the men in her group and went to the pharmacist to see what she could procure for herself. She managed to get the white powder she needed. Fortunately, she had just enough time to dry it out and stuff it into some aluminium aspirin tubes before they needed to set out for their rendezvous.

The *message personnel* that night was, 'Reeds must grow, leaves rustle.' When Jeanne heard that, she knew that her chance had come. It was time to put the lessons into practice and 'hit the enemy directly'.[23] After curfew, she joined the others in a gas-powered van. They all carried pistols with which to protect themselves in case of an ambush. Jeanne's stomach was in knots and fear gripped her insides as the van crept down dirt tracks. The van's headlights were off, making the darkness (and the fear of what might jump out of it) even more intense. Once they reached their destination, they got out of the van, collected all the equipment they needed and headed to the selected part of railway track some 50 metres away from the station:

> I was caught up in the action and forgot my fears . . . with the help of my companions, I placed five or six charges in the switches, securing them with plaster, as I had learned to do, so as to produce as much damage as possible. I pushed the detonators deep into the explosives and tied them together with detonating cord. Finally, after placing half-hour delay pencils at the end of the Bickford cords, I smashed the pencil bulbs. One last look to see if everything was in order and we slipped away quietly.[24]

Despite the fact that her training had taught her to get away straight after she had laid the charge, Jeanne hid under a hedge, keen to see the fruits of her labour. The fuse was set for thirty minutes, which seemed to last an eternity. Checking her watch, she saw that the explosion was imminent, but the seconds ticked by, and nothing happened. Another minute passed, then another. A full thirty-five minutes after they had laid the explosive it still hadn't detonated. Then, just as she turned to leave, she heard a deafening bang. It was 'an enormous explosion', she said. It 'woke the whole countryside'.[25] With her heart in her mouth, she and her companions ran back to the van and got safely back to the village of Plumelec. She later heard that all the attacks had been a success, the resistance had proved themselves and Plan vert was extended across the whole of France.

■ ■ ■

On 10 May 1944, just days after Jeanne's successful railway sabotage, Brigitte Friang was transported to Ravensbrück concentration camp. She was a *Nacht und Nebel* (night and fog) prisoner, meaning she could disappear without a trace and no one would know what had become of her.[26] The camp had been established in May 1939 near the town of Fürstenberg, 95 kilometres north of Berlin, and was expanded throughout the war. By 1942 it was the biggest women's concentration camp, with over forty satellite camps. Approximately 120,000 women from thirty countries passed through Ravensbrück's gates. Among their number were 800 children and babies (some of whom were born within the camp confines), and from April 1941 there were also 20,000 men, who lived and worked in a separate camp.

Little knowing what hell awaited her, Brigitte was crammed into a cattle truck with dozens of women. They were packed in so tightly that there was nowhere to sit or lie down. They jostled for space and knocked into one another as they scrambled to find a footing while the train shunted towards Germany. With only one bucket to use as a toilet and death ever present, the restricted air soon became fetid, and prisoners would fight to get to the edges where they could breathe a little fresh air through the gaps in the wooden planks. Outside, spring was in full bloom, but that brought with it heat and discomfort for the women en route to Ravensbrück. The train took an agonising five days to reach its destination and arrived at night. The camp was pitch dark save for searchlights that swept the compound. The women were brutally dragged off the train and, after delousing and showering, they were taken to a temporary block for the rest of the night, terrified of the skeletal figures they saw around them.

As the sun rose, Brigitte was horrified to discover the reality of the camp: row after row of wooden barracks spread almost as far as the eye could see. There was a prison block (*Fellenbaum*), an infirmary (*Revier*) and a crematorium that belched black smoke into the air following an execution or killing in the nearby gas chambers. Watchtowers were strategically spaced out around the perimeter fence – a fence made of barbed wire and charged with enough electrical voltage to kill a person who inadvertently (or deliberately) fell against it. Male and female SS guards patrolled the camp brandishing whips, their dogs straining at their leashes, ready to attack and savage an inmate at the guard's whim. The SS reign of terror was feared by everyone inside the camp, where brutal beatings, random shootings and whippings were commonplace, even for the smallest misdemeanour. The fine line between life and death had to be trodden carefully by all inmates, but especially those in Block 15 – the French block, where 85 per cent of the women had been arrested for resistance activities, including de Gaulle's own niece Geneviève.

Brigitte was overwhelmed with what she saw and witnessed. After all, she was only twenty years old when she arrived at Ravensbrück, a place where she 'discovered the worst, the very worst in people'.[27] Her wound continued to weep pus, having never received proper medical attention, and she was plagued by hunger and thirst. 'Every hour, every minute [was] a struggle against the deliberate extinction of each of us as a human being.'[28] Every day was a fight for survival, but one day stood out among them all: D-Day. On 6 June 1944, a 'beautiful Ukrainian woman, a fellow prisoner in charge of the barracks, appeared [and] in her funny French she called for silence. "Ladies," she declared, "the Allies have landed in France." We all leapt to our feet and fell into each other's arms.'[29] A glimmer of hope had arrived at Ravensbrück.

■ ■ ■

That morning Alix d'Unienville attended a rendezvous at Bon Marché department store in Paris. Seeing that her contacts were not there, she passed the time by wandering among the street sellers on Rue de Babylon and bought herself a ball of wool. She walked back to the rendezvous point and, this time, the two men she was due to meet were standing outside. She ran up to them and excitedly told them, 'The Allies have landed.'[30] At that moment, a man behind her demanded to see her papers. She reached into her handbag and, when she looked up again, she saw that they were completely surrounded. Immediately, her thoughts turned to the cyanide pill that she had been given in England and which she carried with her. It was horribly incriminating, and she debated whether to drop it through the hole in her pocket onto the street or to take it. She did neither and when it was discovered later it was all but ignored.

They were taken to Gestapo HQ on Avenue Foch, where she and one of the men, Tristan, were interrogated together. This at least meant that they could keep their stories aligned. Her personal belongings were taken from her. Their first interrogation was mercifully brief, as they were simply the first in a large round-up that day. Later that day, she was bundled into a van and taken to Fresnes prison, where she was put into a solitary cell. Now alone, thoughts of her imminent torture played over and over in her mind. The next day she was taken back to Avenue Foch and watched in horror as her handbag was emptied onto the table in front of her. The contents included a considerable sum of money and a ticket with an incriminating address of a doctor scrawled on the back of it. As the interrogator turned his back for a moment, she managed to grab the paper and insisted on going to the lavatory, where she painfully swallowed it.

Tristan bore the brunt of the Germans' ill-treatment. He was brutally tortured, as well as undergoing two mock executions. In his desperation, he prised open the ring in which his poison was hidden, only to find that it had been removed. Alix was not tortured at Avenue Foch, but her treatment at Fresnes made her steadily grow weaker and weaker.[31] During this time, she set a 'high example of fortitude' and refused to answer 'when subjected to brutal interrogation'.[32] 'We were dying of hunger,' she remembered, and cut off from the outside world with little hope of survival. Alix came up with a plan.[33] She feigned insanity, telling the wardresses that her food was poisoned and then going on hunger strike for days on end. She cried out during the night and adopted a vacant stare that made everyone around her ill at ease. Her aim was to get out of Fresnes and to Sainte-Anne, a place for the mentally unstable, where she would 'recover' and hopefully buy her freedom.

■ ■ ■

News of D-Day reached Jeanne Bohec as she was travelling by train. She tried to conceal her joy so as not to get into trouble, but she was overcome with emotion. After D-Day, Jeanne worked directly for the FFI in a forest encampment on the outskirts of Saint-Marcel. The camp was vibrant and busy; there were huts, a hospital, and tents made from parachutes. Hundreds of resisters donned their FFI arm-bands with pride, while weapons and equipment from a recent *parachutage* were scattered throughout the camp or were being used as teaching aids for the newly arrived Jedburgh teams, who were training the new recruits in how to handle them.[34] The time to use them would be sooner than they imagined.

Four years to the day since she had escaped France, Jeanne awoke at dawn to the sound of gunfire and realised that the camp was under attack. The fighting quickly spread 'through the forests, wheat fields and country roads'.[35] Jeanne organised for a wireless message to be sent to London to inform them of what was happening and to ask for instructions. Then she sought out the head of one of the fighting units and asked him for a gun. He refused, telling her that there were enough men and he didn't want or need women to fight. 'I was furious,' she recalled. 'I knew how to fight better than most of the men, who had only been recently and haphazardly trained. I believe that women should be allowed to fight, it is our right to defend ourselves and our country.'[36] She busied herself handing out grenades and ammunition. When she was given a message to take to another group (telling them where and when some new parachutists would arrive), she stuffed the paper in her bra and, consulting a map, set off in the direction of the Maquis.

She had not got too far when she was stopped by some Germans on horseback, who were curious as to why she had a map. 'I tried to stay calm. I caught my breath. I smiled at them.'[37] She told them that she was visiting her grandmother and, as she did not know the area well, she needed a map. She felt like her 'heart was booming' and that she might 'suffocate', but they told her to move along.[38] She cycled away from them, and once they were out of sight, she pulled over and collapsed onto the grass. Her legs were shaking so badly she could barely move.

Meanwhile, the battle continued to rage back at the forest camp. The Maquis fought valiantly until the arrival of the RAF, who strafed the German position and their lookouts in the church towers and windmills. That evening, the Maquis destroyed their ammunition dump before evacuating through a gap that the Germans had inadvertently left open. Carrying their wounded and what arms they could manage, they dispersed across the region in small groups. Jeanne hid with some others in a barn. The next morning, she was supposed to attend a rendezvous but decided against going. A few hours later, she went to the location and was informed that everyone who had turned up had been arrested. Only one of them survived deportation. A few days later, she again avoided arrest when she chose to ride her bicycle instead of joining her comrades who travelled to a rendezvous by car. Luck was certainly on her side.

On 3 August, the FFI and all who worked with them received the message that they had been waiting for: they were to take up posts and harry any Germans who were trying to escape. Jeanne, who made her own uniform to be worn at the liberation, was determined that this time she should at least be given a machine gun or a rifle so that she could join in, but again she was told that 'it was not a woman's affair'.[39] She didn't want to stay in the background; she wanted to fight, but her sex prevented her. She took matters into her own hands and managed to get herself a job firing a bazooka at retreating Germans from a moving tank. The men with whom she fought considered her an equal and a 'comrade'. On 8 August 1944, Quimper was liberated. The men of the resistance proudly marched into the town to cheers and adulation, and the French flag was raised for the first time in nearly five years. The crowd cheered and sang the 'Marseillaise'. Standing proudly among them was Jeanne Bohec, wearing her homemade uniform. She may not have fought with a gun, but her role in making and teaching the use of improvised explosives was as invaluable as it was unique. Her mission was accomplished.

■ ■ ■

Alix d'Unienville had been feigning insanity in the hope of getting out of Fresnes, but instead of being moved to Sainte-Anne she was moved to Hôpital de la Pitié, where Brigitte had been so brutally tortured. There, dressed in nothing but a shirt, she was put into a cell with no toilet or running water. It was far worse than Fresnes: at night she could hear the cries and whimpers of men being tortured, accompanied by the gruff voices of the Gestapo interrogators barking their demands. One day, a woman, bloodied, bruised and broken, was brought into her cell. The soles of her feet had been burnt, and she had been so badly beaten that she could not feed herself. Alix tried to help her. Then, one morning, Alix's clothes were returned to her and she was taken to Saint-Anne's for a cursory check-up, where she discovered, to her horror, that she had a rattle on her lungs. That night she went back to La Pitié and decided that the ruse she had been trying was a waste of time. She stopped pretending to be insane, began to eat and was soon transferred back to Fresnes. From there, she was transported to Fort de Romainville on the eastern outskirts of Paris. It served as a prison, a transit camp and a place of summary execution for civilian prisoners who did not toe the line of the Nazi regime. Those incarcerated there were primarily resistance fighters, political prisoners, communists and intellectuals.

Romainville was described as 'death's waiting room' where *Alles ist verboten* (everything is forbidden) was painted on the door of each cell. According to French communist and resistance fighter Danielle Casanova, there was 'iron discipline, or rather bullying and inhuman treatment'.[40] In some respects it was better than Fresnes. Despite being closely monitored, the prisoners could move around during the day in a large courtyard. But the food was worse: '[we] suffer terribly from hunger, and we are reduced to eating cabbage stalks thrown away and potato peelings . . .'[41]

A fellow prisoner ran PT sessions, and Alix joined in to build up her strength. She was planning to escape and, with a friend with whom she shared a bunk, began to make a rope from the curtains that hung in the empty top floor of their barrack block. Night after night, they sat up after everyone else had gone to bed, plaiting strips of the curtains into a long rope, and each day they hid it under their mattresses. But before they got a chance to use it, her friend was deported to Germany, and on 15 August, Alix was put onto the last transport to Ravensbrück.

It was unbearably hot in the cattle wagon, the summer heat intensified by the sheer number of women's bodies packed in so tightly that there was no room to move. The odour of stale sweat mixed with the putrid stench of urine, excrement and dead bodies. With nothing to eat or drink, all the women could do was fervently hope that the journey would not take too long and that what awaited them was better than the living hell they were enduring on that train.

That first evening the train stopped in a tunnel, where they spent the night and much of the next morning. Uncertain as to what was happening, the women tried their best to remain optimistic. When the train began to move, it was going backwards out of the tunnel and, suddenly, they were ordered off the train and into nearby fields. The railway bridge had been bombed by the Allies; the only way to progress was on foot across a footbridge over the River Marne and then join a train waiting for them on the other side. Alix began to think about escaping once more. In her mind, she went over ways she could get away, and soon the chance she had been dreaming of presented itself.

In a village through which they were passing was a water fountain. The parched women threw themselves at it and, despite the guards' best efforts to keep them away, they quickly turned into a frenzied mob. Alix stepped away; no one was looking at her. She quickly found a doorway in which she briefly hid and then tried her luck with the door. It swung open. She found herself in a house with a rather surprised-looking couple who eyed her suspiciously but who ushered her away from the windows and hid her upstairs. When the column of prisoners had moved on, she thanked the couple who had risked their lives for her and left.

Finding solace in a nearby meadow, the sun shining on her face and the wildlife buzzing and humming around her, she thought how life had changed irrevocably within a few short hours. She then gorged herself on apples until she was sick. She stayed with a wood-cutter's family for a few days and was able to wash and brush her hair and teeth, which had been neglected since the day of her arrest. Alix moved from place to place until the liberation came a few days later, by which time the unfortunate women on her transport were incarcerated at Ravensbrück and subjected to the base dehumanisation that came with it. Hitching a ride back to Paris in an American jeep, the summer wind blew in her face and hair. She began to realise that it was over and she was finally free. Back in Paris, she went to her old apartment. 'I crossed the same threshold that I had on my way out two months earlier,' she said in a post-war interview. 'Just two months. It seemed to me that between those two doorways, a whole lifetime had gone by. And no doubt it was the case as, from then on, a barrier would separate these two eras: Before and After.'[42] The concierge eyed her suspiciously when handing her the spare key. 'Have you been in the country?' she asked. 'Yes,' Alix sighed, 'I have been in the country.'[43]

■ ■ ■

In January 1945, Brigitte Friang spent her twenty-first birthday in the *Revier* at Ravensbrück. She had a soaring temperature and hacking cough that, five days later, was diagnosed as tuberculosis. This was invariably a death sentence. She would either die or be murdered as an inmate who was unfit to work. Upon hearing the news, Brigitte began to cry, the first and only tears she shed during her entire incarceration. It was a relief to her 'to let go for once. To relax nerves that have been bandaged for so many months.'[44] She cried until her eyes felt like they were burning. She wept for the life she had once had, for her parents and for her lost future. She was convinced that she was dying. For her birthday, her friend brought a potato with a stick in it (to represent a candle) to her bedside, from which Brigitte could see a forest of trees and a glimpse of blue sky above them, but in her memoirs, she wrote that in March the trees were taken away from her due to the fact that the Red Army was advancing in the direction of the camp.

That month, four SOE RF Section women were murdered at Ravensbrück: Eugénie Djendi, Pierrette Louin, Marie-Louise Cloarec and Suzanne Mertzizen. They were all members of the 'Merlinettes', the nickname for the Corps féminin des transmissions (CFT, Women's Signal Corps). The CFT was formed by Colonel Merlin, commander of communications for all land, air or sea forces, as a means to free up men for active service in the wake of Operation 'Torch' (the Allied landings in North Africa in November 1942). The CFT was approved by General Giraud just days after 'Torch' on 22 November 1942 and officially created on 18 December 1942. A training centre was established in Staouëli, near Algiers, and approximately 2,000 female volunteers were recruited to work as telephonists, telegraphers and radio operators, many of whom participated in campaigns alongside the Free French Forces in Italy and France. Paul Paillole, commander of the 2nd Office of Algiers, recruited wireless specialists from the Merlinettes to join the Sécurité Militaire (the French military security services) and the four women named above, along with twenty-six others, volunteered to be trained.[45]

Very little is known of the pre-service lives of the three women who trained and served alongside Eugénie Djendi. Born in the Breton town of Carhaix in 1917, Marie-Louise Cloarec was a trained paediatric nurse. She moved to the Free Zone (Vichy) in 1940 and soon found work as a governess with an officer's family. When he was posted to Algiers, she moved with them. In January 1944, she was spotted by Paillole and enrolled in the CFT, from which she was recruited for SOE training. Pierrette Louin was twenty-two years old when she joined the CFT. Born and brought up in Oran, Algeria, she spoke French with a heavy accent and joined the Sécurité Militaire in the autumn of 1943. Twenty-three-year-old Suzanne Mertzizen was born in Colombes, Hauts-de-Seine. In 1938 she married the Algerian-born French military pilot Gabriel Mertzizen. Following the birth of their daughter Danielle in 1940, they moved to Algiers. On 18 January 1943, she enlisted as a radio operator for the CFT, where the four of them met.

According to her biographer, the life of Eugénie Djendi comprised family and military cover-ups, and finding out the truth about her remains a difficult task. Eugénie was born in 1923 in the eastern port town of Bône in Algeria, where her parents Salah and Antoinette Djendi worked as farmers. Brought up by her parents and grandparents, she attended the local school, and after her parents divorced, Eugénie lived with her mother and her new husband. This marriage failed too, and by the time war broke out Eugénie and her mother were living together.[46]

The outbreak of war was something of a surprise to Eugénie. The shock waves were quickly felt throughout Algeria, with 200,000 men enlisting in the first year of the war.[47] While the war in Europe did not directly affect the population of the North African country, news of the Allies' progress was closely followed. In January 1943, Eugénie saw a recruitment poster for the CFT featuring smartly dressed young women in dashing khaki uniforms with jaunty side caps. The poster called for French speakers to join the CFT for the liberation of France. Eugénie decided to go and find out what it was all about. At the interview, she was told that she would not be a soldier – 'after all, you don't send women to fight on the front line' – but that she would be doing 'technical work, transmitting messages and receiving them'.[48] She would live in barracks and receive an allowance. After confirming that she was neither ill nor Jewish, she was asked to produce a certificate of good conduct and was informed that, 'if all went well', she would be asked to take a test to finalise her recruitment.[49]

On 11 January (which was also her grandmother's birthday), armed with everything she needed, Eugénie returned to the recruitment office and was enlisted as an 'operator' for the duration of the war. Her full role would be designated after training, which took place in the École du Corps féminin in the Kasbah of Algiers. Recruits were taught transmission and wireless while becoming used to military life. Since Eugénie had signed up for work in the 'army zone', she had to become accustomed to that aspect of her new life, including military rules and customs, recognition of ranks, marching and conduct, all while wearing her smart khaki uniform – just like the girls in the poster that had drawn her to this work.

It was on this initial training course that Pierrette, Suzanne, Marie-Louise and Eugénie all met. They undertook an intensive telegraphy and wireless course, in which they were taught to take the deserts and surrounding seas into consideration, as well as learning Morse code and message encryption. On 15 March 1943, the first fifty-four operators had left Algiers to take over the telephone operations of the transmission centres at Le Kef, Souk el-Arba, Teboursouk, Le Sers, Ebba-Ksour, Tebessa, Aïn Bedia and the HQ of the 19th Army Corps in Tunisia.[50] A few weeks later, on 1 May 1943, Eugénie and Marie-Louise, having passed their radio operator's exams, arrived at the Le Kef centre, which bordered the British and French zones in Tunisia. They became the first women to help run the radio station there. After working in Le Kef, Eugénie was sent to Tunis to help get the communications network back up and running and stayed there until the end of the month, when communications were finally restored. Her Tunisian campaign came to an end on 6 July 1943, and she returned to Algiers as an 'operator, second class'.[51]

She was soon promoted to 'first class' and proudly sewed the coloured woollen braid onto her khaki uniform to denote her rank. On 1 September, she left Algiers again and was posted to 45/12 Company in Tlemcen in the Oranais region, in western Algeria. It is likely that she 'travelled . . . to Tunis with a reinforcement of around ten signal soldiers'.[52] While she was on this posting, she was called to a meeting by her superiors, who asked her if she would be interested in joining the Sécurité Militaire. She considered this opportunity too exciting to turn down, and readily accepted the new challenge.

On 15 September, she and twenty-nine other women (including Marie-Louise, Pierrette and Suzanne) found themselves standing in front of Paul Paillole. He had decided to recruit women from the CFT to work in occupied France as wireless operators. After all, they were already fully trained and all those in France capable of undertaking the role were either already doing it or had been arrested and needed replacing. The women stared at him in amazement. Had he genuinely just asked them to go and work in France? He told them about the risks of collaborators, arrest and interrogations and about the Nazi direction-finding vans that could trace their signal in twenty minutes. He informed them that their average life expectancy would be six weeks, and they could expect brutal treatment at the hands of the Gestapo if caught. One of the recruits asked how they would get to France. He told them that they could be infiltrated by a submarine to the coast of France or Spain, from where they would commence on foot, or they could be taken by Lysander, or they might even have to parachute from an aircraft.

Paillole was greeted by the stunned silence of thirty women, which was followed by an avalanche of excited questions. As they left his office, each woman had made up her mind that she was going to become a secret agent in France.

A centre had been set up by SOE and their American counterpart, the Office of Strategic Services (OSS), in the Club des Pins, a seafront residence a few kilometres from Staouëli. Under the cover of the 'inter-service transmission unit no. 6', or ISSU6, it was also known within SOE as 'Massingham' and operated as a training base, giving potential agents the same training they would receive at the English Special Training Schools. It was there that the Merlinettes undertook their training, which inevitably put them in contact with SOE staff, instructors and recruiters.

Suzanne Mertzizen, Marie-Louise Cloarec, Eugénie Djendi and Pierrette Louin were offered and accepted a role in the Deuxième Bureau in Algiers for an assignment for the RF Section in France. They were then sent to England to complete their training, which included parachute skills at RAF Ringway.

In early April, Eugénie (now known as Jenny Silvani), Pierrette, Suzanne and Marie-Louise were taken to Gaynes House near RAF Tempsford to prepare for their drop. A Georgian-style manor with almost as many bathrooms as its thirteen bedrooms, the house was filled with men and women awaiting the start of their mission. When that time arrived, Eugénie was disappointed to learn that her flight was cancelled due to operational problems. However, Marie-Louise, Pierrette and Suzanne (along with two male agents) were to be infiltrated that night. Driven to RAF Tempsford, they went through the standard checks for English labels, tickets and cigarettes, before donning their striptease suits and boarding the aircraft that would take them to France. Landing safely, they succeeded in getting to Paris, where they stayed with Pierrette's cousin and established radio contact with London.

Eugénie left on 9 April, along with Georges Penchenier and Marcel Corbusier. There were eleven flights that night, and hers was the last to leave, at around 9.15 p.m. They took just over half an hour to cross the English Channel, after which they climbed to an altitude of 5,000 feet in order to avoid anti-aircraft guns and flak. Once over the River Loire, the aircraft banked and began to search for the DZ. Luckily it was lit by lights in the shape of an 'L' and torches flashing a pre-agreed letter in Morse code. The aircraft returned the signal and swooped in for one final run, during which the three agents jumped, followed down by two containers and several packages. Upon landing they waited nervously for the reception committee to show themselves, but it was not welcoming Frenchmen who stepped out of the shadows. They had landed in a Gestapo trap. With no means to get away or even defend themselves properly, they were handcuffed and driven immediately to Gestapo headquarters at 46 Avenue Alexandre Martin in Orléans for an initial interrogation, before being transferred to the Parisian Gestapo prisons 84 Avenue Foch and Place des États-Unis.

On 27 April, Pierrette, Suzanne and Marie-Louise were also arrested. As with most prisoners, they were kept at Fresnes prison and taken to Avenue Foch and Place des États-Unis for interrogation whenever the Gestapo decided to question them. After many months of incarceration at Fresnes, the women were taken from their cells to Fort de Romainville. They had learned from the bitter experience of their fellow prisoners that this meant they would eventually be deported to Germany as *Nacht und Nebel* prisoners. The relocation meant that the women had a little more freedom to move around and to mingle with friends (albeit under the strict watch of the camp guards) as they were no longer confined to their cells. The food was as poor as before, and the discipline and random punishments at the camp were brutal.

On 8 August, 115 prisoners, comprising thirty-seven women and seventy-eight men, were taken from Romainville and loaded onto buses, which took them to the Gare de l'Est in Paris. But there, something went wrong, and the train did not leave as planned. The men (among them Yeo Thomas) were separated from the majority of the women. Three women had been left on board the train. They were F Section agents Violette Szabo, Lilian Rolfe and Denise Bloch, all of whom showed exceptional bravery in taking water to the men while shackled together when the train was later bombed by Allied aircraft.

The Germans took their time in deciding what to do with the remaining women, and while they deliberated, the women remained shut in their barred railway carriage with no provision of food or water. Eventually, the Germans decided to take the women to Pantin, a goods station on the outskirts of Paris. This station had already been used for deportation due to the length of its platform, which allowed easier movement of prisoners from buses to the cattle trucks that would transport them, many for the last time. One hundred and two women boarded the train (of whom at least seventy-seven survived); the numbers were made up of prisoners at Fresnes who were added to the transport at the last minute.[53]

In the foul cattle trucks, the women were taken away from Paris, and the train shunted through the countryside towards Germany, taking an agonising six days to reach its destination, during which time the women jostled for air or the opportunity to rest. Arriving at Neue Bremm in Saarbrücken, the women experienced their first taste of life in a concentration camp. Built in December 1943 and designed to hold 400 female prisoners, Neue Bremm was a place where French political prisoners and active resistance fighters were crammed into the barracks all day while awaiting final deportation to Ravensbrück concentration camp. The place was designed to break the prisoners' morale and destroy any thought or ability to resist or rebel.

The original transport was then split into two: the first group went to Ravensbrück on 26 August and the second (including the RF women) went on 2 September. They were assimilated into the hellish routine that was imprisonment at Ravensbrück. However, little is known about what happened to them at the camp. As far as can be ascertained, they were not sent to a sub-camp (as the F Section agents mentioned above were) and, in all likelihood, they were put on some sort of work detail building roads, digging out tree roots or working as slave labour in the nearby Siemens factory. Most women who were capable of physical labour were worked until they dropped.

During this time, Eugénie became friendly with F Section agent Yvonne Baseden, a wireless operator who had been arrested after facilitating the largest daylight drop of parachutes to date in June 1944. She had been in the camp for several months and was ill with TB in the *Revier*. Eugénie, whom Yvonne knew by her alias Jenny Silvani, would visit her whenever she could. One day in early January 1945, she visited Yvonne and triumphantly told her that Suzanne had 'been to see one of the SS officers to try and see if she could receive Red

Cross parcels and better treatment for two of her friends who were ill' and that the SS had said that they 'would see what could be done'.[54] Fellow prisoner and SOE agent Trix Terwindt (see Chapter 6, 'Mission Nederlands') also met the women. She worried for them, believing that 'they had not been in German captivity for long enough to know how dangerous it was to attract attention. Moreover, they were not within their rights, as they had been thrown off [parachuted] in civilian clothes'.[55]

A few days later Suzanne was recalled to the office of the SS with Eugénie in tow. They were 'again very well received'. He told them that he had received orders from the SS in Berlin regarding their treatment, and pointed to a blue telegram on the desk, but he refused to tell them what the letter said. Informing them that 'their demands had been considered', he suggested they should be 'available for call'.[56] The blue telegram remained on the desk, tantalisingly untouched. Perhaps it was a letter with orders to give them better treatment, or maybe even to free them. Eugénie reported back to Yvonne that they had been well received again, and their hopes had been raised.

A week later, Eugénie went to see Yvonne again. It was the last time they would meet. 'I heard a day later that four girls had been seen standing in their striped dresses in front of the SS office, guarded by an armed SS guard, which was most unusual. They were taken away by lorry, and I heard later that they had been hanged.' Trix verified this: 'A few weeks later, the girls were taken from their block, without being given the opportunity to even take a toothbrush, something that everyone was allowed to take with them when they were deported. Soon it was rumoured that they had been executed.'[57]

This was effectively confirmed when their clothes came back.[58] At the *Effektenkammer* (where clothes were sorted by prisoners), Suzanne's jumper was spotted by an inmate. There was no blood or bullet hole, confirming what Yvonne believed – that the four young women from Algiers had been hanged.[59] Yvonne was devastated and tried not to believe what she had heard. Their fate could well be her own at any time. The question arises: were they executed for their SOE work or because they had pushed the SS too far with their requests for better treatment? Their date of death is recorded as 18 January 1945, just days before the three F Section women they had met on the transport train were shot while holding one another's hands.

It is notable that the camp commandant was present at the execution of the F Section women, commenting that 'all three were very brave and I was deeply moved' and that he was 'impressed by the bearing of these women'.[60] And yet the deaths of Eugénie Djendi, Pierrette Louin, Marie-Louise Cloarec and Suzanne Mertzizen, who arguably did the same work for the same organisation, were not witnessed by anyone of rank, and they have simply disappeared from history books and public memory.

It is entirely possible that this is because they were French, even though similarities to the F Section women can be drawn – they were all young, they had left their homes and families to travel to France (a country three of them had never seen before) and one of them even left behind a child. A memorial to them was unveiled in 2015 at the Ravensbrück memorial site.

■ ■ ■

It is unclear exactly when Brigitte Friang, who had been festering in the *Revier* at Ravensbrück, was transferred to Zwodau, a sub-camp of Flossenbürg in Czechoslovakia. Her memoirs suggest that it was around the same time as the RF women were killed. Of the 1,350 registered women at Zwodau, 265 were French, and most prisoners undertook forced labour. Brigitte was still wracked with TB and was hospitalised again. Every week, selections were made from those in the *Revier* to be taken to the gas chambers and murdered, so her life hung by a thread. But her doctor managed to ward off the SS by telling them that her patients suffered from a 'terrible and contagious disease' and that they should not come in for fear of catching it themselves.[61] She was so convincing that they did not dare even to open the door. This doctor also helped Brigitte by injecting her with six ampules of calcium she had stolen from SS stores. At first, Brigitte felt worse than ever but by the last injection she was 'visibly reborn'; the 'effect was stunning'.[62] Eating semolina from a silver spoon that she had been gifted by another inmate, Brigitte's strength returned. She was soon able to take walks around the camp, which was relatively small in comparison with Ravensbrück. She would walk up to the perimeter fence, on the other side of which was a Siemens factory where inmates built reels, switches and measuring instruments for an aeronautical company. She was fascinated by the 'apparent fragility' of the fence, beyond which lay freedom. It was the first time in months that she had felt she might eventually be free. Her spirits were lifted and she felt positive again.[63]

But the Red Army was closing in from one direction and the US Army from the other. The SS evacuated the camp and the remaining prisoners were forced onto what became known as a death march. On 16 April 1945, Brigitte joined one of the last convoys and, along with 1,700 other prisoners, was forced to march towards Dachau, some 300 kilometres away. She and her friends attempted to escape a few times and, finally, on 8 May, they managed to break away from the column. She had no idea that Hitler was dead, or that the armistice had been signed and the war was over. She just knew that, against all odds, she was alive and she was free. She was able to 'return from hell' when so many hadn't. Of the 10,000 French women at Ravensbrück, only 300 survived.[64]

■ ■ ■

The fact that so many women who contributed to the work of SOE in France have been overlooked or forgotten can be put down to an imbalance and injustice in the way their stories and the memory of their work has been handled since the war. While some agents from F Section became household names as a result of gazetting for medals, war crimes trials and newspaper articles, the French women who also worked tirelessly for their country have been largely forgotten, not just in England but in France too.

There is a wealth of literature written by historians about the F Section (arguably, the literature is disproportionate as there is more about the women than the men, who made up a much larger part of the section). However, the RF Section and the Merlinettes remain problematic to research, thanks to a lack of archives and difficulty accessing what material there is, and thus difficult to write about. With these few words, it is hoped that their memory has, in some small way, been honoured as it deserves to be.

5

MISSION BELGIQUE

I wasn't a heroine. Just young and excited and willing to do anything except join the ATS!

Elaine Madden, SOE T Section agent[1]

With memories of the Great War still fresh in the minds of the Belgian people, another European, let alone global, conflict still seemed unthinkable. But after months of phony war, it took just eighteen days for Belgium to fall to Nazi occupation. With no tanks, few aircraft and very little artillery, they bravely put up a fight that was always destined to fail. The Germans dropped leaflets over the Belgian troops telling them that their king had deserted them. King Leopold III countered this by telling his people that he would share their fate no matter what happened to them.

On 28 May 1940, without consulting his cabinet, King Leopold surrendered the Belgian army and capitulated to the Germans. Along with France and the Netherlands, they fell to a brutal Nazi occupation that would last for over four years. The king was arrested and interned in Belgium, while the Rexist Party (a far-right authoritarian Catholic political party that soon became fascist with assistance from Mussolini) actively supported the new government and their regime. The Rexist leader, Léon Degrelle, came to lead the Walloon and Flemish stormtrooper units on the Russian front.

But a resistance movement soon grew and, by the end of 1940, Belgium became a focus for SOE activity with the formation of T

121

Section. To begin with, T Section was headed by Eric F. Dadson (T) and W.R. Duff-Torrance as Deputy (T1). SOE had to work alongside the Belgian government in exile. However, 'rumours as to the unreliability of the Belgian Émigré government, who it was felt had only come to the UK *"faute de mieux"* [for lack of anything better] were perpetually confirmed' by SIS.[2] The Belgian military 'showed every sign of wishing to collaborate with SOE', but two Belgian organisations sought to control resistance activity without SOE's help or input:[3] Sûreté de l'État, the security service in exile, which was 'entrusted with the security of the Belgian state and with powers similar to the home office'; and the Deuxième Bureau, which was the intelligence service.[4] Additionally, there was L'Armée secrète – the armed faction of the resistance operating within Belgium, which included many former officers of the Belgian armed forces.

Given this background, it was not surprising that T Section had problems from the start. The section was forbidden any direct contact with the government in exile. Additionally, the Sûreté wanted to know 'every agent's intended role', which was a security risk, and the Deuxième Bureau refused to have anything to do with SOE as long as they were in contact with the Sûreté. These poor relations had a negative effect on recruiting suitable agents for work in and on behalf of Belgium.[5] It was formally acknowledged that 'the lack of coordination and cooperation between SOE and "C" [SIS], which allowed the *Sûreté* and 2eme Direction to play one against the other, had a very adverse effect on operations'.[6]

Brigadier (later Major-General Sir) Colin Gubbins, head of operations and planning for SOE, tried to convince the Belgians that SOE's main role was sabotage and subversion, unlike SIS, which provided security and intelligence. Therefore, the organisation did not have to seek permission to do its job. In essence, SOE wished to be provided with a list of suitable Belgian candidates. They would then decide if they were to undertake training or not, the agents would be paid by the Belgian authorities, and the future employment of any agent would be decided between SOE and the Deuxième Bureau.

On 24 November 1942, a renewed cooperation agreement established that 'all actions in Belgium will only take place after joint agreement between the British and Deuxième Bureau'.[7] Wireless communication via SOE channels would be in collaboration with the Belgian services, respectively the Deuxième Bureau for military sabotage and Sûreté de l'État for Political Warfare Executive (PWE) matters, evasions/escape organisations and industrial sabotage. The Sûreté was to remain technically responsible for the administration of all Belgian communication lines.[8]

Aside from the political confusion that surrounded T Section, there were many practical issues, too, not least air operations. Wartime Belgium was a densely populated country, and even the agricultural areas that would normally make good landing and dropping grounds were covered with small farms and buildings. Owing to its inherent flatness, 'concealment was difficult', there were few 'distinctive landmarks' by which to navigate and its proximity to the 'air highways to the Reich' meant that any aircraft attempting to fly over would be prone to flak or night fighter attacks.[9] Most drops made were to the Ardennes Forest region, while other areas were 'largely starved of material [sic]'.[10]

There were also some early disasters, including an agent's parachute getting entangled in the plane and his mangled body being dragged back to the UK, and a Lysander becoming 'surrounded by a German patrol and the pilot shot up'.[11] These incidents and the inherent terrain issues meant that any flight to Belgium was considered difficult and the route became unpopular among pilots.

Another cause for concern was that neither the heads of T Section nor the majority of the training staff had any practical experience of life or work as an agent behind the lines. They had to rely on returning agents for information about the conditions in the field, instead of sending out agents with 'no other purpose but to get the background information and atmosphere'.[12] This resulted in poor intelligence about current living conditions and, therefore, an inadequate briefing of outgoing agents.

SOE's rivals were not limited to SIS. Rivalry among country sections was also present. Internal wranglings, as well as an external war, seem par for the course within SOE, and T Section was no exception. However, 'In spite of these disadvantages, the SOE effort in Belgium was a marked success.'[13] Rail and canal sabotage was very effective, the prevention of the destruction of the port at Antwerp was hugely successful, and the contribution to the Allied war effort was 'well worth-while'.[14] In all, 183 container operations for supplies were carried out, 110 of which were in the spring and summer of 1944. Of the 182 T Section agents dispatched to Belgium, nine were killed and three injured en route; 170 arrived in the field, thirty-six of whom were killed in action, twenty-three were arrested and subsequently released and sixteen went missing. Only two of the agents sent into Belgium were women. Both were infiltrated just weeks before the liberation. They were Olga Jackson and Elaine Madden.

■ ■ ■

Elaine was born in May 1923 in her grandmother's hotel in Poperinghe. Her father was an Australian who had fought in Belgium during the Great War, after which he married Elaine's Belgian mother, Caroline Duponselle. Elaine was an only child and had a troubled childhood, owing in part to her father's job. After serving in the trenches of the Great War, he took on the macabre and somewhat disturbing task of digging up and reinterring the dead for the Imperial War Graves Commission (IWGC), properly known as 'concentration' work (because they collected bodies from across the battlefield into one area). The hellish nature of what he had already seen while fighting and the nightmarish work he undertook post-war drove him to drink, something that would determine the rest of his life and greatly affect his daughter's.

Elaine was educated at the British Memorial School, next door to St George's church in Ypres. The school had opened in 1929 with sixty-two pupils, the majority of whom were children whose fathers worked for the IWGC and had settled in the Ypres area. By the time Elaine went there, the number of pupils had risen to over a hundred. Her home life was rather lonely. In the family-owned hotel in Poperinghe, her grandmother cooked for the brasserie while her grandfather and two aunts waited on tables.

The family also owned a hotel in Ypres called the Majestique, which Elaine's mother ran. Her father propped up the bar, 'drinking with his old army pals or at Lodge meetings'.[15] The hotel had a room that 'served as a [Masonic] Lodge ... and they wore some kind of costume or cape'. Her father told her it 'was a secret' and none of her 'business'.[16] At the front was a shop, 'which sold chocolates and souvenirs and books' to the tourist trade that had come in on the back of the war. There was also a café and an 'enormous yard', where her father raised Alsatian dogs for the police.[17]

Although she spent very little time with her parents, Elaine was nonetheless hit very hard by the death of her mother from septicaemia following a miscarriage when Elaine was just ten years old. Elaine's father sank even further into despair, not only losing his job at IWGC in 1932 but also abandoning his daughter. 'I don't want her,' he said. 'She looks too much like her mother.'[18] The family was plunged into a deep bereavement and observed strict mourning rituals. Elaine wore black for six months, often with a veil that came down to her waist – even at her first communion. Then, after the allotted time, she wore mauve. She moved in with her grandparents at their hotel in Poperinghe and was sent to a convent school. This she despised so much that she cut her knee-length tunic and thick stockings with some scissors and was expelled after six months. She completed her education back at the British Memorial School in Ypres.

Her father was nowhere to be seen. He had been declared bankrupt and her maternal grandparents had given him money so that he would leave and never come back. Elaine decided to further her studies at a commercial college in England, which was paid for by her uncle. Money was a constant source of aggravation in the family, and when she returned home for Christmas, she was informed that if she wanted to study, she would have to get a job and fund it herself. Full of pride and anger, she told them she wouldn't go back to college – she would stay in Belgium and work. 'I didn't go back to England until I had to,' she said.[19] During this time, she met and became involved with a Belgian officer named Edgar Callan. However, she needed her father's permission to marry Edgar since she was so young, at just sixteen years of age. As she couldn't trace her father, she applied to the council and received her marriage papers just as the occupation was starting. Then her fiancé disappeared, and all she could do was 'hope that he is safe and that after this blessed war, I'll find him'.[20]

'Well darling,' she wrote to her old school friend Renée Fletcher in June 1940, 'we had a pretty rough time. Poperinghe . . . was crowded with refugees . . . and there were thousands of people wandering about the streets and at night sleeping on the pavements. You couldn't get any food, and people were going mad.' A bombing raid two weeks later 'was horrible'. She saw 'women and children lying in the streets, we saw a head lying in the gutter and legs and arms lying about . . . I've seen enough bodies for the rest of my life.'[21]

She turned seventeen at the end of May 1940. In that month, the Germans arrived in Poperinghe and Elaine left.[22] Together with her maternal aunt Simone Duponselle, she took her bags and headed out of Poperinghe. After about 8 miles and totally exhausted, they found shelter in a barn. There they sat in silence and horror as dozens of German aircraft flew over them and destroyed what was left of their beautiful town; it was 'wiped off the landscape'.[23] Devastated, the pair tried to sleep, but on hearing the sound of German tanks, they grabbed their possessions and fled. After about 5 miles, they saw some lorries in which English soldiers were handing out supplies to stranded civilians. 'Want some chocolate?' they asked. 'No,' Elaine replied, 'but you can give us a lift.'[24]

After travelling about 20 miles in their 'Rolls-Royce', Elaine and her aunt had to get out and walk. The roads had been badly shelled and the driving rain had only made matters worse. They soon hitched another lift with some soldiers, but finding the bridges had been blown, they desperately needed a way to get across the river. The soldiers managed to push some lorries into the water and they all crossed safely. After wading knee-deep in water for some time, Elaine was horrified to discover that they had to walk across hundreds of dead bodies floating in the river, using them as stepping stones to get to the other side.

They arrived in Dunkirk at about 11 p.m. 'The whole place was on fire . . . what a mess we were in, we had to find the docks but no one knew the way.'[25] Fighting their way through the rubble and flames, they finally made their way to 'the mole', the long pier where thousands of BEF soldiers were waiting to embark ships for evacuation. This was for military personnel only, and if they wanted to get out, they needed to look the part. Three soldiers, whom they knew as Knocker, Smudger and Gary, lent them 'greatcoats, tin hats and gas masks – everything except the trousers'.[26] They already wore women's army boots, and once their hair was tucked into their helmets (and if no one looked too closely), they were, to all extents and purposes, soldiers.[27]

To get onto the pier, they had to pass a check where they were challenged by French military police. 'You have civilians with you?' they barked. '*Non, non, non*,' said the three soldiers, and then a gunshot rang through the air. Elaine wasn't sure if it was fired by them or just a coincidence, but they hurried through and got into the queue to get them out of France.

Surrounded by the three men, or 'saviours', as Elaine referred to them, they waited anxiously on the mole for the best part of twenty-four hours, 'like sardines, standing next to one another and not being able to move and not being able to sleep'. All around the Germans were bombing, strafing and drenching those who stood waiting, powerless to defend themselves.[28] Elaine said she had never had so 'many shower-baths' as she withstood one soaking after another, clinging onto her newfound friends for fear of being dragged off the pier. They walked carefully across some slippery planks that had been laid across a hole in the deck as they shuffled closer to the front of the queue. 'Come on, our turn next,' she was told:

> We had to go down a rope ladder, so I went first and somebody at the bottom of the rope said 'well, well, well, Ladies legs!' in a sarcastic tone and then he looked up at Simone, who was coming down and said 'more ladies legs! Now, what is this?' Then he pulled us aside and away.[29]

The women's papers were checked, and once safely aboard ship they were put in a cabin, away from the men, for the duration of the crossing. They never saw Knocker, Smudger or Gary again.

Following an interrogation (presumably by MI5) to allow her into the UK, Elaine finally made it to London, where she and her aunt parted ways. After first staying with relatives in Streatham, she moved into lodgings in a flat off Fleet Street. By day she worked as a clerk for the British Relay Wireless Company and by night she was part of the Women's Volunteer Service (WVS), working alongside Air Raid Precaution (ARP) wardens as they dug air raid survivors out of the rubble and helped clear the bomb damage. She 'helped firemen by taking them flasks of tea, with bombs falling' all around her, and decided to make the most of it 'because tomorrow you might die'.[30] She also studied for her Red Cross certificates in home nursing and first aid so that she could offer more practical help until the emergency services arrived on the scene. She was still determined to do even more for the war effort; it was just a matter of finding out what that could be.[31] Had she stayed in Belgium, her life could have been very different: she could have been interned – or worse.

■ ■ ■

Denise Laplat was the same age as Elaine but had stayed in Belgium when war broke out. In 1942, she began to work on behalf of SOE as

a locally recruited courier. She had become aware of the organisation and of resistance activity when her parents' home was used as
a safe house for André Wendelen and his W/T Jean Brion. They had
parachuted back into Belgium near Liège on 27/28 January 1942 on
a mission codenamed 'Mandamus'.[32] Brion continued to live at the
house, and Denise, who was 'very anxious to do some active work for
the resistance', was 'given the job of courier from Liège to Brussels'.[33]

At seventeen years old, she was, like Elaine, very young, but this
meant she could move around with relative ease. Using her own
name and the story that she was visiting her grandmother, every
Monday she would carry messages secreted inside a magazine, which
she would read on the train or hide in her shopping basket. She never
knew or dared ask if they were in code or plain text; she simply took
them where they needed to go. Her brother was also inspired by SOE
and worked as a courier for Group G, also known as General Sabotage Group of Belgium. Group G was a group of resistance fighters
formed as part of Wendelen's mission. When her brother left to go to
England, she took on his courier work too.

On top of the courier work, Denise helped prepare charges for use
in sabotage attacks and took them to a prearranged rendezvous point
hidden in a sack, basket, 'or merely in front of her bicycle'.[34] She was
able to get away with more than a man doing the same job: 'women
were very rarely thoroughly searched' and only a 'superficial' check of
shopping bags and baskets was usually carried out by a gendarme.[35]
Nevertheless, carrying explosives and weaponry was extremely dangerous, as being caught with it would mean instant arrest, followed by
interrogation about where and for whom they were destined. However, she rarely knew to whom she was taking them and had to use passwords to make sure they were being delivered into the right hands.

Often the explosives were of an inferior quality, and the recipients
frequently resorted to using TNT in 'empty tins with a detonator in
the middle'.[36] The partisans she took the weapons to much preferred
the supplies coming in from Britain, such as plastic explosives and

Bickford cord, but these deliveries were few and far between.

Denise only actively took part in one sabotage mission. Together with Wendelen, she prepared the charges at a hotel in Liège before going to the place on the railway line where the charge was to be laid. Armed with a revolver, she gave cover while Wendelen laid '1.5 sticks of plastic in two charges one metre apart connected with Cortex', to ensure maximum effect and efficiency.[37] 'The method of initiating the charge was a detonator on the end of Bickford [cord].'[38] By using enough cord to create a delay fuse, they were able to get a short distance away before the explosion. They ambled off arm in arm, looking to all intents and purposes like lovers. When the sound of the explosion boomed out, 'nobody suspected them'.[39]

Denise made several attempts to recruit others for resistance duties but was not very successful. She believed they were either too frightened to undertake such dangerous work or that they were, in fact, already working for the resistance and did not want to get involved with another organisation. She herself feigned disinterest when asked to join a group rather than admit that she was already a very active résistant; knowing too many people was not advisable. It seems that she was very security-minded, even without formal training.

The job was volatile and arrest was only ever a hair's breadth away. The Laplat family had taken a great risk in housing Jean Brion. He had lived and worked from their family home, successfully sending eighteen wireless transmissions back to SOE HQ. He, too, was very security-conscious and always used a lookout. Sometimes it was Denise herself. In April 1942, he was working in a room on the second floor when the Feldgendarmerie (Military Police) arrived at the house. The danger signal was given, which involved tapping on a central heating pipe that ran from the front door upstairs to the room where Brion was transmitting. He hurriedly hid his set, codes and crystals under the floorboards and started washing the dishes. When questioned, he said he was employed as domestic help in the house.

The police left, but he could no longer transmit from that location, and Denise frantically started to look for a new safe house for him. The only one available was very near to her home, and 'although she thought it foolish to remain in the same district', they had no choice but to accept.[40]

Two months later, on 16 June, Brion's lookout saw a direction-finder van nearby. It was a Citröen with an aerial, and it was coming down the street towards them. Brion 'cut the transmission', which had already lasted an hour and a quarter, and they all scattered.[41] But the next day, he was 'surprised by the Germans' during his transmission and arrested. The house he had been using belonged to two ladies named Durieux. They had helped with the resistance in the 'last war' and were deported to Germany for harbouring him.[42] Brion was taken to Liège prison, after which he was deported to Dachau concentration camp. Fortunately, he managed to survive this incarceration.[43]

Denise was extremely observant and noticed when things were not as they ought to be. Her father was a doctor, and she was in his surgery one day when she saw, in the waiting room, a young man 'of medium height ... good looking', with 'brown hair and no distinguishing features' other than short-sightedness.[44] He seemed to be acting suspiciously, so she decided to observe what he was going to do next. As the young man sat, he allowed several other people to take his turn, stating that he 'was in no hurry', while observing the comings and goings at the surgery.[45] When he met Denise, he asked her numerous questions about her trips to Brussels and what she did when she got there. Her suspicions were aroused still further when he came back again later. She feared she would be denounced and went away to the country, staying with her cousin. The cousin was also a resistance member and undertook *parachutage* work for Sûreté until his arrest in February 1944. After this, Denise moved in with her uncle.[46]

Her work was exemplary, and she showed immense skill in her various activities. As well as being extremely security-conscious, she was daring and brave to undertake the roles that she did at such a young age. Had she been sent to England to train for SOE operations, she would not have been permitted back into Belgium until she was twenty-one, as was the case with Elaine Madden. However, as fate would have it, their paths would cross and the pair would become a formidable team.

■ ■ ■

Back in London, Elaine Madden had been able to defer two call-up notifications to the Auxiliary Territorial Service (ATS), an organisation she desperately wanted to avoid joining. So far, she had been able to due to her employment. But her time was running out and, as a valid candidate for conscription (which was compulsory for single, childless women aged between twenty and thirty), she was soon going to have to enter war work. However, she was fluent in three languages (French, Flemish and Dutch) and felt that her skills would go to waste in the ATS. She also hated the uniform. She talked it over with her flatmate and a US Army officer with whom they were friendly. She was surprised when, a couple of days later, the American took her out to lunch alone and offered to introduce her to someone at the American Embassy who was recruiting individuals for work in the secret service. The Americans could not use her without checking with British authorities and, once they became aware of her skills and enthusiasm, they were also very keen to meet her.

She met 'some people in south London somewhere' and was asked if she would like to return to Belgium, since that 'was the country she knew best'.[47] Next, she met Major Ides Floor, who was a senior SOE staff officer directly connected to the Sûreté and who questioned her about her family and her background. She 'didn't quite know why' and said she 'knew nothing' about why she was there or what she was supposed to do.[48]

Having passed her MI5 clearance, Elaine went to Lillywhites department store in Piccadilly to pick up her First Aid Nursing Yeomanry uniform, which consisted of a smartly tailored khaki jacket and skirt, with 'burgundy buttons' and a cap.[49] As with other SOE country sections, FANY provided a cover for agents during training and a salary while on active duty. FANY employed nearly 3,000 women in other roles such as wireless operators, conducting officers and drivers, both at home and abroad, notably in Italy and the Far East.

Elaine attended SOE training in April 1944 and was already marked as becoming 'an agent in the field when available'.[50] She attended SAB at Winterfold House in Surrey, where she was graded as having average potential for an agent and above-average intelligence. At STS 35, 'Vineyards', a beautiful manor in Beaulieu that overlooks the abbey, she was given a mock interrogation as part of the training to help her learn and maintain her cover story. Woken by a 'German soldier' in the middle of the night, she was quick-marched down to the 'interrogation room', which was lit by a single spotlight hung over a table, at which sat three 'German officers'.[51] She was in her pyjamas and felt extremely vulnerable. Nevertheless, they began to interrogate her about her alibi and cover story. She later remembered that, after a time:

> they made me stand on this chair with this big floodlight in my eyes. And then they made me take my pyjama jacket off, and I was on this damned chair, just in my pyjama trousers, thinking, what the hell are they playing at? Then they switched the lights on, and I could see all the other students sitting around the room, and they started clapping. I could have killed those people! It was ghastly![52]

Despite her somewhat humiliating experience at the hands of the SOE staff and her fellow students, Elaine continued her training and went on to the parachute school at Ringway, where she completed five jumps, having been told by one of her instructors that if she didn't, 'there'll be hell waiting for you'.[53] She recalled how after she had jumped, 'it was as if you had conquered the world, the most wonderful feeling'.[54] But things could go wrong, and on one of her aircraft practices, a young Polish man froze and refused to jump, so was sent to the back to sit it out. Once he had seen everyone else jump, he 'suddenly ran to the hole, yelling in Polish, and jumped' but his static line was not attached, and his canopy did not open. Elaine remembered him falling past her in mid-air. This horrific incident did not deter her from finishing her course, and she received her parachute wings.

Elaine's finishing report described her as having a 'confident manner' and being 'sophisticated for her age'.[55] She was viewed as being 'alert, efficient and methodical' with a strong desire to 'help the Belgian cause'. Her training completed, she just had to wait for her mission and the next full moon to get back to Belgium.[56]

■ ■ ■

Also waiting for her flight back into occupied territory was Frédérique (Freddy) Dupuich. Aged thirty when Belgium was occupied, she was extremely well educated, having been to school and university in Brussels. She was fluent in French, English and Italian with a good understanding of German and Dutch. After the occupation of Belgium, she briefly worked as a nurse in a French military hospital in Suresnes, after which she returned to Belgium and joined SERVICE CLARENCE as an agent. This underground network was run by the Secret Intelligence Service (SIS) and led by Hector Demarque and Walthère Dewé, who had earlier played a leading role in LA DAME BLANCHE.[57] The network was to provide vital information on enemy activity, including coastal defences, troop movements and the effects of Allied bombing raids. It was deemed to be the most successful Belgian network of the war. Freddy collected military and industrial intelligence in Brussels, but by July 1941, she had decided to leave Belgium via an escape line and take the latest intelligence reports with her.

Freddy escaped across the Pyrenees on the escape route 'Deppé De Jongh', which was to become known as the Comet Line. Later, she gained recognition as 'Miss Richards' in Airey Neave's book *Little Cy-*

clone, in which she is described as a 'plump, middle-aged English-woman with a Panama hat'.[58] She must have been pleased that her disguise worked and that no one suspected her of being a spy carrying intelligence over the border and back to London. No sooner had she crossed into Spain following a long and arduous trek than she was thrown into prison and fined for crossing the Spanish border illegally.

However, the Belgian consul intervened and she was soon released to continue her journey (at her own expense). Travelling to Madrid and on to Tangiers (where she visited her sister), then on to Gibraltar, she finally arrived in the UK on 12 October 1941. She headed straight to SIS HQ and handed over the reports she had so dutifully brought with her.

Unable to return to Belgium, she put her skills to good use and joined the Political Warfare and Propaganda department of the Belgian Sûreté, where she became an executive officer of the Belgian PWE Section under Georges Aronstein.[59] She undertook her work 'with ardour and tenacity, she devoted herself totally to the intelligence service in its fight against the enemy'.[60] But she was desperate to get back to work in Belgium, or at least in occupied territory. In January 1944, she undertook SOE training with a view to returning to the field as a courier. She was given permission to miss the para-military aspect of her preparation and attended SAB at Winterfold and finishing school at Beaulieu.

At her training, she tended to try too hard, giving the impression of being nervous and 'anxious to succeed'.[61] But the staff were impressed with her sincerity and keenness to 'do a real job for her country', remarking that her 'upbringing, appearance and manner' would aid her considerably in her role as a courier, since she was not suitable to become a wireless operator (having failed this aspect of the course).[62] It was also noted that two years behind a desk in London had not helped her cause physically, and that she was so 'weak' it was advised that she did not undertake parachute training.[63]

She would have to be infiltrated by Lysander, and this is where the problems to get her back into occupied Europe started. As early as March 1944, a memo was circulated that said, 'It was our intention to try and lay on a Lysander operation . . . for this coming moon to take up Mademoiselle Deeway [Freddy's codename] and some of the stores asked for by Greyhound for Woodchuck 2.'[64] The operation was cancelled as no correctly trained personnel were available to lay a flarepath and as a result they were 'unable to lay on this operation for this moon'. It was possible, however, to get her 'up on a French mission'.[65]

The new plan was to take her by Lysander into France, from where she would make her way back into Belgium to undertake Mission 'Socrates' which would provide financial support to the Belgian resistance and liaise with the CLARENCE network. But three months later she was still waiting.

A memo dated 8 June 1944 from the new Head of T Section, Hardy Amies (a fashion designer who was fluent in French and German and who had worked as an agent in Belgium), to Ides Floor states that the planned Lysander operation 'was put on [hold] at least three times during the past eight days' and was 'cancelled at the last minute owing to weather'.[66] However, it would now be 'postponed indefinitely owing to recent events' (the memo was written on D-Day+2) 'as it is not considered in any way feasible to send a Lysander (which is an almost unarmed aircraft and slow flying) over France'.[67] Amies goes on to say that they are dependent on the 'goodwill of the F Section to deliver her to France and that it is unfortunate for poor CONSTANTIN', aka Freddy.[68]

Having enrolled in FANY, Freddy asked them if she could do something useful while she was waiting; she had a further two months to fill before she finally got on a plane for France. Finally, at 3 a.m. on 6 August 1944, she was infiltrated by a 161 Special Duties Squadron Lysander near Genillé (Indre-et-Loire), north-east of Loches. She undertook her new mission successfully until the liberation and was described as 'a magnificent example of unselfish patriotism'.[69]

■ ■ ■

Olga Jackson née Thioux was infiltrated a day before Freddy, on 5 August 1944. Born to Belgian parents in January 1909 in Liège, Olga arrived in the UK in 1935 and married Major Thomas Jackson of the Royal Artillery. They made their home at 'Wits End' in Camberley (which gives an insight into the sense of humour she possessed). In the summer of 1943, she was briefly 'employed in scientific research with the FFI' and, despite being required to attend the Ministry of Labour after that employment finished, she did not go.[70]

Her next employment record is 1 September 1944, when she worked for the intelligence branch of the Polish Forces in the UK. In April 1944, she was accepted for SOE training and was 'incorporated' into FANY, eventually rising from cadet ensign to the rank of lieutenant. The main aim of her recruitment was to get her onto 'Emilia', a joint mission between SOE, Political Intelligence Department (PID) and the Belgian Sûreté. This was one that she would undertake alone, 'to demoralise a number of senior officers and officials occupying key positions in the German administration in Belgium'.[71]

A report dated 25 April 1944 states that, at first, the training officers thought she was completely unsuited to the proposed role, which she believed would involve contacting German officers and telling them that 'their sacrifice was useless'.[72] Her instructor stated, 'In order to undertake such a mission the following qualities are essential . . . a knowledge of German, a knowledge of the German character, tact and understanding human weakness.'[73] He went on to say that 'none of these qualities are visible in this student. In fact, it would be difficult to find a more tactless, imprudent and headstrong person for the job.'[74] He concluded by saying that it was a 'useless waste of time for this student to undertake the work that she thinks she is going to do'.[75] Clearly, Olga's attitude and demeanour were not gaining her any favours with the instructors.

However, when it transpired that both she and her instructor had misunderstood her mission, he backtracked quite rapidly and decided to give her a second chance, 'in view of the qualities that she has since displayed'. Although she was 'slow at learning', she had shown 'good progress'. At STS 19 in Stevenage (where other agents were preparing Operation 'Periwig', the aim of which was to confuse and disrupt the Nazi regime by suggesting that there was an active resistance movement in Germany), she was described as 'determined [and] unscrupulous'.[76] The instructors believed that she would work well alone but that her 'blindness to her own weaknesses' would mean she would not do well as part of a team.[77] In a somewhat unique situation among SOE women, who were usually to work 'under' a male leader, Olga was to work alone.

Her finishing report from STS 32a, Saltmarsh (a pretty house set in beautiful gardens, at the end of which ran the Beaulieu River, replete with otters and herons) stated that she was 'practical and cunning'. Her hard work and initiative were praised and, although she could be domineering, she was also 'determined and courageous'.[78] Her humour and charm made her a popular student and, eventually, her instructors concluded that they had made a mistake and that she was, in fact, 'suited for the work she is to undertake'.[79]

Codenamed 'Babette', she parachuted into Belgium on 5 August 1944. Almost immediately she made the contacts she needed and from whom she could gather intelligence on the 'private and public lives of the persons in whom she was interested'.[80] She used every means at her disposal, including bribing the mistresses and prostitutes involved with these men to spread 'defeatist feelings' and encourage despondency, as well as planting the ideas of desertion into the minds of leading German officials. She worked in Brussels, Ghent, Liège, Antwerp and Charleroi, and did as much as time would allow. In the end, it was not the enemy but time that worked against her, and less than a month after she was infiltrated, Belgium was liberated and her mission annulled. Rather than return to the UK, she was seconded from SOE to SHAEF (Supreme Headquarters Allied Expeditionary Force) for several months, for whom she undertook 'very good work'. It is here that her story becomes truly remarkable.

While the dates in her personnel file seem a little muddled, the accusations could not be clearer: Olga used her uniform to gain privileges that were not rightfully hers, primarily requisitioning fancy cars from unsuspecting civilians and crashing them. After her mission, Olga requested compassionate leave. When it was granted, she had been informed that she must not wear uniform for the duration of the time that she was off work, but 'this undertaking was broken' and she had, in fact, 'improperly worn' her uniform to gain or persuade people to give her War Department privileges.[81]

In October 1944, days after the liberation, Olga visited the head of transport for her area (whose name is redacted under the Freedom of Information Act in her personnel file). She informed him that she had a mission in the south of France and that she had a brand new MG car in her possession that had been gifted to her by a man who was 'only too keen to get rid of it'.[82] Olga persuaded the transport officer to write her a note that exempted the vehicle from being requisitioned from her by other military personnel. However, she was not on duty, and the MG was not government property, nor had it been formally requisitioned. She had used her uniform and rank to gain something for her own benefit just days after liberation. The head of transport felt that his trust had been abused, especially when he learned that she had presented the papers he had given her to the MG's owner as a requisition voucher, promising to return it forthwith. Then she set off for France. She was not on a mission, but heading off for a 'pleasant trip'.[83]

The trip ended in a very serious crash in which two people lost their lives and the car was wrecked. The RAF military policeman who came to the scene declared the car a write-off. Having no car in which to return, Olga set about 'requisitioning' another one, this time borrowing a Citröen 'for a few days', promising to return it once she had been to Paris. Months later the owner was still waiting for his vehicle to be returned, and the MG owner was writing to the War Office and demanding compensation.[84]

Olga had really done a number on everyone around her and had not reported back to the UK to be formally demobbed. In fact, she had all but disappeared. SOE's disappointment in her was tangible – more so as they believed they had created this fiend:

> You will remember that her mission was of a very special nature and her acceptance of it indicated that she had rather a peculiar temperament. It is very possible that this is again one of those cases where our training and the experience gained in the field had a destructive moral influence.[85]

However, she still received a mention in dispatches in December 1945, and her mission, had it had a chance to develop, could have been very successful. Sadly, it was not to be, and she ended her SOE career in disgrace.

■ ■ ■

On 4 August 1944, Elaine Madden was taken to RAF Harrington USAAF Station 179 in Northamptonshire to prepare for her mission codenamed 'Imogen'. She would be jumping with André Wendelen, who was being infiltrated for the third time, as well as with W/T Jacques van de Spiegel.[86] The three had been briefed on what to expect when they arrived:

> You will find yourself among a population that is magnificently resisting unprecedented oppression. They will ask you questions, offer you contacts, and offer you activities that are not planned in your mission. This is exceptionally dangerous territory on which you should not venture. The essential condition for the security of all operations is that everyone fulfils their mission to the best of their ability and does not intervene in another area.[87]

Sabotage was to be encouraged on railways, waterways, telecommunications, roads and air targets, while reports regarding troop movements (to include numbers of troops, dates and times) were requested to be sent via wireless. Specific to 'Imogen', the team were also required to collect intelligence on the V-1 and V-2 rockets. These 'flying bombs' had the capacity to wreak devastation on London from bases in France and Holland and had been deployed just one week after D-Day. The V-2 was in manufacture and would soon find targets in London, Antwerp and Liège. Information on where they were based and how they were to be deployed was critical to the future war effort, and Elaine was tasked with finding out.

On her person, she would carry 5,000 Belgian francs, with a further 50,000 Belgian francs and 10,000 French francs (to cover her return costs if needed) hidden in a box of talcum powder. The microdots she would need were concealed in a wallet. Her suitcase of 'personal effects' and Jacques's wireless would be dropped after they had jumped. She was to be their courier. Her mission would last three months, and 'for the safeguarding of [her] own safety and that of the organisation' she was to stick strictly to the 'limits of the mission' that had been assigned to her.[88]

From now on, she would be Wendelen's assistant and had to follow his instructions to the letter. She was his 'ears, legs and mouth', since he was a wanted man by the Gestapo and his movements would be limited once on the ground.[89] She was now known as Elaine Meeus, codename 'Alice', which she was to use when among members of the resistance in the field and members of SOE's Verstrepen group.[90] T Section agents had a one-in-three chance of not coming back alive. Only weeks before Mission 'Imogen' left for Belgium, four agents had been caught, tortured and beheaded.

With a sense of determination, and after undergoing the usual checks, Elaine and the two men boarded the B-24 Liberator aircraft under the command of Captain Wright. There was a crew of eight men, who were part of the 850th Squadron. This huge aircraft, the workhorse of the USAAF, was used in every theatre of war, from bombing raids to the dropping of parachutists over occupied territory. To help pinpoint the drop zone, the aircraft detected the 'Eureka beam' using the 'Rebecca' from about half a mile out. This equipment started to be used in 1943 and revolutionised parachute drops. 'Rebecca' (the transceiver and antenna) sent signals from the aircraft to 'Eureka' (the portable transponder) on the ground. Using its highly directional antenna, Rebecca timed the returning signals and calculated the distance to Eureka along with its relative position.

As the hole opened in the floor of the aircraft, Elaine decided she would jump first in case her nerves got the better of her. As she steadied herself, the dispatcher said, 'Honey, I am going to give you the last kiss you'll get in a long time.' Then he picked her up by the straps of her harness, kissed her firmly on the lips and threw her out of the aircraft.[91] Despite jumping afterwards, André and Jacques still flew past her, and although it 'was a beautiful summer's night', she didn't want to spend the majority of it stuck in the sky for all to see, growing frustrated at not descending nearly as fast as she might wish.[92] When she eventually landed, she gathered up the suitcase containing her clothes, another containing Jacques's wireless and the huge amount of money that had been sent with them. After burying their parachutes, they made their way to the safe house. 'I'm home,' she thought. 'I am back in Belgium.'[93]

The next morning Elaine excitedly opened her suitcase to see what clothes London had sent for her to wear. She found a beautiful tweed suit with matching shoes (the like of which hadn't been seen in Belgium since before the Germans arrived) and a handbag with the words 'Made in England' emblazoned in big gold letters on the lining. If she had worn this outfit, she wouldn't have looked more English if she had tried. Her resistance contact told her that she even smelled English and whisked her off to a local shop to be fitted out like a Belgian woman who had endured four years of occupation.

They had been informed by SOE HQ that the purpose of their mission was to 'be our representative with whom we can communicate and from whom we can receive indications that will allow us to provide assistance to the Resistance Groups to achieve the goal of the SHAEF Directives as explained to you.' These were:

a) To delay the establishment and use of enemy troops to face the invasion, more especially artillery, tank and armoured units.
b) To delay the installation of reinforcement troops positioned around the heads of Allied bridges.
c) To hinder air action directed against Allied troops.
d) To hinder transport by river.
e) To transmit to London all information of a more or less important military nature.

The plan is to respect the individuality of the Resistance Groups and make them, as much as possible, autonomous with direct communications with us for everything that concerns actual operations.[94]

The team made their way to Brussels and started work. They shared a house, and soon Elaine and Wendelen became lovers. 'He was a wonderful man,' she said.[95] Elaine had her work cut out for her. She carried van de Spiegel's wireless set; it was deemed safer with her as he was known to the Gestapo. One of Elaine's key contacts, whom she was presumably introduced to by Wendelen, was Denise Laplat. The two women got on extremely well, being of a similar age and background. Together, they found safe houses from which van de Spiegel could work, as well as recruiting a 'protection team' for him to act as lookouts and to warn against the approach of D/F vans while he was transmitting his messages. These messages included vital information about the V-2s. Wendelen had spent a fortune bribing a German soldier who worked at a V-2 launch site, and they managed to get crucial information back to London regarding its targets, as well as intelligence about troop and vehicle movements. Wendelen also coordinated and directed post-D-Day sabotage activities that were carried out by the resistance. Elaine assisted him by carrying messages and weapons between Brussels and the Ardennes. When it comes to details, the personnel files of both Wendelen and Elaine are disappointingly thin. There is no post-mission debriefing, which makes filling the gaps a tricky job.

However, the third part of their mission, codenamed 'Patron Lysander', is fortunately well documented and was quite unique. By late July 1944, SOE had been tasked with getting King Leopold's younger brother, Prince Charles, out of Belgium. He was in increasing danger as he was known to the Gestapo, and his severe sciatica meant he could not travel quickly or easily. His evacuation was considered urgent, and Wendelen was given the 'important and delicate mission of finding a suitable Lysander landing ground for [his] immediate evacuation from Belgium to the UK'.[96]

Elaine's role in all of this was to keep the prince entertained, but she was not aware of who her charge was and only knew him by the name Monsieur Bernard. She went to the château where he was hiding and, believing him to be a 'top-notch resistance man', kept him company by whiling away the hours playing ping-pong, smoking and chatting.[97] Elaine talked about everything, from London's nightlife to how she believed King Leopold to be a traitor and his brother a 'useless so and so' who, instead of helping his country and joining the resistance, 'was probably drunk in some brothel somewhere'.[98] Her charge took it all in his stride and was probably just grateful that, when she wasn't with him, she was working on his behalf, looking for a suitable landing strip for a Lysander to come and extract him. She made several suggestions to the RAF, but each time she was told that the land was not suitable. She began to get agitated – time was running out.

While she was in the Ardennes with her mystery charge, Wendelen and van de Spiegel were in Brussels. One day they sent an urgent message saying they needed her to bring the wireless set to them.

With the train line unusable because of sabotage, she managed to get a lift from a fellow guest at the hotel she was lodging in, who just happened to be a German officer. As he lifted her suitcase into his car, he commented on how heavy it was; she fluttered her eyelashes and told him she had been shopping on the black market and was taking some 'ham, butter, [and] meat to her family'.[99] They made small talk during the journey and he dropped her off near the home of her 'parents' (naturally, a false address). She waited for him to drive off before going to meet the men and handing over the wireless set.[100]

By the end of August 1944, Allied troops were starting to overrun parts of Belgium and had Brussels firmly in their sights. Elaine had another near miss when, while running late, she stuffed some decoded messages into her handbag and went out after curfew to deliver them. Passing a bonfire that had been started to burn SS documents and evidence, she was stopped by a soldier who, on seeing her identity papers, began to speak to her in Flemish, a language she had not spoken aloud for several years. She managed to get away with it and was just happy that he had not searched her handbag, as that would have meant instant death at such a volatile time.

On 3 September, after she had been in the field almost four weeks, Brussels was liberated by the British, with the Germans in a state of disarray after their defeat at Falaise.[101] The Household Cavalry were on the left and the Grenadier Guards on the right, with the Welsh and Irish Guards following close behind. The population had not expected to be liberated so soon, and the troops were met with such a mob of celebrating people that it slowed their progress. Elaine and Wendelen found themselves in charge of a tank, and Elaine climbed into the turret to take potshots at escaping Germans, a skill that SOE had neglected to teach them. Although she believed she didn't hit any of them, she did think she might have damaged a monument, but she didn't care – she was giddy with excitement, she was in love and the war would soon be over. Her life could really begin at last, with Wendelen by her side.

While they were in the tank, Wendelen came clean about who her secret charge had been. Elaine went red with embarrassment, remembering all the terrible things she had said about him, but Wendelen just laughed until the tears rolled down his face. In the event (and in spite of all their hard work), Prince Charles declined his flight to England and instead took on a new role as Prince Regent. Elaine saw him some weeks later and was 'very nervous' about meeting him again. She had no idea how to address him. Should she call him 'Your Majesty'? She needn't have worried. He smiled at her and said, 'Just call me Bernard.' All was forgiven.[102]

With their mission over, Elaine and Wendelen had to decide what their future held. Elaine wanted to get married to 'the love of her life'.[103] But Wendelen said he could not marry her. He had been offered a job as Belgian ambassador to Austria and needed some-one who had money. So he married a diplomat's daughter. Broken-hearted, Elaine soon found someone else to marry – Michael Blaze, who also served with SOE in Belgium and whom she believed had previously had an affair with the head of T Section, Hardy Amies.

Meanwhile, something was wrong at SOE HQ. Both Olga Jackson and Elaine Madden were the subject of a memo penned by Hardy Amies, whom Elaine knew disliked her, often speaking to her as if she were 'a bit of dirt sticking to the floor'.[104] This time he said that the two women had been a 'bloody nuisance ever since liberation'.[105] Damning her by faint praise, he said that Elaine 'had done some quite good work' but had caused trouble later on, which resulted in her and Michael Blaze being sacked.[106] There is no evidence of this in either Elaine's or Blaze's PF. Given that Elaine believed Blaze and Amies to have had a homosexual affair, it seems that Amies might have had a vendetta against her and was determined not only to undermine her, but to bring her down. Could it be that he said they were 'sacked' to cover himself? He did grudgingly accept that 'both these women jumped into Belgium' and that they should do what they could to find them employment in FANY, but *not* SOE.[107]

On 20 March 1945, Michael Blaze and Elaine Madden were the subject of an internal memo regarding their intention to marry. Both had served in Belgium and remained in SOE's employ. Their impending marriage fell under part of Routine Order No. 32 – a rule that agents could not marry and continue to work in the field together. Elaine had accepted this and intended to apply to the Office of Strategic Services (OSS) for a new role in the field. The author of the memo, believing that she would be successful with her request and concerned about losing a good agent, suggested that the pair remain in SOE's employment and an allowance be made for them to marry and be redeployed to work together for Section X (Germany). This suggestion was accepted, despite Amies's attempts to stop any future employment of Elaine by SOE. It would clearly not have been sanctioned if they had both been 'sacked'. On the eve of her wedding, Wendelen and Elaine spent the night together and he asked her to be his mistress. She refused and went on to marry Blaze 'out of spite', resulting in a loveless marriage.[108]

■ ■ ■

As Elaine was wondering what to do next, Renée Lippens was still undergoing SOE training. Although the information that exists about Renée Lippens is scant, her story is still one that deserves to be told in relation to Belgian women agents. Born in Ghent on 17 May 1907, Renée was the daughter of an engineer who later was held as a POW at Stalag VIII-A in Lower Silesia. She was living in Brussels and was employed as a social worker when war broke out. She drove ambulances and trucks for the army, but her thoughts soon turned to resistance activity. She helped organise networks between France, Belgium, Spain and Portugal, presumably assisting on escape lines, which at some point must have taken her to England. Fluent in French and English, and with a good knowledge of German, Flemish and Italian, she was well suited for intelligence work and was recruited into the Sûreté de l'État in London in 1942. As well as the work she undertook for the Belgians, she also worked alongside the Political Warfare Executive and was known to SOE T Section, although she herself knew 'very little of the SOE set up'.[109]

Her work during this time is not well documented but in December 1944 a document from Hardy Amies states that she had 'only just come back to Brussels'. No mention is made of how or why she returned to Belgium. He goes on to say that 'she is undoubtedly of the highest intelligence and integrity' and it is suggested that 'she should be given a mission and be infiltrated into Germany through Switzerland into the Lake Constance region which she knows well. She would obtain information as to present conditions and endeavour also to obtain safe houses and contacts.'[110] At this stage it was not thought that she should go back to England for training, but rather be infiltrated into Switzerland straight from Belgium.

However, she felt differently, and requested that she be permitted to undertake at least a short training course in England. The request was sent to Captain Floor, who agreed. Renée herself was keen to join the military, but this was curtailed quickly. By January 1945, 'no decisions' had been 'arrived at by the authorities as to militarisation of female personnel'.[111] The next best thing was to work as an agent in the field, and SOE changed their minds – she was to be returned to England to undertake SOE training after all. She would 'go through the full training of an organiser, the main object of her mission being one of propaganda of foreign workers'.[112]

At first it was decided that Renée would not undertake parachute training as, at 1 metre 80 centimetres tall, she was 'rather large'.[113] She also had a scar on her, right knee that could have been an injury that weakened her, but (as seemed to be the way of things for her) the instructors changed their minds and allowed her to learn to parachute. Despite being 'very tall', she showed 'good control' due to being 'fit and strong'.[114] Dated 25 March 1945 and issued from STS 34, 'Drokes', a twelve-bedroomed red-brick house set in 14 acres of 'lovely grounds ... overlooking the Beaulieu River', complete with orchard, tennis courts and swimming pool, her finishing report gives a glowing summary of her character and skill.[115] She was described as 'highly intelligent and quick to visualise security problems. She had good powers of imagination and initiative. In her character, she is determined, reliable and very level-headed. She had a pleasant personality, charm and excellent sense of humour.' She produced 'first-class' propaganda work and was said to be 'entirely capable of organising large- or small-scale propaganda campaigns.'[116]

In preparation for her mission, she signed the Official Secrets Act on 8 April 1945 and waited for a flight to be organised. A month later, the war ended. Renée didn't get her chance to shine. It seems such a shame that someone who was clearly a talented, skilled and enthusiastic agent was never infiltrated into the field to prove just how good she could be.

■ ■ ■

Meanwhile, Elaine had volunteered to work for an elite force to undertake 'a dangerous undercover mission'. Four hundred men and women from seven Allied countries volunteered to be part of a mission codenamed 'Vicarage' – later the Special Allied Airborne Reconnaissance Force (SAARF).[117] Their aim was to drop experienced parachutists in small teams, near the POW and concentration camps ahead of the liberating forces to negotiate the safety of remaining POWs and prisoners in the camps. Based on SOE's Jedburgh teams, there were to be two agents and a W/T in each team. But when the first few teams of parachutists were caught and imprisoned, the remainder were sent by road or air transport. When news reached them of the death marches that camp inmates were being forced to undertake, the mission changed to become one of reconnaissance and intelligence gathering rather than of direct intervention.

In April 1945, Elaine began work. Her role was to find surviving SOE agents, Belgian political prisoners and resistance workers. Her search took her to Buchenwald, Dachau, Bergen-Belsen and Flossenbürg and her team followed the liberators into each camp. The horror of what she saw never left her: 'all these things . . . if you hadn't seen these things, you can't believe them'.[118] She recalled bodies hanging from gallows, brutally eviscerated women, and corpses left lying in the gas chambers. She even claimed to have seen the infamous lamp-shade made of human skin. But she only found two survivors from the list of those she was looking for. On returning home, Elaine was neither debriefed nor counselled about what she had seen (no agents were). She was given the money owed her and demobbed from FANY, and 'that', as she said, 'was that'.[119] Elaine was given a mention in dispatches.

■ ■ ■

After the war, Elaine and Blaze moved to Burundi in Africa, where she became pregnant. She returned to Belgium to give birth, but af-terwards went back to Burundi with her daughter, whereupon she discovered that her husband was living with another woman. The marriage over, she moved in with some friends and took a job as an accountant. Elaine eventually found love again and planned to marry. She went to Belgium for a visit, and four days before she was due to return she heard her husband-to-be had been killed in a car crash. Devastated, she lived alone until the end of her life, and only latterly spoke of her wartime experiences.

Elaine's life was one of love, loss and bravery. While she never con-sidered herself a hero, her SOE role and subsequent work on behalf of SAARF was more than worthy of putting her in the annals of SOE remembrance.

6

MISSION NEDERLANDS

I was an amateur, but in war, risks have to be taken. I played a game
of cat-and-mouse with the Gestapo, with the only difference that I
was caged, and the cat was free.

Trix Terwindt[1]

Trix Terwindt was a trailblazer. She was one of a handful of air stew-
ardesses for the Dutch airline KLM, having worked for them since
they had pioneered the use of women in aviation in 1937. The outbreak of war had a huge impact on her life. Flights were grounded
and her job became superfluous. Like the rest of the Dutch population, she was in shock when, on the morning of 10 May 1940, the
news that their neutral country was being invaded by the Germans
was broadcast on the radio.

Dutch citizens watched in horror as Luftwaffe bombers that had
flown out to the North Sea as if en route to England suddenly turned
180 degrees and flew back to launch a brutal attack on the Netherlands. At the same time, paratroopers began to land all over the
country, with one witness remembering hearing on the wireless that
there were 'parachutists landing near Rotterdam; parachutists landing near Utrecht, near Leyden. I had never heard of parachutists
before. I soon found out that there was a lot I did not know.'[2] The
population of the Netherlands, a country that had remained neutral
for the past hundred years and thus had not experienced war in living memory, were shocked to find themselves victims of the *blitzkrieg*

and under threat of occupation. They fought back as best they could, but resources were scarce and the German forces overpowering.

The invading paratroopers bypassed with ease the defences that the Dutch had put in place. These had taken the form of ditches, pillboxes and fortifications. In front of these lay areas of ground that could easily be flooded with a few feet of water. This water would turn the soil into an impassable quagmire. However, this was not an obstacle for the German invaders, who were dropping their forces from the air. During the invasion, many German paratroopers were killed or taken prisoner (and transported to the UK) and approximately 250 Junkers Ju 52s – the paratroopers' transport aircraft – were destroyed. This was one of the reasons that Operation 'Sealion' (the planned invasion of England) was postponed indefinitely in September 1940.

The attack on the Netherlands was part of Operation 'Fall Gelb', the aim of which was the German invasion of France. By attacking through the Netherlands and Belgium, they could bypass the impressive fortifications of the Maginot Line, thus achieving their aim quickly and capturing two more countries along the way. Hitler justified the attack by informing his troops and the German public that the Allies had been planning to attack the Ruhr and that their forces would advance via the Netherlands and Belgium. He had to mount this attack to stop them and save the German people. The ruse worked to such an extent that some German soldiers were surprised when they did not encounter any Allied troops during the invasion.

Another excuse given by Hitler was the 'Venlo incident' in November 1939. Two SIS agents had thought they were in contact with early German resistance, whereas they were actually in contact with Walter Schellenberg, later the well-known SD chief. On 10 November 1939, the SIS agents had a secret meeting in Venlo on the Dutch/German border but they were captured. A Dutch lieutenant was also present and was killed. Hitler used this affair as another justification for the attack in May 1940.

One of the main aims of the invasion was the battle for The Hague. The invaders wanted to capture the city and surrounding airports, as well as seize Queen Wilhelmina and her cabinet and put them under arrest. However, opposition was fierce and the plan failed. Nevertheless, fears for the queen's safety grew. A difficult and contentious decision had to be made: should she stay and risk arrest when the Netherlands inevitably fell, or should she flee and rule in exile? Her cabinet firmly believed that she should leave while she could. Against her initial wishes, she was forced to leave the Netherlands on a warship sent by King George VI to bring her to Britain, where he received her on 13 May.

She set up a government in exile and made her presence widely felt, especially to any *Engelandvaarders* – Dutch escapees who made it to Britain. She received each and every one of them, offering comfort and encouragement. However, some people in the Netherlands believed their queen had acted out of cowardice and felt abandoned. To remain in contact with her people and to offer her support, Queen Wilhelmina regularly made broadcasts on Radio Oranje ('Oranje' was a tribute to the Dutch monarchy's House of Orange-Nassau and was used as a sign of resistance). During one broadcast, she expressed her rage by calling Hitler 'the archenemy of mankind'.[3]

On 14 May, Rotterdam became the scene of unprecedented destruction. German General Schmidt had given an ultimatum: unless Rotterdam surrendered that very day, the city would be bombed. Even before the ultimatum had expired, Luftwaffe bombers appeared on the horizon. In just thirteen minutes, the city was all but razed to the ground, with approximately 850 deaths and countless people injured; 80,000 people became homeless, and 11,000 buildings were destroyed or damaged. Next, the Germans threatened to do the same to Utrecht. The situation was hopeless, with the Netherlands powerless to fight back. There was little choice but to surrender, and the capitulation was signed in a school room the following day. A new administration was installed on 29 May, headed by Reich Commissioner Arthur

Seyss-Inquart, who took up residence in The Hague and ruled with an iron fist. The whole of Western Europe was now occupied, with only Britain remaining free.

As with other countries, SOE was there to offer help and support to the burgeoning Dutch resistance movement. However, things did not go smoothly. Many escaped Dutchmen reported to their queen in London and expressed their desire to return to the Netherlands to fight back against the occupier. She, in turn, referred them to her confidant and personal secretary François van 't Sant, who had set up the Centrale Inlichtingendienst (Central Intelligence Service). It was through this organisation that the first Dutch agent was sent back into the country. However, van 't Sant harboured a personal dislike for the head of SOE's newly founded Netherlands (N) Section, Richard Laming. As a result, he kept the best recruits for his organisation, leaving SOE to find their own agents. The agents were described by a fellow agent as:

> a very mixed batch. Some of them had reached England from Holland; others had been brought to England from all parts of the world to help in the work of liberation. They came from all trades and levels of society and represented every standard of education, from elementary to academic. All of them had one thing in common: a deep love of their country, and in their duties, a blind trust in their superiors.[4]

Establishing SOE's work in the Netherlands took considerable effort for several reasons, not least because the country was at a disadvantage in terms of its geographical location and terrain compared with other countries in which SOE was operating. Despite its relative proximity to Britain, the North Sea coasts were closely guarded by German patrols. The Lysander operations, which had proved so successful in France, were very challenging here due to frequent rain and foggy weather conditions. The country was densely populated with myriad roads and railway tracks traversing it, making it extremely difficult to find suitable landing zones. The lack of wooded areas and the fact that the countryside was completely flat meant that enemy patrols would instantly spot any landing aircraft, making the whole exercise almost impossible. But Laming's attempts to infiltrate agents by sea had also failed and so parachuting agents into the country seemed to be the only viable option.[5]

The first two N Section agents parachuted blind in September 1941, so they did not have any names or addresses of friendly compatriots. In fact, their task was to scout out locals who would be keen to help. However, needing somewhere to stay, they broke the rules and contacted a relative who owned a tobacco shop in The Hague. One was arrested within days, and the other tried to escape by sea and was never heard of again.

The following two agents were infiltrated by parachute on 6/7 November. They were the saboteur Thijs Taconis and his wireless operator Hubertus Lauwers. They did not get off to a good start. As they dressed for their mission in the briefing hut at Newmarket airfield, it became apparent that they had been given matching clothes. Their shoes, overcoats and even briefcases were identical. To add insult to injury, their ID cards bore some significant errors, not least that the lions on the royal coat of arms were facing the wrong way. When the agents protested about the oversights, they were told by their conducting officer that 'nobody was going to bother with details', demonstrating a level of confidence and naivety that could have been extremely damaging. But worse would befall N Section in the months to come.[6]

Due to a faulty wireless set, Lauwers (who was based in The Hague) did not manage to make contact with SOE HQ until early 1942, after which time he established regular communications. Meanwhile, Taconis, who was based in Arnhem, started to develop his network, which came to include a man named Ridderhof, who offered to provide lorries to help get goods away from drop zones after a drop.

Unbeknown to Taconis, this man was a double agent and was feeding information back to Hermann Giskes, a major in the Abwehr, and also to his counterpart Josef Schreider of the Sicherheitsdienst (Security/Intelligence Service). They would give Taconis false intelligence that was then fed back into the SOE group and subsequently appeared in Lauwers's wireless messages. The trap had been set.

On 6 March 1942, Lauwers was preparing to send a message from his safe house, a flat belonging to the Teller family. Just as he settled down and had started to tap out his message using his Morse key, Mr Teller appeared and somewhat shakily informed him that several black cars had pulled up nearby. Knowing that this could only be the Germans, Lauwers wondered if his signal had been picked up by a direction finder. This was something he was keenly aware of and had been preparing for (although it was unlikely to have been a D/F on this occasion as he had barely started his transmission). Lauwers calmly told Mrs Teller to throw his wireless set out of the window. Then he picked up his coat, left the house and nonchalantly walked down the street with three incriminating messages still in his pocket. A few moments later, one of the black cars pulled up behind him and he was arrested.

His wireless set was found dangling in Mrs Teller's washing line and the messages in his pocket were enough to incriminate him a hundred times over. But Giskes was not interested in punishing Lauwers; he wanted to play him for everything he could get. Thanks to Ridderhof's false intelligence (relating to the German warship *Prinz Eugene*), Lauwers's codes were deciphered immediately. He was then coerced into continuing to send messages to London as if he were still at liberty. However, Lauwers was confident that London would know he had been arrested when he missed his security checkout. When this failed, he added the letters CAU at the beginning of a message and ended it with GHT, since it was standard practice to top and tail a message with three random letters. He hoped that this would be enough to save him, but this clue was also missed by the decoders.

From 12 March to the end of October 1942, Lauwers's messages all contained a 'clear warning' that went unnoticed or unheeded.[7]

On 27/28 March, SOE agent Nol Baatsen was dropped near Kallenkote, Overijssel. Ridderhof was on his reception committee and immediately informed him that he was arrested and had been betrayed by England. During the interrogation that followed, Baatsen volunteered a vast amount of information about SOE to his captors. Lauwers realised how dangerous the game he was playing was and refused to send any more messages that would result in the capture of his comrades. Giskes convinced him to carry on by promising that none of them would be executed, so Lauwers continued, naively hoping that SOE were playing the Germans in the same way that the Germans were playing them.

As a result of Lauwers's messages, more and more agents were sent out to the Netherlands, each of whom was arrested on landing, and those who were wireless operators were forced to send messages as if they too were operating freely. 'Englandspiel', or Operation 'Nordpol' (North Pole) as it became known, was run from a white mansion house on the edge of the Scheveningen Woods near The Hague. Those captured were held at Haaren prison in Assen, a former Catholic seminary that was transformed into an impenetrable and harsh internment camp. In total, fifty-nine SOE agents were sent to the Netherlands and immediately captured, among them one woman. Her name was Beatrix Terwindt.

■ ■ ■

Trix was born in February 1911 in Arnhem and had a very strict upbringing. Her family were fervent Catholics and her father was a member of the Roman Catholic Conservative Party (and later a supporter of Nederlandsche Unie).[8] Her mother was frequently away from the family home. Her father was chiefly concerned with Trix's unwavering attendance at church and her achievements at the Sacré-Coeur school, where she received good grades and reports. As the youngest of seven children, Trix often felt alone or excluded at home, but at school, she was known for being outgoing and lively. She excelled in music and art and became proficient in French, English, Dutch and German, as well as speaking a little Italian.

After finishing her education at Sacré-Coeur, Trix attended an English convent school in Bruges for six months and spent another six at a similar educational institute in Brussels. At age seventeen, she returned to the Netherlands and obtained a teaching certificate, after which she went to Amsterdam to study interior design. Here, she ran out of money and was forced to return home, where she undertook secretarial training while dreaming of going to Rome and pursuing her desire to study the history of art.

In 1935, Trix got a job in an art gallery in Maastricht and undertook art classes in her spare time. 'I was in seventh heaven,' she wrote. 'I worked during the day, went to class in the evenings, lived on bread and beans and improved by leaps and bounds.'[9] She also translated French literature as a means to earn money.

In 1937, Trix applied to work as an air stewardess for KLM and, much to her amazement, she was successful. She was one of the first-ever women to undertake such a role and, after an intensive training course, she travelled all over Europe. The media attention on these women was extraordinary; they were photographed and interviewed for a wealth of newspapers and magazines. The attention from gentlemen also took Trix by surprise, and she received countless invitations to theatres and restaurants, as well as proposals of marriage from passengers. Her life had certainly gone in a very different direction from her strict upbringing.

In December 1939, nearly all of KLM's flights stopped due to the outbreak of the war. Trix had almost nothing to do. She was given a retaining fee and undertook various secretarial jobs, including one for KLM at its base at Schiphol airport, but this was cut short by the invasion on 10 May. Her employers arranged for her to move to The Hague to undertake work in the Welfare Office and Advice Bureau, which offered help and shelter to the refugees from the

Rotterdam bombing. She worked there until June 1941, when the office was closed down.

In the meantime, Trix was shocked to discover that all of KLM's pilots had been arrested. In the spring of 1941, the aviation training school was raided and the head of KLM arrested for his part in some preliminary peace talks with Hermann Göring. Trix kept her head down, worked hard and stayed out of trouble.

In the summer of 1941, Trix used some of her retainer money to move into an empty barn in the village of Kudelstaart, near Schiphol. Although it was very basic, Trix thrived on her new lifestyle. She grew vegetables, milked her goat, listened to music and swam or boated in the waters of the Westeinderplassen, sometimes catching fish for dinner. It was, she believed, just what she needed after the months of misery and hard work following the loss of her beloved job as an air stewardess.

She was somewhat taken aback when a former KLM colleague Klaas Voûte (who was previously a secretary to the Ned Unie – the organisation of which her father was also a member) approached her and asked if she knew anyone who could assist with helping downed Allied airmen to escape. Trix realised that her new lifestyle was ideal in that it was solitary and remote. The fact that she had maintained contact with former workmates would also work in her favour. Tentatively, she started to approach people to see how far they would go to help the downed Allied pilots and air crews, and scouted out members of the local resistance. She also acted as a go-between for Voûte and nearby farmers 'with regard to British pilots shot down and their places of hiding', as well as distributing *Vrij Nederland*, an underground newsletter.[10] By now, she was truly ensconced in the local resistance. It gave her a sense of purpose. 'If you want to change the world,' she said, 'start with yourself.'[11]

She decided that she wanted to play a more active role and become a courier, helping the escapees cross the border. The first escape she planned was set for February 1942, but before she was even able to start out, she learned that the route had been compromised and it was unsafe to proceed. The addresses she had been provided with were blown and her contacts had been arrested. She was devastated. 'I feel like I'm slowly falling asleep mentally,' she said. 'I don't think I'll be able to last another year of war.'[12] Though Trix found it difficult to keep quiet about what she was doing, she was obviously unable to tell even her closest friends what she was up to. She managed to continue resisting in her own quiet way, signing off her letters home 'Orange above', or 'Long live Holland', while awaiting her next opportunity to help Allied airmen.

She did not have long to wait. Within a few weeks, the resistance had a new assignment for her – they wanted her to take a young cadet named Theo Lusink from the Royal Military Academy to Switzerland. There were two possible reasons for this: it could be that he had been told that he had to report to a POW camp along with any officers who had been serving in 1940 (this was Hitler's retaliation to the resistance work undertaken by the Dutch military), or that his parents, who were 'strong *Oranje* patriots told him that he would be doing a better service for his country to leave it and fight for the free Forces'.[13] Either way, Trix was to accompany him. For her, it would be a way out of the Netherlands so she could join the resistance fight proper.

Replete with addresses and instructions, the pair set off from Amsterdam on 20 March 1942. Trix found her companion to be rather arrogant and complacent, added to which he complained about everything. He also dressed 'in a truly Dutch way', which was entirely inappropriate for the journey they were undertaking, where they needed to draw as little attention to themselves as possible.[14] The pair crossed the border into Belgium on foot and travelled via Antwerp to Brussels by train. They stayed in a café overnight and for the next few days, with the help of locals, Catholic priests and resistance members, they travelled by train across Europe until they reached the Swiss border. The journey was exhausting. Trix was constantly on her guard in case any of these 'helpers' should turn out to be collaborators. She understood she was risking everything by undertaking this journey. With Switzerland within touching distance, Trix and Lusink 'ran at top speed for about 200 metres over the border'; such was their exhilaration.[15] Their high spirits soon dissipated as they ran into the hands of a Swiss border official who promptly arrested them.

They were taken for interrogation. The fact that neither had the correct papers or documentation made them seem highly suspicious. However, Trix was able to tell them the name of a hotelier who was their contact, and miraculously they were allowed to stay in her hotel while the investigation continued. Trix was immensely frustrated that her plans had been thwarted yet again. Things went from bad to worse. As a result of a new law stating that anyone who arrived after a certain date in March was to be detained, she was put into Bellechasse prison in Fribourg, where her mood and well-being deteriorated rapidly. After twelve days, she was sent to Geneva and, from there, was returned to the Hotel du Lac, where she had initially stayed. While the whole debacle seemed like a convoluted mess, some good eventually came of it when she was issued with a Dutch passport and told that she could go to England upon receipt of the correct visa. Delighted that things might be moving in the right direction, Trix set about trying to get the paperwork she needed.

However, this proved almost impossible, and Trix was sent to Spain, where her situation grew still worse. She was dismayed to miss various boats bound for England due to visa delays. Much to her annoyance, she remained trapped in a series of Spanish and Portuguese hotels until, at last, the paperwork came through. On 25 August, she boarded a flight bound for England. Upon arrival, she was immediately taken to Nightingale Lane, a part of the Royal Patriotic School, where she was questioned. She gave a detailed account of her journey from the Netherlands, complete with the names of those who had assisted her and the places in which she had stayed. Her MI5 report said that she was 'a plucky and sensible little patriot' and that they did

not foresee any security problems. It was suggested that she be immediately released to the Dutch authorities so that she could undertake
'active participation in the war effort'.[16]

While Trix was still in Dutch political quarantine, her story came
to the attention of Airey Neave. He was the head of MI9's organisation Intelligence School Nine (IS9), also known as Room 900 due to
its location within the War Office. The main aim of this organisation was escape and evasion. IS9 initially focused on routes out of
France, the Netherlands and Belgium (and, as we will see, they also
became involved with missions in Eastern Europe). The idea was to
get downed Allied airmen, POWs and persons of interest out of occupied territory by utilising existing escape routes such as the Comet
or Pat lines, or by creating new ones that were specifically suited to
their exact requirements.

Neave believed that with British help, Trix could establish an escape route from the Netherlands to Brussels. From there, the escapees
would be picked up by the network of Belgian and French guides who
would be able to get them over the Pyrenees and eventually back to
England. He thought Trix would be ideal for the job as she had earlier
proved herself willing to try, even though the mission had failed. Her
contacts in aviation (which would be added to the addresses of Dutchmen willing to harbour pilots) and her skill with languages made her
the ideal candidate to undertake such intricate and dangerous work.

Trix was delighted by the idea, saying, 'What I had seen and heard
at the British consulates and what I had experienced at the Dutch
consulates and embassies, and also at the Dutch Intelligence Service
in London, did not make it difficult for me to decide to work with the
British.'[17] She had to wait for the Dutch authorities to release her to
work for the British, during which time she lived a lonely existence
in a flat in Kensington. As soon as permission was granted, she was
signed up to become a member of FANY and started her training.

Even though her mission would be on behalf of MI9, Trix still
needed to learn to parachute so that she could get back into the

Netherlands. In a letter dated 27 November 1942, sent to the head of MI9, Colonel Norman Crockett, on behalf of Charles Blizzard (who had by now replaced Laming as head of SOE N Section), SOE offered to help her in several ways:

> We [SOE] shall be glad to arrange training for her in jumping, and if you wish it and if time allows, we should try and arrange to have her sent to our finishing schools, particularly with a view to giving her some security training in such matters as settling in in her territory of operations, making contacts etc. In view of the importance of her mission and our desire to cooperate with you in any way possible.[18]

Such cooperation between the services would not be isolated to this case, as SOE worked alongside IS9 for the infiltration of the three women who went into Eastern Europe from Mandate Palestine later in the war (see Chapter 10, 'Mission Palmach'). SOE's help would not end at training Trix; they would also infiltrate her using their aircraft and crew from RAF Tempsford. She would be collected by an SOE reception committee, with whom she would spend twenty-four hours before starting her mission. However, before all that she needed training, and MI9 took up SOE's offer to send her on several courses.

At the beginning of December, Trix (now known as Beatrice Thompson) began her SOE training at Wanborough Manor (STS 5), where she undertook a preliminary course. In just over two weeks, she undertook training in PT, basic weapons handling and demolitions. From there, she went on to Ringway, where she began her parachute training. She had visited this airport before as part of her KLM route, but this time she was in for a very different experience. She spent five days undertaking the basic groundwork that would help her to become a proficient parachutist. With a short break for Christmas, she went on to Beaulieu, where she was based at the

House in the Woods, a sprawling mansion with myriad bedrooms, bathrooms and a large briefing room (which had once been the billiard room). As part of her course, she was sent on a ninety-six-hour scheme. Although the report of this no longer exists, it is likely that it would have been an exercise in which she was trailed by a policeman. She would have had to find specific rendezvous points and contacts without drawing unwanted attention to herself.

Trix completed her training at Ringway and was given her final report from the Vineyards (STS 35) at Beaulieu, where she impressed everyone who met her. Her worldly experience had enabled her to mix well with other students of all nationalities and social classes. Her 'mousey' appearance and mannerisms would, it was believed, work in her favour as she would go 'easily unnoticed'.[19] Her instructors described her as 'intelligent, capable, resourceful, practical and most discreet'. Unusually for a woman (particularly as they had only recently been allowed to be recruited as agents), it was felt that she could be a 'great success' as a leader, given time and experience in the field, as she could easily gain people's 'confidence and trust'.[20] She was ready to be sent back to the Netherlands and begin her work in earnest.

Now, it was a waiting game for her mission. An aircraft could only fly during the full moon period, and ground conditions in the Netherlands had been icy. Additionally, the weather that February was stormy with high winds and heavy rain, making flying difficult and parachuting conditions dangerous. The operation was to be twofold. N Section agents Kees van Hulsteijn and Piet Bragaar would accompany Trix, and they would jump first at an LZ near Ijsselmeer, a large freshwater lake not far from Hoorn, using a dinghy.[21] After this, Trix would be dropped along with several containers on heathland near Steenwijk.

Starting on 8 February, Trix reported to Neave (who had taken full responsibility for her mission). Time and again, he gave her the unwelcome news that the flight had been delayed due to adverse weather conditions. Dreadfully disappointed, Trix did her best to remain positive and hope that her time would come. A few days before Trix left England, Major Blizzard invited her for tea and told her that he had received a wireless message from her reception committee, which read, 'Welcome to the most courageous woman.'[22] Trix expressed her concern that the reception committee might not be genuine, but later said, 'Everyone was so definitely confident that this was working perfectly, that I dropped the question.'[23]

On 13 February, she reported to Neave as usual and, much to her surprise, was informed that the flight would depart that night. She was, however, filled with trepidation. The previous night, she had had a vivid nightmare in which she was interrogated by Germans in civilian clothing. The dream had such an impact on her that she mentioned it to Neave, who reminded her that her role was voluntary and that she was under no pressure to undertake the mission. She also told her colleague Lieutenant Mills, who had telephoned her to wish her luck. He offered to be her dispatch officer on the night to 'soften [her] anguish'. She refused but said, 'I felt something awful was going to happen, although I vaguely felt I would survive. I was absolutely sure I would not see London again before the war had ended.'[24]

Trix went to Gaynes Hall near St Neots to receive her final briefing. It was expected that she would need approximately three months to establish the required escape line and complete her mission. She would then use her own line as a means to return to London. Once back, she would maintain contact between MI9 and the resistance in the Netherlands until the end of the war. A few hours later, Trix was driven the 15 or so miles to RAF Tempsford. She and Neave had dined together en route, and he gave her some sandwiches for the journey. At the airfield, she underwent the usual security checks and pre-flight briefings. She was handed 20,000 guilders, a cyanide capsule and her fake ID card. Just as she turned to make her way to the aircraft, Neave pressed a note into her hand. On it were two names: Poos and Slagter. She was to avoid them at all costs.

She met her companions, Kees van Hulsteijn and Piet Bragaar, who would accompany her on the journey. The pilot of the four-engine Halifax bomber was Squadron Leader Boxer. He welcomed the three aboard and ensured they were safely stowed and their static lines were in place before take-off. As the aircraft taxied down the runway, Trix looked out and saw Neave saluting them in the cold, black night. The noise of the engines drowned out any chance of conversation, and the three of them sat in silence, pondering their futures.

As the aircraft approached the first drop zone, they looked out. Beneath them, the choppy waters of the Ijsselmeer were churned up with white foam, and the waves were crashing in due to the storm that had blown up again. The men decided to abort their jump, believing it too dangerous to leap into the icy, tumultuous waves beneath them. The reception committee reported seeing the aircraft near Hoorn but that the agents did not drop.[25] Trix could see the agents' disappointment and wondered what lay in store for her some 60 miles to the east, where her reception committee would be preparing for her imminent arrival.

As the aircraft approached the drop zone, lights from the ground flashed the pre-agreed letter in Morse. At that point, a flurry of parachute containers was released. These were filled with cigarettes and, the most critical item, the wireless set. Trix then lingered on the edge of the hole, 'half in, half out', holding on for dear life, lest she should fall too early and hit a house or farm.[26] She had already told her fellow parachutists that should she falter, they were to push her, but there was no need. Despite the dreadful weather conditions, Trix took a deep breath and jumped. The strong wind caught the canopy of her parachute and dragged her a little off course so that she ended up at the far edge of the moorland. She landed badly, jarring her back. The wind then caught her again and dragged her along the ground over the rough heather, which scratched her face. As she bumped along the ground, she also hurt her nose (she later said it felt as though she had been hit with a football) and lost her parachute helmet.

When she eventually stopped, she cut the cords of her parachute and bundled it up in preparation for burying it in the ground. As she finished, she saw a flashlight and heard voices softly calling 'Felix', which was her codename. The sight of three men walking towards her was very welcome. They sat in the heather together. She mused about how beautiful Holland was, with its flat countryside and charming clouds. She then began to tell them about life in England: 'how well-fed the people were, and how high their morale. [She] spoke about Queen Wilhelmina', but the men maintained a stolid silence, and she noticed that they did not seem particularly friendly.[27] She deduced that they were probably communists and, as she was not, she hoped it might just be a political difference of opinion.

It was beginning to rain, and the men suggested they take shelter in a hut not too far away. As they walked, they began to quiz her. They asked her for the matchbox, which had their new codes hidden in it. This she handed over, along with her uneaten ham sandwiches from Neave and some cigarettes.[28] They then asked for her personal code. When she refused to give it to them, they began to chastise her, saying that London did not understand the situation in the Netherlands, that their communication was poor and that their fake paperwork was amateurish. They informed her in no uncertain terms that they 'did not want a female in the underground organisation and wanted [her] to get out of Holland again as soon as possible'.[29] They pressed her for details of her resistance contacts in The Hague and the address of her safe house in Belgium. They told her that they had orders from London not to release her until she had given them this information. However, believing that the men were genuine SOE agents, she decided that the last piece of information was acceptable to pass over, and she gave them the address of the Bally shoe shop, which was to be her first rendezvous.

The rain had got heavier as they finally reached the hut, and Trix was relieved to be somewhere dry at last. Things had not gone as expected, but she was not suspicious either. These men obviously knew far more about the current situation than she did after almost a year out of the country. It was dark in the hut, and one of the men commented that Trix's coat was too light in colour; it could attract attention in the full moon once they made their way to their headquarters. He took a dark grey horse blanket and threw it over her shoulders, and as he did so, he nudged her in the back.

As she put her hand behind her to feel what had happened, her wrist was caught. The man then grabbed her other arm and twisted it behind her back. She felt cold metal pinching into her skin. The awful truth dawned on her. She had been handcuffed. 'London has betrayed you,' he scoffed. She still didn't want to believe him. But when she saw a man in a German uniform appear out of the gloom, she realised that she had indeed been caught. As she was taken to a waiting car, she heard the German calling her captor by name. It was one of the names that Neave had given her as she'd left. She had been betrayed by her own countrymen.

Trix had unwittingly become another agent arrested as part of 'Englandspiel'. Since she arrived as part of that dreadful game of cat and mouse played between Giskes, Schreider and their men and the SOE agents, she was counted among SOE's number and treated as such by her captors.

It was getting light as the car approached a large villa that had been commandeered as Gestapo HQ in the woods at Driebergen, near Utrecht. When she walked in, she saw that breakfast had been laid, but knew she was not there for such civilities. SS Sturmbann-führer Josef Schreider welcomed 'the bravest woman' and asked her if she had received his message. He was most amused at his own joke. *Damenbesuch* (meaning visiting ladies) had been what the Gestapo had mockingly called each newly arrived secret agent captured as part of 'Englandspiel'. This time, though, it really was a woman. Horrified, Trix realised that she had never stood a chance, that this had been her destiny all along. They went for a walk in the garden, during which time Schreider told her how much respect he had for her and how brave she was. She soon realised that this was a tactic. Instead of employing violence, his methods of dealing with his prisoners were far more subtle.

Then the interrogation began, and it lasted for three days and nights. Over this time, she was asked the same questions over and over again, to which she always gave the same answers. Schreider later said:

> Much has been written about female agents, both favourable and unfavourable, often out of sensationalism and with more or less truthfulness, usually with less. Beatrix Terwindt has proven that in this area too, women can perform the same as a man, and can even remain silent better than many men.[30]

On 17 February, Trix was transferred to Haaren prison, where she was registered and assigned prisoner number 1697. From then on, she was kept in solitary confinement. Her cell, which was on the second floor, was sparsely equipped with a desk, a chair and a bed. What little light there was came from a small barred skylight (the windows had been bricked up) and a single light bulb hanging from the ceiling. A bucket in the corner of her cell served as a toilet. The cell was oppressive, and the camp routine monotonous:

> wake up at 06.00, then wash and wait for breakfast. Then, clean up the cell and wait for lunch at noon. Dinner came at 17.30, and at 20.00, the guards made a final round, and the officers have to lay out their clothes on a chair outside the cell. Half an hour later, the lights go out.[31]

Sometimes, a short spell in the exercise yard was permitted. The next day, the whole cycle would start again, for weeks, maybe months on end. Some prisoners had already been there for a year by the time Trix arrived.

Like in many other prisons, the inmates found a way to communicate by tapping Morse through the walls or water pipes. In this way, Trix initially managed to make contact with fellow prisoners and to hear their prison gossip, such as the escape of SOE agents Pieter Dourlein and John Ubbink in the autumn.[32] But as time went on, she no longer cared and sank into a depressive stupor that became almost impossible to break.

Trix broke down and found herself unable to cope. The relentless interrogations, the sheer brutality of the place (a woman in the cell directly below her had been shot for standing at her window) and the loneliness drove her to despair. She had understood that if she were captured, she would be executed. But now, in this prison, both she and other agents believed that execution would be a better outcome than the perpetual punishment and mental torture that was intrinsically part of incarceration at Haaren.[33]

On Christmas Day 1943, Schreider, who was concerned about Trix's rapid mental and physical decline, ordered that food prepared for the Wehrmacht be brought to her and saw to it that she got a cellmate to keep her company (although Trix believed she was a stool pigeon, sent to spy). She was also given prison clothing to mend in order to keep her occupied. On occasion, Schreider would visit her cell and they would speak about England or about politics and, in spite of the fact that he was her captor, she enjoyed his visits.

Trix remained at Haaren for several more months. By now, most of the other 'Englandspiel' prisoners had been in Assen prison for several months, following their transfer in November. Their lives would change for ever on 1 April 1944, when Giskes sent the following message to SOE:

To Messrs. Blunt, Bingham & Co., Successors Ltd, London.
We understand that you have been endeavouring for some time to do business in Holland without our assistance. We regret this the more since we have acted for so long as your sole representatives

in this country, to our mutual satisfaction. Nevertheless, we can assure you that, should you be thinking of paying us a visit on the Continent on any extensive scale, we shall give your emissaries the same attention as we have hitherto, and a similarly warm welcome. Hoping to see you.[34]

This missive ended Operation 'Nordpol'. 'Englandspiel' was over, but so too was the protection afforded to the captured agents from Giskes and Schreider, who had, up until this point, ensured that no one would be executed. Now the prisoners were moved on again, sent from Assen to Rawicz.

On 8 May, Trix was taken from Haaren to the Gestapo prison at Scheveningen, nicknamed *Oranjehotel* by its inmates who were, for the most part, resistance fighters. There were also some Jews and Jehovah's Witnesses. The prison was on the outskirts of The Hague and was feared by many as an infamous place of torture and terror. Inmates recalled the loneliness and boredom they faced, interspersed with the fear of never knowing when they would be pulled out of their cell for interrogation or execution on the sand dunes at Waalsdorpervlakte.

The prison had been purpose-built and consisted of a series of corridors and small cells, each of which had a skylight, bed, chair, desk and bucket. Sometimes, up to five prisoners were forced into one cell. They were not permitted to sit on the bed during the day and would exercise by pacing up and down. Others were held in solitary confinement. Food was pushed through a hatch in the door and if the prisoner was not there to receive it immediately, it landed on the floor. At night, the prison came alive with knocking on the walls and pipes and the singing of Dutch patriotic songs, especially if prisoners were being taken from their cells to be deported or murdered.

Corrie Ten Boom, who was an inmate at the same time as Trix (accused of harbouring Jews), wrote of her time at *Oranjehotel*, which would have been similar to Trix's experiences there:

A lonely cell awaits me. I am pushed inside, and the door closes behind me. I am alone. Everything here is empty and grey. In the other cell, there were still colours of the clothes of the others. Nothing here. Grey and empty. I feel cold, ice cold. The wind is howling, and there is a chilly draft in the cell . . . My blankets are grey, the walls are white at the top, the window above the door is grey, wide, divided into compartments by bars . . . is this a haunted cell into which I have come? O people, people! If only I could see people! Not this! Oh, please, not this loneliness.[35]

Trix was only at *Oranjehotel* for two days. On 10 May, she was visited by Schreider, who informed her that, against his wishes, she was to be deported to Ravensbrück concentration camp. He had come to bid her farewell and let her know that her few personal belongings would be kept safe. He then ordered the guard to 'take good care of her on the way'.[36]

Later that day, she boarded a train bound for Fürstenberg. Schreider had ensured that she had a second-class ticket so that she could sit down for the duration of the journey, and he made sure that she had cigarettes and magazines to while away the time. A taxi was supposed to meet them at the station, but there was none to be found, so she and her guard walked the last couple of miles to the camp entrance. Trix later wondered why Schreider had gone to such an effort to ensure her comfort when he must have known what hell awaited her at Ravensbrück.

Assigned as a *Nacht und Nebel* (NN) prisoner and given camp number 38382, Trix was taken to Block 24. The block contained only half the number of beds that were actually needed for the number of inmates. Girls who worked in the SS washrooms were allowed a bed each; the rest had to share what was left. The NN prisoners were the worst fed, had to work the hardest of all political prisoners and were denied any contact with the outside world. Most of them were not even registered, as their return from the camp was deemed highly unlikely.

The work, hunger, cold and exhaustion were the toughest parts of life in the camp, but Trix found a new determination to survive. She fought for everything, for her place at the dining table where she could eat her meagre rations of bread 'soup' and ersatz coffee. But the rush to get at the food sometimes meant that the soup pots were overturned or the bread trampled into the ground. She also fought for a place in the overcrowded three-storey beds. Lice were everywhere, meaning that even the few hours' sleep the prisoners did manage to get was disturbed by the scratching and biting of these disease-carrying pests (who at one stage caused a typhus epidemic in the camp). Once in bed, the cold was biting, and with threadbare blankets and straw mattresses, sleep was almost impossible. To compound this, the windows were either broken or had been removed. Trix recalled the toll that all this took on her body:

> I stood in Ravensbrück in the cold winter, in the scorching wind, with bare legs and feet in sandals, in rough cotton clothes, and tried to protect myself somewhat by holding my arms against my body. But it didn't help. I was so thin that my arms didn't fit against my rib cage anymore.[37]

Despite her fragile health and frail body, Trix, like all other prisoners, had to work, and for the first six months she was employed at the Siemens factory. She worked in an assembly line putting together field telephones and was tasked with 'the simplest work of turning small screws into something or other'.[38] Each table had a German civilian worker as supervisor, and alongside her sat German and Polish prisoners who worked hard and whom she believed had been put there to betray her.

'We received permission twice every morning and every afternoon to go to the toilet, in two compartments, which is very inconvenient, was insufficient, since most of us suffer from dysentery' she wrote.[39] 'If I remember correctly, we worked from half past seven in the morning to a quarter to six in the evening with a one-hour lunch break. [This] did not even give us half an hour in camp to eat, as we had to go through the entire camp to [get to] our block.'[40] After work, they had to undergo *Appell* (roll call, also known as *Zählappell*) before they could go to their barracks.

After six months Trix got a job as a nightwatchman in the industrial camp:

There were four of us on guard all night long, two of them in the frozen washing facility, two in the frozen toilet division. We had to keep the fires going and the rooms clean. The only light was a small kerosene lamp. Often, we could only keep one of the heaters on and worked in complete darkness when the kerosene lamp also failed. We were at the mercy of one of the *Blockälteste* [inmates appointed to be the leader of a barrack] of that industrial camp to get some extra food for the night, mostly turnip soup, which had gone sour. We were allowed to leave the place when the *Zählappell* started and could sleep in the noisy block during the day. Once we left the place, as we had no work, no coal for the fire and no kerosene lamp. We went back to our block so as not to freeze. We were betrayed by one of the *Blockälteste* and were punished: for two weeks, we had to clean approximately 40 toilets that were used by dysentery patients, in complete darkness.[41]

In addition to such debasing and cruel treatment, Trix was familiar with the stick or whip of the guards. But she never suffered some of the truly horrendous physical abuse at the camp, such as dog attacks, floggings and arbitrary brutality from the guards.

The whole time that Trix was in Ravensbrück she had open sores all over her body. It was known in the camp as 'avitaminosis' and was the result of malnutrition and vitamin deficiency. Even though going to the camp hospital (the *Revier*) could be a death sentence, Trix knew she needed her wounds tended to. She was told she must continue working but would be put on office duty for three days. At least this involved less physical activity and might give her body a chance to recover a little. When the three days were over, Trix continued in this line of work. But she was still in agony and, after a week, she returned to the *Revier*. She was accused of sabotage as she had stayed in the office too long and was told to get back to her work detail. After spending the day in excruciating pain and with a soaring temperature, she returned to the hospital that evening with a fever and almost unable to walk. With her legs wrapped in paper bandages, she was taken to the infectious wounds block, where she shared a bed with a fellow prisoner. Although the food rations were even less than in her own block, at least she no longer had to work.

As the Russian front line advanced towards Berlin, it became apparent that Ravensbrück would soon be in their path. A frenzied spate of killing began in the camp's gas chambers, as well as calculated murder at the *Jugendlager* (the juvenile protective custody camp). There, among others, F Section's Cicely Lefort had been incarcerated. After a few weeks of enduring dreadful conditions, including extended *Appell*, freezing conditions in the barracks and a complete lack of sanitation, those who did not die quickly enough were brought back to the main camp to be killed. Cicely was among their number. It could easily have been Trix, who was incapacitated by her sickness and was unfit for work. As the staff at the camp began to evacuate prisoners (many of whom were forced onto death marches to other camps) and destroy records, Trix was informed that she was to be moved. On 7 March 1945, she was herded with hundreds of other prisoners onto a cattle truck bound for Mauthausen in Austria. This camp was the destination for thousands of prisoners being evacuated from camps on the front line. The resulting overcrowding, lack of food and rampant disease led to mass death among the prisoners in the final months before liberation.[42]

The camp itself had, up until this point, held only male prisoners, with just a few exceptions. On 24 October 1942, 130 female Czech resistance fighters were taken to Mauthausen to be shot or gassed.

That summer, Himmler had ordered that brothels be set up in certain concentration camps as an 'incentive' to prisoners and functionary prisoners. Mauthausen was among them, and inmates were sent from Ravensbrück as forced sex workers.

In September 1944, several sub-camps originally under Ravensbrück's jurisdiction were also transferred to Mauthausen, after which several women-only sub-camps were set up across the Third Reich. At the end of September, 400 women were sent from Auschwitz to the Hirtenberg women's sub-camp to work at the Wilhelm-Gustloff-Werke munitions factory, followed by a further 500, who were assigned to viscose production at the Lenzing Zellwolle AG factory.

It was only in January 1945, when over 7,000 women and several hundred children were transferred from other camps to Mauthausen, that they were housed in the main camp. Over half of these prisoners were then moved to Bergen-Belsen. Those who remained were kept separately from the men.[43]

When Trix arrived in March, she had little idea of what kind of camp she had arrived at, nor that the many other members of SOE who had been trapped by 'Englandspiel' – with the exception of Ubbink and Dourlein (who escaped from Haaren), van der Ryeden and Lauwers (the first man arrested) – had all perished in the camp the previous September under horrendous circumstances.[44]

One of the work details at Mauthausen was the 'stairway of death', up which inmates were forced to carry slabs of granite on their backs. Any who fell, slipped or collapsed were instantly shot. On 6 and 7 September 1944, the men of 'Englandspiel' had been tasked with carrying huge granite blocks up 186 steps and depositing them at the top. However, the SS had deliberately not provided them with any equipment or ropes to help them get a handhold on the slippery rock. It quickly became apparent that the men would not be able to lift the granite using just their bare hands.

As they staggered up the staircase they were beaten with fists and rifle butts. Any attempt to avoid the blows was interpreted as an 'attempt to flee' and the men were shot. Likewise, if they dropped the granite it was seen as defiance and an attempt to 'avoid work'. This also resulted in execution. By the evening, many of the SOE agents lay dead, and those who survived the first day knew what was to come. Many committed suicide by jumping off the steep staircase into the ravine rather than endure the agonising and sadistic death that the SS had planned for them. By nightfall on 7 September, all the men were dead. 'Shot while fleeing' was given as the cause of death.[45]

Yet, somehow, Trix escaped that fate. As the only woman of 'Englandspiel', the plan for her was very different. She was categorised as a *Schutzhaft* (protective custody) prisoner.[46] Two weeks after she arrived at Mauthausen, on 20 March 1945, she was moved to the Amstetten sub-camp near Linz, which had been established the day before.

Along with 494 other women, she was to be put on the *Bahnbau II* detail, which involved working on railway construction. By now, Trix was skin and bone, riddled with sores and 'almost mad'. How could she endure still more hardship and pain? Before she could even begin work, an Allied air raid landed a bomb right in the middle of her working party, and many of the women she had travelled with were killed outright. About 500 prisoners managed to escape to a forest north of the railway installation. But the forest, where they hoped they could shelter, was also hit during the bombing, and thirty-four more women were killed. Trix had been buried under the rubble of the first raid, but despite torn muscles and severe bruises, she miraculously survived and was sent to the infirmary.

In early April 1945, the first prisoners were transferred back to Mauthausen, and on 18 April, Amstetten sub-camp was permanently shut down. Rumours that the Allies were near were circulating wildly through the camp. By now, Trix was 'more dead than alive'.[47] Just days before the German surrender, Trix was released from the camp and put into the care of the Swiss Red Cross. She was taken to Switzerland for medical treatment. By this stage, she was so weak that it took her six weeks to recover enough strength just to stand.

The war was over, and the conspiracy theories around 'England-spiel' were only just beginning. During the course of Operation 'Nord-pol', over 4,000 messages were sent from the German-controlled wireless sets to Baker Street, yet only 200 had been shared with the Dutch military intelligence service. 'The Dutch authorities were understandably bitter about what had happened, especially as their own intelligence service had never been allowed any operational control' and their wireless messages had always been under the control of SIS – as had SOE's for the first two years of the war.[48]

In SOE's opinion, the absence of Lauwers and other agents' security checks was not enough to prove that they had been arrested.[49] It was not the 'sole arbiter of the continued integrity of a certain agent'.[50] As Dourlein said, even 'agents who were at liberty forgot their check or used it incorrectly'.[51]

The treatment of Dourlein and Ubbink after their escape from Haaren also left much to be desired. Arriving in London on 1 February 1944, they were subjected to lengthy interrogations and put under open arrest in Guildford before being imprisoned in Brixton. They were suspected of being traitors, liars and collaborators. By the time they were released it was too late – the game was over.[52]

Thoughts of a traitor in SOE's midst were also cause for consideration and investigation, but these came to nothing. Perhaps SIS had sought to sabotage the whole operation? Again, this was proved to be nonsense. It would appear that the Germans had simply possessed better intelligence and resources and that SOE had fallen foul of 'sound police work on the German side, assisted by Anglo-Dutch incompetence in London'.[53]

In a conversation with Huub Lauwers in 1979 as part of the 'Englandspiel' documentary series in the Netherlands, Leo Marks (the head of coding, SOE) told him:

No agent anywhere in Europe tried harder than you did to tell London that you were caught . . . nobody could have tried as much as you to alert us not to believe your messages. But the one thing I ask you to accept, there was no deception scheme. For one thing, very few people thought we were capable of running a resistance movement and sabotage – nobody would trust us with a deception operation, nobody. It wasn't what we did, nor would we have been allowed to do it; our job was resistance and sabotage . . . the one thing we did not do anywhere was run a deception scheme of that kind, because what would it have achieved?

. . . We were in the business of bringing [the agents] back, not of having them caught, because – and this is what is so sad – you send an agent in, not just in Holland – anywhere. How do you know he is going to be caught? And if he is caught, how do you know that he is going to pass on anything that you have told him in confidence? Thirdly, who is going to believe him? This was not SOE. I knew for absolute certainty that you were caught . . . I cannot tell you why we had such problems doing something about it, not yet. But I can tell you that you let us know that you were caught.[54]

Undoubtedly, Lauwers suffered as a result of the German operation. Trix never fully recovered from her ordeal and remained permanently affected by the deprivations she had suffered and the brutalities she had witnessed. She underwent LSD treatment to help her deal with her traumatic past. She even attempted to secure the release of her captors, especially Schreider, with whom she remained in contact after the war. Of the fifty-nine agents captured and imprisoned as part of the radio game, Trix was one of only five who survived the war.

7

BEYOND 'ENGLANDSPIEL'

Nazi Germany is so well organised and that is the only reason why they have lasted so long. They spare no one or nothing, if one is suspected, the least one can expect is a concentration camp, if they consider someone dangerous, they are immediately ready with a noose or bullet, and no one dares to think of Resistance.

Jos Gemmeke, 13 March 1945, The Hague[1]

When the details of 'Englandspiel' became known, some of the officials of the Dutch government in exile in London refused to cooperate with SOE. But Prince Bernhard of the Dutch royal family in exile insisted that they should start afresh. In March 1944 the Bureau Bijzondere Opdrachten (BBO), or 'Office of Special Assignments', was founded under the leadership of Kas de Graaf. This was a Dutch secret service that also dispatched secret agents to the German-occupied Netherlands, where they supported the local resistance and carried out sabotage activities.

At the same time Major (later Lieutenant Colonel) R.I. Dobson (who had previously worked for the Belgian Section) became the new head of N Section, replacing Major Seymour Bingham who had been there through the whole 'Englandspiel' debacle. Under Dobson's leadership, SOE started anew and began training and infiltrating several teams of well-prepared and well-equipped agents. Among them were several female agents.

1. Mathilde Carré, also known as 'the cat', was a notorious double agent in Paris where she betrayed several of her fellow resisters and countrymen before being sent to the UK. She was immediately arrested and eventually imprisoned at Holloway prison.

2. Jeanne Bohec, a member of SOE RF Section and the only female explosives instructor in the entire organisation. She undertook the experimental explosions on railway lines ahead of D-Day which were a resounding success.

3. A recruitment poster for the Corps féminin, an organisation that was founded on 7 November 1940, inspired by the precedent set by the British Auxiliary Territorial Service (ATS).

4. The memorial to the 'Merlinettes', four women who were infiltrated into France. After imprisonment at Ravensbrück concentration camp they were hanged in the winter of 1945.

5. Elaine Madden was recruited as an SOE agent following a daring escape at Dunkirk. She parachuted back into Belgium as part of T Section and later worked to help liberate concentration camps and repatriate prisoners.

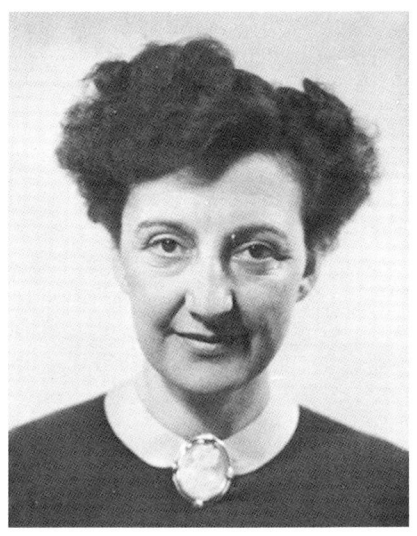

6. Pictured are the Wright aircrew, who were the team that infiltrated Elaine Madden from RAF/USAAF Harrington in Northamptonshire to Belgium.

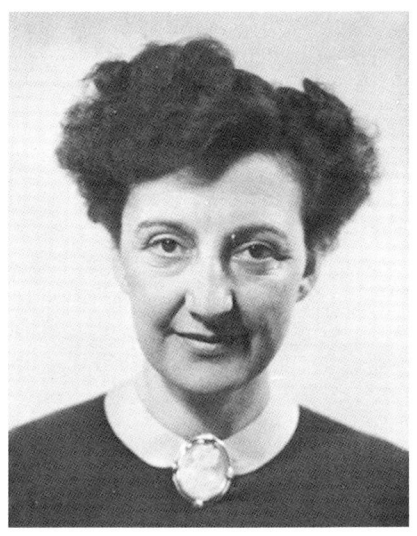

7. Renée Lippens who, before joining SOE, helped on escape lines from France and Belgium to Spain and Portugal. Her SOE career was short-lived as VE Day arrived before she could be infiltrated back into Belgium to begin her mission.

8. Female members of the Special Allied Airborne Reconnaissance Force (SAARF), of which Elaine Madden became a member. Created in March 1945, their remit was to aid Allied POWs and camp survivors in the wake of the fall of Nazi Germany.

9. Trix Terwindt (second from back) in hospital after the liberation of Mauthausen where she had been incarcerated after the end of 'Englandspiel'. She was the only woman impacted by it and was one of only four survivors.

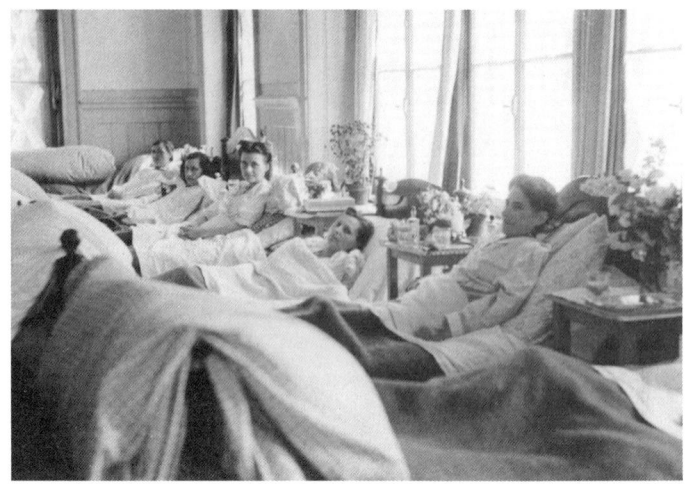

10. The 'Englandspiel' memorial in The Hague. Also known as 'The Fall of Icarus', it was designed by Titus Leeser and is situated near the German HQ from which 'Englandspiel' was played. It commemorates the agents who were dropped into the Netherlands and who were subsequently killed in concentration camps. The inscription reads: 'They jumped to their death for our freedom'.

11. Jos Gemmeke was infiltrated into occupied Holland after the notorious 'Englandspiel' that had resulted in the arrests of fifty-nine SOE agents. Prior to her SOE work she was involved in producing and distributing the underground newspaper *Je Maintiendrai*. While living in London she took afternoon tea with Queen Wilhelmina, and after the war she and the queen were the only two women to receive the oldest and highest Dutch decoration, the Military William Order.

12. Blackbridge House in Beaulieu served as a dormitory house for trainee SOE agents, among them Varinka Muus who worked for SOE in Denmark and who had come to the UK to undertake her SOE training.

13. The *Hongerwinter* (hunger winter) was a time of food and fuel shortages, causing great distress to the Dutch population in the winter of 1944–5. Pictured is the Golsteyn family in Amsterdam who sit around a pot-bellied stove while a woman peels sugar beets.

14. Operation 'Manna' was an RAF mission to deliver humanitarian aid to the starving people of the Netherlands during the *Hongerwinter* of 1944–5, in which close to a million Dutch citizens suffered extreme malnutrition due to food shortages and Nazi military blockades. Starting on 29 April 1945, nearly 7,000 tonnes of food were dropped over ten days to areas of Nazi-occupied Holland.

15. Throughout the Nazi occupation of Denmark, King Christian X would take daily rides on horseback through the streets of Copenhagen to show the population that he stood by them.

16. Varinka Muus was introduced to resistance work by her mother Monica. She undertook work as a liaison between the resistance and SOE, finally joining SOE's ranks in February 1945.

17. Varinka and Flemming (left) Muus. The pair met in Denmark where Flemming was working for SOE. Varinka was determined to become involved with SOE and equally determined not to fall for him. They married in June 1944.

18. A rare image of Surica Braverman (middle foreground), Haviva Reik (back left) and other Palmach fighters, taken in uniform in Palestine before their infiltration back into occupied Europe.

19. Hannah Szenes in the uniform of the Palmach, the Jewish fighting organisation that parachuted thirty-two agents into Europe to help save the Jews.

20. Conti Street prison in Budapest, where Hannah Szenes and other resisters were imprisoned and brutally interrogated by the Gestapo. Her mother visited her there and brought precious gifts of books, clothing and sewing materials.

21. A memorial dedicated to Hannah Szenes who parachuted into Yugoslavia en route to Hungary to help save the Jews from deportation. The memorial is in a park that also bears her name in Budapest.

Just three days after Trix had been deported to Mauthausen, Josepha (known as Jos) Gemmeke was infiltrated into the Netherlands. Born on 3 June 1922 in Amsterdam, she was the youngest of two daughters. The family moved around a lot during her childhood due to her sister's diagnosis of swamp fever. The family were strictly Catholic, and Jos attended authoritarian Catholic schools, something that went against her fun-loving and outgoing nature. So much so that after school hours she was quite the rebel. She would get into all kinds of mischief, such as sprinkling itching powder in the nun's toilets, putting frogs in the shower room of the school gym or showing off on her bicycle. She was such a troublemaker that her head teacher told her parents, 'I would like to have Jos as a daughter, but preferably no longer as a pupil.'[2] Jos enjoyed sports such as ice skating and hockey and was a keen dancer.

After the invasion of Holland in June 1940, Jos reported to the local hospital, where she had already been helping out as an auxiliary nurse. As the Netherlands tried to defend itself against the German onslaught, she treated all manner of wounds in the basement and all manner of people, including Germans. One patient was a German paratrooper who had been shot down from the tree in which he had landed and whose face had been terribly disfigured by a grenade. She was instructed to help him drink and eat and to tend to his every need, which must have been a life-changing experience for the seventeen-year-old Jos.

However, as Jos was not a qualified nurse, she was also given the menial tasks that the trained nurses did not want to undertake, such as emptying bedpans or sterilising surgical instruments. She soon discovered that the work was not as fulfilling as she had hoped, and sought out other war work.

In late 1941, Jos was approached by her old school friend Cock van Paaschen (Pieter Dekker), who was one of the producers of a clandestine newspaper called *Burgerlijk Contact Nieuws*, or *BC Nieuws*. He asked her if she would work for him as a courier and distributor of the newspaper. Underground printing presses were relatively widespread in the Netherlands, and newspapers were illegally printed and distributed as a way of encouraging anti-Nazi resistance and providing a source of unbiased news. Another paper, *Het Parool*, was printed by Johannes Jesse and his three sons. At its height, they produced 20,000 copies a week, all of which had to be typeset, folded and packaged in Jesse's shop. They were never caught, and the newspaper continues to be printed to this day. Another newspaper was *Oranjenieuws vóór en dóór blinden* (Orange News by and for the Blind), which was produced in Braille by Lida Hoeijenbos and her siblings. Incredibly, every word in every single copy was punched by hand.

The *Burgerlink Contact News* was produced in typescript at the Peace Palace in The Hague on a Friday evening, 'after which work continued from Saturday evening to Monday morning', when the copies were duplicated on a mimeograph machine. Then they were 'distributed on the following days'.[3] The newspaper had started in southern Holland, The Hague, Utrecht and Amsterdam but soon spread across the whole country, which was why more couriers and distributors were needed.

Jos readily accepted the role; she was incredibly keen to do something for her country and needed something to keep her busy. Her job was to distribute the newspapers to a main contact in each town. This involved her undertaking long and risky train journeys alone. If she had been stopped and her luggage checked, she would instantly have been arrested and more than likely tortured to reveal who her colleagues were and where the press was based. To add to the danger, she was unable to have a cover story due to the incriminating nature of the material. But she took what precautions she could, such as putting the parcel in a different compartment to hers on the train or leaving the station if she saw German soldiers.[4]

Sometimes, however, she had to fly in the face of such danger. On one occasion, a German saw that she was struggling with her heavy suitcase and offered to carry it for her. She must have been terrified that once he felt the weight of it, he would wonder what she was carrying. Luckily, he did not search her, and she managed to deliver her packages. While the paper aimed for a fortnightly distribution, she sometimes had to make these journeys as often as once a week. Her bravery in undertaking such work is indisputable.

As a courier, Jos had to live by very strict rules and guidelines, which some agents found 'rather tiresome'.[5] These were printed out and handed to agents and included notes on what to do if they thought they were being followed. Agents had to ensure that the newspapers were distributed immediately and swore that they would not leave the house with incriminating materials. They also had to work under codenames and keep everything else private. Jos was known as Els van Dalen, and while she knew her chief contacts' names, they did not know hers or anything else about her.

In January 1943, the newspaper was renamed *Je Maintiendrai*, which was the motto of the Dutch royal family, meaning 'I shall enforce' or 'I shall uphold law and order'. The newspaper took on a more patriotic feel and started to add material that was political in nature, along with a call to resist. The editorial team was combined with another newspaper's already operating in Utrecht. By this point, there were approximately twenty-four clandestine newspapers across the Netherlands and, for the most part, they coordinated with one another.

This was to become the busiest period in Jos's illegal career. Not only did she have to assist with printing the newspaper in the attic of the Peace Palace (where she recalled struggling with the stencil), but she and her colleagues often had to pay for the paper, ink and supplies that were needed. She once used her entire savings to finance the press. Even then, paper was scarce and rationed, and large quantities of paper were not readily available and were only given to established printing companies. Paper was printed with a special number (known as the k-number), which referred to the printing company, so that the Germans could trace all the paper.

Jos was also appointed to take control of the entire distribution of the newspaper. This involved distributing over 5,000 copies: 'Those newspapers consisted of a number of pages, so one can imagine what a weight we had to carry.'[6]

Jos always bought individual tickets for the train, as a season card would have raised too much suspicion. Even then, she was still running a terrible risk. On one occasion, she had a close shave while transporting two pistols in her suitcase. While on a train to Eindhoven, she was forced to open her case so that German soldiers could inspect the contents (they were coincidentally searching for some pistols that had been stolen). She managed to push the incriminating weapons under her clothes and smiled brightly at the German soldiers while they rummaged through her belongings. The search was not very thorough and, after a 'Heil Hitler', the two soldiers left her to continue her journey, no doubt with her heart thumping and nerves jangling. She also recalled another incident:

During the war, you had those cardboard suitcases that we stuffed with as many sheets as possible. I then put white paper on top of those sheets to have a small chance of getting through safely during a check.

Once, when I had to run to Santpoort to catch the train for the transfer to Haarlem, I saw a big, heavy guy standing on the platform, keeping a close eye on everything. Of course, the weight of the suitcase didn't allow me to run so fast. To my surprise, the guy stopped the train for me. Just then, the lid of one of the suitcases popped open, but luckily, everything remained in place, and only the white paper was visible. Gallantly, the man neatly closed the suitcase for me, not realising that it was strange that a young girl was travelling with such a load. When I got in the compartment, I got the giggles from the tension I had gone through.[7]

In July 1943, the first arrest was made. Brand (first name not given), one of the original members of the small group who had started *Je Maintiendrai*, was 'a very talkative person', an attribute Jos neither liked nor trusted about him.[8] He had been warned that his flat was going to be searched and that he should get rid of all the incriminating paperwork such as 'propaganda material, identity cards, papers from Jews etc.'[9] He ignored the warning and when he was arrested he was caught not only with these items but also with an address book full of his contacts.

While Jos and Cock were able to warn most people, not everyone could be reached. As a result of Brand's carelessness, eighteen people were arrested. By August, the Gestapo had discovered the entire distribution apparatus of *Je Maintiendrai* in Amsterdam, Zwolle and Hertogenbosch. The operation was blown, and it was impossible to continue work. It would have to be rebuilt from scratch. The operation in The Hague was also under threat of being discovered. Jos (who was at this point in Eindhoven) went into hiding and, working alone, she started to rebuild the newspaper. Within two months she managed to produce 15,000 copies of *Je Maintiendrai*, as well as acquiring weapons for the resistance.

On 1 April 1944, the day that Giskes sent his message to SOE HQ telling them that he had been fooling them for years, an agent named Tobias Biallosterski (Hans de Brun) was dropped along with his wireless operator Steman. This was Jos's first contact with SOE and England. Biallosterski had been working on a clandestine newspaper himself before escaping to England. His mission was to 'make contact with the whole of the illegal press in Holland and get orders from London for the clandestine press'.[10] However, before he could even begin, the wireless sets he had brought with him were stolen from the farm where they had been hidden. With no means of communicating with London, Biallosterski found a means to return to England and obtain more wireless sets. These arrived in August, but Biallosterski remained in England, having passed on his mission to van Paaschen.

Jos helped him by finding safe houses and delivering wireless sets for him, which involved yet more travelling and endangering herself. When the trains went on strike, Jos travelled by bicycle (for which she had obtained a permit), wearing a Red Cross nurse's uniform as a cover.

In August, fifteen more arrests were made at the *Je Maintiendrai* office in Utrecht. The safety signal (whether the curtains were open or shut would say whether the place was safe or not) had all but been ignored, and Jos only received word of the danger two days later. She had always believed that the office was unsafe as too many people knew about it, and there were constant comings and goings. She had been due to deliver some photographs from England that were to be published, but she had been too busy and sent another courier, who was arrested. Unfortunately, he was an old friend and knew her real name and address, so after his arrest, she dared not return home and, once again, had to start from scratch.

■ ■ ■

Meanwhile, another agent had been dropped into the Netherlands. Antonia (known as Frankie) Hamilton was born on 2 May 1902 in Asten, North Brabant. Her father, H.A.L. Hamilton, was mayor of Etten-Leur from 1930 until 10 December 1943, when he was replaced by a Dutch Nazi mayor. Frankie excelled at school and obtained a diploma in domestic science before undertaking a role as school matron at a boarding school in Leiden, a job she enjoyed and did well. In 1938 she immigrated to Brazil with her brother, rather confusingly called Frank, where they set up a farm together.

When war broke out, the pair wanted to undertake war work. Frank went to England but Frankie stayed on in Brazil, where she worked as a nurse until spring 1943. In April, she boarded a ship full of ex-pats wanting to contribute to the war effort and set sail for England. The convoy was repeatedly attacked by U-boats, and several of her friends were drowned as a result of the immense damage to the ships. This had a huge effect on Frankie's nerves; she described having an 'excited feeling in her stomach', and she lost a huge amount of weight.[11]

In spite of her nightmare crossing, Frankie remained determined. Knowing that her brother had been recruited into SOE, she wanted to follow in his footsteps. And so it was that Frankie was recruited into N Section with the aim of going back into the Netherlands as an agent. But at her initial training course in September 1943, ill health caught up with her. It transpired that she had felt unwell even while nursing in Brazil but had attributed it to a bout of dysentery, the long hours and the tropical heat.

While undertaking wireless training at Thame Park (STS 52) – a large manor house set in hundreds of acres of grounds in glorious Oxfordshire countryside – Frankie's health continued to decline. Feeling weak and constantly hungry, she slept well but always felt tired, so much so that she was unable to concentrate on her lessons. After two weeks, she was withdrawn from the course. Her instructors concluded that she was not capable of becoming a wireless operator and that, in her current state, she was not 'medically fit to go into the field'. She was 'tired and emotional and not fully in control of herself'.[12] Her instructor suggested that she receive psychological treatment, which could help get her fit enough to go into the field.[13] It was not only her illness that deterred her. Frankie hated all the lying that the work would involve, as well as its destructive nature.

It appears that she was given a break (save for attending a few lectures) as her next report was not until December 1943. This was from Roughwood Park (STS 42) in Chalfont St Giles. At this point, Frankie's health and fitness had improved enough to take part in a reconnaissance scheme. She proved herself to be thorough and painstaking, although she was encouraged to 'learn the value of silence as she talked too much during the exercise'.[14]

After passing her parachute training, she attended Wall Hall (STS 59) in Hertfordshire, which was SOE's subversive propaganda school. Her proposed role was assistant to a propagandist in the field. Here she learned how to use a variety of cameras, including Contax and Leica. She practised photographing documents and pictures 'under poor and very good lighting conditions' and acquired a 'sound knowledge' about processing the images.[15] By June 1944, having been described as 'energetic and purposeful' and with her health restored, Frankie was ready to go back to the Netherlands.[16]

On the night of 9/10 August 1944, Frankie, who was now known as Josephine (codenamed 'Tiddlywinks') and her brother Frank Hamilton ('Rowing') were sent out from RAF Tempsford on a propaganda mission. They carried with them leaflets, microfilms and photographs. Arrangements had been made for a blind drop (no reception committee). At 3 a.m., the aircraft approached the selected landing ground. Just as the pair dropped, they became aware that German fighters were in the vicinity and that their aircraft was required to take evasive action to save itself.

Frank landed safely but owing to the fact that they had dropped from too low a height, Frankie suffered a splintered tibia and a broken fibula. To make matters worse, the pair had drifted apart during the drop, and Frankie was now over 10 miles from the original drop zone of Blokker. Frankie was alone and in excruciating pain. Despite her serious injuries she managed to get rid of her parachute and dragged herself into a nearby ditch where she hid. At daylight, she managed to release a pigeon (which had been dropped with her). The message said: 'JOSEPHINE in pain; letter following.' This meant that if the message fell into enemy hands, it would not necessarily start a search for a woman with a broken leg.

As the hours wore on, her pain became worse and was soon accompanied by a fever, which made her delirious. Sometimes she thought she heard voices and noises in the distance, but she could not be sure if they were real or not. If they were real, they could have as easily been German soldiers as Dutch resisters, and her mind raced about what might happen to her. Unable to move, she survived on the emergency food and drink rations that she had brought with her. It was three days until she was finally discovered by her brother.

Once he had found her, a very relieved Frank arranged an ambulance for his sister through a contact he had made. During the transfer to the ambulance, Frankie had a strange experience. She said that she saw a man hiding nearby in the bushes, holding something that looked very much like a camera. This man did not attempt to interrupt the proceedings, but the party was naturally apprehensive. They decided to throw away all incriminating papers at the first opportunity, only keeping hold of their identity cards.

By now, Frankie was very weak and was taken to Haarlem, where under the pseudonym 'Josephine Wouters' she was admitted to the *diaconessenhuis* (deacon's house). Her complex leg injuries were operated on by several doctors and surgeons. She stayed incognito in various hospitals while recovering and received excellent treatment with the cooperation of the local resistance. She was visited by Frank and other colleagues, including Biallosterski. But for the most part, she was alone and frustrated. Her care was very expensive and was paid for from the money that she and Frank had brought with them to fund their activities. It was soon all spent, and more had to be requested. Frankie's healing process would be long and protracted, and she would be unable to start her mission for some time, if at all.

∎ ∎ ∎

In September 1944 the Allies attempted to secure key bridges in Arnhem in Operation 'Market Garden'. There were several bridges, from the Belgian border up to Arnhem. It took considerable time before the bridge at Nijmegen was captured, as German resistance in Arnhem was much stronger than expected. Ultimately the operation was a failure.

At this time the Dutch resistance received a request from Prince Bernhard's headquarters in Brussels for information about troop locations and German V-1 and V-2 launch sites. On 23 October 1944 Jos was tasked with carrying some films, a list of prisoners of war, the latest press releases, information about the civilian population and military data into the newly liberated area of the Netherlands. These items were hidden in the shoulder pads of her jacket and powder compact.[17] She was provided with German papers, which should have enabled her to pass through Gorinchem (a city in southern Holland). However, when she arrived, it turned out that all the papers were out of date. It was only through her perseverance and cool demeanour that she managed to avoid being arrested. She was pushed from the local German commander to the mayor of the city and back again while trying to obtain permission to cross the river, being told that she needed permission from the other one first.

Eventually, she went to the port and was told that no one was allowed through from either direction as the road had to remain clear for retreating troops. At this point, her suitcase was inspected and, when it was discovered that she was carrying letters, she was arrested for a short time. After a change of guards in the prison, she managed to convince the new ones to help her cross the river by pretending that the former guard was to have taken her but ran out of time.[18]

Of her journey, Jos recounted:

> I thought I had now had the hardest part. This was only true to a certain extent, but now I could also notice that I was right between the fronts. It may sound a bit fantastic when I say that the grenades flew around my ears. Yet it came down to this. I took shelter at a house. After some time, it became a bit quieter, and I continued driving. A little later, this house was targeted by artillery, and the side wall against which I had taken shelter recently collapsed.
>
> The crossing over the bridge at Heusden was indescribable. Shortly before, this bridge had been bombed by Allied airmen, but without result. Continuous rows of German tanks drove over it. As I drove over it, the next attack started. The fighter planes narrowly missed the bridge and machine-gunned it. Several Germans were hit by machine gun fire and remained on the bridge. Luckily, I reached the other bank in one piece.[19]

There were also many casualties along the way, and I saw several flying machines crashing down in flames; but I had little time to think about all this, as I had to pay close attention to myself.[20]

As she continued her journey and the shellfire intensified, she saw many German soldiers fleeing in 'wild panic'.[21] Since everyone was far more concerned about the battle going on around them, no one bothered her, and she was able to travel via back roads until she finally reached Eindhoven. There, she was picked up by a motorcycle courier (as her bicycle had become unrideable due to being peppered by shrapnel) and reported to Captain de Graaf at Prince Bernhard's headquarters in Brussels the next day.

After delivering the films, Jos expressed her wish to return to The Hague as quickly as possible but was strongly advised against doing so. It would be better, she was told, to await the further liberation of the Netherlands. However, this was not what she wanted; she wished to continue fighting until the bitter end. When she was asked if she would like to go to England and return as a parachutist, she welcomed the chance. She 'wanted to return to Holland at all costs to continue helping'.[22]

On 1 November 1944, under the pseudonym 'Jeanne Geursen', Jos boarded an army-green, twin-engine Dakota alongside two men (Captain de Graaf and Tony Knight). On landing she was taken straight to the Royal Victoria Patriotic School where she stayed for two days, regaling her interrogators with the 'story of [her] fantastic journey through the enemy lines'.[23] They checked and rechecked all her contacts and clandestine activities. By the end of the second day, she grew frustrated and bored and refused to engage in any further questioning. After a call to de Graaf, the officers agreed to release her. They had concluded that she was 'a very level and cool-headed young woman, completely unemotional, very reserved and determined'.[24]

Bitter disappointment awaited Jos, when it transpired that SOE had decided that women agents should not be used for the foreseeable future. A note in her file dated 6 December 1944 states 'not employed – it has been decided not to send women agents to the field at this stage'.[25] She kept applying and was told to wait. She felt that perhaps if she were to wait, there would be a glimmer of hope that she might be allowed to return to the Netherlands.

That month Jos was invited to visit Queen Wilhelmina, who made a point of entertaining all *Engelandvaarders*. Jos was delighted to see an elaborate tea tray being brought out and spent the next three hours with the Queen Wilhelmina and Princess Juliana, talking about life in the Netherlands and smoking cigarettes. Jos found the whole experience somewhat tiring and felt that she was under constant scrutiny, but later said:

> In retrospect, it was, of course, a great honour to be alone with Queen Wilhelmina and Princess Juliana for about three hours. It was striking how the Queen talked about the situation in the Netherlands with great expertise. It wasn't until the journey back to London that I realised how fantastic this meeting had been.[26]

She was appointed as a liaison officer between SOE, Baker Street and the BBO. This meant that she could maintain contact with agents who had been dropped into the Netherlands, particularly Jan Steman, who she knew was operational in her area. She was also able to inform and influence the decisions of the head of N Section, Major Dobson, and they 'were able to prevent a lot of mischief together'.[27]

Unfortunately, they were not able to stop the bombing of the district of Bezuidenhout in The Hague, despite a number of messages from van Paaschen stating that there were no important targets in the area. Major Dobson contacted the RAF several times but to no avail. During the bombing raid by fifty-six aircraft, more than 550 people died and 250 were seriously injured. Most of the town's houses were destroyed, including the Gemmeke family home, which was an important address for the resistance and agents. As a result of the bombing of Bezuidenhout, the following telegram was received by the BBO in London (intended for the RAF): 'Stop as soon as possible that idiotic pirate work concerning The Hague. If you're thinking of bombing V-2 emplacements, that's your business, but don't just hit the houses. To date, not a single missile deployment has been hit. Germany is a few hundred miles away to the East.'[28]

Jos was still desperate to go back to the Netherlands. 'I eagerly awaited the news that SOE would parachute women again,' she said, so much so that, 'When Queen Wilhelmina asked me to become her secretary, I declined.'[29] In January 1945, she got the news she had been waiting for: she was finally allowed to attend SOE training. But the news from home was very distressing.

That winter the parts of the Netherlands that were still occupied suffered dreadfully. The *Hongerwinter* (hunger winter) ravaged the Nazi-occupied western part of the country from November 1944 until the liberation in May 1945. It was caused by an exceptionally harsh winter and bad crops, in addition to the toll taken by four years of war. In September 1944, the Nazis imposed an embargo on the import of food to the western Netherlands in retaliation for the Dutch government in exile supporting the Allies in liberating the south. This was particularly in reaction to the railway strikes that had started on 17 September in order to support Operation 'Market Garden'.

The situation was desperate, and people had to try to eke out an existence on 400–800 calories a day – if they could find anything to eat at all. People resorted to eating grass, sugar beets and tulip bulbs, as well as dogs and cats, in an attempt to survive. Some people travelled substantial distances by foot or by bicycle to buy food from farmers, some of whom took advantage of the situation to exhort money or jewellery in exchange for food. Soup kitchens were set up and Swedish Red Cross flour enabled people to bake bread.

By spring 1945 the situation was so dire that help had to be brought in from outside. From 29 April to 7 May, Operation 'Manna' was conducted by the RAF and RCAF, and from 1 to 8 May, USAAF conducted

Operation 'Chowhound'. Both operations delivered food by air. The last flights were just before the German capitulation. Two hundred thousand people died as a result of the famine and many suffered the long-term effects of malnutrition and starvation.

■ ■ ■

That winter, in January, Frankie was finally allowed to leave hospital, even though she was still recuperating and relying on crutches and could not bear any weight on her injured leg. She asked if she could work with Biallosterski, who in turn decided to ask for SOE's advice. On 15 January he sent a message saying:

> Within a week, Josephine will leave the hospital, and she wants to live with me if possible. In the beginning, my girls can look after her, and she can do good work when she recovers. However, she cannot leave the house for some assignment. Please, I will gladly await your answer.[30]

Two days later, SOE/BBO gave their permission, and at the end of the month, Biallosterski reported that Frankie was safely ensconced at his house. However, the presence of Frankie and several other agents in his home was also cause for concern. Frankie could not get away in an emergency. If caught, she might give away the details of the network and, undoubtedly, the trail would also lead to the hospitals and doctors who had treated her. The situation was all but impossible, but there was nothing she could do.

Frankie's concerns for the group's security also grew. She noted that Biallosterski frequently visited his mother, which put her in danger because the SD could put her house under surveillance. There were many compromising lists of names and addresses and other written material kept in the office. Frankie also observed that Biallosterski went to a reception committee wearing 'a pair of flying boots, a British army pull-over, and a military-style greatcoat', which were not only easily identifiable but clearly showed his affiliation and links with the British.[31] Inevitably, he was arrested in the same clothes eight days after her arrival at his flat. Her brother replaced him and from February 1945 she went into hiding, spending the last few months on a farm with the Langedijk family in Venhuizen. She was still unable to contribute much and continued to recuperate.

■ ■ ■

Jos was now starting her training and, like Trix had before her, she attended a course at the House in the Woods at Beaulieu. Here she was instructed in 'opening doors, safes and handcuffs' and became quite 'an accomplished burglar'.[32] She also had to go into a city and identify someone by the description she had been given or find a message hidden in a bookcase in a shop, 'after which two pursuers also had to be shaken off'.[33] All the while, she was 'followed by unknown instructors who saw to it' that she carried out the assignment correctly.[34] Jos enjoyed the training as it consolidated what she had already been practising in the Netherlands.

Her instructors were impressed too, believing her to be 'well above average intelligence' with plenty of common sense and a 'good imagination'.[35] She was deemed by instructors to be 'one of the most outstanding students we have had here', and in spite of her thorough knowledge of life in the resistance, she remained 'courteous, attentive and hard-working'.[36]

While undertaking her parachute training in Manchester in February 1945, Jos was billeted at a nearby manor house, presumably Dunham Massey. There she met several other trainee agents. Among them was the Danish agent Flemming Muus and his wife Varinka (see Chapter 8, 'Mission Danska'). The two women trained together and both witnessed a dreadful accident when a Polish agent's parachute did not open. He was killed instantly.

At Ringway, Jos persevered with her parachute training, even though she had weak ankles. She deliberately landed on her seat (with rather painful results), rather than undertake a parachute roll which involved making 'initial contact with her feet'.[37] Although her 'air drill was non-existent', she made good exits and average landings and impressed the instructors with her 'matter-of-fact outlook'. At no time did she exhibit 'the slightest signs of nervousness'.[38] A month later, she was to put her newfound skills to the test on a mission for X Section (Germany), as well as N Section, as part of Operation 'Cackle'.[39] She was expected to fulfil a huge range of objectives.

As part of Plan 'Bonzo', she was to 'obtain all the information possible which will help us to gain contact with Dutch workers in Germany and organise these into disciplined bodies', who could then act on orders from SHAEF. She was also to 'receive instruction during the probable administrative chaos following on [from] a German collapse'.[40] This idea had been mooted in May 1944, but SOE had not been able to find a suitable organiser until Jos came to England and proved to be ideal.

She was to find out the 'exact whereabouts' of Dutch workers in Germany, 'the conditions in the camps in which they were held and the industries in which they were employed'.[41] She was also to explore the conditions in which workers of the Reich Bahn operated and the state of the former trade unions. Jos was to explore the possibilities of 'infiltrating agents into Germany through existing smuggling networks or escape channels already in use by Dutch workers'.[42] She was also to evaluate the canal traffic between northern Holland and Germany as well as the effect that the refugee flow in the Rhineland and from the east had on the movement of others (such as agents).

Jos was to obtain intelligence on controls and obtain safe addresses for agents going to Germany. While her main area of operation was to be The Hague, it was also hoped that she would be able to accompany a Dutch businessman named Kievet to Germany. Kievet had volunteered to work for SOE while on a visit there. Jos's mission to Germany was not to last longer than three weeks, and she was responsible for briefing Kievet and ensuring his safe conduct. She was to drop with two wireless sets, but there would be no one to operate them for some time, and they could not be used while in Germany. In total, her extensive mission outline ran to a lengthy five pages. For SOE to think that any one woman could achieve all the complex and difficult tasks they had assigned to Jos shows how much faith and confidence they must have had in her.

■ ■ ■

While Jos awaited infiltration, nineteen-year-old Annemarie van Hilten was brought out of Holland on 22 February 1945 for SOE training. She was born on 17 July 1925 and lived with her parents and younger brother in Breda. She took her high school exams in Breda and passed her advanced certificates after studying in Amersfoort. She enjoyed sports such as hockey, tennis, swimming and horse riding, and had excellent language skills in Dutch, German, English and French.

Annemarie was involved in resistance activity from the summer of 1942 until her area was liberated in October 1944. Unfortunately, there are no details of this period or the work she undertook. She may have had contact with one or more SOE agents as, in November 1944, they decided to have her trained as one of them. A background search reported on 1 December that there was no trace of any incriminating information about her or her family and, once arrangements had been finalised, she was flown from Eindhoven to begin her training.

She was given a commission in FANY, and after signing the Official Secrets Act, she was given the codename 'Haverman'. She began her SOE training in March and undertook a paramilitary course at Gorse Hill (STS 50) in Witley, Godalming. There she received a positive report: she was 'athletic' and 'a very intelligent student'.[43] She was interested in close combat, in which she made 'good progress' and was capable of firing any weapon she was given, as well as being adept at weapons handling. Her Morse was slow but good, but she lacked patience, and her explosives skills were only passable.[44]

After the usual training at Ringway, she went to Thame Park for her intensive wireless course. While there, the German surrender was announced, which meant her training became irrelevant. This 'dependable' and 'popular' young lady did not have the chance even to begin her mission.[45] On 19 May, she was returned to her unit and sworn to secrecy. She eventually returned to the Netherlands and became a psychotherapist.

■ ■ ■

In the meantime, on 10 March 1944, on a 'dirty, nasty night', Jos (codenamed 'Sphinx') was dropped by Flight Sergeant Ron Sloan and his crew at Nieuwkoop.[46] However, due to the foul weather that night, it took a long time to identify the DZ, by which time Jos had been waiting at the hatch for over an hour. She was 'stone cold' and feeling quite unwell.[47] Sloan recalled that they spent:

> 20 minutes circling and crisscrossing the area when suddenly a shout came from the front, 'Right side, lights on the ground visible.' The correct identification letter! 'Thank God'! I said, repeating the identifying letter. 'Set the light to red,' I said, 'we can make it on our first approach run.' I quickly pulled back on the throttles, set the brake valve switches to one-third, and watched the speedometer and altimeter drop rapidly. We now flew straight towards the lights, which, from my position, quickly disappeared below our aircraft. 'Green light on'![48]

Sloan had instructed the dispatcher to wait a few seconds after the green light had gone on before he opened the bomb bay, as he wanted to make sure that Jos was clear before releasing the five containers, lest they hit her. At an altitude of 600 feet and flying at less than 90 miles per hour, Sloan received the first message from the flight engineer's fuselage: 'Passenger and packages away.'[49]

A few seconds later, he was informed that 'all containers [were] gone', and finally, he received a message from the tail gunner that they had 'dropped right at the lights and all parachutes opened'.[50]

Breathing a deep sigh of relief, Sloan opened the throttles, closed the bomb traps and went up into the moonlit sky.

But on the ground, things had not gone smoothly at all. Jos had been dropped too low and had landed before her parachute was properly open. The cords of the parachute became entangled. Falling backwards due to the weight of her backpack, she was dragged 150 metres or so into a ditch. After being caught underneath her parachute twice, she was able to free herself, but she was soaked to the skin and her back was in considerable pain. She would suffer back problems for the rest of her life as a result of this landing.

The reception committee had yet to find her, and all around was eerily quiet. Jos set about hauling herself out of the muddy ditch she had landed in and removed her striptease suit and parachute helmet. She was just starting to bundle up her parachute when she heard faint voices and saw the flash of torches in the distance.[51] 'I grabbed my own flashlight and started blinking at random. You could never know if they were Krauts, but when I heard my own name softly called and recognised Cock's voice, I knew it was alright.'[52] The friendly reception committee helped her bury her parachute and together they crossed soggy meadows and windswept farmland to a nearby house. Jos was delighted she had made it safely, at last. Not only was she back among her fellow resisters, she was 'back in the Netherlands!'[53]

In the farmhouse, Jos made quite an impression on the farmer's wife, who was amazed to meet the gutsy lady who had just jumped out of an aircraft. By now, Jos was feverish from the prolonged cold and the soaking that she had endured. The farmer's wife lent her a jumper and some warm clothes until her own were retrieved from one of the containers. The two women made small talk, had a drink and then (once suitably attired) Jos left, still 'with soaking wet hair'.[54] She helped to stow the weapons that had been dropped with her inside some huge wheels of cheese at the farm.

She was taken by car to The Hague and encountered her first checkpoint as an SOE agent. Fortunately, her colleague's ID papers were sufficiently convincing that no further inspection was made, and they were soon on their way. On 13 March, Jos managed to send a message back to HQ. She advised that she had been part of a 'terrible water ballet' and wished everyone 'lots of love'.[55] Jos was anxious to begin work, and had soon organised meetings with people who were familiar with the workers' situation in Germany. She also discussed with them the possibilities of setting up resistance networks in Germany and collected evidence of atrocities occurring against foreign workers in the German labour camps.[56]

On 28 March, she left for Germany as planned. SOE/BBO did not hear from her again until 12 April, when she finally managed to send a wireless message:

> Traffic very difficult. Impossible for me to send details travel. After extensive discussions in considering circumstances German plan impossible at moment. Most of information and reports are now from last year. Trying to do what is possible. KIEVIT did not leave for Germany. Am now helping Paaschen because he is very busy. Do you agree. Home totally destroyed. New address Ridderlaan 4 Wassenaar.[57]

Due to the rapid progress of the Allied offensive on the Rhine, she was no longer able to carry out the second part of her mission. The end of the war was tantalisingly close, and it was deemed unnecessary to organise resistance among the workers who were still there. It would not be long until they were liberated. On the one hand, Jos was extremely disappointed that she had not been able to help, but on the other, she was pleased that liberation was finally approaching. She continued her Dutch resistance work with renewed vigour.

Jos also went back to the printing presses, which were busy producing black propaganda for use against the Germans and continuing to report on events throughout the Netherlands. Much of the material to be used was dropped in Nieuwkoop and found its way to the illegal press via the Peace Palace.

Jos helped van Paaschen as much as possible. She took responsibil-ity for maintaining contacts, as this had become extremely difficult for them. She already knew most of the people involved. She also helped Steman, the wireless operator who at that point was working flat out. Jos helped him prepare his messages by coding and decod-ing them for him. She also searched for suitable houses from which he could transmit and broadcasting addresses. Once she found them, she carried his wireless set on her bicycle so as to detract attention from him. In The Hague, this was especially risky because the SD and Abwehr were still intent on catching wireless operators, even though 'Englandspiel' was long over and its agents were dead.

■ ■ ■

In April, another woman began her SOE training. Jantje Sissingh was born on 12 May 1923 in Rotterdam. After attending school, where she learned English and German, she trained as a Dutch shorthand typ-ist and worked as a secretary from 1941 to 1944. She was very sporty and enjoyed fencing, hockey, swimming, sailing, rowing and skating.

In May 1944, Jantje began resistance work. She became a courier and made several journeys across the Netherlands, as well as taking messages between various resistance chiefs in Rotterdam. She man-aged to get to liberated Holland. From there, she travelled to Eng-land via Brussels, arriving in February 1945. Her main aim was to deliver a letter from her resistance chief and some mail from Captain de Graaf.

Her father, Captain W.J. Sissingh (of the shipping firm Erhardt & Dekkers), had been living in London since April 1940, while her mother was believed to have been in hiding in Rotterdam. Her broth-er and sister also remained in the Netherlands.

Jantje (also known as Tilly) received good training reports. She excelled in parachute work and 'was the outstanding student of the party. Her performance on the whole was equal to most of the male students participating. She has the correct outlook on parachuting, made two very good descents and can be considered as an excellent risk.'[58] While deemed too young and immature to work alone, it was felt that she was 'courageous, determined and . . . full of enthusiasm, especially for work involving action.'[59] She was 'far less talkative than the usual female agent, seems to be level-headed, reliable and serious. It is significant that while individual members of [resistance groups] . . . frequently seize occasions to belittle their colleagues, everyone has a good word to say about TILLY.'[60] Unfortunately, this report was dated 8 May 1945. Victory in Europe had been declared and Jantje's training was now redundant.

■ ■ ■

For Jos, the last days of April went by in a blur. She could hardly cope with the ever-increasing workload that she and Cock were faced with. The messages to Steman's wireless were coming in thick and fast from HQ, asking questions related to concentration of troops, 'transports, emplacements, suspicious persons and V-2 launch sites.'[61] 'You could tell from everything that it was pretty much coming to an end,' said Jos. 'However, we were very careful because you never knew what the Krauts had in store for us as a last act of desperation.'[62]

On 5 May 1944, an unencrypted message arrived that everyone had been anticipating for so long. Germany had capitulated and the war was over. 'It was a bit surreal,' Jos recalled. Agents were told to report to their HQ for further instructions, and the message ended with 'Good Luck' instead of the usual code numbers.[63] It took days for the realisation to sink in that the Germans had gone and that Jos could now move about freely and without any risk of arrest. But it was bittersweet. So many had died or been killed as a result of the occupation. It would take some time for life to return to any semblance of normality or for Jos and all the agents to feel like their old selves. 'You think back to the dozens of friends who fell for our liberation . . . I hoped that their sacrifice and our work had made a meaningful contribution to the future of our cherished country, and that the young people who would later grow up in freedom would realise that this precious freedom must be handled with care.'[64]

■ ■ ■

Frankie returned to England on 26 May 1945, having been unable to begin her mission. She had made many observations that she felt showed the thoughtlessness of SOE and the agents in the field. She noted that many of the supplies that were sent over to the Continent were labelled with very clear English names and the date. This could have disastrous consequences for the locals, as the owners of any garden, house or property near where one of these tins happened to be found would be severely punished by the Landwacht (Dutch armed Nazis). She also thought the RAF leaflets should have been distributed by the underground movements after being delivered to prearranged DZs, instead of being scattered all over the place among the wrong people.

After everything she had been through, both in her training and in the field, Frankie had to fight for what was rightfully hers. It had been agreed that Frank's and her salaries would be paid 50 per cent by the British and 50 per cent by the Dutch, but the money was not forthcoming. Frankie resorted to writing a long letter of complaint to SOE and did not receive the payment until March 1946.

The contribution of female agents to the work of SOE in the Netherlands was either mistimed or mismanaged. None of them was able to fully utilise their training, and they were either injured, overrun or captured before they could make an impact. It seems from the stories of the women above that they held huge potential, but unfortunately it was never realised.

In recent years, some doubts have been cast over Jos's testimony, some of which has been said to be a little far-fetched and possibly fabricated. For example, she repeatedly claimed to have been travelling alone when she was in the company of a fellow resister by the name of Jeanne Marie 'Puck' Fermont, with whom she cycled from The Hague through the lines to liberated Holland. Puck was involved in the resistance, just like her father. She listened to the British broadcasts in the attic of the Vredespaleis (Peace Palace) in The Hague, where Jos Gemmeke also did resistance work on the underground press.

Described as being 'about 28 years of age' and 'fairly short but on the stout side, very dark brown eyes, curly hair and a rather tanned complexion',[65] Puck was secretary to Sjef de Groot, the regional commander of the resistance of North Brabant. It is thought that she crossed the River Delta near Dordrecht, which formed the border between the liberated and occupied Netherlands.[66] Puck arranged the overnight addresses for the journey she took with Jos, and she was the contact address for Plan 'Bonzo', the plan of gathering information about Dutch forced workers in Germany. She played a considerable role in Jos's story and yet went unmentioned. In August 1945 Puck married Frans Knapen, who was also a member of the resistance. After the war, they served in the Dutch East Indies, where her husband was shot dead by one of his own officers.

Jos also claimed that during an RAF bombing raid she saw the pilot and later married him. The raid that day was not at the location she specified, and it appears that she embellished her story for dramatic effect.[67]

However, it is clear from her SOE reports and records and from the mission for which she was chosen that she was exceptionally bright and well suited to her role. It is a shame she did not have the chance to fulfil her potential as an SOE agent. In 1950 Jos Gemmeke was awarded the oldest and highest honour of the Kingdom of the Netherlands, the Military William Order (MWO). She was, and remains, the only woman (besides Queen Wilhelmina) ever to have received this decoration, the motto for which is 'Bravery, Leadership and Loyalty'. These are traits she displayed in abundance.

8

MISSION DANSKA

It was not enough to sit here eating and drinking and handing out
little illegal magazines and raising money for the poor communist's wives.

Monica Wichfeld[1]

The invasion of Denmark was so swift that it was over before most people were even getting out of bed. German soldiers soon patrolled the
streets, the Danish flag (*Dannebrog*) was banned and replaced by the
gaudy red, black and white of swastikas and to all intents and purposes
Denmark was occupied – except there were no round-ups, no reign of
terror ensued and business continued as usual. Denmark had opted to
'cooperate' with the Germans, ushering in a unique relationship between
the occupier and the occupied that was not seen in any other European
country. The northern territories of Europe were of vital importance to
both the Allies and Axis powers, not least because of the export of iron
ore. As such Norway was also invaded, while Sweden remained neutral.
This would prove to be extremely useful in the coming years of conflict.

■ ■ ■

Denmark was attacked at 4.15 a.m. on 9 April 1940 by German forces
who were en route to Norway. Sporadic fighting between the Danish and German armies lasted a matter of hours and it soon became
clear that Denmark was unable to repel the attack. The government
soon realised that German military superiority was too great and

were intimidated by the hundreds of leaflets that scattered like con-
fetti from German aircraft threatening to bomb towns and cities if
the Danish citizens resisted the invasion. At 7.20 a.m. the Danes capitulated with the loss of thirteen soldiers and three border guards. It
was all over in a little less than three hours. Most people did not even
know that it had begun.

The Germans offered the Danes a deal: if Denmark stopped fighting back, Germany promised to 'respect the country's territorial integrity' and 'political independence'.[2] In essence, although Denmark
would be occupied by German troops, it would be as a neutral country and a sovereign nation with its own government. Norway, Holland and Belgium were given the same offer in the weeks to come, but
all declined. It was only Denmark who now 'cooperated' with their
German occupiers. The strategy behind this was to preserve Danish
identity and self-preservation while accommodating the demands of
the occupiers, but there is little doubt that Denmark had been backed
into a corner. There was also an underlying fear that the Nazis, including the Danish Nazis (the National Socialist Workers' Party of
Denmark), would bring harsh measures against them if they did not
maintain a certain level of cooperation.[3]

In contrast to other European nations, there was no Danish government in exile. Instead, a new coalition government made up of all
political parties was formed. The intention was to show the Germans
that a democratic system could work well alongside the occupation
and that Denmark was able to adapt to the new regime without up-
setting its political system. Seventy-year-old King Christian X also
remained in Copenhagen and rode his horse through the streets
every morning, showing that he was a 'man of the people', which contributed to his good reputation and his popularity.[4]

For thirty-three-year-old Jutta Graae, a Danish bank clerk, the capitulation of Denmark came as a shock. She had witnessed the aftermath of *Kristallnacht* in Berlin in November 1938, in which some
of her acquaintances had been rounded up and others had their

businesses destroyed, with windows shattered and furniture broken by marauding Brownshirts.[5] The barbarity shown 'only confirmed' her 'long-established attitude' – that she must join in the war against Nazism and stamp it out wherever she found it.[6]

Stylish, and with a penchant for quirky hats, Jutta was recruited into resistance work in November 1939 by her brother-in-law Ebbe Munck, who asked her to receive and deliver messages for him while he was away working as a war correspondent in Finland. In her capacity as a bank clerk, Jutta was able to receive visitors without causing too much suspicion, and she received operatives involved in the sabotage of iron ore. She would also make contact with the English. The agent in question would identify themselves by presenting half a torn picture; the other half was already in her possession.

Jutta and Ebbe were undoubtedly the first (and perhaps only) Danes to engage in the war of resources waged by Section D. When the iron ore sabotage failed and Hitler took over Norway, Jutta and Munck continued with espionage and left sabotage to others.

She described the phony war as a 'strange waiting time', during which she worked alongside Captain Volle Gyth from the intelligence department of the Danish General Staff. The two could easily stay in contact as their families were friends and they lived close to one another. She continued her work at the bank, where she managed safe deposit boxes. Everyday people came and went to collect or deposit money or goods, and this air of hustle and bustle would prove vital for her future work. Otherwise, her life continued as normal and she took a skiing holiday to Norway. On her return she heard reports of German troops congregating at the border, and of gatherings of landing boats in the Baltic Sea ports. She knew things were about to change.[7]

On 8 April, Jutta had dinner with Ingram Fraser, the Scandinavian head of Section D (as well as being an iron ore operative and diplomat). He had various tasks for her; 'but with the many warnings of unrest and the otherwise tense situation, none of us had any doubt that we were entering a new phase . . . we contented ourselves with enjoying the dinner and pondering how we would manage the next step.'[8] After dinner she tried to find Gyth so she could tell him what had happened, but he was nowhere to be found. She consoled herself with the thought that at least the intelligence service was on high alert. In fact they had wanted the army on high alert on 8 April, she recalled, 'but it did not happen.'[9] The following day she woke to the sound of German aircraft flying overhead. She was disappointed that more had not been done to avoid an invasion. She had 'hoped that there would be a reaction . . . it was a political decision.'[10] She knew her work was about to start in earnest.

Denmark soon bore the marks of a country at war. A blackout was instigated to prevent British planes from dropping their bombs on Danish targets as well as preventing the RAF from using the lights of Denmark to navigate their way towards Germany. Outdoor lighting was switched off and blackout curtains put up in homes and businesses. If an air raid warning sounded, those on the streets were legally obliged to make their way to a shelter, whereas those at home could choose to stay in their houses. Rationing and shortages soon took hold, too. Ersatz tea, coffee and fuel became the norm, while oats and butter were put on ration. Although meat and bread were not rationed, they had to be fairly distributed among the population. The shortage of meat led to a lack of leather, and some interesting alternatives were found, including the use of fish skin to make the uppers of shoes and boots.

While there was no conscription, men were encouraged to enlist for the German army, particularly as troops were needed on the Eastern Front. Approximately 7,000 Danish men volunteered for active service, half of whom were members of the Danish Nazi Party.[11] One hundred and fifty women also volunteered and became nurses in the German Red Cross. While resistance to the occupation was present, it was small – the flame of resistance needed gentle but persuasive kindling to reach its full effect.

Jutta and Munck had been gathering intelligence about Nazism since 1938. They knew through their mutual friend Gyth that the Danish military intelligence service (both army and navy) had previously secretly collaborated with MI6 and engaged in espionage against German military plans and forces. The two tried to convince Gyth that they should collaborate further with British intelligence, neglecting to mention that it would not be SIS or Section D, but the newly formed SOE.

Initially there was no separate SOE section for Denmark. It operated as part of the Scandinavian group that had been set up in the autumn of 1940 by Harry Sporborg, a well-connected lawyer, and the banker and Great War veteran Sir Charles Hambro. The latter was a personal friend of Jutta's, for whom she had acted as cut out and later paymaster to agents and résistants. Both men had links with Scandinavia. This group was an expansion of an existing Norwegian section of Section D that had been set up in the aftermath of the Norwegian invasion and the Norwegian government's move to England. Hambro arranged smuggling, intelligence networks and sabotage operations from his office at 64 Baker Street, under the day-to-day management of Commander Frank Noel Stagg.

If a separate Danish section were to be set up there would be obstacles to overcome. Denmark was not a priority. As a country that had effectively accepted occupation, it was of less strategic importance than, for example, Holland, France or Poland. Denmark was a 'neutral state whose King and democratically elected ministers remained [in] power and *in situ*'.[12] Since there was no government in exile, there was an absence of Danish personnel to call upon. The men of the armed forces and patriotic citizens had not fled to England with the pressing desire to return and resist, therefore the pool of men available to lead or undertake clandestine work was extremely limited.

Jutta's brother-in-law Ebbe Munck met with Charles Hambro and helped him forge links with the Danish resistance.[13] Agreeing to work on Hambro's behalf, Munck became a source of intelligence with regard to Denmark and acted as a key contact between the Danish underground and SOE. Munck told Hambro that it would take time and patience before the 'Danish mentality was adjusted to the thought of sabotage', and that it may 'take even longer before organisations with sufficient striking power were built up, properly manned and supplied with enough of the required sabotage material'.[14] But in principle the men agreed that although this would be their goal, they must not rush things and that 'it would not be in the interests of Denmark or Great Britain if uncoordinated sabotage was to break out, in Denmark at the moment'.[15]

SOE's presence in Denmark needed coordination and leadership, and they turned to the Danish diplomatic service to find a leader. They chose twenty-eight-year-old Ralph Hollingworth, an officer in the naval reserve who was involved with intelligence work. Nicknamed 'Holly', Ralph was rather short in stature and was described as 'frank and unceremonious'. He reputedly had a terrible sense of humour, but was a 'decent and cheerful man, without self-importance'.[16] He was in Copenhagen on 9 April when the Germans occupied the British Embassy. He was evacuated alongside several others who would later work for SOE. They went first to a citadel within the city and then via Brussels to London on a 'diplomatic train'.[17] As the train passed through Denmark, Gyth handed a complete plan of the location of German troops in Denmark through the train window to be taken to England. Jutta remembered proudly that 'it was the first report from us, later it was followed by thousands of others'.[18]

Hollingworth was in Iceland (where he was attaché to the admiral in charge of the British occupation forces) when he received word that he should go to London immediately, and to make sure he had at least two sets of clothes. From there, he and fellow SOE recruit Ronald Turnbull attended SOE training, after which he was informed of the exact nature of his job: he was to head the Danish Section of SOE in London, while Turnbull would be posted to Stockholm. Their mission was 'to raise a resistance struggle in Denmark and organise it'.[19]

As Hollingworth settled into his new, somewhat empty office, it dawned on him what an overwhelming task he had just undertaken. To make matters worse, the most basic apparatus and personnel needed to succeed were non-existent. There was no wireless contact or indeed wireless operators, no trained agents or saboteurs; there was hardly anyone on the ground in Denmark. There was nothing but his enthusiasm and two paper trays on his desk for incoming and outgoing correspondence, and even they were empty. He recalled that 'At the beginning we had the feeling that we were absolutely down to bedrock and left to our own devices', and that a feeling of loneliness crept over him as he settled down to make a plan of action and attempt to build up accurate information about potential targets.[20]

Jutta could be one source of such information, if only Gyth, whom she described as having a great 'enthusiasm for his job', with 'tireless energy' and an optimism that was 'contagious', would let her get on with her job.[21] He was not very good at delegating, and she found herself struggling to get 'work out of him'.[22] But he soon became too busy and, much to her delight, started to rely heavily on her to undertake various jobs. This included passing information to the Allies about 'the location of the anti-aircraft defences, the deployment of German troops, the passage of troops to and from Norway, new types of weapons, radar installations, fortifications, passage of warships, their types and numbers, etc.'[23] The intelligence was sent in an almost constant stream via Sweden to England, thus ensuring that the Allies were always up to date and well informed.

One evening, Jutta was invited to dinner at Gyth's house. She was friendly with his wife Agnes and looked forward to spending an evening with her friends. Among the guests was Gyth's boss, Lieutenant Colonel Einar Nordentoft. Jutta later discovered that he was there to see what sort of person she was and if she would pass muster as an agent. 'He was not a fan of ladies in the section,' she said, 'but, after dinner he gave his permission for me to be used ... then my work took off.'[24]

Back in England the head of SOE's Danish Section Ralph Hollingworth was doing his best to recruit suitable agents, but the pool of men from which he could recruit was rather shallow. It included Danes who happened to be in Britain when war broke out, as well as a fleet of Danish fisherman and merchant seaman who had been at sea on the day of the invasion and had taken sanctuary in British ports rather than return to Denmark.

As SOE prepared to drop its first two agents, SIS beat them to it and infiltrated a Dane named Tommy Sneum. This remarkable man had flown out of Denmark in an old biplane he had found in a barn to deliver films and intelligence reports about Germany's new Freya radar machinery, which he wanted to get to the Allies. He repaired the aircraft himself and collected fuel from various sources. When the aircraft was ready, he started the propellors while still in the barn, so as not to alert a nearby German base, and only opened the barn doors to drive out and take off. All this had to be done at exactly the same time that a train passed by, so that the noise of the engines was drowned out. Flying under telegraph wires, the plane headed for England. On arrival in the UK, Tommy had to prove that he was not a German spy, and much to his dismay MI5 mangled the developing process of the films, rendering them useless.

Tommy was given basic SIS training and returned to Denmark by parachute in September 1941. He landed on barbed wire, damaging his coccyx, but still managed to bury his parachute and set about his mission, which was to gather information about German activities and industry in Denmark and report back via wireless to England. He was amazed to discover, upon opening his wallet, that, even though he was working for SIS (the senior of the two services), he had been incorrectly issued with Swedish and not Danish currency.

In fact, Tommy was reputedly unaware of the difference between SOE and SIS, and when it came down to it, he did not know which of the two agencies had recruited him. All he knew was that he was there to help the British. The confusion was widespread. When Tommy contacted the three top members of Danish intelligence – Norden-toft, Gyth and Major Hans Lunding, nicknamed 'the Princes' – they were unaware that the organisation they were working with was SOE or indeed that there was another. They had been communicating with them via Turnbull, Hollingworth's colleague in Sweden. Suspicious of Tommy, the Princes insisted he write a report on his escape and the time he had spent in London, as well as digging up his parachute to prove that he had been dropped and was not a German spy.

Meanwhile SOE dropped its first two agents – Dr Karl Johan Bruhn, who was destined to be SOE's chief on the ground, and Mogens Hammer, his W/T. A little before midnight on 27 December 1941, a freezing night, an aircraft carrying the two men approached their drop zone near Haslev. There would be no reception commit-tee and no safe house waiting for them – they were dropping blind. Bruhn jumped first, carrying the wireless set with him, followed by Hammer and a third parachute and canister containing weapons, explosives and supplies to be used in the sabotage of German facto-ries and machinery.

All of SOE's hopes for Denmark were pinned on these two men. But disaster struck when Bruhn's parachute failed to deploy and he was killed on impact, and the precious wireless set he carried smashed to pieces. Hammer went on the run, having cut the boots from his fallen comrade to retrieve the money hidden in them, setting out to find fellow resistance members who could aid him.

On 17 April 1942, SOE sent a further three agents, Christian Rott-bøll, Paul Johanssen and Max Mikkelsen. The latter two were des-tined to be wireless operators. Disaster struck again when Johanssen and Mikkelsen landed in trees. Both were injured and Mikkelsen was knocked unconscious. Rottbøll landed safely and contacted the local resistance. Slowly but surely SOE limped into action in Denmark.

While SOE worked through its teething problems, Jutta contin-ued to use her role in the bank as a means to exchange information, money and microfilms. Her office was a place of constant comings and goings, and on one particularly busy day a cashier approached her and asked if it was her birthday because of the number of parcels arriving at her desk.[25] There were now more and more shipments to Ebbe Munck and SOE in England. People who were unknown to Jutta came into the bank with all sorts of peculiar objects – toothpaste tubes, shaving brushes, face cream, house keys and a wide variety of cigarette packages, all concealing microfilms. The most unusual item was a small metal capsule that could be inserted into the rectum. But, she recalled, 'when it was found that the metal canister exploded and destroyed the film if you screwed it up incorrectly, not many illegal travellers wanted to take it with them'.[26]

In the summer of 1942, Jutta met a man called Flemming Juncker for the first time. He had been on a business trip and had brought messages back with him from SOE's Turnbull in Stockholm. Jutta was to collect them from him and pass them on to Gyth. Just as she was about to leave, Juncker told her that he could get microfilms to Stockholm if she was interested, having sought Gyth's permission. She accepted Juncker's offer. It was the beginning of a lifelong partnership.[27]

■ ■ ■

The spring of 1942 marked a turning point for another Danish woman, thirty-one-year-old Edith Bonnesen née Andersen. Born in Hellerup in 1911, Edith's parents brought her and her sister up in a strict but loving environment. The family was strongly patriotic, and even early in her childhood, values such as respect for king and country were instilled in her. Educated at Aurehøj Gymnasium, a private school in Hellerup, Edith passed her exams in 1928. The same year, her mother died. From 1930 until her marriage to Poul Winther Bonnesen in 1935, Edith was employed by the London Insurance Company, after which she became a housewife.

In 1937, Edith and her husband witnessed Hitler's racial policy and hatred for the Jews first hand when they were guests at a Jewish home in Berlin. She recalled seeing benches in the parks – yellow for

Jews and white for Aryans – and signs outside doctors' and dentists' offices that read *Juden nicht erwünscht* (Jews not wanted). 'They had to go through a lot,' she said, 'before they ended up in the gas chambers.'[28] What Edith witnessed in Berlin formed the basis of her hatred towards the Nazis, a disdain and loathing that grew into her early involvement in illegal work as part of the resistance movement in Denmark.

In 1940, Edith and Poul divorced, after which she was employed in the Ministry of Transport's department for the supervision of private railways. This work gave her unprecedented access to confidential papers and letters about German activities that could not be published in the legal press. Instead, she took them home, copied them and put them back again before anyone noticed they were missing. She sent the copies anonymously to all her friends, as a means of protesting against the German occupation (they could use the information in whatever way they saw fit). 'I was a courier too,' she said. 'Most people were, both men and women. The courier service was many things. Letters to Sweden. Weapons for resistance fighters . . .'[29]

In the spring of 1942 one of Edith's friends, Sven Hammer, put her in contact with the resistance group De frie Danske, who published an illegal magazine under the same name. The magazine was published in Copenhagen throughout the war and at its height had a circulation of 20,000 readers. Published semi-professionally, it was typeset and even had photographs. Edith worked as a contributor, collected material and wrote articles for the magazine.

As part of De frie Danske resistance group, Edith came into contact with numerous saboteurs. In her opinion, the 'communists were by far the best . . . brave, organised, efficient, trained'.[30] She collected drawings from factories on their behalf and passed on information about what should (and should not) be a target for sabotage. She became involved in acquiring fake ID and ration cards for members of the resistance or those who needed to change their identity. She collected money too, 'partly for the magazine business and partly for the families whose relatives had been arrested'. She continued to do this throughout the occupation.[31]

Edith also allowed her apartment in Tranegårdsvej to be used as a place for illegal meetings, and as a safe house for people whose safety had been compromised or who were wanted by the Germans. One such guest was Mogens Hammer, the brother of Sven (who had introduced her to the resistance) and the survivor of SOE's first parachute drop into Denmark. She had also met SIS parachutists Sneum and his wireless operator Christoffersen through De frie Danske. 'I knew Mogens Hammer was a parachutist,' she said. 'We had to know the circumstances, those of us who were in the inner circle. But it was a mistake for Hammer to seek out his family. Everything went wrong for Hammer . . . he had to bury parachutes, dust the transmitter. He then went to see his brother.'[32] This was an incredibly risky decision. Agents were actively discouraged from seeking out family and contacts from their pre-war existence in case they were being followed or the relationship could be used against them after arrest. However, this time the meeting had a good outcome. Hammer was introduced to the Danish wireless expert and Edith's future work partner, Lorens Duus Hansen.

Edith's work was not without its risks. On the contrary, arrest for resistance activities could mean torture and deportation. She was arrested three times in 1942 by Danish and German police, but each time was released within a few days after stubbornly denying any involvement in illegal work. It seems that she had some assistance from her friends in the Danish police, who were, in her opinion, 'always one step ahead of the Germans. They were aware of what I was involved in. They gave me reports, which is why I got off scot-free.'[33] The Danish police were on their side. For example, it was the Danish police who had found Hammer's broken wireless set when he first landed, and they took it to the police station to hide it. Later, Duus Hansen saw it and recognised it as being similar to the one that

Sneum was using and assumed that it must have come from England too. By this time Duus had already made his own wireless set and was transmitting messages, without England knowing about it.[34]

While Edith still had six of her nine lives intact, other resisters did not fare so well. During 1942, several distinctive resistance groups were established. Their members were young – aged between fourteen and seventeen. The most famous of these was the Churchill Club, whose eleven members were schoolboys at Aalborg Cathedral School. Cycling through the streets in broad daylight, they painted their symbol – a pseudo swastika with blue arrows – on street signs and the doors of the houses of Nazi officials, set fire to plans and blueprints in Nazi offices, stole guns and destroyed German vehicles. They were arrested in May 1942, and were given sentences ranging from a year and six months to three years. But even prison did not stop them, and three boys managed to escape by sawing a loose window bar and using their freedom to perform yet more acts of sabotage. This was to be their last act of resistance: the boys were recaptured, and the Churchill Club ceased to exist.[35]

In September 1942, sabotage became an extremely topical subject. In a radio broadcast the Danish prime minister, Vilhelm Buhl, strongly condemned sabotage and encouraged the Danish people to continue in their acceptance of German occupation. However, former coalition government member Christmas Møller (who had fled Denmark in the hope of creating a government in exile) spoke on the BBC's Danish-language service. In his broadcasts he condemned the government's cooperation with the Germans and encouraged sabotage and other resistance activities. This made him very popular – and the Danish people began to think that resistance was a viable option after all.

However, the Germans had a list of around thirty people who were involved in the illegal press or sabotage, and a manhunt began. When word got out that they were looking for people, some of the wanted managed to escape to Sweden but others were arrested, or worse killed. These included SOE's chief, Christian Rottbøll. At 6.30 a.m. on 26 September, he was a woken by a knock on his door. Half asleep and bleary-eyed, he opened the door still wearing his pyjamas and was immediately shot. A total of twelve bullets hit him in the head, neck and stomach. As he lay motionless his assassin delivered one last bullet shot to his temple, and with that the leader of SOE's Danish Section was dead. And things were about to get even worse.

The following month a diplomatic crisis between Denmark and Germany was sparked when, in acknowledgement of a telegram sent to King Christian X by Hitler congratulating him on his seventy-second birthday, the king somewhat perfunctorily replied, 'Giving my best thanks, King Christian.' Hitler was so angry at the brevity of the message, which he took to be a slight against him, that he withdrew his ambassador from Copenhagen and expelled the Danish ambassador from Germany. A proposal to send the Crown Prince to apologise to Hitler personally was rebuffed. In reprisal Hitler swapped the personnel employed by the Nazis in Denmark for men who offered a more 'heavy-handed' approach, including Dr Werner Best, who became the new plenipotentiary in early November. At the same time the Danish military were removed from Jutland in an attempt to stop illegal intelligence gathering.

Arguably the 'telegram crisis' was an excuse to replace the German leadership in Denmark. Hostility towards the German occupation was increasing and the resistance movement was beginning to grow, undertaking acts of sabotage against railways and factories linked to the German war effort. Denmark was declared as 'enemy territory' and retaliatory attacks were carried out on shops and businesses. Even the iconic and hugely popular Copenhagen landmark, Tivoli Gardens, a nineteenth-century amusement park bedecked with Chinese pagodas, wooden roller coasters and twinkling lights, did not go unscathed, with parts of it being burned down. The gloves were well and truly off.

■ ■ ■

On 12/13 March 1943, SOE in Denmark's new leader, Flemming Muus, parachuted into Denmark. As a young man, Muus had been the black sheep of the family and had a strained relationship with his parents. He was caught cheating and forging his uncle's signature on cheques, and he was sent to become a clerical apprentice.[36] But the cheating continued, so the family sent him first to Berlin and then to a shipping company in Monrovia.[37] He was in Liberia when war broke out. He had been there for eight years when he heard about the invasion of Norway and Denmark on the radio. He immediately sent a telegram to the Danish ambassador in London saying that he wanted to fight for Denmark but was informed that, as there was no government in exile, his services were not needed. But someone somewhere kept a record of his enthusiasm, and two years later he received a telegram from the British consul in Monrovia telling him he was expected in London at once. He underwent SOE training at Hatherop Castle and recalled firing 'several hundred shots daily with pistols – with our left – with our right – in the dark, with a light in our eyes so that we were quite dazzled, at targets which appeared without warning. We became quite expert.'[38]

SOE's usual attention to detail went one step further with regard to Flemming Muus. They could not be sure that he would not be recognised when he returned to Denmark, and to make absolutely sure he blended into the background he underwent plastic surgery to radically alter his physical appearance. The nurses who cared for him were told that he was an actor preparing for a role. The story was so well fabricated that his 'co-star' Vera Lynn even stopped by to wish her screen partner well. The scarring on Muus's face would later become his nemesis, as it was a clear means of identification for the Gestapo 'wanted' posters.

When he jumped into the darkness from the Halifax aircraft that early spring night, he was accompanied by three other agents and their bicycles, which were airdropped with them, adding another layer of difficulty to an already fraught situation. To compound the difficulties, they landed off course. The men were due to land on ground owned by Flemming Juncker at Støvring, but instead blew off course to the west. Danish police were alerted to the drop and, upon finding deserted parachutes, bicycles and striptease suits, knew the men must be nearby. In the meantime, the agents had been spirited away by train to Aalborg and from there Muus met with Juncker and travelled to Copenhagen, where he began his new role as head of SOE and developed contacts.

In June 1943, Muus met his new contact for the first time, British-born Monica Wichfeld. This unlikely résistant was married to a Danish count and lived on a large country estate. Through a communist tenant she had managed to undertake resistance work, including raising money to pay for illegal boats to Sweden carrying fugitives and refugees. At a meeting with an insurance broker, she discovered that he too worked for the resistance and acted in the incredibly dangerous role of lookout for an SOE wireless operator. This involved keeping an eye out for direction-finding vans and informing the wireless operator should he see one so that they could clear out before being trapped. Monica managed to persuade the broker that she and her daughter Varinka (known to the family as 'Inkie') wanted to do something to help, and he brokered an introductory meeting between Monica and Flemming Muus. A few weeks later Muus was to meet Monica's daughter, Varinka. She would not only become his secretary but also the love of his life.

Varinka was twenty-one years old in 1943. Born in Lolland, she was brought up by her grandmother in Italy on account of the poor economic situation in Denmark. She spoke English and Italian fluently and was initially a great admirer of Mussolini, who was, she thought, having a positive impact on Italy. Varinka's mother was very keen that her daughter should learn to stand on her own two feet. 'There will come a day,' her mother told her, when it would be a frequent occurrence that women would 'want an education', not to 'marry or . . . get divorced.'[39] Her mother insisted that she get herself an education, and since Varinka was not inclined to go to university, she was sent, aged sixteen, to Vienna to learn German.

As with Jutta and Edith, Varinka also witnessed *Kristallnacht*. She recalled seeing windows smashed and synagogues set on fire. She saw some of Hitler's work first hand at a very early age and it enraged her. Varinka was back in Italy when the invasion of Denmark was announced on the radio. The news that her homeland had been invaded changed her outlook in a matter of moments: 'I who had never felt Danish suddenly began to feel something and wept with rage against those who had stolen my country.'[40] The situation in Italy had also changed for the worse and Varinka, awash with patriotism, decided to go back to Denmark. Travelling by train, she went via Germany and arrived back in Denmark where, deciding that she would not idly sit by and let the world turn to rack and ruin, she helped her mother with resistance work.[41]

But 'it was not enough', said Monica, to 'sit here eating and drinking and handing out little illegal magazines and raising money for the poor communists' wives'.[42] Varinka and her mother wanted to do more, so Monica took matters into her own hands. Travelling to Copenhagen, she went straight to the Damehotellet (women's hotel) and requested to see their only male guest, Flemming Muus. She told him that while she knew very little about the practicalities of parachute drops, she had land, and plenty of it, which she hoped would make a suitable DZ and thereby put her at the heart of resistance activity in Lolland.[43]

Muus saw huge potential in Monica – her passion and charisma were infectious. Also, her land lay in the perfect position to slow down any withdrawal of German troops and so would be perfect for a base from which to organise resistance activities. Muus accepted her offer of help, and Monica returned home buoyant with success. It was not long before an SOE agent who had recently arrived from England was sent to them. The two women helped him find suitable drop zones for the delivery of arms and explosives in Lolland.

Varinka used all her powers of persuasion to convince a friend to lend them his van, which she then loaded up with sabotage materials to attack local shipping yards. Meanwhile, the working relationship between Monica and Muus flourished.

The pair met regularly, Monica travelling from Engestofte to Copenhagen under one pretext or another – a visit to the dentist or to see her son Viggo. One day in early July some last-minute difficulties made it impossible for her to travel to her meeting with Muus. She decided to send Varinka instead. Slipping the message for Muus into the back of a powder compact, Monica gave Varinka clear instructions that on arrival in Copenhagen she was to go directly to the hotel and hand the message to an elderly lady (codenamed 'Daphne'). Only if Daphne was not available was Varinka to seek out Muus himself, but this was a last resort that should be avoided if possible. Thrilled at the prospect of doing some real courier work, Varinka set off for Copenhagen and, deciding not to bother with Daphne, she went straight to Muus.

The meeting was one that neither would forget. For Muus it was love at first sight. 'The moment I saw her,' he recalled, 'I decided that she was to be my wife.'[44] Varinka, while charmed by Muus, who was 'very handsome' in his blue suit and 'very thick glasses', with a 'calm and cultured voice', was not there for romance.[45] Instead, she took the opportunity to tell him how much she wanted to work for the resistance and SOE. 'All I wanted to do was to go to war with the Germans,' she said determinedly. 'They had to get out of our land, we were not going to sit and take the heat with millions and be killed.'[46] Her blood was up and her patriotism spilling over as she told him that she spoke excellent English and would be an asset to him and his work. Her heart thumping in her chest, she awaited his answer. All he had to do was say yes, and her world would change for ever.

■ ■ ■

That summer, Jutta arranged an important meeting between key resistance members Erling Foss, Mogens Fog and Frode Jakobsen. The last few months had seen a significant increase in sabotage, but it was felt by those present that the targets were sometimes unwisely chosen and had nothing to do with the 'Germans, [nor] made military equipment, nor had particularly German-oriented owners'.[47] The meeting was convened to discuss propaganda in Denmark, and how they could ensure that sabotage was organised properly in future, so that it was not so 'unpopular' with the Danish population. While a final decision was not reached that particular evening, it was agreed that 'more groups should be involved, and more tasks should be taken up' to unify the resistance and its targets in the future. The seeds had been sown for the Danish Freedom Council.

The sabotage and strikes reached a peak during August, and on the morning of 28 August, Jutta received a telephone call at the bank from Gyth telling her to meet him at 1 p.m. He also mentioned that there might be food shortages so she should go to the shops and stock up. Telling her sister to do the same, the pair both bought plenty of liquor. It was obviously what they thought they 'benefited the most from', she quipped.[48]

At 1 p.m., Jutta went to meet Gyth. He arrived in his small car and Jutta discovered that the back seat was already taken up by an officer from the intelligence department, who sat completely surrounded by hand grenades. Jutta 'squeezed in next to the hand grenades' but it 'didn't feel very safe'.[49] They drove around Copenhagen delivering their goods and messages, starting with Flemming Muus at the Damehotellet and finishing at a new address, where Jutta handed over a code word. She later became aware that she had just given orders for the sinking of the Danish fleet that night. After this mission was complete, a few of them gathered around a wireless transmitter to send a message to London. Jutta helped with the coding but misspelled the password. She was furious with herself as she sat by while everything was redone: 'I wasn't worth much,' she thought dejectedly.[50] The next morning a state of emergency was declared by the Germans and the Danish government ceased to function. The world was turned on its head and the work of Jutta, Edith and Varinka would become more important than ever.

The summer of 1943 had seen a change in the mood of the Danish population, who became optimistic and even rebellious as they began to oppose the German occupation. Berets in the style and colour of the RAF roundel became popular and were worn on the streets as a sign of open hostility towards the German occupiers. It also rubbed their noses in the fact that their families back home in Germany were at the mercy of Allied bombers.

A rebellion in Odense on 30 July triggered the main change in resistance activity, when workers at the Steel Shipyard went on strike because the Germans had installed armed sabotage guards to keep an eye on them and their actions. Thereafter, rebellions broke out in many parts of the country, especially Jutland and Funen, where daily clashes between the Germans and Danes, and the sabotage of industrial targets and railways, increased.

Germany was already sensing that it was on the back foot and grappled to keep control of wider global affairs. That summer, Germany had suffered a series of setbacks on the battlefields of the Eastern Front and the Mediterranean, and on 24 July, Mussolini was deposed. In a desperate attempt to keep control in Denmark at least, Hitler ordered that any Danish rebellion and sabotage must be stopped, and he ordered Parliament to declare a state of emergency.

A list of new laws was drawn up with immediate effect. This included the banning of strikes and assemblies, a curfew to be introduced at night and sabotage made punishable by death. The Danish government refused to agree and on 29 August the government, Parliament and King Christian X resigned.[51]

That morning, the Danish defences were rebuffed by the Germans during several skirmishes known as Operation 'Safari'. It resulted in several deaths on both sides and the disarming of some Danish armed forces. The Danes were determined that the Germans should not get their hands on their military equipment, especially the ships

of the Danish fleet, the majority of which were at anchor at Lange-
linie with German guns trained on them to stop them sailing away.
Jutta had delivered a message just hours before with orders to scuttle
the fleet, and as a result thirty vessels were sunk to the bottom of the
harbour or destroyed to prevent them falling into enemy hands. A
handful managed to get away to Sweden. This action also gave a clear
signal to the Allies that Denmark was firmly on their side. Elsewhere,
weapons and equipment were either destroyed or handed to the resistance.

The uprising ended with the arrest of some 250 Danes and an atmosphere of dread reigning over the country. The state of emergency
was lifted after six weeks but neither the government nor the king
returned. The country was under the rule of the German plenipotentiary, Werner Best, and was now truly part of occupied Europe.

The events of August 1943 changed everything. The country was
now under full German occupation, and was subjected to the full extent of occupational rule. It also meant that Denmark's Jews, who until now had been safe, were at risk. The wearing of the yellow star was
never implemented but on 1 October the Germans started to round
up Danish Jews. Many had been warned in advance and had managed either to go into hiding or to escape. Helpers collected food and
money and provided shelter until boats could be organised to help
them flee, at which point they were smuggled by fishermen across
the sound to neutral Sweden. More than 7,000 Danish Jews escaped
to Sweden and 472 were deported to Theresienstadt.

For Jutta, Varinka and Edith, the world had suddenly become a
very dangerous place. Jutta described an 'eerie atmosphere' after the
29 August incident, saying she saw both German and Danish cars
driving around to private addresses to arrest those who were not already detained.[52] She was constantly on edge and looking over her
shoulder. On one occasion, she was waiting on a park bench for Nordentoft when a taxi stopped next to her. A German soldier got out
and she froze with fear. Was he here to arrest her? The soldier walked

up to Jutta and told her that he was lost and could she direct him. Trembling with relief, Jutta made something up about going 'first to the left and then to the right', even though she had no idea where the road in question was. She just wanted to get rid of him as quickly as possible. As he drove away, she breathed a sigh of relief and disappeared lest he should come back.

Jutta and her colleagues rushed to get incriminating packages and papers moved away from the intelligence office as quickly as possible. She also had to pick up papers that had been distributed around the city, collecting some from 'a nice old lady who had them under her bed', and others that had been hidden under the mud of a villa garden.[53] She also had to collect some Polish intelligence reports that had been stored on microfilm and were in a bank safe bearing Gyth's name. This was not as easy as she had hoped, as the 'superior wanted nothing to do with it'. However, forging a key, she managed to get the films and spent an eventful evening trying to flush them down the toilet.[54]

The next few days were spent making critical decisions, namely whether Gyth should flee via Sweden to London – and whether Jutta should go with him. The idea that she might like to go to London to work for SOE in their offices had been mooted before and Jutta had decided to stay put, but now the situation was very different. She felt unsure that she could contribute much more in Denmark and, besides, she was moments away from arrest. She 'knew too many addresses and people within the central work'.[55] But in London she could have a positive impact and really contribute to the war effort. She decided to go, and Gyth would travel with her.

■ ■ ■

Ever since her initial meeting with SOE's chief, Varinka had been employed in SOE's Copenhagen HQ, where she worked full-time. She started out working for Professor Rantzau, head of the underground propaganda department, for whom she translated the leaflets dropped by the RAF. She did her job with such skill that two months later she became Muus's secretary and assistant. He was badly in need of a replacement since his secretary had been forced to flee to Sweden. Impressed with her grasp of both Danish and English stenography as well as her good typing, Muus found Varinka to be 'quick energetic and intelligent . . . in short the ideal secretary'.[56]

Living in a hotel right in the heart of the city, Varinka had arranged to get a cover story from a friend who owned a small firm. Although he was not told why, he gave her papers saying that she worked for him, and when anyone telephoned for her, he was to cover for her absence by saying that she was running an errand.

Her actual job was both difficult and unremitting. She had to be readily available at any time of the day or night and was expected to work 'odd hours' in 'odd places'; for example, taking dictation for a telegram in the back of a taxi or in a hotel room in the middle of the night.[57] Varinka was required to arrange and attend numerous meetings and, if Muus was late or unwell (he frequently suffered from malaria attacks after contracting the disease in Liberia), she was to keep the meeting going until he arrived. She coded and decoded endless messages and telegrams, effectively becoming Muus's right-hand man. She was never happier. It was the 'best time I've ever had', she said, '. . . I felt like I was the centre of attention.'[58] It was around this time that he first asked her to marry him. She refused.

■ ■ ■

Edith Bonnesen too had been busy since 29 August, when she had quit her job at the ministry and gone underground. Up until this point she had worked on illegal magazines, obtained weapons and collected around 10,000–20,000 kroner per month for ink, paper and stamps. She also helped the families of those who were in prison. But now that the Germans had full control, the stakes were simply too high to continue.

She refused to give up, and saw that Duus Hansen was now completely overburdened with his wireless work. Since starting his independent transmissions, he had made contact with officers in the

General Staff's Intelligence Section and was sending dispatches to London on their behalf, as well as assisting with the creation of microfilm reports and sending these via Sweden. In the summer of 1943, he met with an SOE representative in Stockholm who entrusted him with managing the entire radio service in Denmark, contrary to SOE's usual rule of dealing only with English-trained wireless operators.

As this network expanded, Duus needed help, and his colleague Ib Larsen suggested that Edith could be just the person that he needed. Duus was not at all keen at first because she was a woman. 'What can I use her for?' he asked. Larsen replied: 'She can find broadcasting stations. Ration marks, illegal magazines. She's really well connected.'[59] What was more, she had been arrested three times and each time she had got out. She was surely perfectly suited to the role. Duus somewhat reluctantly agreed to give her a chance.

Codenamed 'Lotte', her first job was to find the locations from which they could broadcast. The list of criteria for suitable places was strict. The apartments or buildings could not have children, young people or maids living there – they would see too much, ask too many questions and were more likely to talk. She organised guards (experienced dog handlers or policemen), sourced the nearest telephone boxes and assessed the escape routes. Only when all the criteria had been met could they use a location for such dangerous work, and once it had been blown or someone had been arrested, she had to start all over again. 'It was not difficult to find new apartments,' she said. 'I knew a lot of people. The hard part was being sure it was a safe place.'[60]

Edith also had to recruit and set up a network of telegraphers. 'We took them from the navy and from the telegraph troops,' she said. 'They were already seasoned.' She asked if they were married. Did they have children? What did their wife think about the work? Were they ready for such a dangerous job?[61]

Before long, the radio section was a hundred strong and was made up of coders and the wireless operators whom Edith and Duus trained together. She taught them how to use a transmitter – where the crystals should go and how to switch them to change the frequency. She gave them codes and taught them how to use silk coding sheets and, perhaps most critically in the wake of what had happened in the Netherlands, what to do if they were caught and forced to continue sending. She told them that they should 'leave out their indicator' so that the English could see if someone was sending under duress.[62]

'Mentally, it was a colossal pressure,' she said. The agents took it in turns to live in different places and 'it was hard living so close together . . . you learn to see each other's reactions . . . you have to use your brain and eyes all the time.'[63] The mental and physical exhaustion was overwhelming, but Edith and the others were determined to keep going no matter how tired they got. There 'was a wonderful camaraderie', each knowing the other 'by heart'.[64]

Each person was assigned a codename chosen from the Bible, such as 'Moses', 'Lot', 'Saul', 'Jonas', and so on. Edith ensured each person had a guard who would stand watch, and assigned them their shifts. There could be as many as six shifts in a day, with a minimum of three. She showed them to their safe house and thereafter left them to manage themselves. All of this required huge effort – and money. Duus estimated that it cost around 70,000 kroner to finance the radio section's work, most of which had been stolen. Part of this money went to fund Duus's quest to improve the lot of the wireless operator, which was an extremely dangerous occupation. With survival rates of 50/50 and a life expectancy of six weeks, many wireless operators across Western Europe had been caught, interrogated, tortured and brutally murdered. Duus intended to help them by improving the Danish transmitters and thereby improving security for all those who operated them.

Harnessing the skills he had perfected in his pre-war job as a designer for the radio company Bang & Olufsen, Duus dedicated himself to the pursuit of improving the wireless set that agents used to transmit their messages. Through sheer persistence and hard graft in the extenuating circumstances of wartime, with all the pressures that brought, especially working against the ever-ticking clock, he managed to create a new type of wireless set. It weighed just under 2 kilos – 13 kilos lighter than its predecessor. The wireless set was now the size of a phone directory rather than a suitcase and became known as the 'telephone book radio'. Because of its weight and size, it was far easier to transport and hide if necessary and worked on both alternating current and direct current. He also developed a high-speed transmitter, or Morse burst stick, which could transmit telegraphy at 500–700 words a minute. This was far greater than the speed that could be achieved with a manual Morse key. As the messages could be sent far more quickly, the number of messages sent increased, and the D/Fs found it increasingly difficult to locate the signal and thereby catch the wireless operator.

In addition to all these remarkable achievements Duus was the protagonist for the establishment of the virtually untraceable Ultra High Frequency (UHF) wireless connection from Copenhagen harbour, right across the Øresund strait to Malmö. The station there was equipped with an automatic recording machine, and messages were converted to other wavelengths and passed directly on to London. Known as the 'Spaghetti' then 'Badminton' connection, this was far less risky than transmitting direct to London. Duus was also responsible for 'Minestrone', which was a parallel link between Helsingør and Helsingborg.

Along with Edith, Duus ensured that the Danish wireless service was well organised and safely managed. Every wireless operator only knew what was strictly necessary to carry out their job and they always had a guard or lookout while they operated. In contrast to other European countries, where agents carried their incriminating wireless set with them, Danish operators never carried their own set. The organisation was further strengthened by workshops for the manufacture and repair of wireless sets, and a reserve pool of wireless operators and helpers. Duus soon became responsible for all wireless traffic between England and Denmark.[65]

■ ■ ■

In late August 1943, Jutta left for England via Sweden by rather un-conventional means. She left work early saying that she had a den-tist's appointment and would not be back in that day. She then set out for the rendezvous point at a villa in Klampenborg, where sev-eral military personnel had gathered, including Gyth. Jutta did not know anyone else, but it didn't matter as very few words were spoken. Everybody sat looking at one another and their watches, nervously awaiting news of their departure. After a while they were told 'not tonight'. Jutta's heart sank, but she knew she had to get out and get home before curfew at 8 p.m. Two days later she tried again. Using a repeat visit to the dentist as an excuse, she left work and took the train to Rungsted with Gyth.[66]

Gyth found them a table at the local inn and left Jutta there while he went to find out if they were leaving that evening. Jutta became unsettled as the only other person in the restaurant was a single man 'who sat gravely at a table and looked expectant'.[67] It seemed to take an eternity for Gyth to come back, and when he did Jutta warned him that the single gentleman could well be a Gestapo officer. Gyth burst out laughing and told her it was Captain Mørch from the navy's intel-ligence service, and that he would be sailing their boat. The escape was on.

9

ESCAPE AND EVASION

I had to walk quietly and to look natural. Every moment I expected to be shot in the neck. Then I rolled off my white turban. At least they wouldn't recognize me by that.

Edith Bonnesen[1]

As the sun set over Rungsted harbour, the quay bustled with people out for an evening walk to admire the sunset or the glistening lights over the water. In the midst of these crowds Jutta, Gyth and the others had to make their way to a fishing boat and stow themselves away without drawing too much attention. In fact, the throng of people probably helped to hide them in plain sight. On the boat Jutta and Gyth met the man and woman who would be their travel companions. There should have been a third passenger, but he had received the wrong message and missed the boat. They hunkered down in pitch black. The area below deck reeked of fish but they made themselves as comfortable as they could, which was almost impossible. The men sat in one corner and the women in the other. They exchanged very few words. The silence was broken from time to time by Captain Mørch, who stuck his head down into the fetid darkness to update them: 'Now we lie still and fish,' or, 'There are German patrol boats heading towards us.'[2] As the boat neared the Swedish coast it slowed down. The fishermen did not want to go any closer and it soon became apparent that the stowaways would have to make their own way the last kilometre or so to the beachhead.

Luckily, Jutta was 'wearing long trousers and a jumper', but her female companion, Mrs Lohse, had not fared so well in her choice of attire; she wore a 'smart, tight skirt, which was not the best for swimming in'.³ Jutta ripped the front of the skirt to allow her to swim more freely. The fishermen tied swimming belts, consisting of ropes with corks attached, around the stowaways' waists and got the four escapees as close to the coast as they dared. Then it was time to jump:

> I don't know what the others thought, but I thought it was best to get it over quickly and got into the water in a hurry. I heard the splashing of the others and saw Mrs. Lohse next to me. It was a glorious sight, the flared skirt unfolding like a balloon above her. Neither of us were great swimmers; but with the help of the cork life belts we got ashore quietly and safely.⁴

They were met by two customs officers, who treated them 'excellently', providing warm bathrobes for the women and battledress for the men. Then, much to Jutta's delight, they were each handed a glass of schnapps. 'Lovely!' she declared. Back in Copenhagen, her colleagues at the bank were most puzzled by her disappearance. She had always been so punctual and reliable. Perhaps she had run off with a lover, they postulated, or embezzled cash? They would never guess the truth – that Jutta was about to become a full-time employee of SOE at their offices on Baker Street in London.

■ ■ ■

In October 1943, Flemming Muus was recalled to London (via Stockholm and Scotland) to report to the admiralty and war office on 'how things were going in Denmark'.⁵ They had just discovered the dreadful situation in the Netherlands and needed reassuring that other countries had not fared as badly. Muus was the only active SOE leader who was able to travel to London and, in a hearing at the War Office, he proved to them that their fears were unfounded and that the Danish resistance was not under the control of the Germans. While in London he also met with Hollingworth and, much to his surprise and delight, was awarded the DSO (Distinguished Service Order). 'It was delight-ful', he said, 'to go into a tailors on the way back to my office in Baker Street and have a ribbon sewn on my uniform for the price of a shil-ling.'[6] The following morning he sent a telegram to Varinka to tell her the exciting news. He also proposed to her again, and again she said no.

Muus was due to return by plane to Denmark on 13 December and was to be dropped to a reception committee in South Zealand. However, the aircraft got into a tussle with two German fighters and was shot down in flames. In a blaze of fire, they landed in a field and miraculously all of the crew survived. Muus sent them away. He was in civilian clothes and, if caught, would be shot as a spy, whereas they would become POWs.[7] Varinka was beside herself with worry:

> I knew he was missing, because the next day in the papers the Germans wrote that they had shot down a British plane and they had found a lot of parachutes ... 11 parachutes they said and anyone helping them would be shot on sight. Anyway [he] hid in a haystack for 36 hours, it was very, very cold, it was in December, it was well below zero. He managed to get a train back to Copenhagen and rang me up and said here I am, how are you ... by this time he had proposed to me several times and I had said no.[8]

But, despite her coolness, Varinka was falling for him and wrestling with her conscience about what she should do. As a girl from an upper-class family, she worried how she would explain to her fam-ily that she wanted to marry a man who was in Denmark illegally, whose real name she didn't know and who had surgically changed his appearance. To make matters worse, Muus was effectively commit-ting fraud – he was using the papers of someone who really existed, having taken his identity, his flat and even his telephone directory listing. It was an 'impossible' situation, she recalled. He was 'a nobody, a Mr X'.[9]

She didn't mention him when she went home that Christmas and was relieved to see that her father and brothers had no idea that she and her mother were involved with the resistance. It was safer that way, and she also knew that her father would not approve of her activities. But then disaster struck. The SOE parachutist who had been to the Wichfeld family house some months before was captured and had cracked under brutal interrogation. He had given away the names and addresses of 'all the places he had been and all the people he had contacted' since he had arrived in Denmark. He 'just kept on telling them all the details. A terrible amount of people were arrested', among them Varinka's mother, father and brothers.[10]

The family lawyer telephoned her to deliver the terrible news. Her heart was in her mouth as she bravely reassured him that it was all a terrible mistake and that her family couldn't possibly be involved with the resistance. In a state of shock, she returned the phone to its cradle and went back to her room. Her eyes were pricking with tears and her face devoid of any colour as she threw her belongings into a suitcase. Hurriedly she packed her clothes and cosmetics, but in between the layers of dresses and blouses she hid her horribly incriminating codes and papers. Fleeing as quickly as she could, she took a wood-fired taxi to Muus's flat and told him what had happened. He told her in a rather cool and distant manner to wait and see, and that maybe she would have to go to Sweden. 'That's the rule,' he told her. 'Anyone who is sought by the Gestapo [has] to go to Sweden.'[11]

Varinka angrily replied that she was not going to go and 'that's that'. She said, 'I don't see why I can't do the same as you, take on another name and identity, dye my hair, buy a pair of glasses and continue.'[12] Remarkably, he agreed and she continued with her work, albeit with frizzy red hair. A few days after her family's arrest, she received the welcome news that her father and brothers had been released, the Gestapo having realised that they had nothing to do with the resistance. Monica, however, was not so lucky and was kept in prison in Copenhagen to await trial. Not a day went by when a worried Varinka didn't think of her.

■ ■ ■

The morning following Jutta's somewhat unorthodox arrival in Sweden, she was reunited with the clothes that she had laid out to dry from the sea soaking the night before, remarking that she had never seen 'such a finely pressed pair of trousers'. She was informed that Gyth and Mørch had departed on a Swedish navy boat in the middle of the night and were already in Stockholm.[13] She was not far behind them. With no luggage to speak of she boarded a sleeper train to Stockholm late that night. Arriving a few hours later, she was greeted by 'the handsome Major Petersen, with a bouquet of 24 red roses', who drove her to a villa where she was reunited with Gyth and Mørch (and later Nordentoft).[14] They spent their first few months in Stockholm in this villa. They lived on the floor above their offices, as far away as possible from the housekeepers 'two biting wolf dogs' who also lived there. Jutta was very taken with the accommodation, commenting on the 'loveliest antique furniture' and the 'large dining room which was wallpapered with Swedish general staff cards'.[15] She borrowed some clothes, procured some blackmarket food and wasted no time in getting back to work.

To start with she helped in the passport office of the embassy, but the military department soon got so busy that there was no time for anything else. The days seemed to 'fly by' and she never stopped working. Walking to the office in the early morning, she passed through a park, which was 'a nice experience all year' round with white snow or blooming flowers, and the smell of freshly cut pine in the air.[16] She spent her days dealing with 'legal travellers, illegal travellers, refugees, wives whose husbands were underground in Denmark or had come to England'.[17] Lunch was at a nearby local restaurant, and in the evenings she often took her work home and spent hours poring over 'written work and internal negotiations'. Sometimes Nordentoft and

Mørch would join her and she would cook, or if the workload was slow, they would go to the cinema and watch American films.[18] Rare days off were spent on day trips, boating, visiting castles and then 'home to the office to find out what was new'.[19]

It was during this period that Jutta and Nordentoft became secret lovers, so secretive that literally no one else knew. On the face of it they were an unlikely match – Jutta thought he was a 'stiff military type with no sense of humour' and he felt that women had no place in intelligence.[20] Yet the two were passionately in love and spent as much time together as they could, and Jutta harboured hopes that they would marry after the war.[21]

She soon moved from the villa to a small apartment, but this brought with it the disadvantage of owning the only telephone, meaning she was effectively on call day and night to receive and relay information about the passage of warships. Occasionally she was obliged to make herself scarce while her home was used for top-secret meetings. Jutta's network made use of an unused cable between Denmark and Sweden that had been illegally connected to a tower on the harbour in Malmö and to a small shed at the Charlottenlund Fort on the Danish side. They used it to look after the illegal boat connections and share intelligence on refugee receptions and arms shipments.

Stockholm was 'pretty amazing', according to Jutta. She likened it to Casablanca or Lisbon, since it was a gathering place for refugees and a hotbed for international intrigue. Even the restaurants became known for which nationality dined in them, be they Japanese, German, English or American. It was a place of espionage, with antennae and personnel everywhere, including several women who came to this city of spies and intrigue to spy for the Germans. One of these was Jane Horney Granberg. Jane (unlike like most suspects, who were taken to a refugee camp in the north of Sweden) was Swedish and therefore allowed to roam freely and carry out her work without hindrance. 'Which is why,' said Jutta, 'her potential security risk was so difficult to limit.' She added, 'When you stick your neck out as far as she did in wartime you also have to expect that the head may fall off', thus implying that Jane's death by shooting, and her body being wrapped in chains before being dumped into the sea, was deserved and just.[22]

Jutta's network soon contacted Ebbe Munck, the 'permanent and supreme link between the many different resistance groups and SOE, OSS etc.'[23] Jutta was in awe of him, recalling that 'his ability to work with the vastly different groups was astonishing. He created trust in everyone – without him you would not have stood strong.'[24] She believed it was down to Munck's skill and tenacity that the quantity and speeds with which they could get information to England made the General Intelligence staff choose to work with SOE and not SIS. Gyth had been furious at the amateurish agents who were dropped, and had only realised that there were two different teams when he fled to Sweden. Likewise, it is probable that Jutta used her relationship with Nordentoft to 'convince him of the greater good of Denmark having its own political and diplomatic channel to England. Had they only worked for MI6 the Danish intelligence contribution would have been anonymised as a number among all the other sources of the professional service.'[25]

Jutta and Munck had kept it from Nordentoft and Gyth as much as possible, but once Gyth knew of the difference, he was aware that SIS should deal with intelligence and leave SOE to focus on sabotage.[26] But Munck refused, believing it was beneficial to the Danes to keep everything together and that 'one should not change horses in the middle of a ford'.[27]

Through Munck's discussions with SOE, it was decided that a group of young men should be selected from Denmark to go to England for official SOE training and then be dropped back in to instruct and assist the Danish resistance movements, in much the same way as SOE agents did across the rest of Europe. However, getting to England was becoming increasingly difficult. The aircraft that flew from Bromma to Leuchars in Scotland had very limited capacity for passengers, and they only flew on cloudy nights, to lessen their chances of being spotted over German territory. As a consequence, the process of getting the men to England for training was slow and protracted.

After months of 'pestering', Varinka finally agreed to marry Muus, but their happiness was marred by dreadful news. Varinka, Muus and some others went to stay with a friend for Whit Sunday. They spent the day in 'endless discussions' and decided that an early night was in order.[28] Just before they retired they decided to listen to the Swedish news bulletin. Afterwards, just as their host got up to turn off the radio set, the announcer said, 'From Copenhagen from official German sources it is announced that on the 12th of May 1944 the following have been sentenced according to martial law for helping the enemy.'[29] Some familiar names were read out, causing shocked outbursts from those gathered around the wireless – 'damned swines first torture . . . and now . . .'[30]

The announcer continued, 'Monica Emily Wichfeld . . . [sentenced to] death.' Varinka was known to some in the room only by her nom de guerre, 'Miss Haviid', and could betray no sign that Monica Wichfeld was her mother. Muus took her hand and 'felt its tremble'.[31] Muus was saddened for his young fiancée: 'Her mother, her best friend whom she had always admired, who had created an atmosphere between them that one seldom finds in such a relationship – condemned to death and the poor girl could not even permit herself to express the sorrow which overcame her.'[32] Varinka reached for a cigarette and announced, 'Well we said we were going to bed, good night.'[33]

A few weeks later came the news that everybody had been waiting for: D-Day had started – the Allied invasion of five beaches in Normandy with the purpose of taking Caen, Paris and then Berlin. But it had not always been clear to anyone, the Allies included, where the landings would take place. In April, Ralph Hollingworth sent messages to Muus on behalf of SHAEF to coordinate a wave of sabotage across the whole of Denmark in preparation (he believed) for the

Allied landings there. Believing their time had come, the resistance struck out against railways, power stations and a multitude of other targets across the country and the RAF launched aerial attacks against German shipping off the Norwegian coast. But nothing happened, and by May it had become clear that there would be no invasion. Jutta maintained that she had never believed that the landings would take place in Denmark, but that it was a 'relief' that the question was 'resolved'. Denmark had been 'an unwitting cog in a much greater machine'.[34]

To make matters worse, the Danish resistance had now used almost their entire stock of explosives, which would need replacing immediately if future operations were to be possible. But Hollingworth's hands were tied and he could not tell Muus anything. He simply hoped that eventually it would become clear that the Danish Section had played its part in the Allied deception that made D-Day the unbridled success that it eventually was.

On 8 June, two days after D-Day, Varinka and Muus married. The day was marred by the absence of Varinka's beloved mother. Using false names, the pair were married by the parish clerk of Tystrup near Fuglebjaerg. In the congregation was her brother Viggo, who had been released from prison after several months of incarceration. Celebrating with cherry wine and cakes, and a modest wedding dinner, the two immediately returned to their 'endless codes and meetings in Copenhagen'.[35] In particular they oversaw the Danish Freedom Council, which had been formed in the wake of the collapse of the coalition government in September 1943. The initiative was to coordinate the Danish fight for liberation by unifying the various Danish resistance groups under one umbrella organisation. The council was made up of representatives from the Communists, Holger Danske, Borgerlige Partisaner (BOPA) and other resistance groups, as well as a bishop and a professor. 'They riled Denmark by the underground illegal newspapers that came out,' Varinka said, 'tens of thousands of copies every day, printed illegally and distributed by hand, [this had a] terrific influence on the Danish public who by this time were really going in for doing something active.'[36]

Later that month the Germans enforced a curfew:

[It was the] middle of the summer, when all the working men had vegetable gardens where they supported themselves with vegetables and potatoes and so on, and they put in a curfew at 8 p.m. when the sun was shining. The whole country went on strike, there was a general strike which really was very serious.[37]

The Germans cut off all electricity, water and gas in Copenhagen. Surrounding the town, they threatened to bomb it 'to smithereens if the strike didn't stop'.[38]

But none kept the curfew; they came out onto the streets and lit bonfires. 'Every time a German tank came around the corner the Danes rushed into doorways until the tanks drove past and then they came out again. The Germans couldn't cope with the situation at all.'[39] Varinka went to Freedom Council meetings and wrote the minutes. It was decided that they would demand that the Germans remove the Danish Gestapo, known as the Schalburg Corps, from the streets of Denmark, where they were feared more than the Germans. 'They were criminals and they massacred innocent people, they beat up people and they tortured people. If they took them off the streets and lifted the curfew then the freedom council would see to it that the strike stopped.'[40] The Germans agreed to their terms, and the strike ended.

It was now becoming unsafe for Muus and Varinka to remain in Denmark. An arrested colleague had given a complete description of Muus to the Germans, which, due to the scarring on his face from his plastic surgery, made him very easily recognisable and vulnerable. In any case, he had achieved everything he had set out to do – there was a Danish leader in every region, each with their own wireless set, the Freedom Council was dealing with the 'political side of it' and the reception committees, sabotage, press, intelligence service and escape routes (over which 6,000 Jews had escaped Denmark) were all well organised and run.

Meanwhile, Jutta had been gathering information about Muus, and it seemed that he had returned to his old fraudster ways. She collected evidence to be presented to Turnbull and Hollingworth that Muus was embezzling money meant for the resistance, and gathered enough proof that he would eventually have a major investigation of fraud against him.[41] London wanted him back so they could contain his activities and prevent further incidences, and he was a wanted man by the Danish Gestapo. The time had come for Varinka and Muus to leave Denmark.

■ ■ ■

That summer the stakes were particularly high for all members of the resistance, not least Edith who, despite being arrested three times, was still active in Copenhagen. One day she went to a new depot, the owner of the former establishment having been betrayed and shot some weeks before. The new one was 'an illegal post office on Ny-torv' and Edith was to collect codes, crystals and messages for Duus. The office was also used by couriers for disposing of gear and mes-sages from London that they had collected in Sweden, as well as radio codes that had been packed in a false bottom in cans of soup and were so small that they had to be read with a magnifying glass.

As Edith was picking up the last of her packages, some of which bore her name and others containing telegrams in English, the tele-phone rang. Someone asked if they were speaking to Lagergren. This was the real name of one of her associates, and they never used their real names. Lagergren, who had answered the telephone, told the caller they had the wrong number and hung up, before turning to Edith and uttering, 'We are trapped.'[42]

Before the pair had time to make a plan there was a heavy pound-ing on the door. 'It was horrible,' Edith recalled. 'There were no back doors or back stairs. There was nothing ... to do but to open the door.' Heavily armed Germans and Danish 'henchmen' stormed past them into the room. They could hardly believe their luck when they found the piles of sacks full of mail and packages containing 'all possible secrets'.[43] The men rifled through their loot and then one of them looked up and realised who she was. 'It's Lotte,' he yelled, and raced over to pin her and Lagergren against the wall.[44]

Ordered to put her hands up, Edith felt a gun pushed into her back. But the men's attention soon went back to the sacks on the ground, and Edith took the opportunity to take the new code out of her bag and eat it. 'It was not easy to swallow,' she said. 'I began to shred it with my molars. It tasted disgusting.'[45] As she put her hands back against the wall, they noticed that she had moved. 'She has taken the pill,' one shouted. He grabbed her and shoved her to the floor. When it became apparent that she hadn't poisoned herself, she was pushed down the stairs and taken to a waiting car. Only Lagergren was handcuffed, and he was put in a separate car. 'Were they being gallant to a woman?' she thought as she pondered what awaited her now.[46]

As Edith was driven through the familiar streets of Copenhagen, she stuck her head out of the window in the vain hope that somebody, anybody would see her and realise what had happened. As far as she knew, no one did.[47] Eventually the car stopped at the Shellhus (Shell House). This was the Gestapo's new HQ in the city, since they'd outgrown their previous one at the nearby Dagmarhus. Spanning six floors of offices, interrogation rooms, torture chambers, cells and an archive of Danish resistance members, this was a place to be feared by anyone who involuntarily passed through its doors. Atrocities were committed against resistance members. These included repeatedly beating or burning them, force-feeding them herring and depriving them of water until the thirst drove them mad, and stripping them naked in the freezing winter.[48]

Fearing what was to come, Edith was dragged from the car by two officers. A third pushed a gun into her back and shoved her forward towards the second floor. She defiantly 'met the gaze of a German guard' in the doorway of a large office before being taken inside and told to sit down. Her guards were half drunk and crazed as they proudly declared, 'Well, this is what LOTTE looks like! Finally we have got her,' before passing a bottle of liquor round to celebrate their success.[49] As she watched them, the fear was rising inside her. What was going to happen next with these debauched, drunken men?

It wasn't long before she was taken to the fourth floor, where her interrogation began in earnest. She had done this before, but the terror of being in the Shell House began to dawn on her. She fumbled to make a story out of her fake ID card, telling them that she was a trained seamstress and now the director of a small textile factory, and that she had been at the post office that day to pick up fabric samples. They didn't believe her story, but neither did they need to: 'Don't waste time on her,' a guard spat. 'We have everything on her. Throw her into the cellar.'[50]

Returning to the second floor, Edith was put on a chair in the corridor, and the officer disappeared into the office where he began to talk about her to the others. She feared what might happen to her next. Would she manage to stand up to the horror of torture? Would she keep quiet or would she give away names as they inflicted pain on her in unimaginable ways? How long would she be able to last? Then she looked around. The corridor was still empty and there was no one to be seen. She hesitated, then decided to get up. If anyone asked her what she was doing she would say she was looking for the bathroom. Deciding against taking the lift, she walked down a flight of stairs 'quietly and calmly'. There was 'a quiet voice' deep inside telling her to go on.

She made it down to the next floor, then heard German voices. If these were officers she was doomed. But they were civilians, carrying folders under their arms and going about their business. They looked up at her 'disinterestedly and moved further down'.[51] This was her opportunity to escape. It was now or never. She followed them step by step, so closely that she was almost stepping on their heels. Passing the guard at the entrance, the two civilians gallantly stepped aside – '*Bitte schön*' they said, and gestured to let her pass. With that Edith simply walked out of the Shell House.

Avoiding the easiest route back, which was cordoned off with red and white tape, she walked in the opposite direction, crossing a bridge and getting as much distance between her and the Shell House as possible. 'It was painful,' she said. 'I had to walk quietly and to look natural. Every moment I expected to be shot in the neck. Then I rolled off my white turban. At least they wouldn't recognize me by that.'[52] She asked a nearby ambulance if they would drive her away, explaining that she had just escaped from Gestapo HQ. When the driver refused, she stepped out in front of a tram. 'Are you insane?' the driver yelled at her. 'Yes, I am crazy,' she shouted back, convinced that at any moment she would be shot. She had to get away by any means possible.[53]

Eventually she made it home to Duus. He angrily asked her why she had taken so long. When she told him she had been in the Shell House, he simply looked at her 'seriously for some time'. He didn't hug her, 'but it felt like it. His look and nod was silent admiration. He was never a man of many words.'[54] Soon the phone rang again. Edith froze in terror, but it was Muus calling to tell Duus that she had been arrested. Duus explained that she was sitting there with him and Muus hung up, obviously confused. He called back a few minutes later to say that a mutual acquaintance, Little Pete, had seen her being taken away by the Gestapo, and so it was not possible that she was there with him. 'Well, she left again,' said Duus. 'She didn't like the smell in the bakery.'

Later that evening a friend came to the apartment. He was a Danish policeman and he told them about a manhunt that was taking place near the Shell House. The Germans were running around and asking people if they had seen a woman wearing a black suit and white turban. Edith laughed. Men were so unobservant – she was still wearing her black dress and had put back on her white turban. When the friend realised, he went over to her and hugged her hard. Edith laughed again – she had enjoyed hearing about the reaction to her disappearance. The next day SOE sent a telegram that read, 'Congratulations Lotte.' News about this audacious and bold escape had travelled fast but had also caused tensions among fellow members of the resistance, and Edith 'came incredibly close to being shot' by them.[55]

Senior resistance member 'Citron' said that Edith could not be trusted. In his opinion she could only have got out of the Shell House safely if she had been turned into a double agent, tasked by the Germans to undertake work on their behalf. She was called to a meeting in order to identify her betrayer, but the moment she arrived she knew that 'something was wrong'. To her horror she realised that in each corner of the room stood a young man holding a machine gun. They started to round on her:

'When you get out of the Shell House, you have the whole Gestapo behind you,' said one menacingly.

'The Citronen has warned us,' said another. 'You can't trust Lotte anymore. She must have been given an assignment.'

'You must have slept with the German officers?' said a third in a low voice.[56]

She stumbled backwards, terrified at what they might do to her. They clearly thought she had betrayed them and walked free as a result. The young man who acted as the leader of the group stuck a gun in her stomach, while another came up behind her and stuffed a cotton coat over her head. Powerless to fight back, she was dragged into a car. The injustice of it all hit her hard. She had just escaped the Gestapo and now her own comrades had kidnapped her. 'We work for the same side goddamnit,' she spat. 'I was so angry.' She arrived at a small cottage in Hjortekær and, as the overcoat was removed from her head, she saw the car spin on the gravel, leaving her alone with two men. As she was led into the living room, she deftly took a letter that was lying on the hall table and stuffed it into her pocket. Then 'the all-day interrogation began'.[57]

Armed with Sten guns, the pair asked her about the promises they believed she had made to the German officers, refusing to believe that she had escaped. Round and round the questions went, until the men 'grew weary of the situation'.[58]

She saw her moment and took the letter from her pocket and waved it in their faces. 'You are unprofessional,' she told them. 'You didn't see me take this. If I was an informant, I would have saved it for the Germans.' The two men immediately realised their mistake, and she was released without further questioning or delay. With her nerves still jangling and the horror of what could have been etched on her mind, she was returned to her apartment.[59]

That evening the leader of the group came to her house to tell her they had found the informer. Presenting her with a large bunch of pink carnations, he told her that he was terribly sorry and unhappy about the situation he had placed her in. The following day a meeting was held between Muus, the men who had kidnapped her and Duus. Edith was not invited, even though it was about her. Muus asked if anyone had anything to say: 'Yes,' Duus Hansen said. 'I would like to be allowed to sing a little song.' They looked at him and they knew that something serious was coming. 'Yesterday, someone should have done something that didn't happen. Who is responsible for this?' 'I take responsibility,' Muus said. 'What happened to Lotte can happen to anyone.' Duus then deprived the men of cigarettes and money for a set period, and the matter came to an end. But too many Germans knew what Edith looked like now and, after four arrests, it was felt that her luck might soon run out. She was ordered to go to Sweden and, somewhat reluctantly, she went.[60]

In Sweden, Edith undertook work on the 'Spaghetti' (later known as 'Badminton') wireless connection on behalf of SOE. This was the first time that the foreign consulates were allowed to use it to send messages to London. She also worked on 'Minestrone'. She only sent English material as the Americans could use the official channels, but Edith felt that the consul was too busy messing around with local girls to do his job properly and he was damaging the equipment by tearing out the wires. Edith reported him to the British embassy, and he was dismissed. A replacement was needed and it was felt that she was the perfect fit for the job. She laid wreaths, received downed airmen, helped them in the embassy, bought them train tickets, etc. That Christmas, Duus came to see Edith and told her that the Danish Princes wanted her to go to London. She refused – she wanted to stay and help with 'Minestrone' and undertake her role as consul.

■ ■ ■

In October 1944, Jutta was told to be ready for immediate departure to England, where she would work at SOE HQ. She had been waiting for this opportunity for months. Although Sweden had been exciting and busy, London had always been the end goal. 'It was very exciting,' she recalled, but they were never quite sure when they would leave. Flights were often cancelled at the last moment due to clear weather (in order to aid avoiding German radar and flak) and agents would arrive at the airfield just to be sent home again. Or, worse, they would take off and land and, believing themselves to be in England, step out of the aircraft only to realise they were back in frozen Bromma again.

The night of Jutta's departure was suitably cloudy. She dressed in her woollen flight suit and thick socks, over which she wore a quilted flight suit. Attached to her was a parachute, boat, whistle and red flashlight. Looking and feeling somewhat ungainly, she made her way towards the aircraft, excited that this moment had finally come. The five passengers sat on wooden benches in the pitch black and the inside of the aircraft got increasingly colder until the ceiling had almost frozen up. Despite her multiple layers of clothing, the cold cut through to Jutta's core, making the journey almost unbearable. It was only 'when the ice began to melt from the ceiling and drip into one's lap one knew that one would soon have to land', which, after ten hours of flying in the dark and cold, came as a welcome relief.[61]

In a contravention of the usual rules, it was requested that, after landing and transferring to London, she should be brought in 'through the side door' and not go to the Royal Victoria Patriotic School. It was requested that she be allowed to report to SOE straight away as she was in 'possession of information' to which SOE and SHAEF required immediate access, and they wanted daily contact with her thereafter. Unusually, they provided a 'guarantee' that she would not 'be allowed to contact anyone deemed undesirable' and that she would be made available for MI5 interrogation 'whenever called upon'. It is rare to see such written conviction and faith in an agent, especially one who was locally recruited in the field.[62]

Jutta's first task in London was to deliver a report providing evidence that would convict Muus, not only of cheating the resistance out of millions of kroner, but also of political motivations that went against his role as head of SOE in Denmark. The inner circle there had lost faith in him, and Hollingworth was now his only supporter. 'From early 1944, he began to create intrigue between leading resistance figures, while forging ever warmer relationships with old politicians,' and this could 'smear the Freedom Council as being corrupt'.[63] The only way to handle the issue was to get him to London and hide him, as it would be a catastrophe if this were to come out in Danish resistance circles.[64]

After delivering her report, Jutta went to her aunt's house, which was now home to Christmas Møller. 'Strange', she thought, to see it 'standing quite untouched in a street full of ruins'. She lived at the house for a few weeks until she managed to get a flat of her own. After a short visit to the MI5 clearance at Wandsworth, where they knew everything about her, 'down to the smallest details', and thanked her for her 'cooperation over many years', she left to begin her work for the Danish Military Mission to SHAEF.[65]

London made a huge impact on Jutta – the bomb craters, the broken windows, the blackout curtains, the gas masks and air raid wardens in steel hats. One night, just after she had arrived, she was awoken by a

bomb falling nearby. Her first thought was that she was still in Copenhagen and that this was something to be rejoiced about – another act
of sabotage against the Nazis. But upon remembering that she was in
fact in London she realised it was quite the opposite; it was something
to be feared. The V-2 attacks on London were just beginning, and the
city was in the grip of terror once more. This new weapon travelled
faster than sound. 'If you heard them . . . they had fallen,' Jutta recalled,
'and if you didn't hear them, you were probably dead . . . The world,'
she thought, 'is quite strange.' But in spite of these dangers, she set
about her duties with her usual skill and determination.[66]

She reported to Lieutenant Colonel Villy Lund Hvalkof, who had
two offices in Prince's Garden. One of these he kept for himself while
the rest of the staff shared the other. Jutta found the work underwhelm-
ing and dull after such a busy time in Sweden, 'but,' she said, 'just sitting there meant we were one step closer to being treated as allies.' She
remembered that one day War Captain Ramberg 'sat looking a little
sad. "What the fuck are we sitting here for?"' he said, looking at her.
'We are a symbol,' she replied. They were there to show that Denmark
was an Allied nation and its presence in London proved that. Despite
the fact that Denmark and SOE had worked so closely up until this
point, Jutta was aware that the 'interest on the part of SIS remained . . .
When Nordentoft came over for negotiations around Christmas, Cor-
dot, who was SIS head of northern Europe, contacted him and pressed
hard.'[67] But, heavily influenced by his lover Jutta, Nordentoft was not
in the mood to change anything, and everything continued as before.

Jutta soon got herself a flat in Knightsbridge. It was in the middle of
a bombed-out neighbourhood and stuck out like a sore thumb among
the ruins. There were only two panes of glass left in her windows; the
rest had been nailed up with boards, creating an odd creaking sound
at night. Flemming Juncker and his colleague Svend Truelsen had 'a
lovely apartment in Chiltern Court above Baker Street Station', and it
became a meeting point for all of them. The discussions often went
on well into the night. With SOE in the same building, they brushed

shoulders with agents and visitors from the USA, Norway and Sweden. They even shared a cleaning lady (she had been vetted and cleared for secret work), who must have seen and heard everything. One day Jutta heard Ole Lippmann (Muus's replacement in Denmark) shouting, 'Mrs Hitchmann, Mrs Hitchmann, where are the German orders of battle?'

■ ■ ■

In November 1944, Muus crossed by boat to Sweden. A week later, Varinka followed. As she left Copenhagen, the sky was lit red and orange from the fire that engulfed the East Asiatic building. This had been bombed and now blazed, lighting up the night sky along the docks. Varinka boarded the boat and was crammed below the deck with five others in a space originally meant for two, as well as with all the cargo. The air raid had delayed the boat, making the trip much longer and therefore more uncomfortable than planned. Eventually she transferred to a pilot boat and arrived in Falsterbo cold, wet and rather cross. She was met by a colleague carrying a huge bouquet of red and white carnations and, as with Jutta before her, she had to wait for her flight out of Sweden to Scotland. Varinka and Flemming's flight was held up by unsuitable weather and the Muuses, with no work to speak of, enjoyed their first Christmas together as a married couple. Varinka marvelled at 'all the lights, no blackouts, lots of food, wine and things in the shops. It was a marvellous Christmas.'[68]

■ ■ ■

That December, Jutta tried to make the best of the shortages and rationing in London and bring a little Danish magic to the flat at Chiltern Court where, on Christmas Eve, Hollingworth and some parachutists who were about to go back to Denmark gathered. Jutta had decorated a small Christmas tree with ornaments borrowed from her aunt. They ate goose and Jutta made the best version she could of traditional *risalamande* (a rich rice pudding served with cherries) using porridge oats and boiling water. Everyone appreciated the effort to make it feel homely and 'the atmosphere was good', she recalled, 'but those going home were a little quiet'.[69]

During this time there was discussion between the mission and SOE about where Jutta would be best placed with her skills and expertise. Nordentoft believed that her 'qualifications were not being used to the full' and 'her up to date knowledge of personalities and conditions in the field [was] undoubtedly being wasted' in her work in the mission.[70] The experience she possessed that would allow her to undertake the new job they had in mind was unparalleled. She was 'well informed of all details concerning our activities in the field' and she was 'conversant with identities and code names of most of our representatives, with the intelligence network in the field and with a host of other activities including sea operations'.[71] Nordentoft concluded that if she wasn't accepted for the work in SOE HQ, he would have her back in Sweden, 'where she is ill spared'.[72]

After Christmas, Jutta was transferred from the mission to Denmark's SOE office in agreement with Nordentoft and at Hollingworth's personal request. Jutta was delighted to transfer but, before she could begin, she had to go to the 'holy of holies, SOE's head office in Baker Street' to obtain her pass.[73] She was disappointed at how plain it was but she enjoyed meeting two 'elegant super-aristocratic ladies who were also dazzlingly talented', who encouraged her with a 'kind word'. And so it began.[74] She enjoyed her new job immensely, working alongside Flemming Juncker and Svend Truelsen. They kept her much busier than 'the mission' had, and it proved to be to her liking.[75] Hollingworth had something special in store for Jutta and told her that he wanted her to learn to parachute, alongside Varinka Muus, who would be at the intelligence department any day from Sweden. The training would mean that she could return to Denmark quickly if they needed her. Stunned, Jutta said she would need to think it over. Before she could answer yes or no, she contracted jaundice and was bedridden.

■ ■ ■

In the new year, Varinka and Muus boarded a blacked-out aircraft at Bromma to get to England via Scotland. Despite wearing several layers of clothing and boots, 'and god knows what' else, Varinka's abiding memory was how cold the seven-hour journey had been.[76] Once they'd transferred to London, Muus went to report to SOE HQ in Baker Street and found out they had something lined up for Varinka too. In fact, while she had been enjoying her time off in Stockholm, SOE had been busy preparing for her arrival.

A file noting that she was due to arrive 'any day' also noted that Mrs Muus, who 'has worked for us in the field for approx. 2 years . . . is urgently required in London for operational reasons' and that she would be proceeding to Copenhagen as soon as 'the SHAEF mission (Denmark) has approved the sending of women to Denmark'. She should be given suitable work that would enable her to leave at a moment's notice.[77] Hollingworth requested that she be commissioned into FANY, in the same way 'as other agents [were] . . . for different country sections'. He also noted that Mrs Muus's British mother currently languished in a concentration camp for her part in the Danish underground movement, her death sentence having been commuted to life.[78]

Varinka's training was to begin on 25 February 1945 with a stint at STS 51, Ringway's parachute school. After this she would attend 'Group B' or 'finishing school at Beaulieu followed by a 96-hour scheme.'[79] As she already had 'considerable experience in the field', it was requested that going to the effort of finding a suitable female conducting officer was unnecessary in her case.[80]

Varinka had barely settled into her lodgings in the Mount Royal Hotel in Marble Arch before she was whisked off to her first training school near Manchester. She was accompanied by her husband, who had just been promoted to second lieutenant. The instructors at STS 51 were concerned that her slight build would mean she would not be 'strong enough' to withstand the rigours of parachute training, which could be enough to preclude her from undertaking the course.[81] Her husband also harboured concerns about her slight frame and looked on with fear from the ground as his young wife prepared to jump. Despite being the first to jump, she was the last to land, drifting downwards like a feather. Her slow descent gave her plenty of time to view her husband from above and upon landing she jested with him about his baldness, before watching him undertake the same exercise.[82]

As well as her sharp tongue, Varinka also possessed a stamina and nerve that SOE staff admired: her 'mental skill and determination' saw her through, she was 'calm and collected' at all times and she proved herself 'quite able to undertake the strains of ground training and shocks of landing'.[83] In fact her light weight enabled her to make 'extremely easy landings on all three descents'.[84]

■ ■ ■

Although she was unable to join Varinka at STS 51, Jutta hadn't let being bedridden stop her keeping in touch with the war effort. She allowed Danish friends to host meetings in her 'dark and windy' apartment, so that she could get the latest news from the front and from Denmark.[85] Prescribed a glass of port every evening from an elderly doctor and wearing a ghastly teal-coloured nightie that she had been brought, Jutta wondered if she would ever recover. She thought she was hallucinating the night she awoke to find two policemen standing at the foot of her bed. Her landlady had reported her for having so many foreign people visiting her and had accused her of being a spy. Jutta laughed, showed the policemen her papers and, after a good chat about bombers and spies, they left her – telling her to get better quickly as the war needed her. After this episode, Jutta moved back into her aunt's house and quickly recovered. But she had missed her chance to learn to parachute. 'When I later remarked that I was a little upset that it hadn't come to fruition,' she said, 'the others laughed at me and said, "You! You're way too old!" I had to admit in my quiet mind that I was relieved to be free.'[86]

■ ■ ■

By March 1945, SOE had a much bigger mission to deliver as the RAF, at the request of SOE, made preparations to bomb the Shell House. For months, reports, photographs and drawings had been sent from Denmark to help prepare a scale model of the area of Copenhagen in which the Shell House was located. Complete with access roads and replicas of the nearby buildings, the model was studied by the pilots who would be responsible for the mission, which would involve a low-level attack. They studied 'the buildings, the houses, everything . . . how the approach should be, where the bombs should fall – everything.'[87] They also received lectures and information from Svend Truelsen.

The target had been chosen by SOE at the request of the Danish resistance movement in Copenhagen, which was in danger of being wiped out by the Gestapo. Not only were many of their leaders in-carcerated in the Shell House, it also housed a wealth of Gestapo files and archives on the resistance workers. These had to be destroyed if the underground movement were to survive. The raid was exception-ally risky and would endanger the lives of not only the airmen and civilians, but also the twenty-six members of the resistance move-ment who had been housed in the attic of the Shell House to act as a living shield. The Gestapo hoped that this would prevent another raid like the one at the University of Aarhus in October 1944, which had resulted in the death of approximately 150 to 200 Gestapo mem-bers and 30 Danes.[88]

Varinka, who was waiting to start her Group B training, knew when the attack (codenamed Operation 'Carthage') would be. Early in the morning on 21 March, she sought out the company of Jutta and Hollingworth's PA Maisie Defries, so that she had company when the raid began.[89] As they arrived at the office, Varinka saw that it was 8.15 a.m. At that moment at RAF Fersfield, twenty Mosquito bomb-ers escorted by twenty-eight Mustang fighters took off for Denmark with the sole aim of destroying the Shell House. The hours passed slowly. If all went to plan, the aircraft would attack in three waves at staggered intervals, 'just before the lunch break, while the Germans very likely were working with open safes, so that documents would be set ablaze'.[90]

As the hours seemed to drag by Jutta, Varinka and Maisie tried to work but kept glancing at the clock ticking painfully slowly on the wall. 'We knew the minute the attack would take place,' said Jutta. She also 'knew several of the prisoners who were imprisoned on the top floor of the Shell House', making this whole affair even more torturous for her than it already was. At exactly the moment the first bombs were due to fall on the Shell House the air at SOE HQ was rent with the whistle and whip-crack of a V-2.[91] The blast wave that was created by the rocket that hit Primrose Hill gave way to 'the chaos of the explosion with debris and earth churned skyward'.[92] Amazed at the coincidence, the three decided to get back to work. The day was far from over and they continued to wait anxiously for news of the Copenhagen attack.

That evening, Truelsen came back from the airfield with the news that Operation 'Carthage' had been a huge success. The building had been obliterated, along with files inside it, and a hundred Gestapo had been killed. Of the twenty-six resistance fighters inside the building, eighteen had survived, some of whom managed to escape. Others were transferred to Vestre Fængsel prison.

However, a catastrophe had also occurred when pilots of the second wave mistook the smoke from a downed aircraft as the target and bombed the area. They hit the Jeanne D'Arc school (also known as the French School), which was packed with children going about their daily lessons. The third wave saw the flames and dropped their bombs. Two high explosives directly hit the school, where children and staff were taking refuge in the underground bomb shelter. Another thirteen hit the area nearby. One hundred and twenty-three civilians were killed, eighty-seven of whom were schoolchildren. War Captain Jegstrup, who had gone to the Danish Military Mission at the same time as Jutta, had two little girls at the French school. Jutta dreaded telling him about the bombardment; luckily, he found out almost immediately that they were safe.

256

■ ■ ■

In late March, Varinka completed her time at Group B in Beaulieu, where she not only undertook SOE training but educated the students there about life in the field. She was liked by her instructors, who saw her as 'quick thinking, logical' and with sound judgement.[93] Varinka recalled learning 'all sorts of things' – how to shoot, how to steal from a house and how to 'pick the locks [or] lose a man who "followed her"'.[94] She learned to recognise different types of German weapons and vehicles. 'It was really fun,' she said, 'to see if one could out manoeuvre the enemy.'[95]

Varinka showed herself to be a strong, determined character, but she never once tried to impress others 'with her special knowledge or qualifications'. Instead she helped them by showing an interest in the course and in their welfare. An 'interesting conversationalist' with a 'good sense of humour', Varinka was considered loyal, someone who would put themselves 'unconditionally under the orders of someone she admired and would sacrifice everything for a purpose she considered worthwhile'.[96] Conversely, it was thought that she was so 'strong' and 'determined' that she 'could be ruthless if her plans were interfered with'.[97] Ultimately, the end of the war interfered with her plans to parachute back into Denmark and her mission was cancelled.

Her strength and resolve soon melted away when, on 30 March, Varinka received the news via the Red Cross that she had been dreading:

I arrived in London and Flemming welcomed me and I was full of stories about everything I experienced and saw. He said, 'I have something to tell you and have been told your mother had died at Waldheim in Germany of viral pneumonia, brought on by starvation, hellish living conditions and the harshest privations.'[98]

Varinka was heartbroken, feeling a 'great, great sorrow that it was evil' that killed her mother and that she had not been executed.[99] At least that would have been quick, she mused. But Monica had been 'at the mercy of the Germans. Hunger and cold and then finally dying in Dresden' – it was something Varinka swore she would never forgive and never forget.[100]

■ ■ ■

A week after the Shell House raid, Jutta was preparing to return to Sweden. She had been requested by Nordentoft and Mørch, 'as the workload in the last phase of the war had seriously increased'.[101] After bidding the SOE department farewell, she took the sleeper to Scotland and stayed in St Andrews, along with several others waiting for their flights. The unusually good weather was hampering their plans to return quickly. When she finally got word that her flight was on, she dressed in the same cumbersome clothes and equipment that she had worn outbound and settled down, excited to be heading back to Scandinavia on such an important mission:

> We were only two passengers in the machine, a slightly fat older gentleman and me. I sat behind the gentleman, who promptly fell asleep; but every time he snored, the little red light shone on his shoulder. With that as entertainment, and with the awareness of the boxes I had seen when I boarded, which filled up the rest of the space in the machine and looked eerily like boxes containing explosives.[102]

Jutta thought 'it was great' to be back in Stockholm, which was much busier than before.[103] She was attached to General Dewing during his visit to discuss the Danish Brigade (a military unit made up of Danish refugees who were trained and supplied by Sweden with the intention of helping liberate Denmark). During his visit she helped him find items that were no longer available in Denmark and recalled sitting in a hardware store watching him choose 'nails, screws, hooks and fittings' to fix his roof back home.[104] Dewing was recalled to England at the end of April. Following Hitler's suicide he was needed to help prepare for the end of the war.

When the time came to mobilise the Danish Brigade, the intelligence department in Stockholm moved to Malmö, which was closer to Denmark. Jutta was put in charge of a clandestine telephone exchange that went from Malmö harbour to Charlottenlund Fort. For the next forty-eight hours she heard 'surrender negotiations, the peace message, the sending of the first groups to Denmark. The brigade and fleet were ordered to come home.' She was at the forefront of it all and among the first to know that the war was nearly over.[105]

On the afternoon of 5 May, Jutta and Captain Winkel climbed into one of the tugboats that until recently had sailed illegally with intelligence material on board. Now, in the full light of day, the little boat could sail freely with the *Dannebrog* fluttering proudly behind it. Despite the tug's small size, the naval officers sailing it could not resist circling around the German warships at anchor and blasting their horn in an act of sheer defiance and one-upmanship. The Germans 'stared in astonishment' at them.[106] 'It was strange to set foot on Danish soil again on a day like this,' Jutta thought.[107]

For Varinka, the end of the war interfered with her plans to parachute back into Denmark. Her mission was cancelled and she was demobbed, returning to Denmark a few days after the liberation, which she remembered as being a mess:

> All the people who hadn't done anything came out and they all wore arm bands and they all shouted hurray and they had all been resistance . . . It was sad . . . frustrating, on one hand we did reach our objective that Denmark wasn't looked down on as Hitler's tame canary which was what Denmark was to begin with.[108]

Her frustration at others claiming to be what they were not is clear and understandable. She had risked everything to resist the occupation and was even prepared to parachute back into Denmark to continue the fight underground. But claiming to have resisted helped sweep away the guilt of 'cooperation' for so many years.

The following day, Jutta reported to the General Staff and handed in the papers and cash she had brought with her from the office in Sweden. That evening she watched as long lines of German soldiers, with their heads bowed and shoulders slumped, marched out of Copenhagen. It was a very different atmosphere from when they had arrived five years earlier, hanging out of the trains and singing at the tops of their lungs. 'There was a festive atmosphere,' she said, 'and peace was celebrated.'[109] But Jutta still had work to do. She was sent back to Stockholm to close the offices and settle the accounts. The city was no longer the 'seething centre of espionage' but had ground to a halt and was once again 'a beautiful and quiet Swedish town'.[110]

After this she went to London to 'clean up the last of us', as SOE closed its office doors and weeded down its files.[111] The work of the SOE women from Denmark became a vague memory, obscured by women in other sections, whose work had been perceived as far more glamorous, dangerous and even more worthy of praise. The vital courier, wireless and secretarial work of the Danish women was carried out with bravery and courage in the face of an enemy that would stop at nothing to prevent it. Without Jutta, Edith and Varinka, the work of SOE in Denmark and Sweden could and would have been markedly different.

10

MISSION PALMACH

I could have been
twenty-three next July;
I gambled on what mattered most,
The dice were cast, I lost.

Hannah Szenes, 20 June 1944[1]

That thirty-two Jewish 'parachutists' from Mandate Palestine attempted to halt the deportation of Jews and effectively stop the Holocaust in its tracks deserves to be lauded in Second World War history. While these men and women are revered as heroes and heroines within Israel, their stories are seldom told elsewhere, though most of them had only recently emigrated from Europe to Mandate Palestine. The names of those who undertook these phenomenally brave, if somewhat reckless, missions are virtually unknown in the countries of their birth and upbringing.

This chapter aims to rectify that situation as far as the women are concerned and to put the names of Hannah Szenes, Haviva Reik and Sara Braverman on the international stage where they rightfully belong. These women had all emigrated from Europe prior to the war, and were of European heritage. Their roles took them back to territories across Eastern Europe.

Along with their male counterparts, they set out to undertake missions in Hungary, Romania and Slovakia as part of an SOE/MI9 mission to help Allied airmen and POWs to escape. But they also had their own mission to try to save the remaining Jewish populations in those countries, before every one of them was annihilated as part of the 'Final Solution'. They wanted to halt the constant flow of Jews being sent to the gas chambers and to help them find their way to Mandate Palestine.

To think that a handful of agents could succeed in doing this is incredible, foolhardy even, but they wanted to try. As Hannah Szenes said, 'Even if they catch me – the Jews will be notified. They will know that at least one person tried to reach them.'[2] Her mission was to take her back to her homeland of Hungary, where the situation for the Jews was reaching crisis point.

The story of the Kingdom of Hungary during the Second World War is as complex as it is tragic, with hundreds of thousands of innocent lives lost as the country struggled to come to terms with its fight both for and against Nazi Germany. The struggle had started in the wake of the Great War, when the Austro-Hungarian monarchy was dissolved. The Treaty of Trianon (1920) redefined Hungary's thousand-year-old borders. It left her landlocked and a mere 28 per cent of her former size, with a population that was 36 per cent of its pre-treaty extent.

Eventually, due to Italian and German arbitration, Hungary managed to get some of its territory back from Czechoslovakia and Romania following the First and Second Vienna Awards. This was also as a consequence of Hungary's invasion and occupation of Subcarpathia (Rusynsko).

Throughout the 1930s, Hungary increasingly relied on trade with Italy and Germany to help pull themselves out of the problems caused by the Great Depression. In November 1940, Hungary became a signatory to the Tripartite Pact with Germany, Italy and Japan, making it one of the Axis powers. The following year, Hungarian forces were involved in the invasion of Yugoslavia and the Soviet Union. During the occupation, Hungarian troops faced challenges they were not prepared for and, soon, the whirlpool of partisan warfare dragged them into the abyss of counter-insurgency terror and arbitrary violence.

There was much bloodshed on the Eastern Front in 1943. The Soviets' breakthrough at the Don River sliced through the Hungarian units fighting there, and the Hungarian Second Army was defeated at the Battle of Voronezh. After two years of war against the Soviet Union, Hungary had grown battle-weary. It had lost 50,000 soldiers on the battlefields or to the harsh winters, with 70,000 becoming POWs or missing in action during the onslaught at the Don.

In autumn 1943, Hungary's prime minister, Miklós Kállay, began peace negotiations with the United States and the United Kingdom. However, these powers were more interested in distracting German troops from Normandy than in offering a way out for Hungary.

Berlin was already suspicious of Kállay's government and, antagonised by Hungary's change in alliance, Hitler launched Operation 'Margarethe'. On 19 March 1944, German troops occupied Hungary. They were met with light resistance from some units, but most didn't fight back at all, and in some instances, the German troops were even greeted as allies. The regent Miklós Horthy was placed under house arrest, and Döme Sztójay (an avid supporter of the Nazis) became the new prime minister in what was now effectively a puppet state. Thousands were arrested, and others were forced underground. Non-Germanophile political parties and newspapers were banned, and the Gestapo thoroughly purged the civil and military administration.

As elsewhere in Nazi-occupied countries, the Jewish population became isolated from the outside world. Their movements were restricted, they were forced to wear the yellow star and Jewish-owned property and businesses were seized. From mid to late April, the Jews of Hungary were forced into ghettos, which were essentially urban transit camps. These ghettos were short-lived, and in the fifty-six days between 15 May and 9 July 1944, 440,000 Jews were deported by train, most of them straight to the gas chambers of Auschwitz-Birkenau. By the end of July 1944, the only Jewish community left in Hungary was in Budapest.

In light of the deteriorating military situation, and facing threats from Allied leaders of war crimes trials, Horthy ordered a halt to the deportations on 7 July 1944. A few weeks later, he dismissed Sztójay and resumed efforts to reach an armistice with the Soviet Union, who were now amassing on Hungary's borders. Just as he was entering into the final negotiations, the Germans kidnapped his son and staged a *coup d'état*. Horthy was forced to revoke the armistice and was deposed from power.

He was replaced by Ferenc Szálasi, the leader of the Arrow Cross, a far-right Hungarian ultranationalist party. During its short rule, the Arrow Cross murdered between 10,000 and 15,000 civilians, including many Jews and Romani, and deported 80,000 people to concentration camps in Austria. The Hungarian Nazi leader established a new government. His fanaticism, anti-Semitism and fascist tendencies suited the Nazi occupiers well. The Arrow Cross now began a reign of arbitrary terror against the Jews of Budapest. In November 1944, a ghetto was formed in the city, and the remaining Jews were ordered inside.

Almost as soon as the ghetto was established, deportations began, and more than half of those who had been forced into the ghetto were sent to concentration camps. The remaining Jewish population of Budapest was reduced from 200,000 to 70,000 in the ghetto. The plight of the Jews in Hungary did not go unnoticed or unchallenged, however, and approximately 20,000 Jews were housed in specially marked houses outside the ghetto. They had been granted diplomatic protection by neutral politicians such as Raoul Wallenberg, who issued them with protective passports on behalf of the Swedish legation, and Carl Lutz, who did the same via the Swiss government. They had Hungarian comrades who worked effectively to save as many lives as possible. Besides Wallenberg and Lutz, many Hungarians managed to hide, protect and save more lives. There was also a

Zionist branch of the resistance, which was being formed from various groups, standing against the Arrow Cross.

In spring 1944, Joel Brand, a member of the Budapest Aid and Rescue Committee, a Zionist group that had previously smuggled Jews to the relative safety of Hungary, was approached by Adolf Eichmann, a key figure in the 'Final Solution', who oversaw the deportations and made sure quotas were met. Eichmann proposed 'goods for blood, blood for goods'. He would exchange the lives of a million Jews for 10,000 army trucks for use on the Eastern Front.[3] He asked Brand, 'What Jews do you want to save?'[4]

Eichmann's plan was to send Brand to Istanbul, where he would negotiate with Jewish leaders for the delivery of the trucks. As soon as this was confirmed, the killing facilities at Auschwitz-Birkenau would be blown up and the first 100,000 Jews released. Brand took Eichmann at his word and left Hungary in May but was arrested by the British at the Turkish–Syrian frontier.[5] He was refused permission to return to Budapest and taken to Cairo for interrogation. Unable to fulfil his mission, he believed that the Allied governments (and even some Jewish leaders) had 'failed to believe him, failed to help his mission and failed to save the lives of thousands of Jews'.[6]

Brand was released in October 1944 but by then hundreds of thousands of Jews had died in the gas chambers at Auschwitz-Birkenau in the largest mass extermination in the camp's sordid history. Arriving in Eretz Israel, Brand and the heads of the Jewish settlement there continued to plead for the trucks, but the British turned down the arrangement with the Nazis. Brand later said, 'An accident of life placed the fate of one million human beings on my shoulders . . . I eat and sleep and think only of them.'[7]

The plight of the Jews in Eastern Europe had also reached the ears of three women in Eretz Israel, who decided they had to help: Hannah Szenes, Sara Braverman and Haviva Reik.

■ ■ ■

Born in Budapest on 17 July 1921, Anikó Szenes, known as Hannah from the age of seventeen, grew up in an assimilated Jewish family in Budapest. Her father, Béla Szenes, was a playwright and actor, but he died when Hannah was just six years old, and she and her brother Gyiirgy (Giora) were raised by their mother, Katalin (Katerina). Grief-stricken, Hannah had to adapt to life without her beloved father and, even from an early age, she followed in his footsteps as an accomplished and talented writer, with her grandmother helping her by noting down her early poems.

Attending a Protestant private girls' school (which, in return for triple the usual fees, accepted Jewish pupils), Hannah excelled and was often top of her class. She liked to help teachers by looking after pupils in their absence, which allowed her to tell stories to keep the children entertained. She and her brother also attended 'play afternoons' at the English-Hungarian school, where they learned the English language. For the school's tenth anniversary, Hannah was commissioned to write a poem and was delighted to receive her first-ever writer's fee. Together with her brother, she created a newspaper called *Petit Sensei*, copies of which were passed around in exchange for chocolate. Aged thirteen, Hannah began her diary and studied Hungarian literature, deciding that one day she would become a professional author or poet.

Despite growing up in a Jewish household, it was only at school that Hannah began to learn about 'the foundations of faith and religion' and became involved 'in all Jewish activities'. Despite this seemingly idyllic childhood, Hannah fell victim to anti-Semitism. After the passing of the Nuremberg Laws in Germany in 1935, Hungary became awash with violent demonstrations against the Jewish community. Undeterred or even spurred on by this tidal change, Hannah decided she wanted to learn more about her Jewish heritage. She joined the Zionist Youth Movement, read Zionist-Jewish literature and began to learn Hebrew. This put her in good stead for the new life she was planning for herself: immigration to Mandate

Palestine. She said that 'even if she had not been born a Jew, she would still have been on the side of the Jews, because if a people is suffering such a grave injustice, they must be helped in every way possible'.[8]

Her mother was against the move and tried to persuade Hannah to stay, especially since Giora had gone to study textiles at the University of Lyons in France. But Hannah's many 'clever and persuasive arguments' chipped away at her mother's resistance, and when they visited her brother in the spring of 1939, Hannah discovered that Giora had also become a committed Zionist and wished to emigrate to Mandate Palestine. Delighted to have found a comrade with whom to share her ideals, she and her brother joyfully planned their trip with 'youthful enthusiasm and sparkling eyes'. Hannah had secured a place at the girls' agricultural school in Nahalal. Giora would join her once he had finished his studies, and they hoped that their mother would soon follow. In a moment of foreboding, Katerina wrote: 'Suddenly, it was as if an icy hand gripped my heart: will the three of us ever sit together like this again? Where and when!'[9]

Hannah graduated from high school with flying colours. Despite her teacher's fervent wishes that she should continue her education at university, Hannah pressed ahead with her plans to attend agricultural school, enabling her to work on a kibbutz. She argued that 'there are too many intellectuals in Mandate Palestine, whereas what is needed first and foremost are building hands. Who should do this work if not us young people?' On 21 July 1939, four days before her eighteenth birthday, Hannah received her immigration certificate. She wrote in her diary: 'I've got it, I've got it . . . I am filled with happiness. I can't believe it. I have read and re-read the letter, hearing the good news, now I can't find the words to express what I feel.'[10]

On 13 September, just as war was beginning to ravage Europe and the persecution of the Jews was intensifying, Hannah left her childhood home for the last time. At Budapest railway station, she bid her mother farewell. Katerina recalled:

Standing at the window of the train, [Hannah] was once again overcome by suppressed sobs. The tension and excitement of the last weeks and months have been filled with the knowledge of divorce, final separation and a completely uncertain future. The train pulled out, and a shadow fell over the whole station.[11]

Returning to an empty home, Katerina lit candles to mark the Jewish festival of Rosh Hashana, while with a sense of trepidation, Hannah began her long journey to Mandate Palestine.

Travelling via Istanbul, Hannah boarded a Romanian ship. The passengers were primarily Palestinians on their way home from a visit to Europe, whose presence gave Hannah an excellent opportunity to practise her Hebrew. There were also Poles and Czechs fleeing Europe in the wake of war. The ship docked in Haifa on 21 September, where Hannah spent two days before taking a bus to Nahalal to begin her new life.

She wrote in her diary: 'I am in Nahalal, in Eretz. I am home … here almost every life is the fulfilment of a mission … everything is beautiful, everything is good, and I'm happy that I am able to be here.'[12] Arriving at the school, she was assigned to a dormitory on the farm and found it 'nice and comfortable despite its smallness'.[13] But despite finally fulfilling her dream, Hannah found it difficult to acclimatise to her new life. The physical labour, the hours of housekeeping to which first-year students were assigned and the difficulty of making new friends were hard. The sun beating down and the dryness of the climate were all in stark contrast to the elegant houses and leafy suburbs of the world that she had left behind, and she desperately missed her mother.

As the weeks became months, Hannah eventually settled into the routine of life at Nahalal. As her education neared an end, she debated which course her life should take. She thought of becoming a teacher, a writer or a member of the kibbutz. Meanwhile, she received several marriage proposals, all of which she turned down.

She was also working towards her mother's immigration to Mandate Palestine. She missed her terribly, and since Giora would soon arrive, she wanted the family to be together again.

However, the position of Mandate Palestine itself soon became very precarious due to its geographical location. After the fall of Yugoslavia in April 1941, the German push into northern Greece from Bulgaria and Yugoslavia, and the heavy fighting in Libya, the fighting front was moving ever closer to the Palestinian border. Fear for the country's Jews, should the Nazis invade, was widespread. Meanwhile, in Hungary, Jewish law reached a severity that was even harsher than that of Nazi Germany. Many of those who considered themselves to be non-Jewish were now deemed by the government and by law to be Jewish (considered to be their race as opposed to those who were Jewish by religion). As such, they were subjected to all the restrictions and discrimination that the designation brought with it. In autumn 1941, thousands of Jews were murdered in a brutal massacre by Hungarian policemen supervised by the SS.

At that time, Hannah joined the Sdot Yam (Fields of the Sea) kibbutz at Haifa (with a view to building a new settlement at Caesarea) for a probationary period.[14] She worked in the kitchen and the kibbutz laundry, all the while keeping a detailed diary of her activities and feelings. After a brief interim at Ginosar kibbutz, she returned to Sdot Yam, hoping to make that her permanent residence. Despite fulfilling her dreams of helping to build the settlement, she missed the opportunity to study or read, resulting in her becoming lonely and cut off from the others.

By April 1942, she had found a new outlet for her enthusiasm and dedication: 'I have given considerable thought to enlistment,' she wrote. 'The entire country is being asked to mobilise for the war effort, as the war is coming closer.'[15] Following this sudden desire to enlist, Hannah was elected to the recruitment committee of Sdot Yam and, as a result, was put forward as a suitable candidate for the Palmach.

The Palmach (meaning strike companies) were the strike or attacking arm of the Haganah (meaning defence). This was part of the Jewish Agency and was the underground military organisation of the Yishuv in Eretz Israel from 1920 to 1948.[16] The Haganah wasn't just defensive in intent and training; it was designed for point defence. While the former attacked and could be deployed anywhere in Mandate Palestine, the latter defended, which inevitably involved different training techniques and missions. In 1941, six Palmach companies were established as national and regional combat reserve units. Volunteers received basic military training so they would be prepared for immediate action if needed.

By 1942, due to the threat of invasion by the Germans via the Western Desert and Egypt, the Palmach temporarily gained the support of the British army.[17] Members were trained in 'sabotage, patrols, marksmanship, face to face combat, field training and squad commander training'. This training took place in the forests of Mishmar Ha'emek, Ben-Shemen and Hanita.[18] Various units were established, including the Balkan unit, which trained members for operations in German-occupied territory. Their mission would be to assist in the rescue of downed Allied airmen and aid the beleaguered Jewish populations.

The idea for this unit was mooted in 1942 when the Jewish Agency in Mandate Palestine started to look for ways in which they could aid the Allied war effort. If they contributed to the war, it was hoped that the British might ease restrictions on Zionist activities and Jewish immigration into the country (which had been restricted in 1939 as a means to end an Arab rebellion in Mandate Palestine). The other main motive was the preservation of European Jewry through the provision of aid and escape efforts.[19]

In the winter of 1942, Giora left France hoping to make it to Mandate Palestine, having discovered that it was still possible to get there via Spain or North Africa. He took a bus to the Spanish border but, while attempting to cross the Pyrenees, a fellow escapee became ill.

He took her to a nearby village, but while there, the escapees were arrested and Giora was thrown in prison in Figueres, near the French border. For two weeks, he lived in appalling conditions with little in the way of food or water. After this, he was moved to a prison near Barcelona, then to the Miranda de Ebro camp and finally to a prison in Vichy Catalan. He could do nothing now but wait.

Oblivious of her brother's fate, Hannah was surprised when, in February 1943, a member of the Palmach named Yonah Rosen visited the kibbutz. He had met Hannah before and had been impressed by her demeanour and bearing. He told her of a proposed parachute mission to Europe to help save the Jews. He knew nothing of Brand and the Hungarian Relief and Rescue committee that had been set up in June 1942, but news had spread that the Warsaw Ghetto Uprising had been crushed. So, as far as he knew, nobody was doing anything to stop the slaughter. He went on to tell Hannah that units of Jewish parachutists would be dropped into various countries and 'would only consist of nationals of that particular country'. The enterprise was supported by the British, who would offer training, equipment and aircraft. In return, the agent's priority was to help downed Allied airmen by opening new escape routes in collaboration with local partisans. After that, they would be free to help 'their own people'.[20]

Hannah wrote in her diary, 'My answer, of course, was that I'm absolutely ready. It's still only in the planning stage, but he promised to bring up the matter before the enlistment committee since he considers me admirably suited for the mission . . . we'll see what the future brings.'[21] Several weeks went by before Hannah heard anything from Rosen. During this time, the news from Europe was worsening: Hungarian Jews were being forced to wear yellow stars, could no longer work and were informed that they would eventually be 'evacuated east'. The meaning of this was becoming very clear: a one-way ticket to Auschwitz-Birkenau or Majdanek.

Hannah became increasingly frustrated and depressed. The news from Hungary desperately upset her; she was worried about her mother and also about Giora, from whom she had heard nothing. Life at Sdot Yam continued to leave her tired, and she was lonely. She began to feel that everything she had done so far in her life had been to prepare her for this mission. She did her work as usual, and although she craved company and friendship, she believed it would be easier to leave if she remained alone. 'I pray for only one thing,' she wrote in her diary in April 1943, 'that the period of waiting will not be too long and that I can see action soon. As for the rest – I am afraid of nothing.'[22] Weeks later, she was called for an interview.

Sitting before a panel of British army officials and Jewish representatives of Haganah, Hannah was grilled about her motives, what kinds of decisions she would make 'in the field' and if she was clear about the objectives of the mission. By the end of it, she had convinced the British she was suitable for the job, but the members of Haganah thought she showed 'all the appalling naivety of someone who had just signed their own death warrant'.[23] On 12 June, Sdot Yam agreed to Hannah's enlistment into the British army, and she spent the rest of the summer waiting for the training course to begin. Months passed and Hannah's frustration grew; ever more troubling news came in from new immigrants, and she felt she was treading water and achieving nothing.

In December 1943, the wait was over. Hannah was called to Palmach HQ at a kibbutz named Ramat Hakovesh. Here she was to begin her training, which, along with her mission, was overseen, in part, by SOE. While Hannah has a personnel file, her training notes and reports are not included, and she did not record details of her training in her diary entries or letters for security reasons, as well as to avoid worrying her family. She became one of thirty-two volunteers (twenty kibbutzniks and twelve Jews from the British army), including two other women, Haviva Reik and Surica Braverman, who were to undertake three training courses. The first two, basic training and parachute jumping, were to be held in Mandate Palestine, while the intelligence training was undertaken in Cairo. The women were enlisted in the Women's Auxiliary Air Force (WAAF) and the men into the RAF. At basic training, Hannah learned how to fire various weapons: the Sten gun, Tommy gun, Colt .45 and German Schmeisser, all the while hoping that she would never have to use them in anger. She also undertook close combat and silent killing, learning how to use the 'Kapap' knife, which was usually carried by Israeli shepherds, as well as her bare hands and body weight against her opponents.

The parachute training involved five jumps in as many days and a night jump. Hannah did not seem to suffer from nerves. After she had completed her training, she told fellow trainee and mission colleague Yoel Palgi that 'it's not so bad. It can even be exciting. I'll never forget how Nahalal looked from the air.'[24] Palgi was very taken with Hannah, describing her as 'tall, fine-featured, with blue eyes and wavy brown hair. The blue grey of her uniform enhanced the colour of her eyes. There was something winning about her.' The two hit it off immediately: 'We knew we were united by a deep bond, at the alliance of comrades in arms, front line fighters.'[25] The two remained close until their mission abruptly ended.

After completing her parachute training, Hannah spent a few days in Tel Aviv before heading to Cairo. During this time, on 11 January 1944, she wrote the last ever entry in her diary: 'This week I leave for Egypt. I'm a soldier . . . I want to believe that what I've done and will do are right. Time will tell the rest.'[26] Discussions had already begun about infiltration, and the mission desperately wanted to avoid another disaster like the one that had recently occurred in Romania. Agents were dropped 60 kilometres off course straight into the capital Bucharest. They were caught, convicted as spies and imprisoned. For Hannah's mission, there were two options: to be dropped into Yugoslavia and cross the border on foot or to be dropped directly into Hungary. Either way, the unit would have to travel to Cairo first.

The day before they were due to leave, something quite extraordinary happened. An immigrant ship, the SS *Nyassa*, had recently docked in Haifa and on board was her beloved brother Giora. There followed some careful wrangling of logistics, including setting the start of the mission back by twenty-four hours so that she could meet up with him. She apologised to her colleagues for the delay, telling them, 'Who knows when I will see him again.'[27] Brother and sister spent an afternoon together on the shores of the Mediterranean, an experience that they had long dreamed of sharing. They brought one another up to date with personal and family news. The meeting was painful for Hannah, as she could not tell her brother why she was in uniform or what she was about to do. After a few snatched hours, Hannah took a taxi back to Haifa, and the next day she was on her way to Egypt.

Travelling with Hannah were her colleagues Yoel Palgi, Ben Ephraim, Yonah Rosen and Abba Berdichev. The car journey was long and dusty, and the tension mounted as their nervousness began to manifest. The colleagues bantered with one another, told jokes at which they laughed uncontrollably and made a pact to parachute back into their kibbutz as heroes at the end of the war. The mood of 'forced hilarity' helped dissipate the tension.[28]

While in Cairo, the group were joined by another agent, Enzo Sereni, and the heated debate about infiltration continued. Eventually, it was decided that one team would leave for Yugoslavia and the rest would remain in Cairo. If the Yugoslavia unit ran into trouble, another pair would jump into Hungary and, assuming they were not caught, would assist the agents in Yugoslavia to link up with them. With that settled, they waited anxiously for the mission proper to begin, but they kept being set back by a lack of aircraft. According to Palgi: 'Our total dependence on them was very frustrating. Precious time was slipping through our fingers, and tension was rising in the group.'[29]

Finally, at the beginning of March 1944, they were told that they would be on their way in a few days. All that had to be decided was who would go where and with whom. The mission was jointly organised by SOE and IS9 (Intelligence School 9). IS9 was established in January of 1942 as the executive branch of MI9, and its remit was to assist British and Commonwealth service personnel to evade capture when behind enemy lines and to assist in the escape of POWs. It was decided that Palgi would jump blind with another male agent, Peretz. Hannah desperately wanted to go with them, as her bond with Palgi was now very strong, and she felt safe with him. But their cover story, if caught, would be that they had bailed out of an aircraft, which would not include a woman in the crew. Reluctantly, Hannah agreed to become part of the group that would parachute into Yugoslavia. From there, they would make their way across the border into Hungary.

Hannah became increasingly anxious. Palgi wrote: 'I could not distinguish between her tense impatience and dedication to our mission, which to her was the only thing that mattered. She was totally unconcerned for her own safety . . . she wanted to be sure she got her share of the action, that she would not be left out.'[30] It was not long before her passion found an outlet. In early March 1944, Hannah, along with her colleagues Abba Berdichev, Reuven Dafne and Yona Rosen as the Hungarian mission, and Enzo Sereni, who would parachute into German-occupied northern Italy, were flown to the Italian town of Brindisi. The following day, the mission was told to get ready to leave. Hannah was so excited that she sang all the way back to her lodgings. She tried to get the others to join in, but most were not in the mood, especially Dafne, who had only just learned that his father and brother were in a concentration camp near Trento.

At the airbase, Hannah caused quite a stir. The men couldn't hide their amazement. A sergeant commented: 'I've worked here a long time. I've fitted hundreds of parachutists, but never a woman among them.' Hannah was fitted out in her parachute equipment and continued to cause a stir, so much so that an astonished American paratrooper 'walked up to her and wordlessly shook her hand'.[31] In the last moments before take-off, the agents wrote their final letters to their loved ones. Hannah wrote to her fellow kibbutzniks at Sdot

Yam, as well as to Katerina, from whom she had not heard in many months: 'Mother Darling, in a few days I'll be so close to you, and yet so far. Forgive me and try to understand. With a million hugs.'[32] Hannah was ready.

Sereni offered some parting words. 'Remember,' he said, 'only he who *wants* to die, dies!' The parachutists were surrounded by parcels and weighed down by their suits, winter clothing and weapons. The conversation became stilted as each withdrew into their own thoughts. Dafne looked over to Hannah: 'Her face was aglow, she exuded happiness and excitement. She winked at me, waved her hand encouragingly, and a delightful impish smile enveloped her features ... her luminous smile reminded me of a little girl on her first merry-go-round. Her excitement was contagious.'[33]

The jumping order had been drawn up before take-off: Dafne and Hannah, followed by Berdichev and Rosen and then a British parachutist. As the aircraft circled its target, the first containers of equipment were dropped and Hannah's face was 'wreathed in a huge smile'. She gave Dafne a thumbs-up sign as he jumped. She was right behind him. Her parachute flared open and as she sailed down into the Yugoslavian night, she was full of joy. She had waited for this moment for years and now she was finally going to undertake her mission, starting in the land of the partisans.

Her presence at their first encounter with Tito's partisans after the jump caused quite a stir:

Having a woman with us, a female paratrooper, made a huge impression on the partisans ... It was pretty rare, and the parachute also wasn't what it is today, so a female paratrooper – the news spread like wildfire ... there were female partisan fighters, but no paratroopers ... They knew we were from Eretz Yisrael, and that we were Jewish, and what the Jewish people had suffered, and they treated us very well and with respect.[34]

A few days after their arrival, they heard the news that the Germans had occupied Hungary and Hannah broke down in tears. She had waited so long to get back, and she was so close, but still not where she needed to be. Distraught that millions of Jews were now in German hands, she was angry that she and her colleagues, whose mission was to save them, were stuck in Yugoslavia. She grew restless, constantly seeking ways to cross the border, but she was entirely dependent on the partisans for ways and means of crossing into Hungary. Those partisans were, by necessity, oblivious to the parachutists' true mission.

The parachutists soon joined up with a partisan unit, with whom they had several near misses. On one occasion, they found themselves under attack in a village near the border. They were cut off and had to run for their lives. Sliding down a rope, they began running along an open valley, surrounded by the enemy and desperately trying to dodge their gunfire. Meanwhile, civilians were scrambling and running, but 'people were dropping like birds' and the cries of the injured and dying filled the parachutists' ears. Reaching the forest, they fell to the ground, exhausted but safe . . . for now.

On another occasion, the four of them were lying in the forest, hidden behind some trees with guns drawn in preparation for an enemy ambush. The Germans were at the edge of the forest, shooting in every direction, but miraculously not theirs. Dafne was struck by 'Hannah's amazing composure . . . lying there, pistol cocked, a heavenly radiance on her face . . . her courage, her integrity and unwavering dedication to our mission aroused my utmost admiration.'[35]

Hannah lived with Tito's partisans for about three months, trying relentlessly to reach Hungary with their assistance. It was her firm belief that the paratroopers needed to act without considering their own safety. Even if they didn't manage to save Jews, their personal sacrifice would be a symbol that would give strength and faith to the Jews of Europe. Dafne recalled:

I was not happy with Hannah's papers . . . [I] wanted to convince Hannah not to go with those papers, I was scared . . . We had a very heated argument. She was altogether extremely obstinate . . . Until she suddenly said: 'Even if they catch me – the Jews will be notified. They will know that at least one person tried to reach them.'[36]

On 9 June, just three days after D-Day, Hannah received the news she had been waiting for: she was to cross the border into Hungary. It was a four-hour trek to the border village, and even though Dafne was not happy with Hannah's paperwork, she refused to wait any longer, despite his efforts to persuade her otherwise. After supper, the two walked into an orchard and went through her mission, code words and contacts in minute detail. Hannah asked for a cyanide pill, but Dafne refused her, believing it was his duty to 'increase her self-confidence' at this critical point in the mission. She also asked him to accompany her to the border but he said that, for the sake of the mission, one of them needed to stay behind in the event of the other being captured. Hannah and Palgi agreed on a rendezvous, to meet on a certain day in June at the main synagogue in Budapest or, if that failed, at the cathedral, and they bade each other farewell.

At 7.15 p.m., Dafne and Hannah left the safe house together. Hannah was excited and carefree. She 'seemed to be like someone who was embarking on an experience she had been looking forward to for years'. Shaking hands, they thanked one another for all that they had shared and done before turning and walking in opposite directions.[37] It was 18 May, the very same day that the deportation of Jews from most Hungarian cities had begun.

■ ■ ■

Hannah crossed the border with three colleagues: Kallos, Fleischmann and Tissandier. The route was not straightforward and they became completely lost. Eventually, they reached the River Drava, which they would have to cross to continue their journey towards Budapest. Due to the sheer amount of equipment they were carrying, they had to swim back and forth across the swollen, swirling waters to get everything from one bank to the other, including the various components of Hannah's wireless set. Tissandier had reasoned with Hannah to leave it behind; it was heavy and, more importantly, it would be disastrous if she was caught with it. But she insisted and, eventually, thoroughly soaked and utterly exhausted, the team and the wireless set were safely landed on the other bank of the river. Here, they hid Hannah's uniform and she changed into civilian clothing.[38]

Kallos and Fleischmann set off to find the nearest village, while Tissandier and Hannah hid in the reeds on the riverbank, awaiting their return. On leaving the village, Kallos and Fleischmann were apprehended by the Hungarian police, who wanted to take them in for questioning. Both men were carrying guns in their pockets. Each of them softly released the safety catch on his weapon and kept a finger on the trigger. Just as the police were about to release them, Kallos pulled out his pistol and, putting it to his head, killed himself. Falling to the ground, he took with him all the hopes and dreams that Hannah had carried with her of helping the Jews of Hungary. It was now just a matter of time before she was found.

After waiting for over three hours, Hannah and Tissandier moved away from the riverbank into a small wood, where they buried anything that might incriminate them, including the wireless set. But they soon realised that the wood was surrounded. Soldiers were closing in on them from all directions. At any minute, they would be apprehended. Jumping into one another's arms, they pretended to be a young couple in love. When they were found, convincing as their act was, they were taken in for questioning. 'If they are innocent,' said the officer in charge, 'no harm will be done, and they can resume their lovemaking in an hour.' But, deep down, Hannah knew that this was it – she would never get to fulfil her mission. Handcuffed and bound, they were taken to Szombathely police HQ. There they were shocked to see the battered and silent Fleischmann and the dead body of

Kallos, in whose pocket was a horribly incriminating set of earphones.

Hannah was held for two days at the prison, during which time she was brutally tortured in an attempt to find out more about whether there was a wireless set and, if so, where it was. According to some sources, she was beaten on the palms of her hands and soles of her feet until she became unconscious, but she refused to give anything away. She didn't have to: the woods were combed meticulously and, eventually, the transmitter was found. Her guilt had been confirmed and her fate sealed. She was treated as a spy against her own country, the country she had been so desperately trying to return to and help for so long.

Hannah was bundled onto a train. Under heavy guard, she was taken back to Budapest where, elsewhere in the city, Palgi was eagerly awaiting her arrival. Knowing that only imprisonment and further torture lay ahead of her, she tried in vain to escape from the moving train, but the guard caught her before she was able to jump.

She did manage to hoodwink her guards, however. She had been permitted to bring a French poetry book with her for the journey. Secreted in its pages were the wireless codes that the enemy so desperately wanted. As she was manhandled off the train at Budapest station, she left the book on the seat behind her and the codes were, to all extents and purposes, lost.

At Horthy Miklós Road military prison, Hannah fervently wished that her attempt to jump from the train had been successful. Continually hounded with questions in the hope that she'd reveal information regarding Allied wireless codes, she was bound to a chair and beaten all over. Her hair was pulled out in clumps and one of her teeth was knocked out. Meanwhile, Palgi waited for her in vain at Dohany Street Great Synagogue in Budapest, where they had naively arranged to meet so many weeks before. Within days of entering Hungary, he and Rosner were also captured, still unaware of Hannah's whereabouts.

11
DEATH BE NOT PROUD

We didn't go to Europe to overthrow the Third Reich . . . we didn't
think they would make of us heroes; we wanted to go to the Jews
of Europe and say that we had come to help.

Surica Braverman[1]

News of Hannah's capture reached Surica Braverman just days after she had arrived in Yugoslavia on her mission to Romania. Surica
(also known as Sara) Braverman was born in Botosani in northern
Romania in 1919. Brought up in a family of Zionists, she became
a member of Hashomer Hatzair (a secular Jewish youth movement
founded in Eastern Europe on the eve of the First World War and influenced by the Boy Scout movement) when she was nine years old.
For its members, it was a means of maintaining their Jewish identity and culture outside Orthodox Jewish life. In 1938 she emigrated
to Mandate Palestine, and when war broke out a year later, and
Romania allied itself with Nazi Germany, all contact with the country's remaining Jews was lost.

'My story in the army begins in 1942, when I joined the Palmach,'
she said:

After completing the Unit Commander course, I volunteered,
along with 36 other colleagues, to parachute into European lands
that were occupied by the Nazis. It was a great effort by the Jews
who were in Eretz Israel, where we were in an extreme situation of

poverty, both in terms of weapons and economic means, but we wanted with all our soul to help the Jews who remained in Europe in some way.[2]

Surica's mission would take her to her homeland of Romania, via Yugoslavia, where SOE operatives were working alongside Tito's and Mihailovic's partisans, who were in desperate need of British aid and support. Romania was initially neutral when war broke out but, in mid-1940, the popularity of the Romanian government plummeted. In September of that year, a coup was staged, resulting in the country becoming a dictatorship under Mareşal Ion Antonescu. The new regime officially joined the Axis powers on 23 November 1940. Romania's right-wing party was the 'Iron Guard' and was a militant, revolutionary and fascist political party founded in 1927 by Corneliu Zelea Codreanu as the Legion of the Archangel Michael. It was strongly anti-democratic, anti-capitalist, anti-communist and anti-Semitic while being deeply instilled with Romanian Orthodox Christian mysticism.

In August 1943, the Allies had begun Operation 'Tidal Wave', the bombing of Romanian oilfields and distilleries, in an attempt to deny the Nazis much-needed fuel. Many aircraft were lost and numerous Allied pilots downed over the foreign and unfamiliar landscape of the Romanian countryside. With no knowledge of the language or the local way of life, these men were in desperate need of help. By convincing the British that this was their mission, the Palmach could then undertake their own work in helping the Jewish community. 'You have to understand,' Surica said, 'we didn't go to Europe to overthrow the Third Reich ... We didn't think they would make of us heroes; we wanted to go to the Jews of Europe and say that we had come to help.'[3]

Surica undertook her training with Haviva Reik (a year after Hannah had completed hers). More often than not, the two shared a room, being the only two women on their courses. Sometimes their gender could cause them problems, especially when they arrived at Ramat David parachute camp. Whereas training Hannah had been a novelty, the instructors were less than pleased to find they had to train two more women. There was nowhere for them to live. No female camp or washroom facilities were available, so, much to their delight, they were put up in the Windsor Hotel. Here they were served by waiters in white gloves, ordered themselves wine and wondered between themselves whether, if they 'could have imagined life in the British army, would you have enlisted in Palmach and trudged around in mud on the way to a leaky tent?'[4]

Each day, Surica and Haviva attended parachute training. Surica successfully got through the ground training 'safe and sound'.[5] But on her first proper jump, Surica froze. The last person to jump ahead of her reported that she'd been standing before him on the line and had been afraid to jump. He had thought the instructor would simply push her. Instead, he pulled her to one side to let the others exit the aircraft.[6] She was ashamed and upset by her failure and said, 'I have to admit that it was a really bad experience for someone who trained so hard and knew that it was the only way to take part in the mission.'[7] She knew everything hinged on her being able to parachute, but her fear had got the better of her.

The next day, when the others went to jump again, she did not board the aircraft. After this she did not even join the others at Ramat David. Haviva tried to convince her that it 'was really nothing, just one moment of fear', but neither she nor any of the others who came to visit her at the Windsor Hotel could convince her. 'I was afraid,' Surica said, 'simply afraid . . . on the jump I became paralysed.'[8] The situation was not eased by the fact that the members of the Infiltration Committee felt that their efforts to train a woman (of whom there were only three) had been in vain and that Surica had failed, in spite of all the time, trust and energy they had invested in her.

One final attempt was made to convince her, this time on a night jump. Haviva sourced her some trousers and boots to make her more comfortable, and they boarded the aircraft. As the plane flew high over the Jezreel Valley, Surica realised that she could see nothing but black; there were no lights coming from the settlements, and the 'countryside was shrouded in darkness'.[9] Haviva urged her on, but to no avail. She shrank back into the aircraft like before, wondering if she could ever fulfil her mission of helping the Jews of Romania. Haviva, meanwhile, had jumped into the inky darkness once more. Realising how important Surica was due to her excellent connections in Romania, the British colonel in charge of the mission told her that the group would find another way to infiltrate her.

Dressed in their summer WAAF uniforms, the group were told that they would be leaving for Cairo. The van that took them had two armchairs inside, especially for Haviva and Surica. The two women were also provided with cakes and strawberries for the long and dusty trip through the Sinai desert. They had become good friends, and Haviva wrote that she was close to Surica,

> even though I knew in advance that she was a different type of person, a different spirit and somewhat foreign to me. We live together quite well, our relationship is friendly and we work together too. It is never too late to bring in something new. If this motto had not been with me always, who knows whether I would have found the strength for this work.[10]

They arrived in Bari on 16 July, where Surica 'spent three weeks awaiting completion of arrangements for [her] entry into Yugoslavia'.[11]

At 2 p.m. on 6 August, Surica was flown into the partisan-controlled region of Yugoslavia, with the intention of crossing the border into Romania as soon as possible. She was met by Major Macdam and travelled 'by horse and cart to No.6 Headquarters'. This was a somewhat primitive building where she spent a week before proceeding to Major Macdam's HQ.[12] The devastating news of Hannah's capture was received soon after Surica arrived, which weighed heavily on the minds of the partisans and Palmach alike.

After she had settled down, she tested her wireless set. In her report, she said:

> In the course of a week, I made three tests, all of which were received quite well in Cairo, but unfortunately, it was impossible for Cairo to get into radio communication with me. This was later proved to be the fault of the Receiver Set ... it was decided to make a change. Unfortunately, the change was not made during my stay in Jugoslavia [sic].[13]

Surica (known to the partisans as Sara) was one of several Jewish soldiers awaiting the orders that would enable them to start their true missions. Meanwhile, they served with Tito's partisans. Their cover was as British officers serving alongside SOE in Yugoslavia to aid the partisans in their fight. Surica's specific cover was as a journalist in the army. She recalled:

> When we were in the partisan camp, they didn't know who we were. They knew we were English soldiers and we were not the only foreigners there – there were also Americans. Every morning there would be a partisan girl who came with a cow, and she would give each of us some milk. We were all in English uniforms with officers' insignia. When she saw that I knew about livestock, she was surprised to see an Englishwoman who knew such things. But of course, for me, it wasn't surprising, I had taken a course in farming in Ness Ziona [in Mandate Palestine].[14]

However, the partisans were unwilling to endanger a large group of fighters in order to take her on the long and hazardous distance to the border with Romania. This was made more difficult as the areas en route were constantly changing hands. Perhaps more pressingly, though, Romania had just capitulated. Much to Surica's disappointment, no other mission could be arranged, so she was picked up by aircraft and taken back to Brindisi airbase. There, she was reunited with Haviva, who was still waiting to undertake her mission. Surica had been gone less than a month. Her friend quizzed her about what had happened in Yugoslavia, and Surica expressed her dismay at not having been able to do more, especially for the Jewish population. She said, 'I have nothing further to report as nothing of a very exciting nature happened at any time'.[15] But the women did not let themselves despair, setting to work helping the flow of impoverished Jewish refugees who were flooding into Bari by providing them with food, blankets and clothing. Surica also attended a wireless school 'in order that I keep in good practice for when I finally reach Romania and, am in a position, to use my W/T set'.[16]

Unfortunately, that opportunity did not present itself and Surica was sent home via Cairo. She returned to her kibbutz and continued to work for Palmach. Surica's role as one of the thirty-two Palmach agents has been underplayed and often misunderstood, perhaps because she was not able to carry out her mission to help the Jews. It's often thought that she was not infiltrated because she failed her parachute course, but that's simply not true. She spent a month in Yugoslavia working with the partisans and looking for any chance to get into Romania. It is a sad tale – the odds were constantly against her, and she could not fulfil the work she had set out to undertake of helping the Jews of Eastern Europe in their darkest hours.

■ ■ ■

By this point, Hannah had been in prison for several months and events had taken a somewhat sinister turn. In mid-June, the doorbell at Hannah's family home rang. Katerina answered and was told that she was being summoned to the Military HQ as a witness. She had no idea what was happening or why but, obeying the state police detective who was standing on the doorstep, she grabbed her coat and bag and followed him. The pair travelled by tram to the military prison, which was no more than half an hour from Katerina's house. During the journey, Katerina pondered her situation. The one thing she felt she could be certain of was that both Hannah and Giora were safe. After all, they were in Mandate Palestine and far from the troubles that Hungary and its Jews now faced.

Taken into an interrogation room, Katerina was questioned by a civilian called Rosza, who, after taking down the usual details of residence and background, asked her about Hannah. Why had she left home, where was she now, what was she doing now, how did the two communicate? Katerina wondered if one of Hannah's letters had been intercepted and the censors had found something that they did not like. But the questioning continued and the typewriter in the corner of the room rattled away as her statement was typed up. After she had signed her statement, Rosza menacingly leaned over the desk. 'Where do you really think your daughter is now, this minute?' he asked. When Katerina repeated that her daughter was safely on a kibbutz near Haifa, Rosza told her that Hannah was, in fact, in the next room and that she needed to talk some sense into her and get her to tell them everything she knew. Katerina's world came crumbling down around her, 'like a child's house of cards'. She was 'completely shattered, physically and spiritually'.[17]

Hannah and Katerina had not seen each other for almost five years. Katerina had no idea that her daughter had even left Mandate Palestine. As a bloodied and bruised Hannah entered the room, her mother barely recognised her. 'Her once soft hair hung in a filthy tangle, her ravaged face reflected untold suffering, her large expressive eyes were blackened, and there were ugly welts on her cheeks and neck.' Neither woman could believe that the other was there in front of them. Hannah tore herself away from the guards and threw herself into her mother's arms. 'Forgive me,' she sobbed.[18]

The pair were told to sit in chairs facing one another, and with only a detective remaining, they were able to catch a few snatched words of comfort and explanation. Concerned that Hannah had come to

Hungary to rescue her, Katerina was relieved to hear that not only was Giora safe in Mandate Palestine, but that Hannah was part of a mission by the British army. Perhaps that would offer protection? Katerina took her daughter in her arms and at that moment Rosza burst in. The mother and daughter had refused to give the authorities the performance that would lead to the information they had sought, and Hannah was taken back to her cell. Katerina was released but told she might be brought in again at any time. She was not to repeat anything that she had seen or heard.

Later that day, as she was still trying to reconcile everything that had happened, Katerina was visited by a Gestapo officer named Seifert and an SS man 'whose face resembled his badge'.[19] After a perfunctory inspection of the house, she was told that she was to go with them. They arrived at the freight entrance of the Budapest County Department of Justice building, where her house keys and the contents of her handbag were confiscated. They would be returned, she was told, if she was released. Next, she was taken to a cell.

A few days later, a friendly prisoner who held various privileges came to her and told her to look into the window directly opposite. To her delight, she saw Hannah, who waved and smiled. They began to correspond by drawing letters in the air. This bond kept them both going when all else seemed to be fraught with evil and suffering. Katerina was often interrogated by Seifert. On one occasion, she asked him if Hannah's life was in danger. He replied that, under Hungarian law, her life was in no danger, but German law was 'far more stringent'. As they were currently in a Hungarian prison, Katerina took this to mean that Hannah was safe.[20]

The two continued to communicate from their respective windows across the exercise yard and, one day, Hannah was able to spend a few valuable moments with her mother hidden inside a bathroom. Hannah fell into her mother's arms, who responded by smothering her with kisses. Hannah was recovering from her torture well, and her physical scars were beginning to heal. She told her mother that she was a wireless operator in the British army and had volunteered for a mission that ultimately failed. She believed that Kallos's suicide had caused the 'catastrophe' that had led to their arrest and treatment.[21]

After this, Hannah continued sending messages through the window, but daily interrogations away from the prison meant that she did not get back until late. So she started to send her mother messages via her cellmates, whom she met in the van or the waiting room. On her twenty-third birthday, Hannah received gifts from her mother, including a marmalade jar, a handkerchief, a sliver of soap and a sponge – all precious commodities to someone in a prison cell. Hannah sent a thank-you note, saying that the marmalade reminded her of Mandate Palestine and that her life had been 'happy and beautiful'.[22] She was moved to a communal cell for a short time, where she delighted in playing with some children who were there, holding their hands during exercise or making them dolls from oddments she had found scattered about. But this did not last long, and she was soon returned to solitary confinement.

On 11 September, Hannah was moved from the Gestapo prison to Conti Street prison. The news of this move reached her mother through a fellow inmate. Katerina herself was moved to an internment camp on the outskirts of the city. Three weeks later, on the festival of Yom Kippur, she was released. Bewildered by her sudden freedom, she went to her sister's home and discovered that Hannah had managed to make contact via a Hungarian lawyer named Dr Nanay. He had visited Hannah at Conti Street and offered to defend her case if it came to trial, as well as the cases of the other parachutists who had been captured. Hannah was desperate to see her mother again, and Nanay managed to arrange a visitor pass for her.

At the oppressive prison building with its tiny windows and enclosed courtyard in which stood a tree used for hanging prisoners, Katerina waited in a small and dingy waiting room. Suddenly Hannah appeared, 'flanked by two guards' and looking 'remarkably well'.[23] Unable to talk freely, the two embraced. Hannah was grateful to receive a package that her mother had brought, containing clothing and other bits and pieces, as well as a sewing set that Hannah had had as a child. With tears in her eyes, Hannah asked, 'Does this thing still exist? Was there ever such a time . . . a time of childhood and carefree happiness?'[24] Hannah requested that her mother bring her more books, in particular a Hebrew bible from which she could draw strength, as she was soon to be tried. As her mother left, Hannah asked her to find a lawyer. She would need help in the days and weeks to come. Katerina then spent most of her waking hours seeking legal assistance for her daughter, who, being a Hungarian national, was to be tried as a spy. In the end, she chose Dr Szelecsényi to represent her daughter.

■ ■ ■

On 17 September 1944, just days after Hannah had moved to the Gestapo prison on Conti Street, Budapest, Haviva Reik boarded one of two B-17 Flying Fortresses for her mission in Slovakia.

Marta (later known as Haviva) Reik was born on 22 June 1914 in the Slovakian village of Radvaň. The family had just moved her from Budapest due to a downturn in fortunes. Haviva was the youngest of Arpad and Emilia Reik's six children. The village was quiet and remote, not at all like the vibrant and modern city they had left behind. When Haviva was four years old, the family moved again to Harmanec in the Banská Bystrica region of the Carpathian Mountains. Here, the local paper mill employed hundreds of workers from the town and surrounding villages, including Haviva's father, who was a stock-keeper.

As a child, Haviva became fluent in German, Hungarian, Slovakian and Czech. When she joined the Hashomer Hatzair youth movement in 1933, she also learned Hebrew in preparation for her planned immigration to Eretz Israel. It was at this point that she changed her name from Marta to Haviva. Her favourite book was *Kibbutz Women*. From within its pages, she found inspiration and a sense of being; she carried it with her everywhere. As with Hannah and Surica, her fervent Zionism meant she wanted to leave as soon as possible, and she began to plan for her *hakhsharah* (agricultural training) in preparation for moving to Mandate Palestine. However, her family fell into financial difficulties again and she had to put her plans on hold in order to help, taking a job as a salesperson in an agricultural factory. There, she worked the cash register, supervised accounting and performed secretarial work. Aged eighteen, Haviva volunteered for the Red Cross and helped as a local fire brigade volunteer. She was also interested in politics and was a member of the Democratic Party.

In 1935, Haviva was appointed senior counsellor to a detachment of seventy young members of Hashomer Hatzair. She also became personal assistant to the chairman of the Zionist organisation in Slovakia and helped to transfer the funds and property of Slovakian Jews to Eretz Israel. At Hashomer Hatzair, she met her future husband, a fellow Zionist called Avraham Martinovich. Whether the marriage was for love or to secure and share an immigration certificate is not known. Not long after their wedding, the newlyweds decided that, due to the rise in anti-Semitism under the influence of the Third Reich, it was time to prepare for emigration.

In 1938, Haviva began her *hakhsharah* in Bratislava, and the couple moved to Mandate Palestine together in 1939, where they joined the Ma'anit kibbutz in the Samarian plain. Haviva loved it there and rapidly became a valued and active member of the community. She helped to organise the citrus fruit harvest and was involved in all manner of activities at the kibbutz. But her marriage fell apart. Avraham became disillusioned with left-wing Zionism and became a fanatical communist. The couple argued over their significant political differences and eventually decided to separate, although neither filed for divorce.[25]

Haviva then moved to a new settlement called Kibbutz Shamir. It was here that she met Surica Braverman, who, sharing her passion and zeal for justice and desire to help European Jewry survive, persuaded her to join the Palmach. If Haviva was successful in her training, she would be sent into the heart of Slovakia.

Slovakia joined the Axis powers in November 1940, when its leaders signed the Tripartite Pact. The Pact's terms meant that Slovakia participated in the invasion of the Soviet Union in June 1941 and declared war on Britain and the United States in December of the same year.

In March 1942, Slovakia became the first Axis partner to sign an agreement with Germany that permitted the deportation of the Slovak Jews.[26] The Slovakian authorities were so fervent in their desire to rid the country of its Jews that they drove some 57,000 Slovak Jews into labour and to concentration camps at Sered, Novaky and Vyhne.[27]

In the months to come, these Jews were transported to the border with the German Reich and handed over to the SS. Nearly all of them were killed in Auschwitz-Birkenau, Majdanek, Sobibor and other camps in German-occupied Poland. Once he realised what was happening, the Slovak president Jozef Tiso called a halt to the deportation of the remaining 24,000 Slovak Jews in the autumn of 1942. Among the Jews deported were Haviva's brother Imre and his wife Irene, her older sister Ferencz and her mother. They all died at Auschwitz-Birkenau. Haviva never learned of their fate.

When Haviva was in training, an uprising occurred in her former home of Banská Bystrica against the puppet government. The revolt began on 29 August 1944 and was initiated by various political parties and army officers.[28] Later that year, these parties aligned with the Slovak National Council (SNR), as well as armed underground Jewish cells, which had been formed in each of the Slovakian labour camps. While the partisans made promising advances, they were stopped in their tracks when Germany occupied the country and brutally crushed the uprising.

In autumn 1944, approximately 12,600 Slovak Jews were deported to Auschwitz-Birkenau, Theresienstadt and other camps in Germany. Units of Germans and the Hlinka Guard (the militia maintained by the Slovak People's Party in the period from 1938 to 1945 and known for its participation in the Holocaust in Slovakia) also murdered several thousand Jews who were caught in hiding or fighting with the partisans in Slovakia. It was into this horrific situation that Haviva would have to go and attempt to stop the deportations. Was it to be a heroically brave mission or a fool's errand?[29]

To prepare her for what lay ahead, Haviva undertook the same training as her predecessor, Hannah Szenes, who had completed her courses a year before. Unlike her fellow trainee Surica, Haviva especially delighted in parachute jumping, an activity she found so exhilarating and enjoyable that she often asked if she could go again. On one occasion, she did three jumps from three different altitudes in one day. The views of the settlements and the valleys of Eretz Israel beneath her often moved her to tears.

In late summer, Haviva was sent to Bari in Italy to await her posting. With her was Surica Braverman, and the two shared a room again, continuing to be confidantes to one another. Haviva left many of her belongings with Surica, but not her treasured book *Kibbutz Women*, which she would take with her on her mission. There was a snag: women were not permitted to participate in 'blind drops' (drops with no reception committee to meet the parachutists on the ground), so Haviva was not allowed to jump with her male comrades. 'How can I stay here in Bari when there will be no representative of Hashomer Hatzair among the parachutists?' she said to Surica.[30] Refusing to be defeated, Haviva found an American military transport bound for Tri Duby airfield in Banská Bystrica, which was now held by anti-German rebel forces. Here, she would rendezvous with the Yishuv parachutists Rafael Reiss, Haim Hermesh and Zvi Ben-Ya'akov.

Her 'British' name was Ada Robinson, and it was under this name that, on 17 September, she boarded one of two B-17 Flying Fortresses bound for Slovakia. However, her SOE/IS9 file lists her under her married name of Marta Martinovich. This has caused immense confusion and some authors have written about Marta, without realising that both she and Ada Robinson were, in fact, Haviva Reik.

The Flying Fortress would fly from Brindisi airbase in Italy to a partisan-held airfield in Banská Bystrica, where several Allied airmen were waiting to be evacuated. At 8.25 a.m., Operation 'Amsterdam' began. The two Flying Fortresses took off, escorted by forty-one P-51 Mustangs that would help protect them from German fighter planes and anti-aircraft guns.[31] Inside the aircraft were 4.5 tonnes of military equipment and some much-needed supplies for the local partisans. Haviva herself carried $1,000 on her person, with gold sovereigns and jewellery also hidden in the heels of her shoes. The money and valuables were to fund, bribe or otherwise ensure the success of her mission.

To while away the time, Haviva wrote a note for her fellow agents back in Bari:

> My dear friends, it's about an hour from my destination, and I am thinking about you, and that gives me strength. During the first two hours, I was somewhat excited. Now I am totally calm and am looking forward to the future with a lucid mind. Give my regards to our comrades. The men who accompanied me took good care of me. We will see one another soon. Have a drink for me too. Thank you for everything,
> Yours, Haviva.

She looked out of the window to see what she could recognise of her homeland from the air. Marvelling at the forests, rivers and mountains, she delighted in reflecting that she would be back in Slovakia that day. At 10 a.m. local time, the B-17 landed at Tri Duby airfield. There was an 'enthusiastic welcome from numerous and well-armed reception committees'. This also involved being surrounded by photographers and being introduced to Dr Julius Kirschteuer, the liaison officer for American and British delegations on behalf of the Czechoslovakian government in exile.[32] The aircraft left to return to Italy with '15 evaders on board'.[33] Haviva enquired after the three comrades who had set off from Bari two days earlier. She was informed that no one had seen or heard from them.

Determined to find them, Haviva managed to commandeer a car with help from Major Sehmer, a British SOE agent in charge of Operation 'Windbreak', and the pair set off to find the missing parachutists.[34] They searched along the winding roads and ramshackle villages that led to the location of the safe house they had been allocated. Haviva knocked on the door and offered the prearranged password but was disappointed to learn that the woman in question had not seen them either. Then it dawned on her: she was alone and with no means of starting her missions or even communicating back to HQ about what was happening. Seeing her distress, Major Sehmer let her use his wireless set, and she transmitted back to Bari that she was safe but there was no sign of the others. The next day, she received a reply saying that the pilot who had dropped them confirmed that they had flashed their torches back to him to say they had landed safely.[35] She was bemused and, more to the point, she was alone. There were two missions to fulfil: the British one of helping Allied airmen and the Zionist cause of helping the Jews. She would now have to manage both of them on her own.

She lay low and tried to avoid meeting people she knew from before she had emigrated. In order to blend in, she wore civilian clothing and began trying to raise the funds she needed to help the many Jewish refugees she found in the town. She also monitored and sent regular transmissions from the wireless set. Every few hours, she would contact Dr Kirschteuer to see if he had any news about the three parachutists, but he had heard nothing.

On 23 September, just minutes after Haviva had left, the three men arrived. They were filthy, unshaven and in torn uniforms. They marvelled at hearing how Haviva had arrived safely and had been diligently looking for them, as well as beginning work on the missions without them. When they were finally reunited, the men told Haviva that they had been dropped 60 kilometres off course. It had taken two days for them even to meet up with one another. Worse, they had lost their wireless and all their equipment. They had suffered close calls with Nazis, Hlinka Guards and even partisans who were collaborators. Realising they could only rely on themselves, they had risked everything to get to the town and find her. They had met Egon Rot, the leader of the local Hashomer Hatzair organisation, and it was through him that they had finally found Haviva. After their emotional and heartfelt reunion, the four checked into the hotel that was to be their lodgings and base, ate a meal and planned their missions. By the end of the month, they were joined by a wireless operator named Abba Berdichev.

Over the next six weeks, the agents liaised with SOE operative Major Sehmer and established contact with Slovak army commanders who were supporting the Slovakian rebels. Together, they managed to rescue and assist approximately sixty Allied airmen who had been shot down over the Carpathian Mountains. They also established a truce between rival factions and various Jewish organisations, which resulted in a coordinating committee being established in Banská Bystrica.

The agents also attempted to undertake their second and, to them, their primary mission, which was the salvation of the Jews. Approximately 5,000 remained alive, having been broken out of various camps by the partisans. With the help of the British, they organised soup kitchens, housing and medical care. Haviva opened a tailor's shop where Jews could find work and helped them procure false documentation. They also evacuated several groups of Jewish refugees closer to the Hungarian border in the desperate hope that the Russians would reach them before the Germans did.

But, despite their best efforts and all their bravery, it soon became clear that their mission, as with all the Palmach missions, was doomed to fail. The task was too big, the enemy too brutal and the odds were stacked against them. When it was suggested that the agents should try to get out while they still could, they resolutely replied,

'We have come here to be with you, and we will be with you under any conditions.'[36]

■ ■ ■

On 28 October, Hannah's trial started at Margit Boulevard prison. Katerina was 'appalled by the mob milling about' outside and fought her way in. Reaching the courtroom, a sign on the door read 'Hannah Senesh and Accomplices' but Katerina was denied entry. Hannah stood alone in front of judge and jury.

After a few hours, the doors were flung open so the judges could deliberate on their verdict. Hannah, who was 'flushed, excited, her eyes brilliant, her smile self-confident', caught sight of her mother and rushed to her, flinging her arms around her.[37] A guard pulled them apart, telling them they would only be permitted to speak after the verdict had been given. The court was soon called back into session. Hannah emerged a few moments later. She told her mother that judgement had been postponed for eight days. Hannah then 'disappeared from view, lost in the mob'.

Katerina tried to get a visitor's pass several times but was informed that the lawyer could no longer get this for her and that it must be obtained through a Captain Simon. The eight days had now passed and still there was no verdict. On 7 November, Katerina finally managed to track the captain down at Margit Boulevard prison, but it was too late.

When Hannah had come up before a tribunal, she had eloquently pleaded her cause, warning the judges that as the end of the war was approaching their own fate would soon hang in the balance. She was convicted as a spy, which carried the death sentence. However, her speech had resonated with the officer in charge, who happened to be Captain Simon. He came into her cell on the morning of 7 November and offered her the option of begging for a pardon. It was that or face death by firing squad.

Hannah resolutely refused to beg clemency from her captors. She penned short notes to her mother and her comrades and went out to face the firing squad. Yoel Palgi, one of the Yishuv paratroopers with whom she had parachuted, wrote:

> Suddenly, a shot rang out, one or two shots. They were shooting in the courtyard. What had taken place? Perhaps someone was executed again? But no, that couldn't be ... Surely, it was just a stray bullet from the guard's rifle ... Close to noon ... 'What happened?' asked Fleischmann, and was answered: 'The shooting what we heard was "the shooting" ... They executed Hannah an hour ago.' We stood as though turned to stone. Hannah? Impossible! Error, error, error! Every drop of blood within me roared, every nerve ending. It couldn't be! Why her, of all people and not us?! ... I felt I had to say something, but the words lodged in my throat. I saw that all eyes were on me. I stammered: 'She was the most wonderful person I met in my life!'
>
> ... We got up and stood in silent tribute for a long time. Afterwards, we sat down without a word ... They killed Hannah! They killed Hannah![38]

Hannah went to her death at age twenty-three in a snow-covered Budapest courtyard, refusing a blindfold in order to face her murderers in the moments before her death. Her body was buried by unknown persons in the Jewish graveyard in Budapest.

Katerina had arrived moments too late. She was told that her daughter 'was guilty of major crimes against the interests of Hungary'.[39] As Hungary was under martial law and Hannah had been caught with a wireless transmitter, she had been found guilty of treason by a military tribunal that had 'demanded the supreme penalty'.[40] This had been carried out moments before Katerina arrived. Her world went black: the light that was her daughter's love and life had been snuffed out.

After her daughter's execution, Katerina tried to get Hannah buried among the martyrs, but no one was permitted to attend the burial.

Katerina was forced on a death march by the Arrow Cross but, remarkably, she survived and eventually returned to Budapest.

■ ■ ■

In Slovakia, it became clear in late October that German forces were closing in on Banská Bystrica. Haviva and her colleagues began to organise the evacuation of the Jews. Leaving the city on 26 October, two days before it fell, Haviva and the other agents took the remaining forty or so Jews with them. Since Haviva had refused to leave the elderly and sick behind, their progress was painstakingly slow. Climbing up to the mountains near the village of Pohronský Bukovec took much longer than planned. It was foolhardy to believe they had gone unnoticed by enemy patrols, and local collaborators reported seeing large groups of people setting up camp in the forests along the sides of the mountains.

On 30 October, the refugees and partisans awoke to the sounds they had been dreading. It was the din of Ukrainians from the Waffen-SS Halychyna division shouting and cursing, the rattle of guns firing at fleeing refugees and the sound of hand grenades exploding as they were thrown into the thick of the encampment. The attack was brutal and indiscriminate. The dense forest on the side of the mountain was shrouded in a deep fog. Survivors recalled not being able to distinguish who was friend and who was foe. Many were afraid to shoot in case they hit one of their own, and so many did not even open fire. Some tried to hide, a few committed suicide rather than fall into enemy hands, while others ran as far and as fast as they could. The only Palmach agent to get away was Haim Hermesh. He and several others managed to break through and hide. Everyone else was killed or captured.

The next day, those who had been taken prisoner were taken down the mountain. The sun was shining and glinting off the rooftops of the villages beneath them. Haviva and the two men tried to convince the others to say that they did not know them, that they had just met, as it might save their lives. The village, which until recently had been in rebel hands, was teeming with German trucks and troops ready to meet the Russian onslaught. The prisoners were led to a building that Haviva knew well: only a few days earlier, it had served as the partisan HQ where she had been helping refugees and Allied airmen. Now it was Gestapo HQ, and there would be no one there to save them.

The three agents (Zvi, Rafi and Haviva) were interrogated separately and then together, and the violence gradually increased towards them. They tried to stop it by telling their captors that they were British officers operating within the bounds of the Geneva Convention and, as such, only gave their names and numbers. But when the Germans discovered that Haviva and Rafi were Jewish, their behaviour worsened, and they became far more brutal. But how did they discover they were Jewish? Did Haviva's precious book *Kibbutz Women* give them away? How had she got away with taking such an incriminating item with her on such a perilous journey? Zvi maintained that he was British and his treatment was bearable. At the end of the interrogation, Haviva was separated from the others and her brutal interrogation continued for another day and night.

The next morning, bloodied and bruised, Haviva was driven through the streets, which were now adorned with flags bearing swastikas and the double cross emblem of the Hlinka Guard. Slovakia had fallen to the Germans and Haviva was powerless to fight back or help those in the most desperate need. Her mission had failed. Eventually, the car pulled through the gates of the imposing prison where she was to be incarcerated. Haviva was kept in an overcrowded, squalid and filthy cell on the third floor, along with sixty other Jews, but even so, she was feeling isolated, lonely and despondent.[41] The cold was biting and the cell doors were only opened so that the guards could throw in meagre food rations, hurl abuse or remove the corpses of those who had died in the night.

On 20 November, the cells on the third floor were emptied and the prisoners were shoved and harried into canvas-covered trucks waiting in the snow-laden courtyard. Across the crowds of people, Haviva caught sight of Rafi who, like her, was still in his blue RAF uniform. They smiled weakly at one another, both knowing that this was the end. The trucks began to leave in a convoy. Those inside grappled for a foothold and tried to help one another stay upright as they were jostled and jolted out of the prison compound towards the village of Kremnička.

It was 6.30 a.m. and, although dawn was breaking, it was still dark. The air was thick with fog and it was snowing. The prisoners were dragged from the trucks and ordered to put their belongings onto a slowly building pile. Standing bewildered in the harsh glare of the trucks' headlights, the first group of prisoners were driven with sticks and shouts to an anti-tank ditch on the edge of the forest. There, every one of them was shot in the back of the neck, their crumpled bodies falling down into the ditch. When the bloody massacre was over, the bodies were covered with earth and branches, ready for more batches of victims to be murdered over the coming months.

In the UK and Mandate Palestine, Haviva's whereabouts remained a mystery for many months. Her SOE/IS9 file has pages of reports attempting to determine what happened to her. A note dated 1 October 1945 said she had suffered and 'Death took place by accident at Mauthausen concentration camp, Austria, 24 Jan 1945'. Another note dated 25 June 1945 states, 'Marta Martinovich has now been reported as safe.'[42] Neither of these was correct.

Following the liberation of Slovakia in April 1945, the bodies of Haviva and her two comrades, Zvi and Rafi, were found in the mass grave amid the pile of corpses. They were identifiable by their dog tags and RAF uniforms. Near Haviva, scraps of pages from the book *Kibbutz Women* were found. It was the book she had taken with her everywhere – even to her grave.[43]

■ ■ ■

At the end of the war, Yoel Palgi, the only one of the three parachutists who had survived the Hungarian mission, found Katerina Szenes and arranged for her to leave Budapest for Mandate Palestine. But before she went, she wanted to say one final farewell to Hannah.

She found the graveyard and discovered a small plaque: 'Hannah Szenes, 7th November 1944.' Turning and leaving Hannah behind broke her heart all over again. Katerina left Hungary soon afterwards. In October 1945, she emigrated to Eretz Israel and was reunited with her son Giora. In 1950, Hannah's remains were placed in the parachutists' section in the military cemetery on Mount Herzl in Jerusalem. Two years later, they were joined by the remains of Haviva Reik. In the same year, a kibbutz was founded and called Yad Hana in Hannah's memory. The Givat Haviva Institute, an Aliyah Bet illegal immigrant ship and numerous streets are all named for Haviva Reik.

■ ■ ■

That these missions should ever have been undertaken at all has been a great source of debate. Ultimately, they were suicide missions, doomed to fail before they had even begun. How could such small teams of individuals call a halt to the mass deportations across Europe? All they could realistically do was help save a few lives and, arguably, the only woman who accomplished anything she had set out to achieve was Haviva Reik. Fifteen people left on the OSS aircraft by which she arrived; she organised aid for the Jewish population in Banská Bystrica and assisted forty or so Jews to evacuate the town and hide in the mountains when the Germans occupied the area. That they were later captured and slaughtered was a tragedy that no one could have foreseen.

Surica's mission never had the chance to get started. Before she could get across the border into Romania, the country had surrendered to the Germans. If she had continued, she would have risked not only her own life but also those of everyone around her. She was clearly bitter about being sent back to Italy, but she persevered in her training and self-improvement against the day she would return. She never went back. The scale of Romanian collaboration with the Third Reich had a devastating impact on the Jewish population, and between 380,000 and 400,000 Jews died in Romanian-controlled areas.

Hannah's mission was highly controversial, even at the time. Although she was arrested as soon as she crossed the border into Hungary, when her colleagues Yoel Palgi and Perec Goldstein later entered Hungary (on 19 June), they saw for themselves that deportations from the countryside were already well under way, with trains heading directly to Auschwitz-Birkenau. There, the Jews would be selected as either 'fit' or 'unfit' for work on a brand new 'ramp', or platform, built especially for the purpose.

The Jews remaining in Budapest were easily identified by the yellow star they were forced to wear on their coats. Two men alone would hardly be able to stop these systematic and mechanised round-ups. In fact, some historians believe that Palgi and Goldstein actually jeopardised some rescue missions, including a Zionist operation in Budapest led by Rezső Kasztner. Kasztner also worked with Joel Brand in the 'blood for goods' negotiations with Adolf Eichmann mentioned above.

On 30 June 1944, Kasztner arranged a train to take 1,686 Jews to neutral Switzerland, at a huge personal cost.[44] But Eichmann broke his promise that the train would travel directly to Switzerland. The transport went to Bergen-Belsen, where the passengers were held for several months in the Ungarnlager (Hungarian camp). By December, though, all the Jews had been transferred to Switzerland, where Kasztner joined them. While plans were being made for the journey, Kasztner met with Palgi. Calling the paratroopers 'mad', he told the men to report to the Gestapo, saying they were from the Palestinian Jewish Agency and wanted to negotiate. Palgi escaped the meeting unscathed only to be arrested by Hungarian intelligence. Later, again at Kasztner's suggestion, Goldstein gave himself up. This worked to Kasztner's advantage as he believed Goldstein's presence would jeopardise the whole deal to save the Jews by train.

The very presence of the Palmach agents in Hungary, who arrived without prior notification or contacts and who were unaware that rescue missions were already being planned, effectively jeopardised the work of the Jewish Relief and Rescue Committee. After the war, people came to believe that the Jews of Europe did not resist or put up a fight and went to their deaths like lambs to the slaughter. The story of the Palmach fighters, even though their missions were futile, is a moving and eloquent counterpoint to this. It proved that there were those who cared, who would move heaven and earth and risk their own lives to help their fellow man. Many of them ended up making the ultimate sacrifice.

Hannah's last Hebrew poem, 'Blessed is the Match', expressed her spirit of self-sacrifice for the sake of the Jewish people and her willingness to fight to the last breath. She gave Reuven Dafne the poem when they parted on the eve of her border crossing into Hungary. She made this request of him: 'If I don't come back, give this to my friends in Sdot Yam.'

> Blessed is the match consumed in kindling flame.
> Blessed is the flame that burns in the secret fastness of the heart.
> Blessed is the heart with strength to stop its beating for honour's sake.
> Blessed is the match consumed in kindling flame.
> 2 May 1944

Her final poem was found in her cell after her execution:

> One – Two – Three . . .
> eight feet long,
> Two strides across, the rest is dark . . .
> Life hangs over me like a question mark.
>
> One – Two – Three
> maybe another week,
> Or next month may still find me here,
> But death, I feel, is very near.

I could have been
twenty-three next July;
I gambled on what mattered most,
The dice were cast, I lost.

Budapest 1944.

EPILOGUE

After the Nazi invasion of Europe, the tentative sparks of resistance in occupied countries were fanned by Britain's Special Operations Executive. With a remit to 'set Europe ablaze', SOE women answered the call to arms to resist the Nazis, to fight back and to risk everything in the cause for freedom.

Until now the emphasis on remembrance and commemoration has primarily been on France and has focused in particular on F Section. Of the thirty-nine women employed by F Section, thirteen died or were killed in pursuit of their duties, often in brutal and disturbing circumstances. Their fates fuelled public outcry and the stories of the survivors left little to the imagination. Several of these women became household names, while others were consigned to the footnotes of history.

The women who contributed to other SOE sections, either as agents, those trained by SOE for MI9 or IS9 or those recruited locally across the rest of Europe, had all but been forgotten in the media and the general hype that surrounds SOE in modern literature and the press. Likewise, the group of Jewish agents recruited and trained in Mandate Palestine for missions in Eastern Europe were also virtually unheard of outside Israel, even though their work and contributions to the war effort were equally valid and the women themselves just as brave and selfless.

In the course of this book, the stories of these women have finally been highlighted. From Poland to Denmark, Belgium to Hungary, women of all different ages and backgrounds, with varying experience and motives, have been brought to the fore in order to align them with better-known agents and to recognise their work against the enemy. For some, this ended in brutal murder at the hands of those against whom they were fighting. Others survived incarceration but carried the scars for the rest of their lives. Others simply went back to their normal lives without seeking fame or glory for what they did.

Many of these women are known and often lauded in their countries of origin. Hannah Szenes is a national heroine in Israel; Elżbieta Zawacka was given the highest military decoration of the Order of the White Eagle and became a General (alongside her colleague Maria Wittek). She even has Girl Scouts packs named after her. But the ingenuity of women like Edith Bonnesen in Denmark, who undertook phenomenal wireless work as well as breaking out of Gestapo HQ, or Jeanne Bohec, the only female explosives expert in SOE, have all but been overlooked and ignored in favour of others. Until now, few books have been written about these SOE women outside their native countries and it is rare to find them mentioned in works in the English language. This has made researching them a challenge, albeit a very worthwhile one.

Other challenges have been weeding out fact from fiction. For example, in retelling Jos Gemmeke's story, care had to be taken as she was known to exaggerate. A recent podcast ('Tante Jos') by her niece tried to untangle her stories. In the archives, the story of Beatrice Jackman did not stand scrutiny, in particular post-war assertions about various items she claimed to have received. Likewise, in an obituary pertaining to Nicola Trahan, claims made on her behalf that she was a member of SOE were exaggerated. After much effort and research these claims were eventually redacted and rewritten. The danger of using such material has highlighted the problem that once a story has been told, especially if told by or on behalf of someone, it is very difficult to redact, and those seeking the truth are often harried for doing so.

However, it is my hope that this book has brought to light lesser-known women, and has highlighted their personalities, strengths and indeed weaknesses. *Mission Europe* has attempted to tell the true story of some of Europe's women agents. It has re-examined some of the better-known stories and revealed some hitherto unknown and uncelebrated stories of heroism and bravery, as well as frustration, failure and betrayal. It has been enlightening to find that, in revealing these women's personalities and contributions, they cease merely to be names in a footnote or an afterthought in a text and become real women, often just normal women to whom we can relate and with whom we can empathise.

Mission Europe has drawn these backstage stories out of obscurity and pushed them into the limelight by celebrating the work of many SOE women in occupied Europe. Stories of human trial and error, capture, escape and execution have filled these pages. This tome has revealed and celebrated the lesser-known women of SOE, and reiterated that they were ordinary women who did extraordinary things.

ENDNOTES

PROLOGUE

1. The underground army of the Yishuv (Jewish community) during the period of the British Mandate for Palestine.
2. Hannah Szenes, *Hannah Senesh: Her Life and Diary*, Hakibbutz Publishing House, Tel Aviv, 1973, p. 178.
3. Ibid.
4. Ibid., p. 177.
5. Ibid.
6. Ibid., p. 179.
7. William Mackenzie, *The Secret History of SOE: Special Operations Executive 1940–1945*, St Ermin's Press, London, 2000, p. 65. The attendees at this meeting were Lord Lloyd (secretary of state for the colonies and chairman of the British Council), Lord Hankey, Dr Dalton (minister of economic warfare), Sir Alexander Cadogan, Colonel Menzies, Mr Desmond Morton (representing the prime minister) and Mr Gladwyn Jebb.
8. Ibid.
9. Ibid.
10. Hugh Dalton, *The Fateful Years*, Frederick Muller, London, 1957, p. 366.
11. The branch focusing on France would come to have six sections: EU/P, focusing on Polish settlements in Europe; DF, working on escape lines; AMF or 'Massingham', operating from Algiers into southern areas of France after Operation 'Torch' in November 1942; 'Jedburgh', which was operational after D-Day; RF; and F. See Kate Vigurs, *Mission France: The True History of the Women of SOE*, Yale University Press, New Haven and London, 2021.
12. Charles de Gaulle, *Discours et Messages, 1940–1946*, Éditions Berger-Levrault, Paris, 1946, p. 476.
13. Mackenzie, *Secret History of SOE*, p. 719.
14. Correspondence with Mark Seaman, SOE Historian at the Cabinet Office, 18 June 2011.
15. M.R.D. Foot, *SOE in the Low Countries*, Amberley, Stroud, 2017, p. 62, fn.
16. Charles Cruickshank, *SOE in Scandinavia*, Oxford University Press, Oxford, 1986, p. 255.
17. Ibid., p. 256.

18. Ibid.
19. Ibid.
20. Ibid.
21. Ibid., p. 257.
22. David Stafford, *Mission Accomplished: SOE and Italy 1943–1945*, Bodley Head, London, 2011, p. 59.
23. Mackenzie, *Secret History of SOE*, p. 336.
24. The other roles were essentially jobs similar to those filled by the ATS but working for a far more secretive service. Approximately 1,200 women were based in these jobs in the UK; the others were spread out globally: North Africa and Italy (121), Middle East (91) and India and China (18). According to figures from April 1944, Mackenzie, *Secret History of SOE*, p. 718.
25. Ibid., p. 59.
26. Charles Cruickshank, *SOE in the Far East*, Oxford University Press, Oxford, 1983, pp. 44–5.
27. Ibid.
28. Ibid.
29. Awards included: three George Crosses; two George Medals; a King's Medal for Courage in the Cause of Freedom; a King's Commendation for Brave Conduct; two Commendations for Good Service; and thirty-two Mentions in Dispatches. Also: one CBE; six OBEs; twenty-three MBEs; ten BEMs. There were numerous foreign decorations too: one Chevalier of the Legion of Honour; six Croix de Guerre; two Medaille de la Reconnaissance; one Norwegian Liberty Medal; one US Bronze Star; and one US Medal of Freedom with Bronze Palm.
30. Dennis Rigden, *SOE Syllabus*, PRO, London, 2001, p. 2.
31. Ibid.
32. Vigurs, *Mission France*, pp. 32–3.
33. Susan Ottoway, *Violette Szabo: The Life That I Have*, Leo Cooper, Barnsley, 2002, p. 54.
34. William Pilkington (16854), Audio Archive, Imperial War Museum.
35. Stella King, *Jacqueline: Pioneer Heroine of the Resistance*, Arms and Armour Press, London, 1989, p. 94.
36. M.R.D. Foot, *SOE in France*, HMSO, London, 1966, p. 57.
37. Leo Marks, *Between Silk and Cyanide: A Codemaker's War 1941–1945*, HarperCollins, London, 1999, p. 599.
38. See Russell Miller, *Behind the Lines: The Oral History of Special Operations in World War II*, Pimlico, London, 2003, p. 267.

1 MISSION POLSKA

1. Transcript of interview, Tape 8, Fundacja General Elżbiety Zawackiej, Toruń.
2. 1 September 1939, Reichstag speech, Adolf Hitler.
3. Poland had gained independence after the First World War, a period in which Russia was weak and wreaked by revolution. Since the eighteenth century, it had been partitioned and occupied by Tsarist Russia, Germany (Prussia) and the Austro-Hungarian Empire. The Second Republic of Poland came into being through the Treaty of Versailles at the end of the First World War and survived until 1939.

4. Jeffrey Bines, *Poland's SOE: A British Perspective*, Polish Underground Movement Study Trust, London, 2018, p. xviii.
5. Wiesław Rogalski, *SOE Polish Section: The Death of the Second Polish Republic*, Helion, Warwick, 2022, p. 72.
6. Bines, *Poland's SOE*, p. 1.
7. Ibid.
8. Ibid., p. 2.
9. Rogalski, *SOE Polish Section*, p. 77.
10. Bines, *Poland's SOE*, p. 19.
11. Ibid., p. 20.
12. Jonathan Walker, *Poland Alone: SOE and the Collapse of the Polish Resistance, 1944*, Spellmount, Stroud, 2008, p. 22.
13. Rogalski, *SOE Polish Section*, p. 74.
14. Ibid., p. 73.
15. Ibid., p. 75.
16. Ibid.
17. Ibid., p. 72.
18. Germany had to recognise the independence of Poland and renounce 'all rights and title over the territory'. Portions of Upper Silesia were to be ceded to Poland, with the future of the rest of the province to be decided by plebiscite. The border would be fixed with regard to the vote and to the geographical and economic conditions of each locality. The Province of Posen (now Poznań), which had come under Polish control during the Greater Poland Uprising, was also to be ceded to Poland. Pomerelia (Eastern Pomerania), on historical and ethnic grounds, was transferred to Poland so that the new state could have access to the sea, and became known as the Polish Corridor. The sovereignty of part of southern East Prussia was to be decided via plebiscite while the East Prussian Soldau area, which was astride the rail line between Warsaw and Danzig, was transferred to Poland outright without plebiscite. An area of 51,800 square kilometres (20,000 square miles) was granted to Poland at the expense of Germany. Memel was to be ceded to the Allied and Associated powers, for disposal according to their wishes. Germany was to cede the city of Danzig (now Gdansk) and its hinterland, including the delta of the Vistula River on the Baltic Sea, for the League of Nations to establish the Free City of Danzig.
19. Katarzyna Minczykowska, *Elżbieta Zawacka alias 'Zelma', 'Sulica', 'Zo'*, Fundacja General Elżbiety Zawackiej, Toruń, 2016, p. 9.
20. Elżbieta Zawacka, unpublished autobiography, Fundacja General Elżbiety Zawackiej, Toruń.
21. Ibid.
22. Minczykowska, *Elżbieta Zawacka*, p. 12.
23. Zawacka, unpublished autobiography.
24. Elżbieta Zawacka interview, Warsaw Uprising Museum.
25. Ibid.
26. Ibid.
27. Ibid.
28. Ibid.
29. Ibid.

30. Ibid.
31. Ibid.
32. Zawacka, unpublished autobiography.
33. Ibid.
34. Elżbieta Zawacka interview, Warsaw Uprising Museum.
35. Minczykowska, *Elżbieta Zawacka*, p. 16.
36. Elżbieta Zawacka interview, Warsaw Uprising Museum.
37. Minczykowska, *Elżbieta Zawacka*, p. 17.
38. After the war Elżbieta discovered that Ela had been arrested in Warsaw and had died at Ravensbrück concentration camp in Germany.
39. Elżbieta Zawacka interview, Warsaw Uprising Museum.
40. Aidan Crawley, who met Skarbek during WW2, https://spartacus-educational.com/SOEgranville.htm, accessed January 2024.
41. TNA, HS9/612, Granville Christine, Personnel File.
42. Ibid.
43. Ibid.
44. Vigurs, *Mission France*.
45. Madeleine Masson, *Christine: A Search for Christine Granville, GM, OBE, Croix de Guerre*, Hamish Hamilton, London, 1975, p. 95.
46. Ibid.
47. Klara survived, became a lawyer and died in 2012.
48. Ibid.
49. Ibid.
50. Ibid.
51. Transcript of interview, Tape 5.
52. Minczykowska, *Elżbieta Zawacka*, p. 21.
53. Zawacka, unpublished autobiography.
54. Ibid.
55. Ibid.
56. Ibid.
57. Ibid.
58. Ibid.
59. Transcript of interview, Tape 5.
60. Katarzyna Minczykowska, *Cichociemna, Generał Elżbieta Zawacka 'Zo'*, Fundacja General Elżbiety Zawackiej, Torún, 2014. p. 120.
61. Ibid.
62. These were destroyed in Allied raids in 1944.
63. Transcript of interview, Tape 5.
64. Some weeks later Elżbieta discovered that the French had been taken to a concentration camp.
65. Elżbieta Zawacka interview, Warsaw Uprising Museum.
66. Ibid.
67. Transcript of interview, Tape 5.
68. Ibid.
69. Ibid.
70. Ibid.
71. Ibid.
72. Ibid.

73. Ibid.
74. Ibid.
75. Elżbieta Zawacka interview, Warsaw Uprising Museum.
76. Ibid.
77. Transcript of interview, Tape 5.
78. Elżbieta Zawacka interview, Warsaw Uprising Museum.
79. Her PF states Liverpool but all other memoirs refer to Bristol.
80. A.J. Photiadou, 'The Detention of Non-Enemy Civilians Escaping to Britain During the Second World War', *Historical Journal*, 65(2) (2022), pp. 482–504.
81. TNA, HS9/1635/3, Elizabeth Watson, Personnel File.
82. Ibid.
83. Elżbieta Zawacka interview, Warsaw Uprising Museum.
84. Sue Ryder, *Child of My Love*, Collins Harvill, London, 1986, p. 116.
85. Ibid.
86. Ibid.
87. Ibid.
88. TNA, HS9/1635/3, Elizabeth Watson, Personnel File.
89. Elżbieta Zawacka interview, Warsaw Uprising Museum.
90. Ibid.
91. Ibid.
92. Minczykowska, *Cichociemna*, p. 125.
93. Transcript of interview, Tape 7.
94. Elżbieta Zawacka interview, Warsaw Uprising Museum.
95. Ibid.

2 THE UPRISINGS

1. Sir Owen O'Malley, *The Phantom Caravan*, John Murray, London, 1954, p. 208.
2. Archive Fundacja General Elżbiety Zawackiej, Toruń.
3. Zawacka, unpublished autobiography.
4. Ibid.
5. Ibid.
6. Ibid.
7. Ibid.
8. Ibid.
9. Ibid.
10. Ibid.
11. Ibid.
12. Ibid.
13. Ibid.
14. Sue Ryder, *And the Morrow Is Theirs*, Burleigh Press, Bristol, 1975, p. 40.
15. Ibid.
16. Ibid., p. 41.
17. Zawacka, unpublished autobiography.
18. Ibid.
19. Ibid., and Elżbieta Zawacka interview, Warsaw Uprising Museum.
20. Elżbieta Zawacka interview, Warsaw Uprising Museum.
21. Ibid.

22. Ibid.
23. Ibid.
24. Ibid.
25. 'Maquis' literally means scrubland and these resisters lived in the countryside.
26. Masson, *Christine*, pp. 192–3.
27. Ray Jenkins, *A Pacifist at War: The Silence of Francis Cammaerts*, Arrow, London, 2010, p. 174.
28. The mission of the Jedburgh teams was to supplement existing SOE 'circuits', to help organise and arm the resistance, arrange supply drops, procure intelligence, provide liaison between the Allies and the resistance and to take part in sabotage operations.
29. TNA, HS9/612, Christine Granville, Personnel File.
30. Ibid.
31. Zawacka, unpublished autobiography.
32. Ibid.
33. Ibid.
34. Ibid.
35. Norman Davies, *Rising '44: The Battle for Warsaw*, Pan Books, London, 2004, p. 254.
36. Elżbieta Zawacka interview, Warsaw Uprising Museum.
37. Ibid.
38. Ibid.
39. Ibid.
40. Ibid.
41. 'Out of 149 drops made over Warsaw, the insurgents picked up only 44. It is presumed that a certain number of parachutes failed to open and the containers smashed, also that a small proportion, consisting of food fell into the hands of civilians who kept it . . . the night sorties from Italy show a much better result. Out of 42 drops the insurgents picked up 25 i.e. 59.5%. This however relates only to the first period up to August 14th.' Jozef Garlinski, *Poland, SOE and the Allies*, George Allen & Unwin, London, 1969, p. 205.
42. Ryder, *Child of My Love*, p. 118.
43. Elżbieta Zawacka interview, Warsaw Uprising Museum.

3 MISSION FRANÇAISE

1. Shelley Saywell, *Women in War*, Costello, London, 1985, p. 37.
2. A 'mole' is a pier, breakwater or causeway used to separate two bodies of water.
3. General de Gaulle speech, delivered 18 June 1940 on radio and printed on posters. It was delivered from 4 Carlton Gardens, London, the HQ of the Free French in Britain.
4. Foot, *SOE in France*, p. 21.
5. Ibid., p. 22.
6. Ibid., p. 23.
7. Mackenzie, *Secret History of SOE*, p. 257.
8. Ibid., p. 258.
9. Ibid.

10. American-born Virginia Hall arrived in Vichy in August 1941. She was a pioneer secret agent and had to learn on her own the 'exacting tasks of being available, arranging contacts, recommending who to bribe and where to hide, soothing the jagged nerves of agents on the run and supervising the distribution of wireless sets'. After she was compromised, she escaped across the Pyrenees and returned as an OSS agent in March 1944. Information from Foot, *SOE in France*, pp. 156, 171. For more information see Vigurs, *Mission France*.

11. Gilliana Gerson née Balmaceda was Chilean by birth and thus possessed a Chilean passport, which allowed her to travel to Vichy France. At the end of May 1941, she spent three weeks there staying in Lyons and Vichy, and returned with invaluable information about timetables, curfews, the papers civilians had to carry and the extent of bus and railway controls. Information from Foot, *SOE in France*, p. 156.

12. Mathilde Carré, *I Was the Cat*, Souvenir Press, London, 1959, p. 22.

13. Ibid., p. 38.

14. Ibid.

15. Ibid., p. 67.

16. Ibid.

17. Ibid., p. 70.

18. Ibid.

19. Ben Macintyre, *Double Cross*, Bloomsbury, London, 2012, p. 14.

20. Carré, *I Was the Cat*, p. 72.

21. E.H. Cookridge, *Inside SOE: The Story of Special Operations in Western Europe, 1940–45*, Arthur Barker, London, 1966, p. 130.

22. Carré, *I Was the Cat*, p. 77.

23. Macintyre, *Double Cross*, p. 15.

24. Carré, *I Was the Cat*, p. 98.

25. Ibid., p. 73.

26. Ibid.

27. Macintyre, *Double Cross*, p. 17.

28. Poland's highest military decoration for heroism and courage in the face of the enemy at war. Equivalent to the British Victoria Cross.

29. Macintyre, *Double Cross*, p. 18.

30. Ibid., p. 45.

31. Carré, *I Was the Cat*, pp. 99–100.

32. Ibid., p. 104.

33. Ibid.

34. Ibid.

35. According to historian Ben Macintyre, a former airman named Kieffer, who had been a courier, was betrayed and under torture revealed the name of his contact in the INTERALLIÉ network. The contact in turn gave the Gestapo the address of the flat in Montmartre. When Bleicher burst in, he did not even know the name of the man he was arresting.

36. Carré, *I Was the Cat*, p. 107.

37. Ibid.

38. Ibid., p. 108.

39. *Time* magazine, 'Foreign News: La Chatte', 17 January 1949, retrieved 2 March 2024.

40. Most were sent to Buchenwald; only fourteen ever got back to France.
41. Jean Overton Fuller, *The German Penetration of SOE*, George Mann Books, Bristol, 1996, p. 18.
42. Cookridge, *Inside SOE*, p. 135.
43. Ibid.
44. TNA, KV2/297.
45. Ibid.
46. Ibid.
47. Ibid.
48. Cookridge, *Inside SOE*, p. 145.
49. TNA, KV2/297.
50. Jeanne Bohec, *La Plastiqueuse à bicyclette*, Du Felin, Paris, 2022 (downloaded pdf version on 13 January 2024 with no page numbers).
51. Ibid.
52. Ibid.
53. Saywell, *Women in War*, p. 34.
54. Ibid.
55. Bohec, *La Plastiqueuse à bicyclette*.
56. Ibid.
57. Ibid.
58. Ibid.
59. Ibid.
60. Ibid.
61. Ibid.
62. Ibid.
63. Ibid.
64. Ibid.
65. Ibid.
66. Sébastien Albertelli, *Elles ont suivi de Gaulle: Histoire du Corps des volontaires françaises*, Perrin, Paris, 2020, p. 378.
67. Ibid.
68. TNA, HS9/1390/3, Marcelle Somers, Personnel File.
69. Ibid.
70. TNA, HS9/173/2, Jeanne Bohec, Personnel File.
71. Ibid.
72. Ibid.
73. Ibid.
74. Bohec, *La Plastiqueuse à bicyclette*.
75. Ibid.
76. Ibid.
77. Ibid.
78. TNA, HS9/173/2, Jeanne Bohec, Personnel File.
79. Ibid.
80. Marguerite Petitjean was destined to become a sabotage instructor but worked as a liaison officer once in the field.
81. TNA, HS9/173/2, Jeanne Bohec, Personnel File.
82. Bohec, *La Plastiqueuse à bicyclette*.
83. Saywell, *Women in War*, p. 50.

84. Ibid.
85. Bohec, *La Plastiqueuse à bicyclette*.
86. Ibid.
87. Ibid.
88. Ibid.
89. Ibid.
90. Ibid.
91. Saywell, *Women in War*, p. 47.
92. Ibid.
93. Ibid., pp. 47–8.
94. Ibid.
95. Ibid., p. 50.
96. Bohec, *La Plastiqueuse à bicyclette*.
97. Ibid.
98. Ibid.
99. Ibid.
100. Ibid.
101. Marcus Binney, *The Women Who Lived for Danger*, Coronet, London, 2002, p. 286.
102. Ibid., p. 287.
103. TNA, HS9/1498/2, Alix d'Unienville, Personnel File.
104. Ibid.
105. Ibid.
106. Ibid.

4 NACHT UND NEBEL

1. Bohec, *La Plastiqueuse à bicyclette*.
2. Brigitte Friang, *Parachutes and Petticoats*, Jarrolds Publishers, London, 1958, p. 14.
3. Ibid.
4. Ibid.
5. Ibid., p. 15.
6. Ibid.
7. Ibid.
8. Brigitte Friang, *Regarde-toi qui meurs*, Du Felin, Paris, 1997, p. 73.
9. Ibid.
10. Ibid., p. 15.
11. Ibid.
12. Ibid., p. 16.
13. Ibid.
14. Ibid.
15. Ibid., p. 19.
16. Ibid.
17. Ibid., p. 20.
18. Ibid.
19. It had been Guy who betrayed Yeo Thomas. He had taken the Gestapo straight to Passy metro from the aquarium where Yeo Thomas was waiting for Brigitte.
20. Friang, *Regarde-toi qui meurs*, p. 20.

21. Josiane was infiltrated in July 1944 to work as a wireless operator, a task in which she was very successful. She arranged for agents and provisions to be dropped to the area, which was one of the last to be liberated. She and her mother survived the war when Americans overran their area.
22. Bohec, *La Plastiqueuse à bicyclette.*
23. Ibid.
24. Ibid.
25. Ibid.
26. The 'Night and Fog Decree' was issued by Hitler on 7 December 1941, whereby prisoners were to be cut off completely from the outside world, moved frequently and apparently at random, and no records kept either of their imprisonment or even their death. All administrative and physical traces of them would be erased for ever, and they would disappear without a trace. Anyone connected to them would remain uncertain as to their fate or where-abouts.
27. Saywell, *Women in War*, p. 61.
28. Friang, *Parachutes and Petticoats*, p. 23.
29. Ibid.
30. Binney, *The Women Who Lived for Danger*, p. 303.
31. https://www.alliancefrancaise.london/Alix-Marrier-dUnienville.php.
32. TNA, HS9/1498/2, Alix d'Unienville, Personnel File.
33. Binney, *The Women Who Lived for Danger*, p. 303.
34. The Jedburgh personnel, known as 'Jeds', were selected from SOE and its American equivalent, OSS (Office of Strategic Services). A team typically consisted of a British or American officer, with another from the country they were working in, along with a radio operator who was often a sergeant. Unlike many SOE operators, the men worked in uniform.
35. Saywell, *Women in War*, p. 65.
36. Ibid.
37. Ibid.
38. Ibid.
39. Ibid., p. 67.
40. http://www.curagiu.com/la_sante_et_romainville.htm.
41. Ibid.
42. https://www.alliancefrancaise.london/Alix-Marrier-dUnienville.php.
43. Saywell, *Women in War*, p. 313.
44. Friang, *Regarde-toi qui meurs*, p. 162.
45. At least thirty of the women radio operators from North Africa completed training both in Algiers and then England, and currently twelve women who proceeded to work in the field are known by name. They are: Frédérique Bigrel, Denise Colin, Suzanne Combelas, Colette Martini, Jeanne Mereau, Geneviève Torlet, Elisabeth Torlet, Evelyne Valve, Marie-Louise Cloarec, Eugénie Djendi, Pierrette Louin and Suzanne Mertzizen.
46. Dominique Camusso and Marie-Antoinette Arrio, *La Vie brisée d'Eugénie Djendi*, L'Harmattan, Paris, 2020.
47. After being a French colony from 1830 to 1848, Algeria was designated a depart-ment, or part, of France from 4 November 1848, when the Constitution of the French Second Republic took effect, until its independence on 5 July 1962.

48. Camusso and Arrio, *La Vie brisée d'Eugénie Djendi*, p. 44.
49. Ibid.
50. Lucien Merlin, 'Les transmissions en A.F.N. de 1934 à 1944', *Armée française*, 1946. Cited in Camusso and Arrio, *La Vie brisée d'Eugénie Djendi*.
51. Camusso and Arrio, *La Vie brisée d'Eugénie Djendi*, p. 66.
52. Ibid., p. 70.
53. Fondation pour le mémoire de la déportation, Memorial Book, transport departing from Paris on 11 August 1944 (I.262.), accessed 29 February 2024.
54. TNA, HS6/437, Yvonne Baseden affidavit.
55. Trix Terwindt files, Box 1, Aviodrome archive, Lelystad, Netherlands.
56. TNA, HS6/437, Yvonne Baseden affidavit.
57. Trix Terwindt files, Box 1, Aviodrome archive, Lelystad, Netherlands.
58. Ibid.
59. There is speculation that they were shot by firing squad, but the evidence leans towards hanging. There are no definitive documents to prove either way, other than Yvonne Baseden's testimony, which has proved reliable.
60. TNA, WO 235/309 Bl.11, Judge Advocate General's Office, War Crimes Case Files, Second World War, Ravensbrück case, exhibits 1–8, March 1946.
61. Friang, *Regarde-toi qui meurs*, p. 162.
62. Ibid.
63. Ibid.
64. Saywell, *Women in War*, p. 69.

5 MISSION BELGIQUE

1. Elaine Madden, letter to Sue Elliott, 2009, quoted in Sue Elliott, *I Heard My Country Calling: Elaine Madden, Unsung Heroine of the SOE*, History Press, London, 2015, p. 244.
2. TNA, HS7/100, History of T Section.
3. Ibid.
4. Ibid.
5. Ibid.
6. Ibid.
7. Ibid.
8. Paul McCue and Peter Verstraeten, Belgian Intelligence conference, 24 November 2023, RAF Club, London, author in attendance.
9. Ibid.
10. Ibid.
11. Ibid.
12. Ibid.
13. Ibid.
14. Ibid.
15. Sue Elliott, with James Fox, *The Children Who Fought Hitler: A British Outpost in Europe*, John Murray, London, 2010, p. 70.
16. Ibid.
17. Elaine Madden interview with Sue Elliott, 7 June 2008.
18. Elliott, *The Children Who Fought Hitler*, p. 70.
19. Ibid.

20. Letter from Elaine Madden to her friend Renée Fletcher, dated June 1940.
21. Ibid.
22. Elaine Madden interview with Sue Elliott, 7 June 2008.
23. Ibid.
24. Ibid.
25. Ibid.
26. Ibid.
27. Ibid.
28. Ibid.
29. Ibid.
30. *Radio Times* magazine, article on Elaine Madden, 7–13 November 2005.
31. Elliott, *The Children Who Fought Hitler*, p. 235.
32. Inserted by Sgt E.E. Jones and Wing Commander Jack Benham in a Whitley bomber. The aircraft ditched 20 miles out to sea on the return leg of the journey, and crew and aircraft were lost.
33. TNA, HS6/112, Belgium Missions.
34. Ibid.
35. Ibid.
36. Ibid.
37. Ibid.
38. Ibid.
39. Ibid.
40. Ibid.
41. Ibid.
42. Ibid.
43. Foot, *SOE in the Low Countries*, p. 209.
44. TNA, HS6/112, Belgium Missions.
45. Ibid.
46. Ibid.
47. Elliott, *The Children Who Fought Hitler*, p. 236.
48. Ibid.
49. Elaine Madden interview with Sue Elliott, 7 June 2008.
50. TNA, HS9/973/7, Elaine Madden, Personnel File.
51. Elaine Madden interview with Sue Elliott, 7 June 2008.
52. Ibid., p. 240.
53. Ibid.
54. Ibid., p. 241.
55. TNA, HS9/973/7, Elaine Madden, Personnel File.
56. Ibid.
57. LA DAME BLANCHE was an underground intelligence network who provided information on German troop movements by rail in Belgium during the Great War.
58. Airey Neave, *Little Cyclone*, Biteback Publishing, London, 2013, p. 1.
59. https://www.conscript-heroes.com/escapelines/EEIE-Articles/Art-24-Freddy-Dupuich.htm.
60. Belgian MoD Ondersectie Notariaat Archieven.
61. TNA, HS9/460/3, Frédérique Dupuich, Personnel File.
62. Ibid.

63. Ibid.
64. Ibid.
65. Ibid.
66. Ibid.
67. Ibid.
68. Ibid.
69. Belgian MoD Ondersectie Notariaat Archieven.
70. TNA, HS9/784/1, Olga Jackson, Personnel File.
71. Ibid.
72. Ibid.
73. Ibid.
74. Ibid.
75. Ibid.
76. Ibid.
77. Ibid.
78. Ibid.
79. Ibid.
80. Ibid.
81. Ibid.
82. Ibid.
83. Ibid.
84. Ibid.
85. Ibid.
86. His second mission, 'Tybalt', had taken place between 10 August 1943 and 29 February 1944. The aim was to coordinate resistance and to try to stop deportations of forced labourers to Germany. Having escaped across the Pyrenees, he was incarcerated in Spain. He managed to get out and return to Britain via Gibraltar. He was one of only two agents to successfully complete three missions, returning to the UK each time.
87. TNA, HS6/112, Mission Imogen.
88. Ibid.
89. Elliott, *The Children Who Fought Hitler*, p. 242.
90. Ibid.
91. Ibid.
92. Ibid.
93. Ibid., p. 243.
94. TNA, HS6/112, Mission Imogen.
95. Elaine Madden interview with Sue Elliott, 7 June 2008.
96. TNA, HS9/1576/5, André Wendelen, Personnel File.
97. Elliott, *The Children Who Fought Hitler*, p. 245.
98. Ibid.
99. Ibid.
100. Ibid.
101. The last major battle of the Normandy campaign was fought in August 1944 in the so-called Falaise–Argentan pocket, where the Allies encircled and destroyed a substantial part of the German forces. Nevertheless, tens of thousands of German soldiers managed to escape.
102. Elliott, *The Children Who Fought Hitler*, p. 247.

103. Elaine Madden interview with Sue Elliott, 7 June 2008.
104. Ibid.
105. TNA, HS6/112, Mission Imogen.
106. Ibid.
107. Ibid.
108. Elaine Madden interview with Sue Elliott, 7 June 2008.
109. TNA, HS9/928/1, Renée Lippens, Personnel File.
110. Ibid.
111. Ibid.
112. Ibid.
113. Ibid.
114. Ibid.
115. FL Mercer & Co., sale notice for Drokes House, 26 November 1938.
116. Ibid.
117. One hundred and twenty French, ninety-six British, ninety-six American, thirty Belgian, thirty Dutch, eighteen Polish and ten parachutists from Luxembourg.
118. Elaine Madden interview with Sue Elliott, 7 June 2008.
119. Ibid.

6 MISSION NEDERLANDS

1. *The Times*, Trix Terwindt obituary, 4 May 1987.
2. Theo van Duren, *Orange Above*, Staples Press, London, 1956, p. 10.
3. Radio Oranje was the voice of the Dutch government in exile, and it was broadcast on the BBC. Radio Herrijzend Nederland broadcast from the southern part of the country. Listening to either programme was forbidden under German occupation.
4. H.J. Giskes, *London Calling North Pole: The True Revelations of a German Spy*, Echo Point Books & Media, Brattleboro, VT, 1953, pp. 175–6.
5. The first agents were put ashore by boat, but they were SIS/CIS, not SOE.
6. M.R.D. Foot, *SOE 1940–1945*, BBC, London, 1984, p. 131.
7. Giskes, *London Calling North Pole*, p. 185.
8. A Dutch group founded during the occupation, which was criticised for collaboration with the Nazis and its ban on Jews becoming members; it nonetheless had around 600,000 supporters at its peak.
9. Ingrid van der Chijs, *Luchtmeisjes*, Nijgh & Van Ditmar, Amsterdam 2013, p. 43 (AI translation).
10. TNA, HS9/1452/8, Trix Terwindt, Personnel File.
11. Van der Chijs, *Luchtmeisjes*, p. 125.
12. Ibid., p. 127.
13. TNA, HS9/1452/8, Trix Terwindt, Personnel File.
14. Van der Chijs, *Luchtmeisjes*, p. 133.
15. TNA, HS9/1452/8, Trix Terwindt, Personnel File.
16. Ibid.
17. Van der Chijs, *Luchtmeisjes*, p. 173.
18. TNA, HS9/1452/8, Trix Terwindt, Personnel File.

19. Ibid.
20. Ibid.
21. Nowadays the water of the LZ is called Markermeer, due to a dyke built in 1963–76.
22. Trix Terwindt Archive, Box 1, Letter to Airey Neave, Aviodrome.
23. Ibid.
24. Ibid.
25. TNA, HS7/274, SOE War Diary 48, Volume I, Netherlands, July 1942–December 1943, p. 72.
26. Trix Terwindt Archive, Box 1, Letter to Airey Neave, Aviodrome.
27. Ibid.
28. In the same letter Trix says that they asked her for the lighter containing her codes. The matchbox is more likely as other agents all had matchboxes, not lighters.
29. Ibid.
30. Van der Chijs, *Luchtmeisjes*, p. 183.
31. Information supplied by Coen Hijszeler.
32. They escaped through Switzerland and made it back to England, where they reported on 'Englandspiel' to the Dutch legation there, who passed the information along to the British government. By this time flights had temporarily ceased due to the number of aircraft and aircrew casualties.
33. Pieter Dourlein, *Inside North Pole*, William Kimber, London, 1953, p. 106.
34. Giskes, *London Calling North Pole*, p. 135.
35. Corrie Ten Boom, *A Prisoner and Yet . . .*, CLC Publications, 1980. PDF version, no page numbers.
36. Van der Chijs, *Luchtmeisjes*, p. 190.
37. Ibid.
38. Trix Terwindt Archive, Box 1, Ravensbrück file, Aviodrome.
39. Ibid.
40. Ibid.
41. Ibid.
42. https://www.mauthausen-memorial.org/en/History/The-Mauthausen-Concentration-Camp-19381945.
43. Around 3,000 female prisoners were officially registered in the Mauthausen women's concentration camp. However, in total around 10,000 women passed through the Mauthausen camp system.
44. Forty Dutch, six British and one American SOE agents were executed in Mauthausen on 6/7 September 1944. Eleven Dutch agents went missing after Rawicz and some agents died in other camps. Ubbink and Dourlein, who escaped from Haaren, and van der Ryeden and Lauwers (the first man arrested) survived.
45. Van der Chijs, *Luchtmeisjes*, p. 194.
46. This was based on a decree for the protection of people and state and was defined as a forced measure against persons who were seen to pose a threat to the security of the people and the state. Correspondence with Peter Egger, Collections Department, Mauthausen memorial site.
47. Ibid., p. 195.

48. Nigel West, *Secret War: The Story of SOE*, Coronet Books, London, 1992, p. 127.
49. A similar situation played out with SOE F Section and Noor Inayat Khan who, although operating under duress and leaving out her security checks, was deemed to be careless, and still at liberty.
50. Ibid.
51. Dourlein, *Inside North Pole*, p. 190.
52. They were not released until after D-Day, possibly so that they could not betray that information either.
53. Foot, *SOE in the Low Countries*, chapter 7; 'SOE: A New Instrument of War', IWM, 2006, p. 83.
54. *Englandspiel*, episode five, 'The Survivors, or the Consequences and Cause of the Spiel', aired 1 February 1979, Netherlands One. Accessed via YouTube, 3 May 2024.

7 BEYOND 'ENGLANDSPIEL'

1. Jos Gemmeke files, Crash Museum, Fort bij Aalsmeer, Aalsmeerderbrug.
2. Eddy de Roever, *Sphinx: The Story of Jos Gemmeke, a Fascinating Woman*, Hollandia BV, Baarn, 1987 (AI translated), p. 20.
3. Jos Gemmeke files, Crash Museum.
4. TNA, HS9/572/4, Jos Gemmeke, Personnel File.
5. Ibid.
6. De Roever, *Sphinx*, p. 36.
7. Ibid., p. 37.
8. TNA, HS9/572/4, Jos Gemmeke, Personnel File.
9. Ibid.
10. Ibid.
11. TNA, HS9/650/2, Antonia Hamilton, Personnel File.
12. Ibid.
13. Ibid.
14. Ibid.
15. Ibid.
16. Ibid.
17. This can be seen in Crash Museum, Fort bij Aalsmeer, Aalsmeerderbrug.
18. Jos Gemmeke files, Crash Museum.
19. This story became embellished after the war, and she claimed that the raid was carried out by the Dutch airforce and that her future husband had been flying one of the aircraft that had fired on her.
20. Jos Gemmeke files, Crash Museum.
21. Ibid.
22. Ibid.
23. De Roever, *Sphinx*, p. 101.
24. Jos Gemmeke obituary, *The Times*, 14 January 2011, accessed online 8 May 2024.
25. TNA, HS9/572/4, Jos Gemmeke, Personnel File.
26. De Roever, *Sphinx*, pp. 106–7.
27. Ibid., p. 104.

28. Ibid.
29. Ibid., p. 107.
30. Eddy de Roever, *London roept Amsterdam*, Hollandia BV, Baarn, 1992 (AI translated), pp. 152–3.
31. TNA, HS9/1506/2, Annemarie Hilten, Personnel File.
32. De Roever, *Sphinx*, p. 116.
33. Ibid.
34. Ibid.
35. TNA, HS9/572/4, Jos Gemmeke, Personnel File.
36. Ibid.
37. Ibid.
38. Ibid.
39. Although the second part of her mission was for X Section, Jos was part of N Section for the rest of her work and under their auspices for administrative purposes (PF).
40. Ibid.
41. Ibid.
42. Ibid.
43. TNA, HS9/1506/2, Annemarie Hilten, Personnel File.
44. Ibid.
45. Ibid.
46. Crash Museum permanent exhibition.
47. De Roever, *Sphinx*, p. 135.
48. Ibid.
49. Ibid.
50. Ibid.
51. Jos's suit and helmet are on display in Museum 1940–1945, Dordrecht. A dress made from her parachute may be seen at Crash Museum, Fort bij Aalsmeer, Aalsmeerderbrug.
52. De Roever, *Sphinx*, pp. 135–6.
53. Ibid.
54. Ibid., p. 38.
55. Ibid.
56. Sauckel, the Nazi labour minister, was tried and hanged at Nuremberg for the way in which he ran these camps.
57. Jos Gemmeke files, Crash Museum.
58. TNA, HS9/1367/3, Jantje Sissingh, Personnel File.
59. Ibid.
60. Ibid.
61. De Roever, *Sphinx*, p. 142.
62. Ibid.
63. Ibid.
64. Ibid.
65. TNA, HS9/572/4, Jos Gemmeke, Personnel File.
66. Ibid.
67. Information from 'Tante Jos' podcast. Extracted and translated by Coen Hijszeler.

8 MISSION DANSKA

1. Varinka Muus (80012826), audio archive, Imperial War Museum.
2. Guidebook, Museum of Danish Resistance, p. 10.
3. Ibid.
4. Ibid., p. 14.
5. On 9/10 November 1938, Nazi leaders unleashed a series of pogroms against the Jewish population in Germany and recently incorporated territories. This event came to be called *Kristallnacht* (the Night of Broken Glass) because of the shattered glass that littered the streets after the vandalism and destruction of Jewish-owned businesses, synagogues and homes. As the violence spread and following Heydrich's instructions, units of the SS and Gestapo arrested approximately 30,000 Jewish males and transferred most of them from local prisons to Dachau, Buchenwald, Sachsenhausen and other concentration camps.
6. Jutta Graae, *Værnepligt*, Odense University Press, Odense, 1995, p. 10.
7. Ibid., p. 12.
8. Jutta Graae (RA 255553-8), audio archive, Museum of Danish Resistance.
9. Ibid.
10. Ibid.
11. Around 2,000 did not survive the war.
12. Rowland White, *Mosquito: The RAF's Legendary Wooden Wonder and its Most Extraordinary Mission*, Bantam, London, 2023, p. 34.
13. Between December 1940 and November 1941, Hambro was also in charge of overseeing the French, Belgian, German and Dutch sections of SOE, and from November 1941 he was deputy leader of SOE for five months.
14. Deborah Hopkinson, *Courage and Defiance: Stories of Spies, Saboteurs, and Survivors in World War II Denmark*, Scholastic, New York, 2016, p. 47.
15. Ibid.
16. Knud Jespersen, *No Small Achievement: Special Operations Executive and the Danish Resistance 1940–1945*, University Press of Southern Denmark, Odense, 2002, pp. 44–5.
17. Lieutenant Commander Ralph Hollingworth was attached to the naval attaché's office in Denmark and became head of SOE's Danish department in England. Ronald Turnbull, who was press attaché here, became head of SOE's department in Stockholm. Henry Denham, who was naval attaché and had come to Denmark a few months beforehand, became naval attaché in Stockholm. Reginald Spink, who was also in Denmark on 9 April, became Hollingworth's second-in-command at the start of SOE. Graae's memoirs.
18. Graae, *Værnepligt*, p. 19.
19. Ibid.
20. Eventually he came up with a meticulous operations plan called 'Booklet'. It had six parts and was a blueprint for an effective resistance effort in Denmark: 'Chair' – building a secret army with Denmark; 'Dresser' – developing lines of communication; 'Settee' – a financial structure to fund local resistance operations; 'Chest' – anti-German propaganda; 'Divan' – a special intelligence network; and 'Table' – the effort to build sabotage groups within Denmark. Hopkinson, *Courage and Defiance*, p. 48.

21. Graae, *Værnepligt*, p. 14.
22. Ibid.
23. Ibid., p. 15.
24. Ibid.
25. Ibid., p. 26.
26. Ibid.
27. Juncker married a Danish woman in London in 1945. After his divorce, he and Jutta became lovers and were eventually married in 1960.
28. Edith Bonnesen, radio broadcast on Denmark's Radio, January 1976, Museum of Danish Resistance.
29. Ibid.
30. Ibid.
31. Ibid.
32. Ibid.
33. Ibid.
34. Ibid.
35. Their exploits were made into four comic books and after the war the young men met with Winston Churchill.
36. Trine Engholm Michelsen, *Storfyrstinden*, People's Press, Copenhagen, 2021, p. 86.
37. The Muus family in Denmark were wealthy businesspeople who were closely connected with SIS. It was SIS who 'exported' Flemming to Liberia, where he observed for them. This caused the later rivalry between SOE and SIS on recruiting him in London.
38. Flemming Muus, *The Spark and the Flame: The Saga of Wartime Sabotage in Denmark*, London Museum Press, London, 1956, p. 54.
39. Varinka Muus (21931), audio archive, Museum of Danish Resistance.
40. Christine Sutherland, *Monica: Heroine of the Danish Resistance*, Canongate Books, Edinburgh, 1991, pp. 93–4.
41. Varinka Muus (80012826), audio archive, Imperial War Museum.
42. Ibid.
43. Varinka Muus (21931), audio archive, Museum of Danish Resistance.
44. Muus, *The Spark and the Flame*, p. 106.
45. Ibid.
46. Ibid.
47. Jutta Graae (RA 255553-8), audio archive, Museum of Danish Resistance.
48. Graae, *Værnepligt*, p. 29.
49. Ibid.
50. Ibid.
51. He did not abdicate.
52. Graae, *Værnepligt*, p. 29.
53. Ibid.
54. Ibid., p. 30.
55. Ibid.
56. Muus, *The Spark and the Flame*, pp. 106–7.
57. Varinka Muus (21931), audio archive, Museum of Danish Resistance.
58. Ibid.

59. Edith Bonnesen, radio broadcast on Denmark's Radio, January 1976, Museum of Danish Resistance.
60. Ibid.
61. Ibid.
62. Ibid.
63. Ibid.
64. Ibid.
65. https://biografiskleksikon.lex.dk/L._A._Duus_Hansen, accessed January 2024.
66. Graae, *Værnepligt*, p. 33.
67. Ibid.

9 ESCAPE AND EVASION

1. Edith Bonnesen, radio broadcast on Denmark's Radio, 9 April 1985, Museum of Danish Resistance.
2. Graae, *Værnepligt*, p. 33.
3. Ibid.
4. Ibid.
5. Varinka Muus (80012826), audio archive, Imperial War Museum.
6. Muus, *The Spark and the Flame*, p. 123.
7. Half of the crew eventually got to Sweden and back to England, while the other half went to a POW camp for the rest of the war.
8. Varinka Muus (80012826), audio archive, Imperial War Museum.
9. Ibid.
10. Ibid.
11. Ibid.
12. Ibid.
13. Graae, *Værnepligt*, pp. 45–6.
14. Ibid., p. 34.
15. Ibid., p. 35.
16. Ibid., p. 45.
17. Ibid.
18. Ibid., p. 46.
19. Ibid.
20. Correspondence with Trine Engholm Michelsen, author of *Storfyrstinden*, 14 February 2024.
21. This was not to be the case, and the relationship ended after the liberation.
22. Graae, *Værnepligt*, p. 45.
23. Ibid., p. 35.
24. Ibid.
25. Correspondence with Trine Engholm Michelsen, author of *Storfyrstinden*, 14 February 2024.
26. Ibid.
27. Ibid., p. 44.
28. Muus, *The Spark and the Flame*, pp. 154–5.
29. Ibid.
30. Ibid.
31. Ibid.

32. Ibid.
33. Ibid.
34. White, *Mosquito*, p. 191.
35. Muus, *The Spark and the Flame*, pp. 157–8.
36. Varinka Muus (21931), audio archive, Museum of Danish Resistance.
37. Varinka Muus (80012826), audio archive, Imperial War Museum.
38. Ibid.
39. Ibid.
40. Ibid.
41. Engholm Michelsen, *Storfyrstinden*, p. 88.
42. Edith Bonnesen, radio broadcast on Denmark's Radio, 9 April 1985, Museum of Danish Resistance.
43. Ibid.
44. Ibid.
45. Ibid.
46. Ibid.
47. Fellow resisters Little Pete and Lok Lindblad did see her but at the time she didn't know.
48. Danish National Archives, Rigsarkivet, Edith Bonnesen, 05184.
49. Edith Bonnesen, radio broadcast on Denmark's Radio, 9 April 1985, Museum of Danish Resistance.
50. Ibid.
51. Ibid.
52. Ibid.
53. Ibid.
54. Ibid.
55. Ibid.
56. Ibid.
57. Edith Bonnesen, radio broadcast on Denmark's Radio, January 1976, Museum of Danish Resistance.
58. Ibid.
59. Ibid.
60. Ibid.
61. Graae, *Værnepligt*, p. 50.
62. TNA, HS9/605/3, Jutta Graae, Personnel File.
63. Engholm Michelsen, *Storfyrstinden*, p. 156.
64. Scotland Yard and SOE confirmed Muus's behaviour. He continued his forging in London during the winter of 1944–5. Hollingworth and the small group of SOE Danes in London kept the secret. He was accused of fraud after the war and Varinka furiously defended his innocence.
65. Graae, *Værnepligt*, p. 49.
66. Ibid., p. 50.
67. Ibid., p. 51.
68. Varinka Muus (80012826), audio archive, Imperial War Museum.
69. Graae, *Værnepligt*, p. 57.
70. TNA, HS9/605/3, Jutta Graae, Personnel File.
71. Ibid.
72. Ibid.

73. Graae, *Værnepligt*, p. 57.
74. Ibid.
75. Ibid.
76. Varinka Muus (80012826), audio archive, Imperial War Museum.
77. TNA, HS9/1081/2, Varinka Muus, Personnel File.
78. Ibid.
79. Ibid.
80. Ibid.
81. Ibid.
82. Muus, *The Spark and the Flame*, p. 170.
83. TNA, HS9/1081/2, Varinka Muus, Personnel File.
84. Ibid.
85. Graae, *Værnepligt*, p. 57.
86. Ibid.
87. Jutta Graae (RA 255553-8), audio archive, Museum of Danish Resistance.
88. David Zabecki, *World War II in Europe: An Encyclopedia*, Taylor & Francis, London, 1999, pp. 350–1.
89. White, *Mosquito*, p. 379.
90. 'About the Shell House Attack' by Anders Straarup – translated from the article in Danish: https://www.airmen.dk/pdfs/VHTmarts2020ASe.pdf, accessed 28 January 2024.
91. Incorrectly referenced as a V-1 in Jutta's memoirs.
92. www.v2rocket.com, accessed 28 January 2024.
93. Varinka Muus (21931), audio archive, Museum of Danish Resistance.
94. Ibid.
95. Ibid.
96. TNA, HS9/1081/2, Varinka Muus, Personnel File.
97. Ibid.
98. Ibid.
99. Ibid.
100. Ibid.
101. Graae, *Værnepligt*, p. 59.
102. Ibid.
103. Ibid., p. 60.
104. Ibid., p. 62.
105. Ibid.
106. Ibid., p. 63.
107. Ibid.
108. Varinka Muus (80012826), audio archive, Imperial War Museum.
109. Graae, *Værnepligt*, p. 60.
110. Ibid.
111. Ibid.

10 MISSION PALMACH

1. Hannah Szenes, 'One–two–three', in Szenes, *Hannah Senesh: Her Life and Diary*, p. 257.
2. Yad Vashem Archives O.3/6988.

3. Alex Weissberg, *Advocate for the Dead: The Story of Joel Brand*, Four Square, London, 1960, p. 1.
4. Ibid.
5. Syria was a French mandate that had been given its independence (in 1943), but the British army (using a lot of ex- and future-Palmach Palestinian Jews) had been fighting the (Vichy) Syrians.
6. Weissberg, *Advocate for the Dead*, p. 1.
7. Ibid.
8. Egy Igazi Mensch, *Hanna Szenes*, Mensch International Foundation, 2014, p. 22.
9. Ibid., p. 23.
10. Anthony Masters, *The Summer That Bled: The Biography of Hannah Senesh*, Michael Joseph, London, 1972, p. 48.
11. Ibid., p. 26.
12. Szenes, *Hannah Senesh: Her Life and Diary*, pp. 81–2.
13. Masters, *The Summer That Bled*, p. 58.
14. Sdot Yam started out as a nucleus near Haifa, but it deployed to Caesarea in 1940 to – in effect – be a PalYam base.
15. Masters, *The Summer That Bled*, p. 104.
16. The Yishuv – literally 'settlement' – was the community of Jews living in the Palestine Mandate. It was a population with some social cohesion. It had representative organisations: the Jewish Agency (which was a quasi-government), the Histadrut (the Trades Unions Council), the Jewish National Fund (the land fund) among others (correspondence with Lynette Nusbacher). Eretz Israel (meaning the Land of Israel) is a philosophical, theological and halakhic (Jewish legal) concept and is not equivalent to the political State of Israel (https://rossingcenter.org/judaisms/eretz-israel).
17. The support was removed as soon as the German threat dissipated.
18. https://palmach.org.il, accessed online 5 April 2024.
19. *Jerusalem Post*, Surica Braverman obituary, 28 February 2013, accessed online 5 April 2024.
20. Masters, *The Summer That Bled*, pp. 118–19.
21. Ibid., p. 120.
22. Szenes, *Hannah Senesh: Her Life and Diary*, p. 129.
23. Masters, *The Summer That Bled*, p. 126.
24. Yoel Palgi, *Into the Inferno: The Memoir of a Jewish Paratrooper Behind Nazi Lines*, Rutgers University Press, New Brunswick, 2003, p. 2.
25. Ibid.
26. Szenes, *Hannah Senesh: Her Life and Diary*, p. 131.
27. Palgi, *Into the Inferno*, p. 6.
28. Ibid., p. 8.
29. Ibid., p. 10.
30. Masters, *The Summer That Bled*, p. 151.
31. Szenes, *Hannah Senesh: Her Life and Diary*, p. 167.
32. Ibid., p. 173.
33. Ibid.
34. Yad Vashem Archives O.3/6988.
35. Szenes, *Hannah Senesh: Her Life and Diary*, p. 177.

36. Yad Vashem Archives O.3/6988.
37. Szenes, *Hannah Senesh: Her Life and Diary*, p. 178.
38. Yad Vashem Archives O.3/7393.

11 DEATH BE NOT PROUD

1. *Jerusalem Post*, Surica Braverman obituary.
2. Ibid.
3. Ibid.
4. Tehila Ofer and Zeev Ofer, *Haviva Reik: A Kibbutz Pioneer's Mission and Fall Behind Nazi Lines*, Fawns Publishing, USA, 2014, p. 319.
5. Ibid., p. 323.
6. Ibid.
7. Ibid.
8. Ibid.
9. Ibid.
10. Ibid., p. 365.
11. TNA, WO208/3414, Sara Braverman, Personnel File.
12. Ibid.
13. Ibid.
14. *Jerusalem Post*, Surica Braverman obituary.
15. TNA, WO208/3414, Sara Braverman, Personnel File.
16. Ibid.
17. Szenes, *Hannah Senesh: Her Life and Diary*, p. 207.
18. Ibid., p. 207.
19. Ibid., p. 212.
20. Ibid., p. 218.
21. Ibid., p. 220.
22. Ibid., p. 222.
23. Ibid., p. 232.
24. Ibid.
25. Avraham carried a photograph of Haviva in his wallet until the day he died.
26. United States Holocaust Memorial Museum. 'The Holocaust in Slovakia', *Holocaust Encyclopaedia*, https://encyclopedia.ushmm.org/content/en/article/the-holocaust-in-slovakia, accessed 5 April 2024.
27. These groups were Slovak gendarmes and military personnel, units of the Slovak People's Party's paramilitary organisation, the Hlinka Guard, and members of the Slovak ethnic German paramilitary formation Freiwillige Schutzstaffel (Volunteer SS).
28. The Czechoslovak Agrarian Party (part of the Social Democratic Party), the Communist Party and sectors of the Slovak nationalists.
29. In all, German and Slovak authorities deported more than 70,000 Jews from Slovakia; the Germans murdered more than 60,000 of them.
30. https://israeled.org/nazis-kill-palmach-paratrooper-haviva-reik, accessed 5 April 2024.
31. The other aircraft carried seven OSS agents as part of an American delegation to free Slovakia.
32. TNA, WO208/3414, Sara Braverman, Personnel File.

33. Ibid.
34. The SOE operation 'Windproof' was destined for Hungary via Slovakia but the team were caught up in the collapsing Slovak Uprising. Major Sehmer was later captured, tortured and killed at Mauthausen concentration camp.
35. Ibid.
36. https://www.jewishheroes.live/hero-en/reik, accessed 5 April 2024.
37. Szenes, *Hannah Senesh: Her Life and Diary*, p. 236.
38. Yoel Palgi, *And Behold, A Great Wind Came*, 1978, pp. 194–6. Accessed through Yad Vashem online archive.
39. Szenes, *Hannah Senesh: Her Life and Diary*, p. 240.
40. Ibid.
41. Rafi and Zvi had significantly better cells.
42. TNA, WO208/3415, Marta Martinovich, Personnel File.
43. Berdiczew was deported to Mauthausen concentration camp and killed. Hermesh escaped and eventually returned to Palestine.
44. Kasztner was accused of having been a Nazi collaborator and was tried. The judge ruled that he 'sold his soul to the devil' by negotiating with Eichmann. He also selected some Jews to be saved while neglecting to alert others. He was assassinated in Tel Aviv in March 1957.

BIBLIOGRAPHY

GENERAL

Albertelli, Sébastien, *Elles ont suivi de Gaulle: Histoire du Corps des Volontaires françaises*, Perrin, Paris, 2020

Armstrong, David, *At Close Quarters: SOE Close Combat Pistol Instructor Colonel Hector Grant-Taylor*, Fonthill Media, Stroud, 2013

Atkin, Malcolm, *Section D for Destruction: Forerunner of SOE*, Pen and Sword, Barnsley, 2017

Batalion, Judy, *The Light of Days: Women Fighters of the Jewish Resistance*, Virago, London, 2022

Beevor, Antony, *The Mystery of Olga Chekhova: A Life Torn Apart by Revolution and War*, Penguin, London, 2005

Bines, Jeffrey, *Poland's SOE: A British Perspective*, Polish Underground Movement Study Trust, London, 2018

Binney, Marcus, *The Women Who Lived for Danger: The Women Agents of SOE in the Second World War*, Coronet, London, 2002

Bishop, Patrick, *The Man Who Was Saturday: The Extraordinary Life of Airey Neave*, William Collins, London, 2019

Bogle, Joanna, *Sue Ryder: A Life Lived for Others*, Gracewing, Leominster, 2002

Bohec, Jeanne, *La Plastiqueuse à bicyclette*, Du Felin, Paris, 2022

Bondy, Ruth, *The Emissary: A Life of Enzo Sereni*, Robson Books, London, 1977

Brady, Tim, *Three Ordinary Girls: The Remarkable Story of Three Dutch Teenagers Who Became Spies, Saboteurs, Nazi Assassins – and WWII Heroes*, Citadel Press Inc., New York, 2021

Camusso, Dominique, and Marie-Antoinette Arrio, *La Vie brisée d'Eugénie Djendi*, L'Harmattan, Paris, 2020

Carré, Mathilde, *I Was the Cat*, Souvenir Press, London, 1959

Clark, Tim, and Nick Cook, *Monopoli Blues*, Unbound, London, 2018

Cookridge, E.H., *Inside SOE: The Story of Special Operations in Western Europe, 1940–45*, Arthur Barker, London, 1966

Cruickshank, Charles, *SOE in the Far East*, Oxford University Press, Oxford, 1983

—, *SOE in Scandinavia*, Oxford University Press, Oxford, 1986

Davies, Norman, *Rising '44: The Battle for Warsaw*, Pan Books, London, 2004

de Gaulle, Charles, *Discours et Messages, 1940–1946*, Éditions Berger-Levrault, Paris, 1946

Dourlein, Pieter, *Inside North Pole: A Secret Agent's Story*, William Kimber, London, 1953

Elliott, Sue, with James Fox, *The Children Who Fought Hitler: A British Outpost in Europe*, John Murray, London, 2010

—, *I Heard My Country Calling: Elaine Madden, Unsung Heroine of the SOE*, History Press, London, 2015

Engholm Michelsen, Trine, *Storfyrstinden*, People's Press, Copenhagen, 2021

Escott, Squadron Leader Beryl E., *The Heroines of SOE: Britain's Secret Women in France*, History Press, London, 2010

Foot, M.R.D., *Holland at War Against Hitler*, Frank Cass, London, 1990

—, *MI9: Escape and Evasion 1939–1945*, Book Club Associates, London, 1979

—, *Six Faces of Courage*, Eyre Methuen, London, 1978

—, *SOE: The Special Operations Executive 1940–46*, BBC, London, 1985

—, *SOE in the Low Countries*, Amberley, Stroud, 2017

Fourcade, Marie-Madeleine, *Noah's Ark*, Dutton, New York, 1974

Frame, Alan, *Toto & Coco: Spies, Seduction and the Fight for Survival*, Kelvin House, Glasgow, 2020

Friang, Brigitte, *Parachutes and Petticoats*, Jarrolds Publishers, London, 1958

—, *Regarde-toi qui meurs*, Du Felin, Paris, 1997

Friedhoff, Herman, *Requiem for the Resistance: The Civilian Struggle Against Nazism in Holland and Germany*, Bloomsbury, London, 1988

Fry, Helen, *The London Cage: The Secret History of Britain's World War II Interrogation Centre*, Yale University Press, New Haven and London, 2017

—, *MI9: A History of the Secret Service for Escape and Evasion in World War Two*, Yale University Press, New Haven and London, 2021

—, *Women in Intelligence: The Hidden History of Two World Wars*, Yale University Press, New Haven and London, 2023

Garlinski, Jozef, *Poland, SOE and the Allies*, George Allen & Unwin, London, 1969

Giskes, H.J., *London Calling North Pole: The True Revelations of a German Spy*, Echo Point Books & Media, Brattleboro, VT, 1953

Graae, Jutta, *Værnepligt*, Odense University Press, Odense, 1995

Hastings, Max, *The Secret War: Spies, Codes and Guerrillas 1939–1945*, William Collins, London, 2016

Hazelhoff, Erik, *Soldier of Orange*, Sphere Books, London, 1982

Hopkinson, Deborah, *Courage and Defiance: Stories of Spies, Saboteurs, and Survivors in World War II Denmark*, Scholastic, New York, 2016

Jenkins, Ray, *A Pacifist at War: The Silence of Francis Cammaerts*, Arrow, London, 2010

Jespersen, Knud, *No Small Achievement: Special Operations Executive and the Danish Resistance 1940–1945*, University Press of Southern Denmark, Odense, 2002

King, Stella, *Jacqueline: Pioneer Heroine of the Resistance*, Arms and Armour Press, London, 1989

Le Chêne, Evelyn, *Mauthausen: The History of a Death Camp*, Methuen, London, 1971

Macintyre, Ben, *Agent Sonya: Moscow's Most Daring Wartime Spy*, Penguin, London, 2021

—, *Double Cross: The True Story of the D-Day Spies*, Bloomsbury, London, 2012

Mackenzie, William, *The Secret History of SOE: Special Operations Executive 1940–1945*, St Ermin's Press, London, 2000

Marks, Leo, *Between Silk and Cyanide: A Codemaker's War 1941–1945*, HarperCollins, London, 1999

Masson, Madeleine, *Christine: A Search for Christine Granville, GM, OBE, Croix de Guerre*, Hamish Hamilton, London, 1975

Masters, Anthony, *The Summer That Bled: The Biography of Hannah Senesh*, Michael Joseph, London, 1972

Mensch, Egy Igazi, *Hanna Szenes*, Mensch International Foundation, 2014

Miller, Russell, *Behind the Lines: The Oral History of Special Operations in World War II*, Pimlico, London, 2003

Milton, Giles, *Churchill's Ministry of Ungentlemanly Warfare: The Mavericks Who Plotted Hitler's Defeat*, John Murray, London, 2017

Minczykowska, Katarzyna, *Cichociemna, Generał Elżbieta Zawacka 'Zo'*, Fundacja General Elżbiety Zawackiej, Toruń, 2014

—, *Elżbieta Zawacka alias 'Zelma', 'Sulica', 'Zo'*, Fundacja General Elżbiety Zawackiej, Toruń, 2016

Montagu, Elizabeth, *Honourable Rebel*, Montagu Ventures, Beaulieu, 2003

Mulley, Clare, *The Spy Who Loved: The Secrets and Lives of One of Britain's Bravest Wartime Heroines*, Macmillan, London, 2012

Muus, Flemming, *The Spark and the Flame: The Saga of Wartime Sabotage in Denmark*, Museum Press, London, 1956

Neave, Airey, *Little Cyclone*, Biteback Publishing, London, 2013

—, *Saturday at MI9*, Grafton, London, 1989

Ofer, Tehila, and Zeev Ofer, *Haviva Reik: A Kibbutz Pioneer's Mission and Fall Behind Nazi Lines*, Fawns Publishing, USA, 2014

Olson, Lynne, *Madame Fourcade's Secret War: The Daring Young Woman Who Led France's Largest Spy Network Against Hitler*, Scribe, London, 2019

Ottaway, Susan, *Violette Szabo: The Life That I Have*, Pen and Sword, Barnsley, 2003

Overton Fuller, Jean, *The German Penetration of SOE*, George Mann Books, Bristol, 1996

Palgi, Yoel, *Into the Inferno: The Memoir of a Jewish Paratrooper Behind Nazi Lines*, Rutgers University Press, New Brunswick, 2003

Pawley, Margaret, *In Obedience to Instructions: FANY with the SOE in the Mediterranean*, Leo Cooper, Barnsley, 1999

Photiadou, A.J., 'The Detention of Non-Enemy Civilians Escaping to Britain During the Second World War', *Historical Journal*, 65(2) (2022), pp. 482–504, doi: 10.1017/S0018246X2100008X

Picardie, Justine, *Miss Dior: A Wartime Story of Courage and Couture*, Faber, London, 2022

Rigden, Dennis, *SOE Syllabus*, PRO, London, 2001

Ritchie, Alexandra, *Warsaw 1944: The Fateful Uprising*, William Collins, London, 2013

Roever, Eddy de, *London roept Amsterdam*, Hollandia BV, Baarn, 1992

—, *Sphinx: The Story of Jos Gemmeke, A Fascinating Woman*, Hollandia BV, Baarn, 1987

Rogalski, W., *SOE Polish Section: The Death of the Second Polish Republic*, Hellion, Warwick, 2022

Ryder, Sue, *And the Morrow Is Theirs*, Burleigh Press, Bristol, 1975

—, *Child of My Love*, Collins Harvill, London, 1986

Saywell, Shelley, *Women in War*, Costello, London, 1985

Stafford, David, *Mission Accomplished: SOE and Italy 1943–1945*, Bodley Head, London, 2011

Strauss, Gwen, *The Nine: How a Band of Daring Resistance Women Escaped from Nazi Germany*, Manilla Press, London, 2022

Sutherland, Christine, *Monica: Heroine of the Danish Resistance*, Canongate Books, Edinburgh, 1991

Szenes, Hannah, *Hannah Senesh: Her Life and Diary*, intro. Abba Eban, Hakibbutz Publishing House, Tel Aviv, 1966

Tremain, David, *Double Agent Victoire: Mathilde Carré and the Interallié Network*, History Press, Stroud, 2018

Urquhart, Clara, and Peter Ludwig Brent, *Enzo Sereni: A Hero of Our Times*, Robert Hale Ltd, London, 1967

Valentine, Ian, *Station 43: Audley End House and SOE's Polish Section*, History Press, Stroud, 2006

van der Chijs, Ingrid, *Luchtmeisjes*, Nijgh & Van Ditmar, Amsterdam, 2013

van der Zee, Henri A., *The Hunger Winter: Occupied Holland 1944–1945*, J. Norman & Hobhouse, London, 1982

van Duren, Theo, *Orange Above*, Staples Press, London, 1956

Vigurs, Kate, *Mission France: The True History of the Women of SOE*, Yale University Press, New Haven and London, 2021

Walker, Jonathan, *Poland Alone: SOE and the Collapse of the Polish Resistance, 1944*, History Press, London, 2008

Weissberg, Alex, *Advocate for the Dead: The Story of Joel Brand*, Four Square, London, 1960

West, Nigel, *Secret War: The Story of SOE*, Coronet Books, London, 1992

White, Rowland, *Mosquito: The RAF's Legendary Wooden Wonder and its Most Extraordinary Mission*, Bantam, London, 2023

Zabecki, David, *World War II in Europe: An Encyclopedia*, Taylor & Francis, London, 1999

ARCHIVES

AVIODROME ARCHIVE, THE NETHERLANDS

Trix Terwindt files

BELGIAN MOD ONDERSECTIE NOTARIAAT ARCHIEVEN

CRASH MUSEUM 1940–1945, THE NETHERLANDS

Jos Gemmeke files

DANISH NATIONAL ARCHIVES (BLACK DIAMOND), COPENHAGEN, DENMARK

Rigsarkivet, Edith Bonnesen, 05184

DANISH RESISTANCE MUSEUM, COPENHAGEN, DENMARK

22-25553, Janni Andreassen
22-21329, Jutta Regitse Pilegaard Graae
22-25554, Jutta Regitse Pilegaard Graae
42-26096-1, Kirke and Sogneblad Udbyneder-Kastbjerg, no. 2, 2002, with a portrait
   article about Flemming Juncker and Jutta Juncker f. Graae
15B-21619, Vivi Jørstad
08A-26088-5, Interview with Flemming and Varinka Muus 29.5.1974
11A-21931, Varinka Wichfeld Muus
11A-24796-56, Peter Edelberg, Peter Edelberg's research archive regarding SOE's
   work in Denmark: Material regarding Flemming B. Muus and Varinka Muus
11A-24796-69, Peter Edelberg, Peter Edelberg's research archive regarding SOE's
   work in Denmark: Personal file for Varinka Muus

FUNDACJA GENERAL ELŻBIETY ZAWACKIEJ (GENERAL ELŻBIETĄ ZAWACKA FOUNDATION), TORÚN, POLAND

Report, EZ1, 1975
Report of Elżbieta Zawacka, 1938–1943
Transcript of audio interviews
Zawacka, Unpublished Autobiography

NATIONAL INSTITUTE OF REMEMBRANCE, BUDAPEST, HUNGARY

Ezredveg 2021-1643141423
MagyarNaplo 1992-1605557665
MagyarZsidoSzemle 2009-2010
MultEsJovo 1991-1583548407
NEB VLB Szenes-Hanna

NEW ARCHIVE, WARSAW, POLAND

Report by E. Zawadriline, 'Zo' from her trip to London, 1944–45

THE NATIONAL ARCHIVES, UK

HS6/112, Belgium Missions including Mission Imogen
KV2/297, German Intelligence Agents
HS7/100, History of T Section
WO235/309 Bl.11, Judge Advocate General's Office, War Crimes Case Files, Second
   World War, Ravensbrück case, exhibits 1–8, March 1946
HS6/309, SOE in France
HS6/602, SOE in France 2
HS6/437, Yvonne Baseden affidavit
WO208/3414, Sara Braverman, Personnel File
HS9/173/2, Jeanne Bohec, Personnel File
HS9/436/3, Jenny Djendi, Personnel File
HS9/1498/2, Alix d'Unienville, Personnel File

HS9/460/9, L. Dupre, Personnel File
HS9/460/3, Frédérique Dupuich, Personnel File
HS9/572/4, Jos Gemmeke, Personnel File
HS9/605/3, Jutta Graae, Personnel File
HS9/612, Christine Granville, Personnel File
HS9/1506/2, Annemarie Hilten, Personnel File
HS9/784/1, Olga Jackson, Personnel File
HS9/928/1, Renée Lippens, Personnel File
HS9/973/7, Elaine Madden, Personnel File
WO208/3415, Marta Martinovich (Haviva Reik), Personnel File
HS9/1022/2, Jeanne Mereau, Personnel File
HS9/1081/2, Varinka Muus, Personnel File
WO208/3401, Hannah Senesh, Personnel File
HS9/1390/3, Marcelle Somers, Personnel File
HS9/1452/8, Trix Terwindt, Personnel File
HS9/1635/3, Elizabeth Watson, Personnel File
HS9/1576/5, André Wendelen, Personnel File

YAD VASHEM ARCHIVES

O.3/6988
O.3/7393

AUDIO ARCHIVES

Edith Bonnesen, radio broadcast on Denmark's Radio, January 1976, Museum of
    Danish Resistance
Edith Bonnesen, radio broadcast on Denmark's Radio, 9 April 1985, Museum of
    Danish Resistance
Jutta Graae (RA 255553-8), Museum of Danish Resistance
Clare Hollingworth (21130), Imperial War Museum Audio Archive
Beatrice Jackman (17390), Imperial War Museum Audio Archive
Jutta Juncker (14250), Imperial War Museum Audio Archive
Elaine Madden interview with BBC journalist Sue Elliott, 7 June 2008
Varinka Muus (13104), Imperial War Museum Audio Archive
Varinka Muus (80012826), Imperial War Museum Audio Archive
Varinka Muus (21931), Museum of Danish Resistance
William Pilkington (16854), Imperial War Museum Audio Archive
László Bernát Veszprémy, 'Faith Makes a Man Strong: The Self-Sacrificing Example
    of Hanna Szenes', Committee of National Remembrance, Budapest, 2023
Elżbieta Zawacka interview, Warsaw Uprising Museum
Elżbieta Zawacka, transcript of interview, Fundacja General Elżbiety Zawackiej,
    Toruń

NEWSPAPERS AND MAGAZINES

Jerusalem Post, Surica Braverman obituary, 28 February 2013, www.jpost.com/
    magazine/features/a-brave-fighter, accessed 5 April 2024

BIBLIOGRAPHY

New York Times, 15 July 1964, accessed online 26 May 2024

Radio Times magazine, 'My Life as a Secret Agent', article on Elaine Madden, 7–13 November 2005

Time magazine, 'Foreign News: La Chatte', 17 January 1949, accessed online 2 March 2024

WEBSITES

Alliance Française, 'Alix Marrier d'Unienville', https://www.alliancefrancaise. london/Alix-Marrier-dUnienville.php, accessed 5 November 2024

Biographical Lexicon, 'L.A. Duus Hansen', https://biografiskleksikon.lex.dk/L.A._ Duus_Hansen, accessed January 2024

CIE, 'Nazis Kill Palmach Paratrooper Haviva Reik', www.israeled.org/nazis-kill-palmach-paratrooper-haviva-reik, accessed 5 April 2024

Conscript Heroes, 'Frédérique Dupuich – The Real Miss Richards', https://www. conscript-heroes.com/escapelines/EEIE-Articles/Art-24-Freddy-Dupuich.htm, accessed 5 November 2024

Curagiu, www.curagiu.com/la_sante_et_romainville.htm, accessed 28 January 2024

Danish Airmen, 'About the Shell House Attack', www.airmen.dk/pdfs/VHTmarts 2020ASe.pdf, accessed 28 January 2024

Jewish Heroes, 'Haviva Reik', www.jewishheroes.live/hero-en/reik, accessed 5 April 2024

Palmach, www.palmach.org.il

Spartacus Educational, 'Christine Glanville', www.spartacus-educational.com/ SOEgranville.htm, accessed 28 January 2024

United States Holocaust Memorial Museum, www.ushmm.org

V2 Rocket, www.v2rocket.com, accessed 28 January 2024

ACKNOWLEDGEMENTS

My sincere thanks and gratitude go to the Gerry Holdsworth Special Forces Charitable Trust for funding the research phase of this book, which enabled me to travel to archives and sites of interest in Hungary, the Netherlands, Poland, Denmark, Berlin and London.

Among the many people to whom I am indebted for help in the preparation of this book I would especially like to thank Coen Hijszeler, Trine Engholm Michelsen, Sue Elliott and Alina Nowobilska for their unwavering support, generosity, hospitality and friendship.

My appreciation goes to Steven Kippax for sharing with me his copies of official files and documents, enabling me to undertake research swiftly and effectively; to Martyn Cox for sharing interview files with me; and to Richard Aldrich and the University of Warwick for having me as a research fellow, and allowing me access to the university library.

I would like to acknowledge those who have helped me with various tasks such as reading this text to ensure its accuracy and tone, and for offering me words of encouragement and motivation. They are too numerous to name individually, but I would like to mention in particular Keith Errington, Lynette Nusbacher, Caitlyn Brinkman-Schwartz and Nigel Mercer.

Thanks also to my fantastic publishers, especially Heather McCallum, Katie Urquhart and Rachael Lonsdale. Also to my peer reviewers and copy editor. Thanks also to my fantastic agent Charlie Campbell.

The information provided by KZ Gedenkstätte Mauthausen, KZ Gedenkstätte Ravensbrück and Yad Vashem has proved extremely useful. My appreciation also goes to Theodore van Heesch at CRASH '40–'45; Ed Vermeulen at 1940–1945 Museum, Dordrecht; Gry Scavenius Bertelsen, curator at the Danish Resistance Museum/Archives; archivist Anna Rojewska and all staff at the General Elżbieta Zawacka Foundation; Mariusz Olczak, director of the Central Archive of Modern records in Warsaw and all the staff there who welcomed and assisted me. Also, the research undertaken by Dr Áron Máthé, vice chair at the Committee of National Remembrance (Hungary) and his team has been very helpful.

Thanks also to Ingrid van der Chijs, Joyce Wilding, An Osborne, Paul McCue, Angy and Antony Lewis, Henry Smith, Karen Sivebæk Munk and Lugina McConnell.

And most especially to my parents, Gus and Susan Vigurs, who have stood by me every step of the way. And to Phil Lowes, who has kept the home fires burning, the kettle on and the animals entertained while allowing me to write.

INDEX OF TRAINING SCHOOLS

Beaulieu 14, 87, 92–3, 133, 135, 138, 148, 163–4, 253, 257

Inverailort House 11, 13

Largo House, Fife 13, 50

Massingham 10, 57, 113, 309

Ramat David 13, 283

Students Assessment Board (SAB) xii, 11, 92, 133, 135
Special Training Schools (STS) xii, 10, 71, 113
   STS 5, Wanborough Manor 163
   STS 7, Winterfold House 133, 135
   STS 6, Finchampstead 86
   STS 19, Gardeners End 138

STS 20/20a Pollards Park 53–4
STS 20b, Nightingale Lane 53
STS 21, Arisaig House 11
STS 31, House in the Woods 195
STS 32b, Swordland 12
STS 32a, Saltmarsh 138
STS 34, Drokes House 148
STS 35, Vineyards 133, 164
STS 42, Roughwood Park 187
STS 43, Audley End House 53
STS 45, Hatherop Castle 219
STS 50, Gorse Hill 197
STS 51, Ringway Aerodrome 10, 13, 50, 114, 133, 163–4, 195, 197, 253–4
STS 51a, Dunham Massey 52, 195
STS 52, Thame Park 13, 187, 197
STS 59, Wall Hall 187

GENERAL INDEX

Aarhus 255

Abwehr 76–8, 80, 156, 201

Albania 5

Algiers 10, 57, 72, 110–12, 114, 117, 309, 318

Allies 34, 59, 67–8, 74–5, 80, 100, 103, 108, 111, 152, 177, 189, 193, 205, 211–12, 225, 239, 263, 282, 314

Amies, Hardy 136, 146, 148

Amsterdam 16, 158, 160, 181–2, 185, 294

Amstetten 177

anti-Semitism 264, 266, 291

Antwerp 123, 138, 141, 160

Arisaig 11 13

Armia Krajowa (AK) 20, 22, 30, 55, 60, 62, 65

Arnhem 155, 157, 189

Arrow Cross 264–5, 298

Assen prison 157, 171–2

ATS xii, 6, 83, 121, 132, 310

Auschwitz-Birkenau 37, 46, 48, 176, 263, 365, 271, 292, 303

Auxiliary Transport Service (ATS) xii, 6, 83, 132, 310

Avenue Foch 95, 97, 104, 115

B-24 Liberator 141

'Badminton' 247

Baker Street 15, 21, 79, 178, 192, 209, 233–4, 250, 252–3

Banska Bystica 290, 292–4, 296, 299, 302

Bari 284, 286, 293–5

Baseden, Yvonne 116–17, 319

BC Nieuws 181–2

BCRA 70–1, 85, 90

Beaulieu 11, 14, 87, 92–3, 133, 135, 138, 148, 163–4, 195, 253, 257

BEF xii, 3, 9, 68

Begue, Georges 79

Belgium 3, 5, 7, 15, 121–4, 126, 128–9, 132, 131–8, 141–2, 144–8, 150, 152, 160, 162, 167, 206, 306

Berdichev, Abba 274–5

Bergen-Belsen 149, 176, 303

Berlin 3–31, 38, 102, 117, 175, 206, 214–15, 219, 259, 263, 341

Bernhard, Prince 180, 189, 191

Best, Werner 218, 225

Biallosterski, Tobias (also de Brun) 185

Bickford cord 84, 91, 94, 100–1, 129

Bingham, Seymour 170, 180

Blaze, Michael 146–7, 150

Bleicher, Hugo 76–80

blitzkrieg 19, 66, 151

Blizzard, Charles 163, 165

Bloch, André 79

Bohec, Jeanne ('Râteau') 67, 81–9, 100, 101, 105–7

Bonnesen, Edith ('Lotte') 214–17, 221, 224–5, 227–30, 232, 242–8, 260, 307

Brand, Joel 265

Braverman, Surica 272–86, 29–1, 293, 302

Brindisi 275, 286, 294

Brion, Jean 129 131

British Memorial School 124–5

Brossolette, Pierre 95

Bruhn, Karl Johan 213
Brussels 129, 131, 134, 138, 143–5,
    147–8, 158, 160, 162, 189, 191, 201,
    210
Bucharest 273
Buchenwald 97
Buckmaster, Maurice 71, 79
Budapest 1, 16, 29, 33, 264–7, 278, 280,
    288, 298–9, 301, 303, 305
Bureau Bijzondere Opdrachten (BBO)
    180, 192–4, 200

Caen 239
Caesara 2, 269, 331
Cairo 9, 33–4, 265, 272–4, 284–6
Cammaerts, Francis 58–9
Carré, Mathilde ('La Chatte') 72–81
Casanova, Danielle 107
Ceylon 9
CFT see Merlinettes
Charles, Prince of Belgium 144, 146
Chevigné, Colonel de 85–6, 99
Chiltern Court 250–1
Christian X, King 206, 218, 224
Christoffersen 216
Churchill Club 217
Cichociemni 13, 22, 49, 5–3, 55
Citroën 97, 98, 131, 139
Cloarec, Marie-Louise 110, 113, 114,
    115, 118, 318
Clouët des Pesruches, Jean-François
    90–1, 96, 98
Comet escape line 17, 134, 162
communists 7, 69, 107, 167, 215, 221, 246
Conti Street prison 289
Copenhagen 16–17, 206, 210, 215, 218,
    220–3, 226, 230, 233–4, 236, 239,
    240–4, 250–1, 253, 256, 260
Corps féminin 83, 99, 110, 112
Culioli, Pierre 80
Czerniawski, Roman 73–6

Dachau 19, 119, 131, 149, 326
Dafne, Reufen 1, 275–8, 304
Dakota 191
Dalton, Hugh 4, 309
Damehotellet 221, 223
Danish Brigade 258–9

Danish Freedom Council 223, 240–1
Danish Nazis 206, 208
Dannebrog 205, 259
D-Day 5, 57–8, 95, 99–100, 105, 136,
    141, 144, 239–40, 278, 309, 324
De frie Danske 215–16
de Gaulle, General Charles 5, 68–70,
    75, 81, 83–5, 92, 99, 103, 314
de Gaulle, Geneviève 103
de Graaf, Captain 191, 201
de Jongh, Andrée 17, 134
de Vomécourt, Pierre 78–80
Denmark 3, 5, 55, 205–6, 208, 212–13,
    215–21, 223–6, 228, 230, 233–41,
    250–5, 252–60, 306–7
detonator 84, 91, 95, 100–1, 129–30
Deuxième Bureau (SR) 45, 70, 114,
    122–3
Dewavarin, André 69
DF Section 75
Djendi, Eugénie 110–12, 114, 116–18,
    318
Dourlein, Pieter 170, 176, 178, 323
Dunham Massey 52
d'Unienville, Alix 92–4, 103–4, 107–9
Dunkirk 3, 67–8, 127
Dupuich, Frédérique (Freddy) 134, 136
    137

Eastern Front 208, 224, 263, 265
Egypt 34, 270, 273–4
Eichmann, Adolf 265, 303, 333
Eindhoven 184–5, 191, 197
Electra House (EH) 3
Engelandvaarders 153, 192
'Englandspiel' 157, 168, 170–1, 176–8,
    180, 201, 323
Ephraim, Ben 274
Eretz Israel 265, 270, 281, 290–1, 293,
    302, 331
explosives 12, 34, 53, 70, 82, 84–7, 91,
    94, 100–1, 107, 129–30, 197, 213, 221,
    239, 256, 258, 307

F Section 5–6, 69–72
Fairbairn, William 13
FANY xii, 6, 8–10, 15, 52–3, 133, 136–7,
    146, 150, 162, 197, 253

Far East 5, 9, 133, 310, 334
Feldgendarmerie 130
Fermont, Jeanne Marie ('Puck') 203–4
FFI 83–5, 99, 105–6, 137
Final Solution 262, 265
Finland 9, 207
Fleischmann 278–9
Floor, Ides 132, 136, 148
Flössenburg 118, 149
Flying Fortress 58, 290, 293–4
Fog, Mogens 222
Force 136 5
Fort de Romainville 107, 115
Foss, Erling 222
Fourcade, Marie-Madeleine 17
France 3–59 14, 20, 30, 37–9, 42, 57,
    67–9, 71–6, 79–86, 88–9, 92–5,
    100–3, 105, 110–11, 113–14, 118–19,
    121, 127, 136, 139, 141, 147, 152, 154,
    162, 209, 267, 270, 306, 309, 316, 318
Fraser, Ingram 207
Free French 5, 68–70, 83–4, 92, 110, 314
Fresnes prison 97–8
Friang, Brigitte 89–90, 95–9, 109–10,
    118–19
Funkspiel 80

Gaynes Hall 165
Gemmeke, Jos 183–6, 189, 190–204,
    307
Gerson, Gilliana 71
Gestapo 8, 14, 17, 33–5, 50, 58, 76, 79,
    85, 89, 95–7, 99, 104, 107, 113–15,
    141, 143–4, 151, 168, 171, 185, 219,
    231, 235, 241–3, 245–6, 255–6, 263,
    288–90, 300, 303, 307, 315, 317, 326
Ghent 138, 147
ghettos 46, 60, 263–4, 271
Gibraltar 38, 44–6, 135, 321
Giskes, Hermann 156–7, 168, 170–1,
    185
Gittus, Yvonne 86
Goldstein, Perec 303
Göring, Hermann 159
Gorse Hill 197
Graae, Jutta 206–7, 209–11, 213–14,
    221–6, 231–3, 236–8, 240, 242,
    248–52, 254–6, 258–60

Granville, Christine *see* Skarbek,
    Krystyna
Greece 5, 7, 267
Grendon Underwood 9
Grüner, Germaine 86
Gubbins, Sir Colin 13, 71, 122
Gyth, Volle 207–10, 213–14, 223, 226,
    231–2, 236, 238

Haaren prison 157, 169
Haarlem 189
Haganah 270, 272
Haifa 268–9, 273–4, 331
Halifax (aircraft) 51–2, 55–6, 86, 93,
    166, 219
Hall, Virginia 71
Hamilton, Antonia ('Frankie') 186–8,
    194, 203
Hamilton, Frank 188–9, 203
Hammer, Mogens 213, 216
Hansen, Duus 216, 227, 247
Hashomer Hatzair 281, 290–1, 293, 296
Hebrew 266, 268, 290, 304
Heim, Germaine 86
Hermesh, Haim 293, 299
Himmler, Heinrich 176
Hitler, Adolf 19–20, 29, 68, 119, 152–3,
    160, 184, 207, 214, 218, 221, 224,
    258–9, 263, 310, 318
Hlinka Guard 292, 296, 300, 332
Holger Danske 240
Hollingworth, Ralph 210, 212, 239, 326
Holocaust 261, 293
Hongerwinter (hunger winter) 193
Hôpital de la Pitié 97–8
Horthy, Miklós 263–4, 280
Hungarian Relief and Rescue 271, 304
Hungary 1, 5, 16, 31–4, 49, 261–9, 271,
    273–5, 277–80, 287–8, 298, 302–4,
    306, 333

Ijsselmeer 164, 166
Imperial War Graves Commission
    (IWGC) 124–5
Inchmery House 70
India 9–10
instinctive shooting 11
INTERALLIÉ 73–4, 76–9

Inverailort 13
Inverlair 11
Inverlochy Castle 50
iron ore 205, 207
IS9 3, 17, 162–3, 274, 293, 301, 306
Israel 13, 261, 265, 270, 273, 276, 281, 290–1, 293, 302, 306–7, 331
ISSU6 13
Italy 5, 7, 9

Jackson, Olga 124, 137–40, 146
Jakobsen, Frode 222
Je Maintiendrai (newspaper) 183, 185–6
Jedburgh 59, 105, 149, 309, 314, 318
Jews 60, 64
Johanssen, Paul 213
Juliana, Princess 192
Juncker, Flemming 250, 252, 327

Kallos 278–80, 289
Kasztner, Rezső 303, 333
Katowice 19, 24–6, 30, 35
Katyn massacre 20
kibbutz 1, 267–9, 271–2, 274–5, 286–7, 290–1, 293, 301–2
Kibbutz Women 290, 293, 301
kibbutznik 272, 275
KLM 151, 158–9, 163
Komorowski, General Tadeusz ('Bor') 59–60, 62
Kowerski, Andrzej 32–3
Krakow 19, 27–8, 35, 65
Kristallnacht 206, 221, 326
Kuczynski, Ursula (Agent Sonya) 17

LA DAME BLANCHE 134
Laplat, Denise 128–31, 143
Largo House, Fife 13, 50
Larsen, Ib 228
Lauwers, Huub 155–7, 176, 178–9, 323
Lefort, Cicley 175
Leopold, King 144
Liège 129–31, 137–8, 141
Lippens, Renée 147–9
Lippman, Ole 251
Loch Morar 12

Lolland 220–1
London 8, 22, 29, 31, 34–7, 44–8, 51, 59, 65–6, 70, 74–6, 78–81, 83–5, 90, 92–3, 99, 105, 113, 128, 132, 135, 141–4, 147, 154, 156, 162, 165, 167–8, 170, 178, 180, 185, 192–3, 201, 210, 213–14, 219, 223, 226, 228, 230, 233–4, 242, 247–51, 253, 257, 260
Louin, Pierrette 110, 112–15, 118, 318
Luftwaffe 68, 151, 153
Lunding, Hans 213
Lutz, Carl 264
Lwów 27–8
Lysander 75, 113, 123, 136, 144, 154

Maastricht 158
Madden, Elaine 121, 124–9, 132–4, 140–7, 149–50
Magrit Boulevard 16, 297
Majdanek 271, 292
Malmö 259
Manchester (Ringway) 9, 13, 50
Mandate Palestine 163, 261, 263, 267–70, 272, 281, 285, 287–9, 291, 301, 306
Maquis 7, 58, 105–6, 314
Marks, Leo 15, 178
Martinovich, Haviva see Reik, Haviva
Massingham 10, 57, 113, 309
Mauthausen 175–7, 181, 301, 323, 333
Merlinettes 110, 113, 120
Mertzizen, Suzanne 110–18, 318
message personnel 100
MI(R) xii, 4, 22
MI5 45, 128, 132, 161, 212, 249
MI6 17, 209, 238
MI9 3, 17, 162–3, 261, 275, 306
microfilm 32, 34, 37–8, 42, 188, 213–14, 226
Mikkelsen, Max 213
Milorg 8
'Minestrone' 230, 247–8
Mørch, Captain 232, 236–7, 258
Morse code 11, 13
Mosquito 255
Mount Herzl 302
Munck, Ebbe 207, 209, 214, 238

Muss, Varinka 'Inke' 195, 220–7, 334–6, 239–42, 251–60
Mussolini, Benito 121, 220, 224
Mustang 255, 294
Muus, Flemming 195, 219–23, 227, 233–5, 239, 240–2, 245, 247, 249, 251–3

N Section 7, 155, 163–4, 180, 187, 192, 196, 325
Nacht und Nebel 101, 115, 172
Nahalal (agricultural school) 267–8, 269, 272, 304 273
Narodný Komissariat Vnutrennikh Del (NKVD) 20
Nazi 3, 14, 17, 19, 60, 67–9, 74, 78, 107, 113, 121, 138, 180, 182, 186, 193, 203, 206–9, 215, 217–18, 250, 262–5, 269, 281–2, 296, 306, 322, 325–6, 333
Neave, Airey 134, 162, 164 168
Netherlands 3, 5, 7, 121, 151–4, 157–8, 160–2, 164–5, 178, 180–3, 186–8, 190–3, 195, 198–202, 203–4, 229, 233
Nightingale Lane (STS 20b) 53–4
Nordentoft, Einar 211, 213, 225, 236–8, 250, 252, 258
North Africa 9, 34, 110–11, 270, 310, 318
North Sea 151, 154
Norway 3, 5, 8, 205–7, 211, 219, 251

Operation 'Carthage' 17, 255
Operation 'Chowhound' 194
Operation 'Manna' 193
Operation 'Market Garden' 189, 193
Operation 'Sealion' 162
Operation 'Nordpol' 157, 171, 178
Operation 'Tempest' 60
Operation 'Torch' 110, 309
Oranjehotel 16, 171–2
Oslo gang 8
OSS 113, 147, 237, 302, 315, 318, 332

'Paku' 40–2
Palgi, Yoel 273–4, 298, 301, 303
Palmach 1, 3, 13, 163, 261–72, 281–3, 285–6, 291, 296, 299, 303–4, 331

parachute 1, 10, 13, 48–52, 56–8, 75, 86, 88–90, 92, 94, 100, 105, 113–14, 116–17, 123, 129, 133–5, 138, 142, 148, 155, 162–3, 166–7, 187–8, 193, 195, 198–9, 210, 212–13, 216, 219, 221, 234, 248, 252–4, 257, 259, 271–6, 281, 283, 286, 293, 298, 314, 325
paramilitary training 11
paratrooper 58–9, 151–2, 181, 276–7, 298, 303
Paris 3, 5, 31, 37–8, 72–6, 89–91, 94–5, 100, 103, 107, 109, 114–16, 119, 140, 239–40
partisan 1, 21, 59, 129, 240, 263, 271, 276–7, 282, 284–6, 292–4, 296, 299–300
Pétain, Marshal Philippe 68–9, 74
Petitjean, Marguerite 86
Place des États-Unis 115
Plan vert 100–1
plastic explosive 12, 91, 100, 130, 219
Poland 5–6, 18–19, 23, 25, 27, 29, 31–2, 34, 36–7, 39, 47–54, 59, 61, 65–6, 73, 209, 292, 306, 310–11, 315
Political Warfare Executive (PWE) 123, 135
Pollards Park House (Station 20a) 53
Poundon 9
Poznań 23, 29, 311
preliminary training 10–11
propaganda 22, 25, 32, 54, 75, 90, 92, 135, 148–9, 185, 187–8, 200, 223, 226, 326
Przysposobienie Wojskowe Kobiet (PWK) 24–7, 29, 34, 49, 65
Pyrenees 17, 37, 40–2, 75, 134, 162, 170, 313, 321

Radio Oranje 153
RAF Tempsford 54, 57
Ramat David 13, 283
Ravensbrück 16, 34, 101–3, 108–10, 118–19, 172–6, 312
Red Army 28, 60, 64, 110, 119
Red Cross 9, 59, 73, 92, 128, 177, 186, 193, 208, 257, 291
Reich Bahn 196

Reik, Haviva 261, 265, 272, 282–4, 286, 290–302
Reiss, Rafael ('Rafi') 300–1
Reuven, Dafne 1–3, 275–8, 304
Revier 102, 109, 116, 118, 174–5
RF Section 69–71, 78, 81
Ridderhof 155–7
Robinson, Ada *see* Reik, Haviva
Romania 33, 261–2, 268, 273, 281–2, 284–6, 302
Rosen, Yonah 274
Rosh Hashana 268
Rottbøll, Christian 213, 218
Rotterdam 151, 153, 201
Roughwood Park 187
Royal Air Force (RAF) xii, 54, 56, 87, 106, 114, 139, 140, 144, 163, 165, 188, 192, 193, 203, 204, 208, 224, 226, 240, 254, 255, 273, 301
Royal Victoria Patriotic School 45, 191, 249
Rue de Saussaies 99
Ryder, Sue (Baroness of Warsaw) 54–5

SAB xii, 11, 92, 133, 135
sabotage 3–4, 12, 22, 29, 46, 49, 55, 84–5, 87, 91, 100–1, 122–4, 129–30, 141, 144–5, 178–80, 207, 209–10, 213, 215, 217–18, 222–4, 238–9, 242, 250, 270, 314, 316, 326
Sachsenhausen 19, 326
Sansom, Odette 71, 76
Schiphol 158–9
Schreider 156, 168–72, 179
Schutzhaft 177
Scotland 9–12, 50, 86, 233, 239, 251–2, 258
Sdot Yam 2, 269, 272, 304
Section D 4, 31–2, 34, 207, 209
Sehmer, Major 295–6, 333
Sereni, Enzo 274–5
SERVICE CLARENCE 134, 136
Shell House 243–6, 254–6, 258
Sikorski, General Radosław Tomasz 46–7, 75
Silvani, Jenny *see* Djendi, Eugénie

SIS xii, 4, 31, 75, 122, 124, 135, 152, 178, 209, 212, 216, 238, 250, 322, 327; *see also* MI6
Sissingh, Jante 201–2
Skarbek, Krystyna 31, 34, 57–8
Slovakia 32–3, 261, 290–4, 296, 299–301, 332–3
Służba Zwycięstwu Polski (SZP) 20
Sneum, Tommy 212, 216–17
Sobibor 292
Social Emergency Service (SES) 25–6
Somers, Josiane 86, 99–100, 318
Somers, Marcelle 86, 99–100
Soviet Union 20, 32, 262–4, 292
'Spaghetti' 230, 247
Spain 38–40, 43, 75, 115, 135, 147, 161, 270
Special Allied Airborne Reconnaissance Force (SAARF) 149–50
Sporborg, Harry 209
Sten gun 12, 91, 246, 273
Stockholm 31, 210, 214, 228, 233, 236–7, 253, 258–60, 326
striptease suit 86–8, 114, 199, 220
Supreme Headquarters Allied Expeditionary Force (SHAEF) 139, 143, 196, 239, 249, 253
Sûreté de l'État 122–3, 147
Sweden 55, 205, 211, 213, 215, 217, 220, 225–8, 231, 235–8, 242, 247–8, 250–2, 258, 260, 328
Switzerland 48, 148, 160–1, 177, 303, 323
Swordland 12
Sykes, Eric 13
synagogue 221, 278, 280, 326
Szabo, Violette 71, 115
Szenes, Giora 266–7, 269–73, 287–8, 302
Szenes, Hannah 1–3, 261–2, 265, 269, 271–80, 282, 286, 290, 293, 297–8, 302, 307
Szenes, Katarina 266–8, 286–90, 297–8, 301–2

T Section 7, 121–4, 136, 141, 146, 148
Taconis, Thijs 155–6

Tel Aviv 273, 333
'telephone book' wireless 230
Terwindt, Trix 117, 151, 157, 169–77, 179
Thame Park 13, 187, 197
The Hague 16, 153–5, 157–8, 167, 171, 180, 182, 185, 191–2, 199, 201, 203
Theresienstadt 225, 292
time-delay pencils 84, 91, 95, 100–1
Tissendier 278–9
Tito, Josef Broz 1, 7, 276–7, 282, 285
Tivoli Gardens 218
Toruń 16–17, 23, 28–9, 34, 53, 65–6
Tripartite Pact 262, 292
Truelsen, Svend 250, 252, 255–6
Turnbull, Roger 201, 326

U-boats 19, 46, 186
USAAF xii, 140, 142, 193
Utrecht 151, 153, 168, 182–3, 186

V-1 141, 189, 330
V-2 141, 143, 189, 193, 202, 250, 256
van de Spiegel, Jacques 140, 143–4
van Hilten, AnneMarie 197–8
van Paaschen, Cock 181, 185, 192, 199–200, 202
Venlo incident 152
Vercors 57–8
Versailles, Treaty of 19, 23, 72, 310
Verstreppen 141
Vichy 34, 37, 39, 68–9, 75, 110, 271, 315
'Vineyards' 133, 164
Vistula 23, 26, 55, 60, 64, 311
Voute, Klaus 159

WAAF 6, 273, 284
Wall Hall 187
Wallenberg, Raoul 264

Warsaw 16–17, 19, 23–4, 29, 31, 32, 35–8, 46–50, 53–7, 59–60, 62–6, 271, 311
Warsaw Ghetto Uprising 46, 60, 271
Warsaw Uprising 23, 59–64
Wendelen, André 129–30, 140–1, 143–6
Wichfield, Monica 205, 220–2, 236, 239, 257
Wilhelmina, Queen 153, 167, 192–3, 204
Windsor Hotel 283
wireless xii, 9, 11, 13–15, 32, 34, 53, 57, 65, 70, 74, 76, 78–9, 86, 90, 105, 110, 112–13, 116, 123, 128, 130, 133, 135, 141–5, 151, 155–7, 165–6, 178, 185–7, 196–7, 200–2, 211–13, 216–17, 220, 223, 227–30, 239, 241, 247, 260, 279–80, 285–7, 295–6, 298, 307, 315, 318
Wittek, Maria 23–5, 27, 29, 35–6, 42, 47, 57, 63, 65, 307
Women's Volunteer Service (WVS) xii, 128

yellow star 225, 263, 271, 303
Yeo Thomas, Tommy 95, 97–9
Yishuv 270, 293, 298, 309, 331
Yom Kippur 289
Yugoslavia 1, 5, 7, 33, 261–2, 268–9, 273–7, 281–2, 284–6

Zagroda 29–30, 35–6, 65
Zawacka, Elżbieta 16–18, 23, 25, 27–31, 34–45, 47, 49–57, 61–6
Zionist 265–7, 274, 281, 291, 295, 303
Zvi, Ben-Ya'akov 293, 300–1, 333
Związek Walki Zbrojnej (ZWZ) 20, 29–30